*SCHAUM'S OUTLINE OF*

# THEORY AND PROBLEMS

of

# COST ACCOUNTING I
## Second Edition

•

by

### RALPH S. POLIMENI, Ph.D., CPA
*Professor and Chairman*
*Department of Accounting*
*Hofstra University*

and

### JAMES A. CASHIN, CPA
*Emeritus Professor of Accounting*
*Hofstra University*

**SCHAUM'S OUTLINE SERIES**
McGRAW-HILL BOOK COMPANY
New York   St. Louis   San Francisco   Auckland   Bogotá   Hamburg   Johannesburg
London   Madrid   Mexico   Montreal   New Delhi   Panama   Paris
São Paulo   Singapore   Sydney   Tokyo   Toronto

RALPH S. POLIMENI is Chairman of the Accounting Department at Hofstra University and in 1978 received the Hofstra University Distinguished Teaching Award. He has also taught at City University of New York and the University of Arkansas and is the Director of Chaykin's CPA Review Program at Hofstra University. Dr. Polimeni received a Ph.D. in accounting from the University of Arkansas 1973 and holds a C.P.A. Certificate from New York State. He has served as a consultant to Cooper's and Lybrand, the City of New York, the New York State Special Prosecutor's Office, as well as several law firms, and has coauthored several books, including Schaum's Outline of *Cost Accounting II*.

JAMES A. CASHIN, Emeritus Professor of Accounting, was formerly Chairman of the Accounting Department at Hofstra University. He has also taught in the Graduate School of City University of New York and at New York University. His publishing credits include 20 titles; he is a coauthor of Schaum's Outlines of *Accounting I*, *Accounting II*, *Intermediate Accounting I*, *Cost Accounting II*, *Tax Accounting*, and *Advanced Accounting*. Professor Cashin holds a B.S. degree in Accounting from the University of Georgia and an M.B.A. degree from New York University; he is a Certified Public Accountant and a Certified Internal Auditor and has had wide experience in business and government agencies.

Schaum's Outline of Theory and Problems of
COST ACCOUNTING I

1 2 3 4 5 6 7 8 9 10 11 12 13 14 15 16 17 18 19 20 SHP SHP 8 9 8 7 6 5 4

ISBN 0-07-010273-2

Sponsoring Editor, Elizabeth Zayatz
Editing Supervisor, Marthe Grice
Production Manager, Nick Monti

Library of Congress Cataloging in Publication Data

Polimeni, Ralph S.
     Schaum's outline of theory and problems of cost
accounting I.

     (Schaum's outline series)
     Rev. ed. of: Schaum's outline of theory and problems
of cost accounting / by James A. Cashin and Ralph S.
Polimeni. c1978.
     Includes index.
     1. Cost accounting—Problems, exercises, etc.
I. Cashin, James A.   II. Cashin, James A.   Schaum's
outline of theory and problems of cost accounting.
III. Title.
HF5686.C8P5955   1984      657'.42'076      83-17495
ISBN 0-07-010273-2

# Contents

# Preface

This book, the second edition of a volume that covers the first part of the Cost Accounting course, reflects the latest issues, concepts, and procedures in the field of cost accounting.  As in the first edition, the solved problems approach is used, with emphasis on the practical application of fundamental cost accounting concepts and techniques.  The student is provided with:

1. concise definitions and explanations in easily understood terms
2. examples which illustrate the concepts and techniques developed in each chapter
3. chapter review questions with answers
4. fully worked-out solutions to a large range of representative problems (against which students can check their own solutions)

*Cost Accounting I* and its sequel, *Cost Accounting II*, parallel the full-year cost accounting course offered in most schools.  The subject matter has been carefully coordinated with leading textbooks, so that any topic can easily be found in the table of contents or the index.

The modern use of cost accounting in all phases of business activity reflects its usefulness as a management tool for planning and control as well as decision-making.  Indeed, the diversity of its uses has stimulated its own growth, so that today cost accounting embraces such sophisticated advances as those in quantitative techniques and decision models, productivity and performance standards, behavioral science concepts, human resources accounting, learning curve theory, and advanced marketing concepts.  In addition, important changes have been made in the field.  These include the establishment of the Cost Accounting Standards Board (CASB) and the examination program for the Certificate in Management Accounting (CMA) given by the National Association of Accountants (NAA).  Thus, cost accounting, once concerned primarily with manufacturing operations, is now recognized as appropriate for nonmanufacturing activities of all kinds.

The topics treated in this book comprise perhaps the most difficult area of study in the accounting curriculum.  Cost accounting is a highly specialized field, requiring an in-depth understanding and mastery of complex concepts and techniques that are unparalleled in other accounting courses.  The theory-and-solved-problems approach of *Cost Accounting I* is designed to clarify the detailed subject matter and provide students with the practical applications they need to be completely familiar with the methodology.

In addition to its usefulness in formal course work, *Cost Accounting I* will provide excellent preparation and review for the Uniform CPA Examination and for the CMA Examination.  It will also serve the needs of those interest in acquiring cost accounting knowledge through independent study, such as students majoring in business and economics areas outside accounting, as well as business owners, managers, and executives.

Among the many individuals the authors have to thank for contributions to this volume are Anthony Basile, Nenette Bembo, and Denise Segal.

RALPH S. POLIMENI
JAMES A. CASHIN

CONTENTS

# CONTENTS

# Chapter 1

# The Role of Cost Accounting

## 1.1 PLACE IN THE COMPANY

Cost accounting provides management with costs for products, inventories, operations or functions and compares actual to predetermined data. It also provides a variety of data for many day-to-day decisions as well as essential information for long-range decisions.

## 1.2 MANAGERIAL FUNCTIONS

The managerial functions are carried out by the *top management group*, the president, vice-presidents and other executives; the *middle management group*, the division managers, branch managers and department heads; and the *lower management group*, the supervisors. These groups require comprehensive analytic cost data provided on a systematic basis. Essentially the various managerial groups assist in establishing company objectives and determining that the objectives are realized. There are four basic managerial functions that are common to all activities, no matter how large or small the enterprise: (1) planning, (2) organizing, (3) directing, and (4) controlling.

*Planning.* The process of establishing organizational goals (i.e. setting objectives) and a strategy for their accomplishment is known as planning. It is concerned with the future—immediate and/or long range. Middle and lower management planning stems from the goals (i.e. the plan) set by top management. Examples of primary objectives are improvements in market standing, productivity, profitability, managerial performance, and public responsibility.

*Organizing.* Once objectives are set and a basic plan is established, the process of organizing involves developing a framework for the activity and making specific work assignments. *Authority* originates with top management and is delegated to the various management levels. A closely related factor is *responsibility*—the obligation to work to the best of one's ability. The supervisor has the authority to delegate the particular work, the employee has the responsibility for performance. *Accountability*—a facet of responsibility—is the obligation to report results to higher authority. This is an important feature of budgetary control and standard costing, since it aids in the comparison of actual performance with predetermined standards and an analysis of causes of difference.

*Directing.* This is the process by which management achieves its objectives. It requires the ability to supervise and motivate employees in order to obtain optimal levels of productivity conforming to established plans (e.g. budgets or standards for sales, production, costs, etc.).

The modern concept of motivation involves creating a work environment that stimulates superior levels of productivity. On the manager's part, it means providing subordinates with a clear picture of what is expected, necessary guidance, and the feeling that their work represents an important contribution to the achievement of the enterprise's ultimate goals. By effectively communicating with employees and encouraging feedback from them, managers are able to satisfy employee needs.

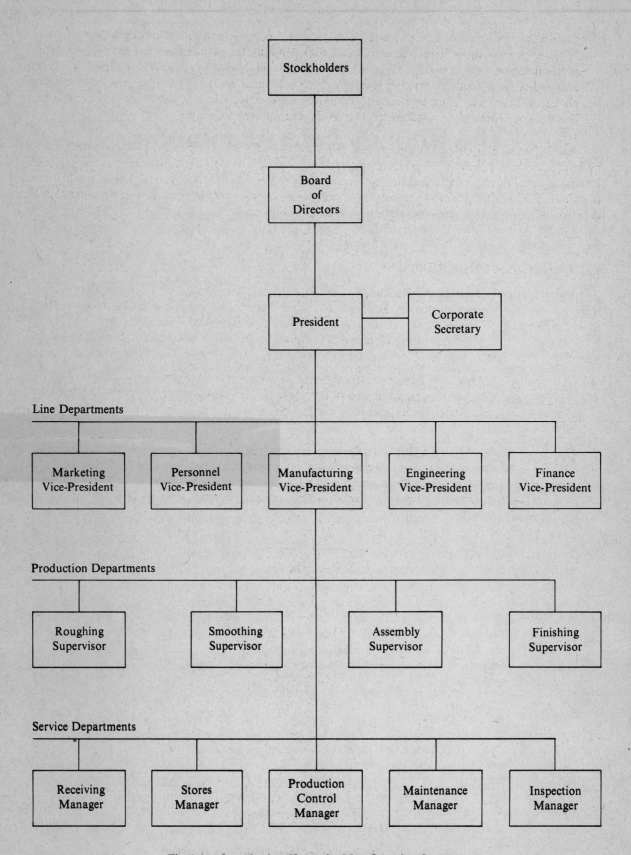

Fig. 1-1. Organization Chart of a Manufacturing Company

*Controlling.* The process of review, evaluation and reporting monitors the achievement of goals. It involves comparing actual results with those projected in planning as well as against actual performance in past periods. There are two facets to reviewing the enterprise's activities: (1) the comparison of actual to projected results and (2) individual traits. This is done because discrepancies on paper can often be traced to employee achievements and/or failures (e.g. good and bad decisions, exceptional or insufficient supervision and motivation, etc.).

Another kind of appraisal is the *internal audit.* This is a systematic review and evaluation made by a staff of internal auditors to assure management that established controls are operating as planned. Internal auditing today covers accounting, financial and other business operations, such as evaluations of policies, managerial performance, methods, etc. An important part of any review is the reporting of deficiencies and effective recommendations for their prompt correction.

## 1.3  ORGANIZATION CHARTS

An organization chart establishes the flow of authority and responsibility by defining the relationships among the major management positions of the enterprise. As such, it identifies those persons to whom the various kinds of cost accounting information (see Section 1.5) should go.

For purposes of cost accounting there are two organization charts that we should consider:

(1) *Company Chart.* This chart depicts the flow of authority and responsibility downward from the stockholders, through the Board of Directors, the President, the respective Vice-Presidents and other executives to the operating levels. See Fig. 1-1.

(2) *Controller's Division Chart.* The controller is the top accounting officer in the company. As a member of the top management team, his or her attention should be directed to providing services to all levels of management and to all functions of the company. The technical and detailed activities for which the controller is responsible are prepared by a staff of specialized accountants. See Fig. 1-2.

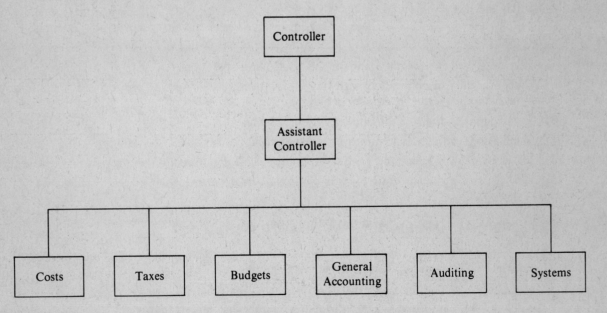

**Fig. 1-2.  Organization Chart of the Controller's Division**

## 1.4  LINE AND STAFF RESPONSIBILITY

Most responsibilities in a company can be divided into line and staff functions. The *line function* has the responsibility for decision making, guidance and supervision. The *staff function* provides advice and service to the line function, but cannot require implementation of its findings. Thus, the controller has line responsibilities (i.e. those that affect his or her own department) as well as staff responsibility with respect to other departments.

## 1.5  THE COST DEPARTMENT

The cost department is usually supervised by a controller or chief cost accountant. It is responsible for developing and reporting cost data with respect to materials, labor and overhead, and maintaining the necessary underlying records.

The extent to which the cost department participates in management decisions is prescribed by the definition of cost accounting used by the company. In some cases, the cost department is responsible only for compiling product costs, and has no part in analysis for decision making. In others, the wide variety of cost data needed in making day-to-day operating decisions is provided by a staff of cost accountants who have the ability to provide all types of cost information. See Section 1.6.

**EXAMPLE 1**

Suppose that a manufacturing firm must decide whether to produce a part necessary for one of its products, or purchase it from a supplier. Under the limited definition of cost accounting, the cost computations needed for the decision would not be made by the cost department. In the broader sense, the cost department would be responsible for such computations as well as any related analyses.

## 1.6  NATURE OF COST ACCOUNTING

The broad definition of cost accounting is *the process of identifying, summarizing and interpreting information needed for* (1) *planning and control,* (2) *management decisions, and* (3) *product costing.* Note that product costing is number 3, since in most companies the more important activities relate to planning and control and special decisions rather than to the more mechanical aspects of accumulating and computing product costs.

The various activities of a cost department under the broad definition cover a wide range of responsibilities:

(1)  Preparing data required in planning and controlling operations.

(2)  Preparing data in connection with day-to-day decisions or special projects that require a choice among alternative courses of action.

(3)  Participating in the creation and execution of budgets.

(4)  Establishing procedures to improve operations and reduce costs.

(5)  Developing cost systems and analyses to improve cost determination and review of variances.

(6)  Cost recording and reporting of costs by product or department.

## 1.7  PROFESSIONAL ASSOCIATIONS AND AGENCIES

The following professional associations and government agencies (listed in order of importance) have had a major influence on the field of cost accounting:

(1)  *National Association of Accountants (NAA).* The NAA has had the greatest impact on developing new and sophisticated procedures in the cost and management accounting field. NAA research studies provide reviews of current practices and analyses of both the factors considered and the approaches taken in arriving at the accepted solutions.

(2) ***Cost Accounting Standards Board (CASB).*** The CASB was a five-member government agency chaired by the Controller General of the United States. Its principal objective was to promote standards for achieving uniformity and consistency in the cost accounting practices employed by companies holding government contracts. Such standards applied to both defense and nondefense contracts. Since federal government contracts are an important source of revenue for many companies, these pronouncements have had a significant effect on cost accounting concepts and procedures. The standards are still applicable today even though the CASB was dissolved in 1980 because its major objective was accomplished.

(3) ***Financial Accounting Standards Board (FASB).*** The FASB establishes standards governing external financial reports of the private business sector. Because they delineate the content of external financial reports, these standards have a direct effect on how cost accounting systems are organized and operated.

(4) ***American Accounting Association (AAA).*** AAA membership includes most accounting teachers of college rank as well as leading public, industrial, commercial, and government accountants. The association's quarterly publications, *The Accounting Review* and *Accounting Education News*, cover a broad range of topics, including accounting theory, cost and management accounting, auditing, and taxes.

## *Summary*

(1) Supervisors comprise the _____ management group.

(2) The group which includes the president and vice-presidents is called _____.

(3) _____ is comprised of division managers, branch managers and department heads.

(4) _____ refers to goals to be obtained, whereas _____ refers to the means to be used to achieve them.

(5) The establishment of departments, divisions, etc. is known as _____, while _____ refers to the supervision and monitoring of these units by management.

(6) _____ is the power to perform assigned duties, while _____ is the obligation to carry them out to the best of one's ability.

(7) In order to measure performance there must be some form of _____, _____, and _____.

(8) The process of identifying, summarizing, and interpreting information needed for planning and control, for management decisions and for product costing is termed _____.

(9) Authority to command is termed _____ authority; authority to advise but not command is termed _____ authority.

(10) The controller has _____ authority over his or her own department, but a _____ relationship with the other departments.

(11) The two most useful organization charts for the cost accountant are the _____ chart and the _____ chart.

*Answers:* (1) lower; (2) top management; (3) middle management; (4) setting objectives, directing; (5) organizing, controlling; (6) authority, responsibility; (7) review, evaluation and reporting; (8) cost accounting; (9) line, staff; (10) line, staff; (11) company, controller's division.

# Solved Problems

**1.1 Centralization vs Decentralization.** The Georgia Atlantic Paper Company, which has its headquarters and manufacturing operations in the southeast, has as its principal product kraft wrapping paper. The company recently increased its production substantially and, for product outlets, acquired four corrugated box plants located in Canton, Massillon, Akron and Springfield, Ohio. Two bag manufacturing plants, located in Hempstead and Locust Valley, Long Island, were also acquired. This expansion required decentralization of much of the manufacturing operations, and there has been considerable discussion of decentralization of the accounting operations as well.

Your firm has been performing this company's audit for years and you have been asked to carry out a Management Services Survey. Prepare a report covering the following points:

(a) Should the accounting and cost functions be decentralized?

(b) If so, to whom should the accountant report? Should the local accountant have line, staff or functional responsibilities?

(c) What are some of the advantages of decentralization?

**SOLUTION**

(a) When manufacturing operations are decentralized, it is generally desirable to decentralize the accounting function in order to better serve the newly diversified and widespread operations. It would not be practical to expect a plant manager to wait for cost accounting answers to the many everyday cost problems which arise. Instead, there should be a trained accountant at each plant or available at a nearby plant to answer cost questions promptly.

(b) The local accountant should report on a *line* basis or administratively to the local plant manager. He or she would have *staff* responsibility with respect to other departments. The accountant could advise but not command departments other than his or her own. The local accountant is a member of the plant unit or organization and is thus subject to the jurisdiction of the plant manager in all areas except accounting. Thus, the accountant and his or her staff would be expected to observe the working conditions established for the plant.

However, the chart of accounts, the preparation and filing of financial statements and reports would be a *functional* matter established by the controller in accordance with authority delegated by the president. Uniformity in accounting reports is required since consolidated financial data are submitted to stockholders, government agencies, etc. The local accountant would also prepare the many studies, analyses, and other cost information essential to local management. With the greater diversity and geographic distribution of operations and the greater need for lateral command, there is now a far greater understanding of the functional authority necessary in a large company with widespread operations.

(c) The advantages of decentralization include the following:

(1) Company accounting policies and procedures established by the corporate controller can be interpreted, implemented and enforced by the local accountant.

(2) Decision making at the local level provides good management training for advancement within the company.

(3) An alert accountant can provide information needed by management in controlling and reducing costs and improving operations. The accountant can also greatly enhance the value of the department and increase the appreciation of the contribution that accounting can make.

**1.2    Corporate Responsibilities.**   You have just been appointed Controller of the Fulton Company, which has grown rapidly in recent years. This expansion has brought about the need to reorganize various corporate responsibilities. The present responsibilities are as follows:

| Name | Present Responsibilities |
|---|---|
| Helen L. Johnson | President and Production Manager |
| Lloyd Smith | Vice-President in Charge of Production |
| Alfred Knowles | Manager of Accounting |
| Roberta Harter | Vice-President in Charge of Sales |
| Jennifer Lyons | Chief Accountant |
| Thomas Reilly | Manager of Design |
| Frank Weag | Purchasing Agent |
| Ray Lanuto | Manager of Maintenance |
| Georgina Kuezek | Vice-President of Engineering |

(a) Prepare an organization chart showing the proper arrangement of functions and (b) describe the proposed changes in duties and titles.

**SOLUTION**

(a)   See Fig. 1-3.

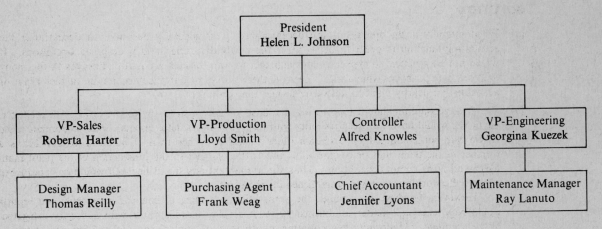

**Fig. 1-3**

(b) In order to avoid confusion regarding the direct responsibility for production, Lloyd Smith, the Vice-President, should be given the direct responsibility commensurate with his ability for the production function. Of course, he would be responsible to the President and perhaps a limit might be placed on contracts which the Vice-President could approve. Contracts for higher amounts would have to be approved by the President.

The title of Alfred Knowles as Manager in Charge of Accounting should be changed to Controller, the currently accepted terminology for the chief accounting officer.

The title of Roberta Harter as Vice-President in Charge of Sales might be changed to VP-Sales to be consistent with the titles of the other Vice-Presidents.

**1.3**     **Organization Chart.** The Samson Manufacturing Company has the following job classifications:

Vice-President, Marketing
Manager, Costs
Manager, Purchasing Department
Supervisor, Finishing Department
President
Manager, Shipping Room
Vice-President, Personnel
Manager, Branch Sales
Vice-President, Research and
    Development
Manager, Budgets
Controller
Manager, Employment
Vice-President, Finance
Manager, Receiving Department
Corporate Secretary
Manager, Market Research
Vice-President, Engineering
Manager, Internal Auditing
Supervisor, Machining Department

Manager, Production Control
    Department
Supervisor, Drilling Department
Manager, Inspection Department
Supervisor, Assembly Department
Manager, New Products
Manager, Basic Research
Manager, Product Improvement
Manager, Job Evaluation
Manager, Engineering Services
Treasurer
Manager, Engineering Design
Assistant Treasurer
Manager, Systems
Vice-President, Manufacturing
Manager, General Accounting
Superintendent of Production
Manager, Receiving Department
Manager, Stores Department
Manager, Maintenance Department

Prepare an organization chart showing the relationship among the various areas of responsibilities.

**SOLUTION**

See Fig. 1-4.

**1.4**     Indicate whether the relationship of the first individual to the second in the following pairs is of a line (L) or staff (S) nature.   (a) VP-Finance, Controller; (b) VP-Manufacturing, Controller; (c) Controller, Cost Accountant; (d) Controller, Production Superintendent; (e) VP-Finance, Employment Manager; (f) VP-Finishing Dept., Manufacturing Supervisor; (g) Cost Accountant, Cost Clerk; (h) Cost Accountant; General Accountant; (i) Treasurer, Assistant Treasurer.

**SOLUTION**

(a) L,  (b) S,  (c) L,  (d) S,  (e) S,  (f) L,  (g) L,  (h) S,  (i) L.

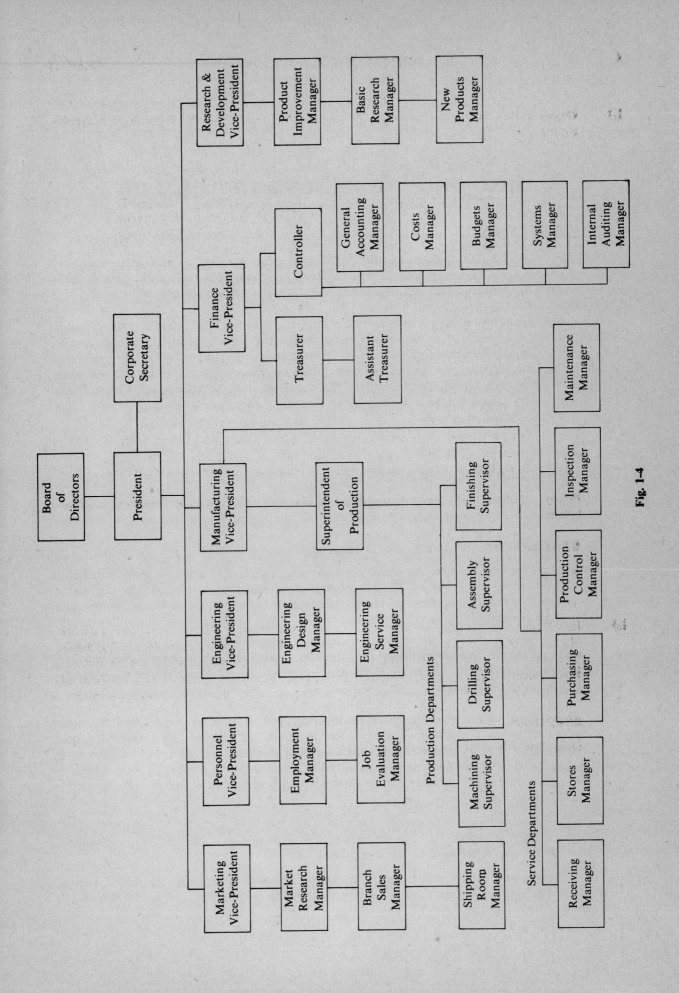

Fig. 1-4

# Chapter 2

# Nature and Classification of Costs

## 2.1 COST ACCOUNTING DEFINED

As practiced today, cost accounting may be defined as *the process of measuring, analyzing, computing and reporting the cost, profitability and performance of operations.* This can be contrasted to earlier definitions which limited cost accounting to "obtaining a figure representing the cost of a manufactured product."

The nature of modern business is such that all enterprises—whether large or small, manufacturing or nonmanufacturing, public or private, profit or nonprofit—require a wide variety of cost data in making day-to-day operating decisions. Thus, for the modern cost accountant, the positive emphasis on analysis and interpretation (managerial cost accounting) requires involvement in the *dynamic phase* of business—the current period and the future. The dynamic phase is concerned primarily with *planning* (i.e. selecting objectives and the means for their attainment) and *controlling* (i.e. achieving conformity to established plans).

## 2.2 COST ACCOUNTING CONCEPTS

A concept is a basic principle or assumption, as opposed to a procedure for carrying out the concept. Cost accounting concepts may be separated into two groups: (1) *planning* and (2) *controlling*.

(1) ***Planning.*** There are two key types of planning, as described below.

*Project Planning. The process whereby management, confronted by a specific problem, evaluates each alternative in order to arrive at a decision as to the course of future action.* Since planning requires a comparison of the costs of various alternative solutions, the cost of each alternative must be determined.

*Period Planning. The process whereby management systematically develops an acceptable set of plans for the total future activities of the enterprise, or some functional subdivision thereof, for a specified period of time.* This type of planning, covering a period of one year or more, usually refers to an overall budget.

(2) ***Controlling.*** This involves the systematic monitoring of performance to determine the degree of adherence to established objectives. Actual results are continuously measured against yardsticks such as budgets, standard costs, time study standards, etc. previously established for manufacturing, marketing, finance and all other activities of the company. Any significant deviation from such yardsticks can be detected quickly and management can take corrective action promptly.

The concepts of *cost, expense,* and *loss* are often used interchangeably. The AICPA, in *Accounting Terminology Bulletin No. 4*, defines these terms as follows:

*Cost* is "the amount, measured in money, of cash expended or other property transferred, capital stock issued, services performed, or a liability incurred, in consideration of goods or services received or to be received."

*Expense* is "all expired costs which are deductible from revenues." In a narrower sense "the term 'expense' refers to operating, selling, or administrative expenses, interest, and taxes." Items included in cost of manufacturing, such as materials, labor, and overhead, should be described as costs, not expenses.

*Loss* is "(1) the excess of all expenses, in the broad sense of that word, over revenues for a period, or (2) the excess of all or the appropriate portion of the cost of assets over related proceeds, if any, when the items are sold, abandoned, or either wholly or partially destroyed by casualty or otherwise written off. When losses such as those described in (2) are deducted from revenues, they are expenses in the broad sense of that term."

## 2.3  CLASSIFICATION OF COSTS

Classification of costs is necessary in order to determine the most suitable method of accumulating and allocating cost data. The principal methods of accumulating costs are described below.

(1)  *Function*

   *Manufacturing.*   Costs applied to producing a product.

   *Marketing.*   Costs incurred in selling a product or service.

   *Administrative.*   Costs incurred in policy-making activities.

   *Financial.*   Costs related to financial activities.

(2)  *Elements*

   *Direct material.*   Material which is an integral part of the finished product.

   *Direct labor.*   Labor applied directly to components of the finished product.

   *Factory overhead.*   Indirect materials, indirect labor, and the manufacturing expenses that cannot logically be charged directly to specific units, jobs or products.

(3)  *Product*

   *Direct.*   Costs which are charged to the product and require no further allocation.

   *Indirect.*   Costs which are allocated.

(4)  *Department*

   *Production.*   A unit in which operations are performed on the part or product and whose costs are not further allocated.

   *Service.*   A unit not directly engaged in production and whose costs are ultimately allocated to a production unit.

(5)  *When Charged to Income*

   *Product.*   Costs included when product costs, as defined above, are computed. Product costs are included in inventory and in cost of sales when the product is sold.

   *Period.*   Costs associated with the passage of time rather than with the product. These are closed out to the income summary each period since no future benefits are expected.

(6)  *Relation to Volume*

   *Variable.*   Costs which change in total in direct proportion to changes in related activity. The unit cost remains the same regardless of volume.

*Fixed.* Costs which do not change in total over wide ranges of volume. The unit costs decrease as volume increases.

(7) **Period Covered**

*Capital.* Costs which are expected to benefit future periods and are classified as assets.

*Revenue.* Costs which benefit only the current period and are thus expenses.

(8) **Degree of Averaging**

*Total.* The cumulative cost for the established category.

*Unit.* The total cost divided by the number of units of activity or volume.

## 2.4 COST SYSTEMS

The cost system must be closely tailored to the organizational structure of the company, the manufacturing process, and the type of information desired and required by executives. Numerous cost systems exist, each with their own advantages and disadvantages. The principal types of cost systems, classified according to their particular attribute, are described below.

(1) **Periodic Cost Accumulation Systems.** These provide only limited cost information during a period and require quarterly or year-end adjustments to arrive at the cost of goods manufactured. Periodic physical inventories must be taken to adjust inventory accounts and arrive at the cost of goods manufactured. A periodic cost accumulation system is *not* considered a complete cost accumulation system since the costs of work-in-process and finished goods can only be determined after physical inventories are taken. Because of this limitation, periodic cost accumulation systems are generally used by small manufacturing companies.

(2) **Perpetual Cost Accumulation Systems.** These provide continuous information about work-in-process, finished goods, and cost of goods manufactured. Cost data are accumulated through a work-in-process account. These systems are used by most medium and large manufacturing companies. Perpetual cost accumulation systems are usually organized under either a job order or process cost format.

*Job Order Cost.* The cost unit is the job, and costs are accumulated by job. This format is most suitable where each job or order is different, such as in a printing shop.

*Process Cost.* The cost unit is the average cost for the units produced in a specified period of time. This format is most suitable where a high volume of similar products are produced, such as in a paper mill.

## 2.5 UNIT COSTS

The total cost figure is usually unsatisfactory from a control standpoint since the quantity of production varies greatly from period to period. Therefore, some common denominator, such as unit costs, must be available for comparison of varying volumes and amounts. The unit cost figure can be readily computed by dividing total costs by the number of units produced. Unit costs may be stated in terms of tons, gallons, pounds, feet, individual units, etc.

### EXAMPLE 1

Unit costs facilitate the computation of amounts for closing inventory and for cost of goods sold. For example, assume that 3,000 units are produced at a total cost of $4,500, or $1.50 per unit. If 2,500 units are sold and 500 remain in inventory, the computation is as follows:

| Description | Units | Cost | Unit Cost |
|---|---|---|---|
| Production cost | 3,000 | $4,500 | $1.50 |
| Cost of goods sold (2,500 units @ $1.50) | 2,500 | 3,750 | 1.50 |
| Closing inventory (500 units @ $1.50) | 500 | $ 750 | $1.50 |

## 2.6 FIXED AND VARIABLE COSTS

For proper budgeting and cost control it is necessary to make a distinction between *fixed* and *variable* total costs. Most costs fit easily into one category or the other; however, various items of factory overhead can be classified as *semivariable* costs and must be carefully examined to determine their relationship to changes in the volume of production.

*Fixed Costs.* Those which continue unchanged in total within a relevant range despite wide fluctuations in volume or activity. There is a fluctuation in fixed cost *per unit* with volume change. Examples of fixed costs are property taxes and production executives' salaries.

*Variable Costs.* Those which change in total in direct proportion to changes in volume or activity. There is a relatively uniform cost *per unit* with changes in volume or activity. Direct materials and direct labor are generally considered variable costs. Included in this category are such items as factory supplies and payroll taxes.

*Semivariable Costs.* Those which vary but not in direct proportion to volume or activity. For example, the payroll department costs may remain unchanged up to a certain number of production employees. Additional volume usually requires additional production employees and causes an increase in payroll costs. Other examples of semivariable costs are salaries of production department supervisors and heat.

## 2.7 INCOME STATEMENTS

The income statements of a manufacturing company and a merchandising company reflect the basic difference in operations of these two types of enterprises. The manufacturing company transforms raw material into finished goods through the use of labor and factory facilities (for example, a company producing finished furniture from lumber). A merchandising company, such as a retail furniture store which buys finished furniture and sells it in the same form, sells the goods it buys without changing the basic form.

### EXAMPLE 2

In the Cost of Goods Sold section of the Augusta Manufacturing Company's income statement, there is a caption *Cost of Goods Manufactured*. On the comparable line of the Locust Valley Merchandising Company's statement is the caption *Purchases*. The latter caption indicates that goods similar to that in the opening and closing Merchandise Inventory have been bought during the accounting period. The caption *Cost of Goods Manufactured* represents the total of materials, labor and overhead used in manufacturing the product and is detailed in the supporting Schedule of Cost of Goods Manufactured. As can be seen, the schedule shows the direct materials, the direct labor and the various components of factory overhead that apply. The term Cost of Goods Manufactured relates to the cost of products which have been *fully completed and transferred to Finished Goods*. The products which have not been completed will remain in the Work in Process Inventory at the end of the period.

*Augusta Manufacturing Company*
*Income Statement*
*for year ended December 31, 19X1*

| | |
|---|---:|
| Sales | $2,100,000 |
| Less: Cost of Goods Sold | |
| Finished Goods, Jan. 1, 19X1 | $ 180,000 |
| Cost of Goods Manufactured | 1,500,000 |
| (see Schedule of Cost of Goods | |
| Manufactured) | |
| | $1,680,000 |
| Finished Goods, Dec. 31, 19X1 | 150,000 |
| Cost of Goods Sold | $1,530,000 |
| Gross Margin | $ 570,000 |
| Less: Selling and Administrative | |
| Expense | 250,000 |
| Net Income | $ 320,000 |

*Locust Valley Merchandising Company*
*Income Statement*
*for year ended December 31, 19X1*

| | |
|---|---:|
| Sales | $2,150,000 |
| Less: Costs of Goods Sold | |
| Merchandise Inventory Jan. 1, 19X1 | $ 150,000 |
| Purchases | 1,550,000 |
| | $1,700,000 |
| Merchandise Inventory Dec. 31, 19X1 | 175,000 |
| Cost of Goods Sold | $1,525,000 |
| Gross Margin | $ 625,000 |
| Less: Selling and Administrative | |
| Expense | 275,000 |
| Net Income | $ 350,000 |

*Augusta Manufacturing Company*
*Schedule of Cost of Goods Manufactured*
*for year ended December 31, 19X1*

| | | |
|---|---:|---:|
| Direct Materials: | | |
| Inventory, Jan. 1, 19X1 | $ 170,000 | |
| Purchase of Direct Materials | 1,050,000 | |
| | $1,220,000 | |
| Inventory, Dec. 31, 19X1 | 120,000 | |
| Direct Materials Used | | $1,100,000 |
| Direct Labor | | 250,000 |
| Factory Overhead | | |
| Indirect Labor | $ 70,000 | |
| Supplies | 15,000 | |
| Heat, Light and Power | 23,000 | |
| Depreciation, Plant | 20,000 | |
| Depreciation, Equipment | 30,000 | |
| Miscellaneous | 7,000 | 165,000 |
| Manufacturing Costs | | $1,515,000 |
| Add: Work in Process, Jan. 1, 19X1 | | 90,000 |
| | | $1,605,000 |
| Less: Work in Process, Dec. 31, 19X1 | | 105,000 |
| Cost of Goods Manufactured (to Income Statement) | | $1,500,000 |

# Summary

(1) Cost accounting is the process of _IDENTIFYING_____, _SUMMARIZING_____ and _INTERPRETING_____ information needed for _____, _____ and _____.

(2) Cost accounting concepts include all of the following except (a) planning, (b) controlling, (c) profit sharing, (d) product costing.

(3) Evaluating each option to arrive at a decision is called _____, while developing a set of plans for the future activities of the enterprise is known as _____.

(4) A _____ company changes raw materials into finished goods, while a _____ company sells its inventory in the same form as acquired.

(5) The three major elements of product costs are all *but* (a) direct materials, (b) factory overhead, (c) indirect labor, (d) direct labor.

(6) Cost is the amount exchanged in consideration for goods or services received or to be received, while expense is that portion of cost which has expired. (a) True, (b) false.

(7) The unit cost is desirable as a _COMMON DENOMINATOR_____ for comparing costs from period to period.

(8) Cost of goods manufactured includes (a) manufacturing costs and finished goods inventory, (b) manufacturing costs and work in process, (c) manufacturing costs, work in process and finished goods inventory.

(9) _____ costs are those chargeable as expenses or losses in the current period, while _____ costs are those carried forward to future periods.

(10) _FIXED_____ unit costs remain constant with changes in volume, while _VARIABLE_____ unit costs fluctuate with volume.

(11) Two examples of fixed factory overhead are (a) _____, _____; two examples of variable factory overhead are (b) _____, _____.

(12) _PRODUCT_____ costs are those which follow the item into inventory, and _PERIOD_____ costs are those chargeable against current income.

(13) _MFG_____ departments work directly with the product, while _SERVICE_____ departments render a benefit for other departments.

(14) _REVENUE_____ expenditures benefit the current period only, while _CAPITAL_____ expenditures benefit more than one period.

(15) An overstatement of work in process at the end of a period will (a) overstate cost of goods manufactured, (b) understate current assets, (c) understate gross profit, (d) overstate net income.

*Answers:* (1) identifying, summarizing, interpreting; planning and control, management decisions, product costing; (2) c; (3) project planning, period planning; (4) manufacturing; merchandising; (5) c; (6) a; (7) common denominator; (8) b; (9) expired, unexpired; (10) variable, fixed; (11) supervisors' salaries, property taxes; lubricants, factory supplies; (12) product, period; (13) manufacturing, service; (14) revenue, capital; (15) d.

# Solved Problems

**2.1**  **Cost Elements.**  Indicate whether the cost element for each of the following cost components is direct materials (DM), direct labor (DL) or factory overhead (FO).

(a)  Fire insurance on equipment  (e)  Machinery repairs
(b)  Machine operator's wages  (f)  Supervisor's wages
(c)  Bags in cement mills  (g)  Bottles for product
(d)  Cutting tools  (h)  Cost Accountant's salary

**SOLUTION**

(a) FO,  (b) DL,  (c) DM,  (d) FO,  (e) FO,  (f) FO,  (g) DM,  (h) FO.

**2.2**  **Fixed and Variable Costs.**  Indicate whether each of the following items represents a fixed (F), variable (V) or semivariable (S) cost.

(a)  Rent  (e)  Production control salaries
(b)  Indirect employee's wages  (f)  Factory power
(c)  Cutting tools  (g)  Factory manager
(d)  Property taxes  (h)  Machinery repairs

**SOLUTION**

(a) F,  (b) S,  (c) V,  (d) F,  (e) F,  (f) V,  (g) F,  (h) S.

**2.3**  **Direct and Indirect Materials.**  Indicate whether each of the following items represents direct (D) or indirect (I) materials.

(a)  Sandpaper used in production  (e)  Adhesives for boxes
(b)  Jars for cosmetics  (f)  Nails
(c)  Shop patterns  (g)  Wood pulp
(d)  Freight-in on raw materials  (h)  Lubricants

**SOLUTION**

(a) I,  (b) D,  (c) I,  (d) D,  (e) I,  (f) I,  (g) D,  (h) I.

**2.4**  **Computation of Sales.**  The following data relate to the operations of the Overbrook Road Company for 19X7:

|  | Work in Process | Finished Goods |
|---|---|---|
| Beginning inventories | $22,000 | $13,000 |
| Ending inventories | 28,000 | 17,000 |

Given that the cost of goods manufactured was $284,000 and the gross profit for the year was $35,000, compute the sales for 19X7.

**SOLUTION**

| | |
|---|---:|
| Cost of Goods Manufactured | $284,000 |
| Add: Beginning Inventory of Finished Goods | 13,000 |
| | $297,000 |
| Less: Ending Inventory of Finished Goods | 17,000 |
| Cost of Goods Sold | $280,000 |
| Add: Gross Profit | 35,000 |
| Sales | $315,000 |

**2.5    Income Statement.**    The records of Folk, Incorporated show the following data for November, 19X7.

| Inventory Balances | November 1 | November 30 |
|---|---|---|
| Raw materials | $12,000 | $13,500 |
| Work in process | 15,100 | 17,600 |
| Finished goods | 19,500 | 21,200 |

| Operating data: | |
|---|---:|
| Direct labor cost | $ 50,000 |
| Factory overhead | 62,500 |
| Cost of goods sold | 150,000 |
| Sales | 250,000 |
| Selling expenses | 23,000 |
| General and administrative expenses | 25,000 |

Prepare (a) an Income Statement with (b) a separate schedule showing the cost of goods sold.

**SOLUTION**

(a)

*Folk, Incorporated*
*Income Statement*
*for month of November, 19X7*

| | | |
|---|---:|---:|
| Sales | | $250,000 |
| Less: Cost of Goods Sold (see schedule) | | 150,000 |
| Gross Profit on Sales | | $100,000 |
| Operating Expenses | | |
| Selling Expenses | $23,000 | |
| General and Administrative Expenses | 25,000 | 48,000 |
| Net Income from Operations | | $ 52,000 |

(b)

**Folk, Incorporated**
**Schedule of Cost of Goods Sold**
**for month of November, 19X7**

| | | |
|---|---:|---:|
| Raw Materials Cost | | |
|    Raw Materials Inventory, November 1 | $12,000 | |
|    Purchases | 43,200 | |
|       Goods Available | $55,200 | |
|    Less: Raw Materials Inventory, November 30 | 13,500 | |
| Raw Materials Cost | | $ 41,700 |
| Direct Labor Cost | | 50,000 |
| Factory Overhead | | 62,500 |
| Total Manufacturing Cost | | $154,200 |
|    Add: Work in Process, November 1 | | 15,100 |
| | | $169,300 |
|    Less: Work in Process, November 30 | | 17,600 |
| Cost of Goods Manufactured | | $151,700 |
|    Add: Finished Goods Inventory, November 1 | | 19,500 |
| | | $171,200 |
|    Less: Finished Goods Inventory, November 30 | | 21,200 |
| Cost of Goods Sold | | $150,000 |

*Note:* On a problem such as this the form may be set up first and then all amounts given inserted in the proper places in the form. Generally, the problem has to be solved by working backwards from the ending figure given, which in this case was the cost of goods sold of $150,000.

**2.6    Gross Profit.** The M. G. Milligan Company produces basketball fixtures which retail for $420 a unit. This year a gross profit of 30% of the cost of goods sold was made on the 3,000 units sold. Materials were 50% and labor cost 30% of the current cost of goods sold.

Next year it is expected that material and labor costs will increase 20% per unit, and factory overhead will increase 15% per unit. A new selling price of $500 has been established to meet rising costs.

Compute the number of units that must be sold next year to make the same gross profit as this year.

**SOLUTION**

**Current Year: Cost and Gross Profit**

| | |
|---|---:|
| Selling price per unit | $420 |
| Cost of goods sold ($420 ÷ 1.30) | 323 |
| Gross profit per unit | $ 97 |

**Next Year: Cost and Gross Profit**

| | |
|---|---:|
| Materials ($323 × 50% × 120%) | $193.80 |
| Labor ($323 × 30% × 120%) | 116.28 |
| Factory overhead ($323 × 20% × 115%) | 74.29 |
| Total cost per unit | $384.37 |
| Gross profit per unit ($500.00 − $384.37) | $115.63 |

In the current year, the gross profit totaled $291,000 (3,000 units × $97). To determine the number of unit sales required to maintain this figure in the next year, the current gross profit is divided by the projected new gross profit per unit. Thus, $291,000 ÷ $115.63 = 2,517 units.

NATURE AND CLASSIFICATION OF COSTS

**2.7** **Fixed and Variable Costs.** The Englewood Company produces a large excavator selling for $400 per unit, of which cost of goods sold amounted to $320 and selling and administrative expenses, $25. During 19X5, 2,500 units were sold. The breakdown of cost of goods sold was: materials, 50%; labor, 25%; factory overhead, 25%.

The following cost increases are expected in 19X6: materials, 15%; labor, 20%. The selling price is to be raised to $460, but management anticipates an accompanying 20% decrease in the number of units sold.

(a) Prepare an Income Statement for 19X5, including costs per unit.

(b) Prepare an Income Statement for 19X6, including unit costs. Materials and labor costs are to be held to 75% of cost of goods sold; selling and administrative expenses increase to $35 per unit.

(c) It was later found that 19X5 factory overhead consisted of $125,000 in fixed expenses and $75,000 in variable expenses. Prepare a revised Income Statement for 19X6, ignoring the previous relationship of materials and labor to cost of goods sold. Fixed costs will remain constant despite the decrease in units sold.

**SOLUTION**

(a)

*Englewood Company*
*Income Statement*
*Year 19X5*

| | Total | Per Unit |
|---|---|---|
| Sales (2,500 units) | $1,000,000 | $400.00 |
| Cost of Goods Sold | | |
| Materials (50%) | $ 400,000 | $160.00 |
| Labor (25%) | 200,000 | 80.00 |
| Factory Overhead (25%) | 200,000 | 80.00 |
| Total Cost of Goods Sold | $ 800,000 | $320.00 |
| Gross Profit | $ 200,000 | 80.00 |
| Selling and Administrative Expenses | 62,500 | 25.00 |
| Net Profit | $ 137,500 | $ 55.00 |

(b)

*Englewood Company*
*Income Statement*
*Year 19X6*

| | Total | Per Unit |
|---|---|---|
| Sales (2,000 units) | $920,000 | $460.00 |
| Cost of Goods Sold | | |
| Materials ($160 × 115%) | $368,000 | $184.00 |
| Labor ($80 × 120%) | 192,000 | 96.00 |
| Factory Overhead (25% of Cost of Goods Sold) | 186,667* | 93.33 |
| Total Cost of Goods Sold | $746,667 | $373.33 |
| Gross Profit | $173,333 | $ 86.67 |
| Selling and Administrative Expenses | 70,000 | 35.00 |
| Net Profit | $103,333 | $ 51.67 |

* *Computation of factory overhead:*
   Total cost of goods sold = ($368,000 + $192,000) ÷ 75% = $746,667
   Factory overhead = $746,667 × 25% = $186,667

(c)

*Englewood Company*
*Income Statement*
*Year 19X6 Revised*

|  |  | Total |  | Per Unit |
|---|---|---|---|---|
| Sales (2,000 units) |  | $920,000 |  | $460.00 |
| Cost of Goods Sold |  |  |  |  |
|   Materials |  | $368,000 |  | $184.00 |
|   Labor |  | 192,000 |  | 96.00 |
| Factory Overhead |  |  |  |  |
|   Fixed | $125,000 |  | $62.50 |  |
|   Variable | 60,000* | 185,000 | 30.00 | 92.50 |
| Total Cost of Sales |  | $745,000 |  | $372.50 |
| Gross Profit |  | $175,000 |  | $ 87.50 |
| Selling and Administrative Expenses |  | 70,000 |  | 35.00 |
| Net Profit |  | $105,000 |  | $ 52.50 |

\* The factory overhead in 19X5 was $200,000, made up of $125,000 fixed expense and $75,000 variable expense. The variable expense per unit is $30 ($75,000 ÷ 2,500 units). The variable portion of factory overhead in 19X6, therefore, is 2,000 units times $30, or $60,000.

**2.8**    **Cost of Goods Manufactured.** The Hempstead Company, which manufactures a single product, shows the following ledger balances for the month of January, 19X6.

| | |
|---|---|
| Direct labor | $180,000 |
| Indirect labor | 65,000 |
| Factory rent | 11,000 |
| Heat, light and power | 3,500 |
| Miscellaneous factory overhead | 16,500 |
| Interest expenses | 4,500 |
| Office salaries | 11,000 |
| Sales commissions | 4,000 |
| Sales returns and allowances | 5,000 |
| Freight-out | 5,500 |

*Other data:*

Purchases of raw materials: 16,000 units at $3.00 each; 10,000 units at $2.50 each.

Production: 25,000 units.

Sales: 20,000 units at $12.

Raw materials inventory, January 1: 2,000 units at $3.50 each.

The first-in, first-out method is used in valuing raw materials inventory.

Each unit of finished goods requires one unit of raw material.

Work-in-process inventory: January 1, 3,000 units costing $12,000; at January 31, 5,000 units costing $17,000.

Finished goods inventory, January 1: 5,000 units at $9 each.

Factory machinery: cost $30,000, depreciation 10% per year.

Office equipment: cost $10,000, depreciation 8% per year.

Prepare a Statement of Cost of Goods Manufactured for the month of January, 19X6.

**SOLUTION**

*The Hempstead Company*
*Statement of Cost of Goods Manufactured*
*for month of January, 19X6*

| | | |
|---|---:|---:|
| Raw Materials | | |
|    Inventory, January 1 | $ 7,000 | |
|    Purchases | 73,000 | |
|      Raw Materials Available | $80,000 | |
|    Less: Inventory, January 31* | 7,500 | |
| Cost of Raw Materials Used | | $ 72,500 |
| Direct Labor | | 180,000 |
| Factory Overhead | | |
|    Indirect Labor | $65,000 | |
|    Factory Rent | 11,000 | |
|    Heat, Light and Power | 3,500 | |
|    Depreciation, Machinery | 250 | |
|    Miscellaneous | 16,500 | 96,250 |
| Total Manufacturing Costs | | $348,750 |
| Add: Work in Process, January 1 | | 12,000 |
|    Balance | | $360,750 |
| Deduct: Work in Process, January 31 | | 17,000 |
| Cost of Goods Manufactured | | $343,750 |

| *Raw Materials Units | |
|---|---:|
| Inventory, January 1 | 2,000 |
| Purchases (16,000 + 10,000) | 26,000 |
|    Units Available | 28,000 |
| Used in Production | 25,000 |
| Inventory, January 31 | 3,000 |

**2.9    Cost of Goods Manufactured and Sold.**   The Mason Manufacturing Company had the following data in its ledger for the six months ended December 31, 19X6.

| | | | |
|---|---:|---|---:|
| Raw materials purchased | $74,000 | Fire insurance | $ 400 |
| Factory supplies purchased | 2,600 | Workers' compensation insurance | 1,800 |
| Direct labor | 60,000 | Power, heat and light | 2,200 |
| Indirect labor | 3,800 | Depreciation, machinery | 2,800 |
| Supervision | 6,400 | Depreciation, factory building | 1,300 |

Inventories: finished goods, June 30, $63,000, December 31, $73,000; work in process, June 30, $12,000, December 31, $18,000; raw materials, June 30, $57,000, December 31, $17,000; factory supplies, June 30, $250, December 31, $350.

Prepare (a) a Statement of Cost of Goods Manufactured and Sold for this six-month period, including (b) a supporting Schedule of Factory Overhead.

**SOLUTION**

(a)

Mason Manufacturing Company<br>
Statement of Cost of Goods Manufactured and Sold<br>
for six months ended December 31, 19X6

| | | |
|---|---:|---:|
| Raw Materials | | |
|     Inventory, June 30, 19X6 | $ 57,000 | |
|     Purchases | 74,000 | |
|         Materials Available for Use | $131,000 | |
|     Less: Inventory, December 31, 19X6 | 17,000 | |
| Cost of Materials Consumed | | $114,000 |
| Direct Labor | | 60,000 |
| Factory Overhead (see schedule) | | 21,200 |
| Total Manufacturing Costs | | $195,200 |
|     Add: Work in Process Inventory, June 30, 19X6 | | 12,000 |
| | | $207,200 |
|     Less: Work in Process Inventory, December 31, 19X6 | | 18,000 |
| Cost of Goods Manufactured | | $189,200 |
|     Add: Finished Goods Inventory, June 30, 19X6 | | 63,000 |
| | | $252,200 |
|     Less: Finished Goods Inventory, December 31, 19X6 | | 73,000 |
| Cost of Goods Sold | | $179,200 |

(b)

Mason Manufacturing Company<br>
Schedule of Factory Overhead<br>
for six months ended December 31, 19X6

| | |
|---|---:|
| Indirect Labor | $ 3,800 |
| Supervision | 6,400 |
| Factory Supplies ($250 + $2,600 − $350) | 2,500 |
| Power, Heat and Light | 2,200 |
| Depreciation, Machinery | 2,800 |
| Depreciation, Factory Building | 1,300 |
| Workers' Compensation Insurance | 1,800 |
| Fire Insurance | 400 |
|     Total Factory Overhead | $21,200 |

**2.10   Cost of Goods Manufactured and Sold.** The Kiven Manufacturing Company showed the following ledger balances at December 31, 19X6 after adjustments.

| | | | |
|---|---:|---|---:|
| Purchases | $160,000 | Insurance | $ 4,000 |
| Purchase returns and allowances | 2,000 | Heat, light and power | 20,000 |
| Raw materials used | 128,000 | Depreciation, factory building | 7,000 |
| Direct labor | 150,000 | Depreciation, machinery | 28,000 |
| Indirect labor | 30,000 | Factory supplies | 8,000 |
| Property taxes | 3,000 | Maintenance | 6,000 |

Inventories were as follows:  Raw materials, January 1, $40,000; work in process, January 1, $12,400, December 31, $23,400; finished goods, January 1, $30,000, December 31, $50,000.

Prepare a Statement of Cost of Goods Manufactured and Sold for the year 19X6.

**SOLUTION**

*Kiven Manufacturing Company*
*Statement of Cost of Goods Manufactured and Sold*
*for year ended December 31, 19X6*

| | | | |
|---|---:|---:|---:|
| Raw Materials | | | |
|   Inventory, January 1, 19X6 | | $ 40,000 | |
|   Cost of Purchases | | | |
|     Purchases | $160,000 | | |
|     Less: Purchase Returns and Allowances | 2,000 | 158,000 | |
|   Total Inventory and Purchases | | $198,000 | |
|   Less: Inventory, December 31, 19X6 | | 70,000 | |
|   Raw Materials Used | | | $128,000 |
| Direct Labor | | | 150,000 |
| Manufacturing Overhead | | | |
|   Indirect Labor | | $ 30,000 | |
|   Heat, Light, and Power | | 20,000 | |
|   Maintenance | | 6,000 | |
|   Factory Supplies | | 8,000 | |
|   Insurance | | 4,000 | |
|   Property Taxes | | 3,000 | |
|   Depreciation, Factory Building | $ 7,000 | | |
|   Depreciation, Machinery | 28,000 | 35,000 | 106,000 |
| Total Manufacturing Cost | | | $384,000 |
| Add: Work in Process, January 1, 19X6 | | | 12,400 |
| Total Manufacturing Costs to Account for | | | $396,400 |
| Less: Work in Process, December 31, 19X6 | | | 23,400 |
| Cost of Goods Manufactured | | | $373,000 |
| Add: Finished Goods, January 1, 19X6 | | | 30,000 |
| Total Cost of Goods Available for Sale | | | $403,000 |
| Less: Finished Goods, December 31, 19X6 | | | 50,000 |
| Cost of Goods Sold | | | $353,000 |

**2.11**  **Net Income and Cost of Goods Sold.**   Susan Manufacturing Company produces television sets that sell for $100.   The following data is from the company's books as of December 31, 19X6:

| | |
|---|---:|
| Sales | $200,000 |
| Purchases | 35,000 |
| Direct labor | 24,000 |
| Indirect labor | 3,500 |
| Rent | 1,500 |
| Freight-in | 300 |
| Freight-out | 1,700 |
| Office salaries | 18,800 |
| Sales salaries | 14,000 |

| | | |
|---|---|---|
| Royalties paid | $12,000 | |
| Bad debts expense | 150 | |
| Interest earned | 50 | |
| Purchase discounts | 600 | |
| Depreciation (Factory) | 1,700 | |
| Miscellaneous: | | |
|    Factory overhead | 9,000 | |
|    Selling expenses | 7,000 | |
|    Administrative expenses | 4,000 | |

| Inventories | January 1 | December 31 |
|---|---|---|
| Raw materials | $2,200 | $6,400 |
| Work in process | 5,400 | 3,200 |
| Finished goods | 3,600 | 6,800 |

The finished goods inventory on January 1 consisted of 100 units; the December 31 inventory contained 140 units. The rent is apportioned 70% to manufacturing, 15% to sales, and 15% to administration.

Prepare (a) an Income Statement for the year ended December 31, 19X6 along with (b) a Schedule of Cost of Goods Sold.

## SOLUTION

(a)

*Susan Manufacturing Company*
*Income Statement*
*for year ended December 31, 19X6*

| | | | |
|---|---|---|---|
| Sales | | | $200,000 |
| Cost of Goods Sold (see schedule) | | | 69,350 |
| Gross Profit on Sales | | | $130,650 |
| Operating Expenses | | | |
|   Selling Expenses | | | |
|     Sales Salaries | $14,000 | | |
|     Royalties Paid | 12,000 | | |
|     Freight-out | 1,700 | | |
|     Rent | 225 | | |
|     Miscellaneous | 7,000 | | |
|   Total Selling Expenses | | $34,925 | |
|   Administrative Expenses | | | |
|     Office Salaries | $18,800 | | |
|     Loss from Bad Debts | 150 | | |
|     Rent | 225 | | |
|     Miscellaneous | 4,000 | | |
|   Total Administrative Expenses | | 23,175 | |
|   Total Operating Expenses | | | 58,100 |
| Net Profit from Operations | | | $ 72,550 |
| Nonoperating Income and Expense Items | | | |
|   Income Additions: | | | |
|     Interest Earned | | $ 50 | |
|     Purchase Discounts | | 600 | |
|   Total Additions | | | 650 |
| Net Income for Period | | | $ 73,200 |

(b)

**Susan Manufacturing Company**
**Schedule of Cost of Goods Sold**
**for year ended December 31, 19X6**

| | | | |
|---|---:|---:|---:|
| Raw Materials | | | |
| Inventory, January 1, 19X6 | | $ 2,200 | |
| Purchases | $35,000 | | |
| Add: Freight-in | 300 | 35,300 | |
| Raw Materials Available for Use | | $37,500 | |
| Less: Inventory, December 31, 19X6 | | 6,400 | |
| Cost of Raw Materials Consumed | | | $31,100 |
| Direct Labor | | | 24,000 |
| Factory Overhead | | | |
| Indirect Labor | | $ 3,500 | |
| Depreciation (Factory) | | 1,700 | |
| Rent | | 1,050 | |
| Miscellaneous | | 9,000 | |
| Total Factory Overhead | | | 15,250 |
| Total Manufacturing Costs | | | $70,350 |
| Add: Work in Process Inventory, January 1, 19X6 | | | 5,400 |
| | | | $75,750 |
| Less: Work in Process Inventory, December 31, 19X6 | | | 3,200 |
| Cost of Goods Manufactured | | | $72,550 |
| Add: Finished Goods Inventory, January 1, 19X6 | | | 3,600 |
| | | | $76,150 |
| Less: Finished Goods inventory, December 31, 19X6 | | | 6,800 |
| Cost of Goods Sold | | | $69,350 |

**2.12    Manufacture and Sale.**   The Purdy Manufacturing Company had the following operating data for the year 19X6:   Materials purchased, $136,000; direct labor, $120,000; and factory overhead, $135,000.   Inventories were as follows:   Raw materials, January 1, $28,000, December 31, $24,000; work in process, January 1, $60,000, December 31, $65,000; finished goods, January 1, $115,000, December 31, $90,000.

For the year 19X6, compute (a) the cost of goods manufactured, and (b) the cost of goods sold.

**SOLUTION**

(a) Cost of goods manufactured, year 19X6

| | | |
|---|---:|---:|
| Raw Materials | | |
| Raw Materials Inventory, January 1, 19X6 | $ 28,000 | |
| Purchases | 136,000 | |
| Materials Available | $164,000 | |
| Less: Raw Materials Inventory, December 31, 19X6 | 24,000 | |
| Raw Materials Used | | $140,000 |
| Direct Labor | | 120,000 |
| Factory Overhead | | 135,000 |
| Total Manufacturing Costs | | $395,000 |
| Add: Work in Process, January 1, 19X6 | | 60,000 |
| Total | | $455,000 |
| Less: Work in Process, December 31, 19X6 | | 65,000 |
| Cost of Goods Manufactured | | $390,000 |

(b) Cost of goods sold, year 19X6

| | |
|---|---|
| Finished Goods Inventory, January 1, 19X6 | $115,000 |
| Cost of Goods Manufactured, year 19X6 | 390,000 |
| Goods Available for Sale | $505,000 |
| Less: Finished Goods Inventory, December 31, 19X6 | 90,000 |
| Cost of Goods Sold | $415,000 |

**2.13** **Cost Data.** The following data pertain to the operations of the Samuel Company for the month of May: 127,000 lb of raw materials were purchased @ $0.50/lb. Raw materials put into process, $58,000. In Department A, 16,500 direct labor hours were worked, the labor rate was $2.10 per hour and the overhead rate was $1.30 per hour. In Department B, 22,750 direct labor hours were worked at rates of $2.50 for labor and $0.90 for overhead. Inventories were as follows: Raw materials, May 1, $22,500, May 31, $28,000; work in process, May 1, $26,000, May 31, $29,000; finished goods, May 1, $17,000, May 31, $14,100.

Compute (a) the total cost of production, (b) the cost of goods manufactured, and (c) the cost of goods sold.

**SOLUTION**                                    **Computations**

*Raw Materials*

| | | | |
|---|---|---|---|
| Inventory, 5/1 | 22,500 | 58,000 (1) | To production |
| Purchases | 63,500 | 28,000 | Inventory, 5/31 |
| | 86,000 | 86,000 | |

*Work in Process*

| | | | |
|---|---|---|---|
| Inventory, 5/1 | 26,000 | | |
| Materials | 58,000 (1) | | |
| Labor, Dept. A | 34,650 | 188,450 (2) | To finished goods |
| Labor, Dept. B | 56,875 | | |
| OH, Dept. A | 21,450 | | |
| OH, Dept. B | 20,475 | 29,000 | Inventory, 5/31 |
| | 217,450 | 217,450 | |
| Inventory, 5/1 | −26,000 | | |
| Put into production | 191,450 | | |

*Finished Goods*

| | | | |
|---|---|---|---|
| Inventory, 5/1 | 17,000 | 14,100 | Inventory, 5/31 |
| Production for May | 188,450 (2) | 191,350 | Cost of goods sold |
| | 205,450 | 205,450 | |

(a) *Cost of production:* $191,450.

(b) *Cost of goods manufactured:*

| | | |
|---|---|---|
| Cost of production | $191,450 | |
| Plus: Work in process, 5/1 | 26,000 | |
| | $217,450 | |
| Less: Work in process, 5/31 | 29,000 | |
| Cost of goods manufactured | | $188,450 |

(c) *Cost of goods sold:*

|  |  |  |
|---|---|---|
| Cost of goods manufactured | $188,450 |  |
| Plus: Finished goods, 5/1 | 17,000 |  |
|  | $205,450 |  |
| Less: Finished goods, 5/31 | 14,100 |  |
| Cost of goods sold |  | $191,350 |

# Chapter 3

# Costing and Control of Materials

## 3.1 CHARACTERISTICS OF MATERIALS

Materials are the basic substances that are transformed into finished goods. Materials costs may be either *direct* or *indirect*.

**Direct Materials.** The three characteristics of direct materials are:

(1) Easily traced to the product and quantified
(2) A major material of the finished product
(3) Can be identified directly with production of the product

**Indirect Materials.** These include all other materials used in production (i.e. nails in furniture manufacturing) and are considered to be a factory overhead cost.

## 3.2 PURCHASING MATERIALS

Three forms are used in the purchase of materials. Both direct and indirect materials are purchased in the same way; differences, however, exist in their issuance.

(1) **Purchase Requisition.** This is a written order to the purchasing department to inform them of the need for materials. Two copies are made; one is sent to the purchasing department and the other is retained by the originator of the order.

(2) **Purchase Order.** This is a written request to a supplier of materials by the purchasing department. It contains the quantity ordered, price, and terms of the agreement. Five copies are made; the original goes to the supplier; one is retained by the purchasing department; others are sent to the accounting department, the accounts payable department, and the receiving department.

(3) **Receiving Report.** This is a written report compiled by the receiving department upon receipt of the goods. It is a means of reconciling quantity discrepancies and discovering damaged goods. Five copies are made; they are sent to the purchasing department, the accounts payable department, the accounting department, the department placing the order, and the storeroom.

Under a periodic inventory system, the purchase of materials is recorded in an account entitled Purchases of Raw Materials. If a beginning materials inventory exists, it is recorded in a separate account entitled Materials Inventory—Beginning.

Under a perpetual inventory system, the purchase of materials is recorded in an account labeled Materials Inventory, rather than in a purchase account. If beginning materials inventory exists, it is also recorded in the materials inventory account.

### EXAMPLE 1

Sweet Dreams Brass Bed Company receives 1,000 feet of brass tubing (direct) and 2 cases of assorted brass screws (indirect). The tubing is $2 per foot and the screws are $25 per case. The journal entries under both periodic and perpetual inventory systems are as follows:

| Periodic Inventory System | | Perpetual Inventory System | |
|---|---|---|---|
| *Purchases of Raw Materials* | *2,050* | *Materials Inventory* | *2,050* |
| *Accounts Payable* | *2,050* | *Accounts Payable* | *2,050* |

*Note:* Direct and indirect materials are not placed in different accounts at the time of purchase.

## 3.3 ISSUANCE OF MATERIALS

(1) A material requisition must be prepared by the production department requesting the goods. The requisition should contain the job order number and/or the name of department making the request, the quantity and description of the goods, and the unit and total costs.

(2) Recording materials issued also differs, depending on whether a periodic or perpetual system is used. No entry is made under a periodic cost accumulation system when materials are issued; however, under a perpetual cost accumulation system, a debit is made to a work-in-process account and a credit is made to the materials account.

## EXAMPLE 2

Sweet Dreams Brass Bed Company places 500 feet of brass tubing in production ($2 per foot).

| Periodic Inventory System | | Perpetual Inventory System | |
|---|---|---|---|
| *No entry* | | *Work in Process* | *1,000* |
| | | *Materials* | *1,000* |

## 3.4 COSTING MATERIALS ISSUED AND ENDING MATERIALS INVENTORY

A comparison of the two inventory systems is shown below:

| Periodic Inventory System | Perpetual Inventory System |
|---|---|
| Materials Inventory (begin.) | Materials issued are charged to |
| + Purchases | the work-in-process account as |
| Materials available for use | they are used, and ending inven- |
| − Materials inventory (end.) | tory can be read directly from the |
| Cost of materials issued | materials inventory account. |

*Note:* Under a periodic system, materials inventory and work-in-process accounts hold historical balances. They must be adjusted to reflect the ending balance each period. This balance remains unchanged in the new period until it is adjusted again via the above calculation.

Periods of changing prices pose problems for the valuation of inventory. For example, what price should be charged for materials placed into production during such a period; what price should be charged for materials still on hand at the end of the period (ending materials inventory); and should the cost of materials issued be determined by the beginning unit price of materials, the average unit price for the period, or the ending unit price? Because the answers to these questions vary, depending on the business, four methods have been developed to value ending inventories and cost of materials issued during periods of changing prices:

(1) Specific identification
(2) Average cost—simple and weighted
(3) First-in, first-out (FIFO)
(4) Last-in, first-out (LIFO)

Use of each method under both the periodic and the perpetual inventory systems is illustrated in Examples 3 to 7. For convenience, BI and EI are used to denote Beginning Inventory and Ending Inventory, respectively. All five examples are based on the following data:

Sweet Dreams Company's inventory and purchases of brass tubing are as follows:

| | Date | Units Purchased | Cost per Unit ($ per ft) | Units Issued |
|---|---|---|---|---|
| (BI) | 1/1 | 1,500 | $1.75 | — |
| | 1/7 | 1,000 | 1.80 | — |
| | 1/9 | — | — | 1,000 (from BI) |
| | 1/15 | — | — | 500 (from BI) |
| | 1/21 | 2,000 | 2.00 | — |
| | 1/25 | 500 | 2.10 | — |
| | 1/30 | — | — | 2,000 (from 1/7 & 1/21 purchase) |

Ending Inventory 1/31: 1,500 units

(1) **Specific Identification.** Under this method each item is placed into inventory with a price tag. Both ending inventory and materials issued are valued at the prices tagged on each unit. This technique is generally used for expensive items.

## EXAMPLE 3

**Periodic and Perpetual Inventory Systems**

When specific identification is used, both the application of the technique and the results are *identical* under *either* the periodic or the perpetual inventory system, as illustrated below:

Cost of materials issued:

| (BI) | $1,000 \times \$1.75 =$ | $1,750 |
|---|---|---|
| (BI) | $500 \times \$1.75 =$ | 875 |
| (1/7) | $1,000 \times \$1.80 =$ | 1,800 |
| (1/21) | $1,000 \times \$2.00 =$ | 2,000 |
| | | $6,425 |

Ending inventory:

| (1/21) | $1,000 \times \$2.00 =$ | $2,000 |
|---|---|---|
| (1/25) | $500 \times \$2.10 =$ | 1,050 |
| | | $3,050 |

(2) **Average Cost.** This method is more appropriate for small, homogeneous items (i.e. brass tubing) and when specific identification is impossible (i.e. peanuts). There are two ways to compute average cost—simple average and weighted average.

(a) *Simple Average.* The *unit price* of the items in beginning inventory is added to the *unit price* of each purchase, and the sum is divided by the number of purchases plus one (for beginning inventory). This method is most accurate when purchases are of the same quantity. The object is to compute the average purchase (unit) price.

## EXAMPLE 4

**Periodic Inventory System**

Because inventory and materials issued are not valued until the end of the period under periodic inventory systems, the average cost is calculated only once, at the end of the period.

$$\text{Simple average unit cost} = \frac{\text{BI unit price} + \text{Unit price of each purchase}}{\text{Number of purchases} + 1 \text{ (for BI)}}$$

$$= \frac{\$1.75 + \$1.80 + \$2.00 + \$2.10}{3 + 1} = \frac{\$7.65}{4} = \$1.9125$$

Cost of materials issued:    $3,500 \times \$1.9125 = \$6,693.75$

Ending inventory:           $1,500 \times \$1.9125 = \$2,868.75$

## Perpetual Inventory System

Under perpetual inventory systems an average must be calculated *each time* a purchase is made because a running inventory is being kept. Materials are issued at the last average cost at their date of issuance. This is called a *simple moving average*. See Table 3-1.

### Table 3-1   Simple Moving Average

| Date | | Purchases | | | Issued | | | Balance | | |
|------|-------|------|-------------------------------------|-------|------|----------------------------|-------|--------------|---------------|
| | | Units | Unit Cost | Cost of Materials Avail. for Use | Units | Unit Cost | Cost of Materials Issued | Units | Unit Cost | Total Cost |
| (BI) | 1/1 | 1,500 | $1.75 | $2,625 | — | — | — | 1,500 | $1.75 | $2,625.00 |
| | 1/7 | 1,000 | 1.80 | 1,800 | — | — | — | 2,500 | 1.775(a) | 4,437.50 |
| | 1/9 | — | — | | 1,000 | $1.775 | $1,775.00 | 1,500 | 1.775 | 2,662.50 |
| | 1/15 | — | — | | 500 | 1.775 | 887.50 | 1,000 | 1.775 | 1,775.00 |
| | 1/21 | 2,000 | 2.00 | 4,000 | — | — | — | 3,000 | 1.85(b) | 5,550.00 |
| | 1/25 | 500 | 2.10 | 1,050 | — | — | — | 3,500 | 1.9125(c) | 6,693.75 |
| | 1/30 | — | — | | 2,000 | 1.9125 | 3,825.00 | 1,500 | 1.9125 | $2,868.75 (EI) |
| | | | | $9,475 | | | $6,487.50 | | | |

*Computations*:

(a) $\dfrac{\$1.75 + \$1.80}{2} = \$1.775$

(b) $\dfrac{\$1.75 + \$1.80 + \$2.00}{3} = \$1.85$

(c) $\dfrac{\$1.75 + \$1.80 + \$2.00 + \$2.10}{4} = \$1.9125$

| | |
|---|---|
| Cost of materials issued | $6,487.50 |
| Ending inventory | 2,868.75 |
| Actual Cost of materials available | $9,356.25 |

*Note*: The actual cost of materials available differs from $9,475 (Table 3-1, column 4) because of the unequal number of purchases at each price. This problem is overcome by the weighted average method (Example 5).

(b) *Weighted Average.* This method overcomes the limitations of simple average by considering the purchase quantity as well as the price. Under this method each purchase (including beginning inventory) is calculated by multiplying the quantity purchased by the respective unit cost to get a total purchase cost. The purchase costs are summed and divided by the units of materials available for use. The implementation of this method differs depending on whether a periodic or perpetual system is under use.

## EXAMPLE 5

### Periodic Inventory System

Under a periodic system the weighted average is calculated only once, at the end of the period.

$$\text{Weighted average} = \frac{\text{Total purchase cost}}{\text{Materials available for use}}$$

$$= \frac{(1,500 \times \$1.75) + (1,000 \times \$1.80) + (2,000 \times \$2.00) + (500 \times \$2.10)}{5,000} = \$1.895$$

Cost of materials issued:   $3,500 \times \$1.895 = \$6,632.50$

Ending inventory:        $1,500 \times \$1.895 = \$2,842.50$

## Perpetual Inventory System

Under a perpetual system an average is calculated at the time of each purchase (hence it is called a weighted *moving* average) and is used to issue materials until a new purchase is made, at which time the average cost must be recalculated.   See Table 3-2.

### Table 3-2   Weighted Moving Average

| Date | | Purchases | | | Issued | | | Balance | | |
|---|---|---|---|---|---|---|---|---|---|---|
| | Units | Unit Cost | Cost of Materials Avail. for Use | Units | Unit Cost | Cost of Materials Issued | Units | Unit Cost | Total Cost |
| (BI) 1/1 | 1,500 | $1.75 | $2,625 | — | — | — | 1,500 | $1.75 | $2,625.00 |
| 1/7 | 1,000 | 1.80 | 1,800 | — | — | — | 2,500 | 1.77(a) | 4,425.00 |
| 1/9 | — | — | | 1,000 | $1.77 | $1,770.00 | 1,500 | 1.77 | 2,655.00 |
| 1/15 | — | — | | 500 | 1.77 | 885.00 | 1,000 | 1.77 | 1,770.00 |
| 1/21 | 2,000 | 2.00 | 4,000 | — | — | — | 3,000 | 1.9233(b) | 5,769.90 |
| 1/25 | 500 | 2.10 | 1,050 | — | — | — | 3,500 | 1.9485(c) | 6,819.75 |
| 1/30 | — | — | | 2,000 | 1.9485 | 3,897.00 | 1,500 | 1.9485 | $2,922.75 (EI) |
| | | | $9,475 | | | $6,552.00 | | | |

*Computations*:

(a) $\dfrac{(1,500 \times \$1.75) + (1,000 \times \$1.80)}{2,500} = \$1.77$

(b) $\dfrac{(1,000 \times \$1.77) + (2,000 \times \$2.00)}{3,000} = \$1.9233$

(c) $\dfrac{(3,000 \times \$1.9233) + (500 \times \$2.10)}{3,500} = \$1.9485$

| | |
|---|---|
| Cost of materials issued | $6,552.00 |
| Ending inventory | 2,922.75 |
| Rounding difference | 0.25 |
| Cost of materials available | $9,475.00 |

(3)   **FIFO (First-in, first-out).**   Materials issued for use under this method come from beginning inventory and then the earlier purchases.   The ending inventory here is considered to be the last materials purchased and therefore reflects current costs.

## EXAMPLE 6

### Periodic and Perpetual Inventory Systems

Both inventory systems yield identical results for materials issued and ending inventory when FIFO is used.
*Cost of materials issued*: The 3,500 units issued come from the earliest purchases, so we start with beginning inventory and work forward.

| Date | Units | Unit Cost ($) | Cost of Materials Issued |
|---|---|---|---|
| (BI) 1/1 | 1,500 | $1.75 | $2,625 |
| 1/7 | 1,000 | 1.80 | 1,800 |
| 1/21 | 1,000 | 2.00 | 2,000 |
| | 3,500 | | $6,425 |

*Ending inventory*: To get the ending inventory we start with the last purchase and work backward.

| Date | Units | Unit Cost ($) | Total |
|------|-------|---------------|-------|
| 1/25 | 500 | $2.10 | $1,050 |
| 1/21 | 1,000 | 2.00 | 2,000 |
|  | 1,500 |  | $3,050  EI |

Cost of materials available: $6,425 + $3,050 = $9,475

(4) **LIFO (Last-in, first-out).** Under this method we assume that the last goods received will be the first issued (exactly the opposite of FIFO). Therefore, our ending inventory will include the period's beginning inventory and the early purchases. Results of LIFO application differ, depending on whether a periodic or perpetual system is used.

### Table 3-3    LIFO in Perpetual Inventory System

| Date | | Purchases | | | Issued | | | Balance | | |
|------|---|-------|------|-------------------------|-------|------|-------------------------|-------|------|-------|
| | | Units | Unit Cost | Cost of Materials Avail. for Use | Units | Unit Cost | Cost of Materials Issued | Units | Unit Cost | Total Cost |
| (BI) | 1/1 | 1,500 | $1.75 | $2,625 | — | — | — | 1,500 | $1.75 | $2,625 |
| | 1/7 | 1,000 | 1.80 | 1,800 | — | — | — | 2,500 | (a) | 4,425 |
| | 1/9 | — | — | | 1,000 | $1.80 | $1,800 | 1,500 | 1.75 | 2,625 |
| | 1/15 | — | — | | 500 | 1.75 | 875 | 1,000 | 1.75 | 1,750 |
| | 1/21 | 2,000 | 2.00 | 4,000 | — | — | — | 3,000 | (b) | 5,750 |
| | 1/25 | 500 | 2.10 | 1,050 | — | — | — | 3,500 | (c) | 6,800 |
| | 1/30 | — | — | | 2,000 | (e) | 4,050 | 1,500 | (d) | $2,750 (EI) |
| | | | | $9,475 | | | $6,725 | | | |

*Computations*:
(a)  (1,500 × $1.75) + (1,000 × $1.80) = $4,425
(b)  (1,000 × $1.75) + (2,000 × $2.00) = $5,750
(c)  (1,000 × $1.75) + (2,000 × $2.00) + (500 × $2.10) = $6,800
(d)  (1,000 × $1.75) + (500 × $2.00) = $2,750
(e)  (500 × $2.10) + (1,500 × $2.00) = $4,050

| | |
|---|---|
| Cost of materials issued | $6,725 |
| Ending inventory | 2,750 |
| Cost of materials available | $9,475 |

## EXAMPLE 7

**Periodic Inventory System**

The calculation of materials issued and ending inventory is done at the end of the period, as is normal with periodic systems.

*Cost of materials issued*: To value the 3,500 units issued, we begin with the last purchase and work backward.

| Date | Units | Unit Cost ($) | Cost of Materials Issued |
|------|-------|---------------|--------------------------|
| 1/25 | 500 | $2.10 | $1,050 |
| 1/21 | 2,000 | 2.00 | 4,000 |
| 1/7 | 1,000 | 1.80 | 1,800 |
|  | 3,500 |  | $6,850 |

*Ending inventory*: To arrive at a value for the ending inventory, we begin with the beginning inventory and work forward.

| | Date | Units | Unit Cost ($) | Total | |
|---|---|---|---|---|---|
| (BI) | 1/1 | 1,500 | $1.75 | $2,625 | EI |

Cost of materials available: $6,850 + $2,625 = $9,475

### Perpetual Inventory System

The ending inventory and the value of materials issued will differ from those calculated under a periodic system because costs are assigned as materials are issued and *not* at the end of the period. Our ending inventory value will be greater here for this reason. See Table 3-3.

## 3.5 COMPARISON OF INVENTORY METHODS

The method selected determines the values of materials issued and ending inventory. The inventory system used also has an effect on these values. A firm should select its method of inventory valuation carefully since the *principle of consistency* (*Statement of Financial Accounting Concepts No. 2*) states that the method chosen should be adhered to each period. A change can be made only if it can be shown that doing so would improve the accuracy of the firm's financial statements.

## 3.6 LOWER OF COST OR MARKET (LCM)

LCM is a rule (*Accounting Research Bulletin No. 43*) which states that inventory should be valued at the lower of its historical cost (time of purchase) or current market value (usually replacement cost).

(1) Generally, in inflationary times, historical cost is lower than market, so no adjustment is necessary.

(2) If market is lower than cost, the ending inventory must be reported at market. This is based on the *principle of conservatism* (*Statement of Financial Accounting Concepts No. 2*) which states that losses should be recognized in the period in which they occur.

(3) If inventory is reduced under LCM, the resulting loss is generally added to the cost of goods manufactured.

LCM can be computed two ways:

(1) Applied to the total inventory value
(2) Applied item-by-item to ending inventory

### EXAMPLE 8

Using the ending inventory calculated under LIFO (perpetual) in Example 7, assume the replacement cost of brass tubing decreased to $1.80 per foot.

(*a*) LCM applied to the total inventory value:

| | Date | Units | Unit Cost ($) | Total |
|---|---|---|---|---|
| (BI) | 1/1 | 1,000 | $1.75 | $1,750 |
| | 1/21 | 500 | 2.00 | 1,000 |
| | | 1,500 | | $2,750 |

Applying LCM to ending inventory, we get 1,500 × $1.80 = $2,700.

| | |
|---|---|
| Ending inventory before LCM adjustment | $2,750 |
| Ending inventory after LCM adjustment | 2,700 |
| Loss (to be added to Cost of Goods Manufactured) | $ 50 |

(b)  LCM applied item-by-item to ending inventory:

| | Date | Units | Unit Cost ($) | Replacement Cost | Adjusted Total | |
|---|---|---|---|---|---|---|
| (BI) | 1/1 | 1,000 | $1.75 | $1.80 | (1,000 × 1.75) | $1,750 |
| | 1/21 | 500 | 2.00 | 1.80 | (500 × 1.80) | 900 |
| | | 1,500 | | | | $2,650 |

| | |
|---|---|
| Ending inventory before LCM adjustment | $2,750 |
| Ending inventory after LCM adjustment | 2,650 |
| Loss (to be added to Cost of Goods Manufactured) | $ 100 |

*Note*: The application of LCM on an item-by-item basis results in the *most conservative* ending inventory value.

There are several criticisms of LCM:

(1)  LCM was introduced when *conservatism* was more important than *consistency*.

(2)  It violates the principle of consistency because inventories may be valued one way at one time and another way at another time.

(3)  It is also inconsistent because the technique recognizes losses in inventory value before inventory is sold and doesn't recognize increases in replacement cost until goods are sold.

## 3.7  CONTROL PROCEDURES

Because inventory represents a major investment to a firm, adequate control is essential.   The level of raw materials inventory is based on scheduled production, which is in turn based on sales forecasts. Five control procedures are commonly used:

(1)  *Order cycling.*   Materials are reviewed on a regular cycle, and orders are placed to maintain a desired inventory level.

(2)  *Min-max method.*   Minimum and maximum inventory levels are determined.   Reordering is done when the minimum level is reached.

(3)  *Two-bin method.*   This is used for inexpensive items.   When the first bin is empty, an order is placed.   The second bin provides coverage until the order is received.

(4)  *ABC plan.*   This is used with a wide variety of items having different values.   The more expensive items receive more frequent review and closer monitoring.
A items—most expensive items, usually few on hand
B items—moderately priced items and moderate quantity on hand
C items—inexpensive items, generally kept in large quantities

(5)  *Automatic order system.*   An order is automatically placed when the inventory reaches a predetermined level.   This system works best when used with a computer.

## Summary

(1)  To order materials, a _____ is sent to a supplier.

(2)  Valuation of ending inventory yields the same results whether a periodic or perpetual system is employed under (a) FIFO and LIFO, (b) LIFO and average cost, (c) LIFO and specific identification, (d) FIFO and specific identification.

(3)  When materials are issued for use on a job, the materials inventory account is credited under a
     _____ inventory system.

(4)  Under a periodic inventory system the _____ account is debited when materials are
     received from a supplier, but under a perpetual system the _____ account is debited.

(5)  Under a periodic system _____ plus _____ equals the materials available for
     use. If _____ is subtracted from the materials available, the resulting figure is the
     _____ .

(6)  Under a perpetual system, the work-in-process account contains a historical balance. (a) True,
     (b) false.

(7)  No entry is made to record the issuance of materials under a periodic system. (a) True, (b) false.

(8)  The purchases account will have an identical balance regardless of whether a periodic or perpetu-
     al system is used. (a) True, (b) false.

(9)  Under a perpetual system direct and indirect materials are differentiated at the time of purchase.
     (a) True, (b) false.

(10) When a perpetual system is used a physical inventory is not required to obtain a balance for the
     materials inventory account. (a) True, (b) false.

(11) The four methods of evaluating ending inventories are _____ , _____ ,
     _____ , and _____ .

(12) When the _____ and the _____ methods are used, their application differs
     depending on whether a periodic or perpetual system is used.

(13) When using the average cost method, a _____ average is used for periodic systems and
     a _____ average for perpetual systems.

(14) _____ and _____ yield the same result for cost of materials issued whether a
     periodic or a perpetual system is used.

(15) LCM can only be applied if specific identification or FIFO has been used to compute the ending
     inventory. (a) True, (b) false.

(16) While being consistent, LCM violates the principle of conservatism. (a) True, (b) false.

(17) When LCM is applied, the ending inventory is reduced if _____ is higher than
     _____ .

(18) To get the most conservative ending inventory value, one would apply LCM _____ .

(19) A loss on ending inventory valuation under LCM is charged to (a) cost of goods sold, (b) work in
     process, (c) cost of goods manufactured, (d) an expense account.

(20) The _____ classifies items according to value.

(21) The _____ works most efficiently when used with a computer.

(22)  The _____ is the least likely method of inventory control to be used with expensive items.

*Answers*:  (1) purchase order; (2) *d*; (3) perpetual; (4) purchases, materials; (5) beginning materials inventory, purchases, ending materials inventory, cost of materials issued; (6) *b*; (7) *a*; (8) *b*; (9) *b*; (10) *a*; (11) specific identification, average cost, LIFO, FIFO; (12) LIFO, average cost; (13) simple, moving; (14) FIFO, specific identification; (15) *b*; (16) *b*; (17) historical cost, replacement cost; (18) item-by-item; (19) *c*; (20) ABC plan; (21) automatic order system; (22) two-bin method.

# Solved Problems

**3.1**  Tepee Ltd., a tent manufacturer, showed the following transactions for the month of May:

| Date | Units Purchased | Unit Cost ($) | Units Issued |
|---|---|---|---|
| (BI) 5/1 | 10 | $15 | — |
| 5/5 | 20 | 20 | — |
| 5/15 | — | — | 15 |
| 5/19 | — | — | 10 |
| 5/24 | 15 | 18 | — |
| 5/30 | — | — | 15 |

Assume the company uses a periodic inventory system and compute the ending materials inventory and cost of materials issued under (*a*) specific identification (materials issued on 5/15 came from the 5/5 purchase, materials issued on 5/19 came from beginning inventory, and those issued on 5/30 came from the 5/5 and 5/24 purchases); (*b*) weighted average cost; (*c*) FIFO; (*d*) LIFO.

**SOLUTION**

(*a*)  **Specific identification**

| Date of Issue | Purchase Lot | Units × Cost | | Cost of Materials Issued |
|---|---|---|---|---|
| 5/15 | 5/5 | 15 × $20 | = | $300 |
| 5/19 | BI | 10 × $15 | = | 150 |
| 5/30 | 5/5 & 5/24 | (5 × $20) + (10 × $18) | = | 280 |
| | | | | $730 |

Ending inventory:  5 (from 5/24 purchase) × $18 = $90

(*b*)  **Weighted average cost**

$$\frac{(10 \times \$15) + (20 \times \$20) + (15 \times \$18)}{45} = \$18.222$$

Cost of materials issued: 40 × $18.222 = $728.88

Ending inventory: 5 × $18.222 = $91.11

(c)  **FIFO**

| Date | Units | Unit Cost ($) | Cost of Materials Issued |
|------|-------|---------------|--------------------------|
| BI   | 10    | $15           | $150                     |
| 5/5  | 20    | 20            | 400                      |
| 5/24 | 10    | 18            | 180                      |
|      | 40    |               | $730                     |

Ending inventory:   5 × $18 = $90

(d)  **LIFO**

| Date | Units | Unit Cost ($) | Cost of Materials Issued |
|------|-------|---------------|--------------------------|
| 5/24 | 15    | $18           | $270                     |
| 5/5  | 20    | 20            | 400                      |
| BI   | 5     | 15            | 75                       |
|      | 40    |               | $745                     |

Ending inventory:   5 (from BI) × $15 = $75

**3.2**    Assume the same set of facts as presented in Problem 3.1, except that Tepee Ltd. now uses a perpetual inventory system.  Compute the cost of materials issued and ending inventory under (a) specific identification, (b) weighted average cost, (c) FIFO, and (d) LIFO.

**SOLUTION**

(a)  **Specific identification.**   The solution is the same as for Problem 3.1(a).
(b)  **Weighted (moving) average cost**

| | | Purchases | | | Issued | | | | Balance | |
|---|------|-------|--------------|-------|--------------|--------------------------|-------|--------------|------------|---|
| | Date | Units | Unit Cost ($) | Units | Unit Cost ($) | Cost of Materials Issued | Units | Unit Cost ($) | Total Cost | |
| (BI) | 5/1  | 10 | $15 | — | — | — | 10 | $15.000 | $150.00 | |
|      | 5/5  | 20 | 20  | — | — | — | 30 | 18.333(a) | 550.00 | |
|      | 5/15 | — | — | 15 | $18.333 | $275.00 | 15 | 18.333 | 275.00 | |
|      | 5/19 | — | — | 10 | 18.333 | 183.33 | 5 | 18.333 | 91.67 | |
|      | 5/24 | 15 | 18 | — | — | — | 20 | 18.084(b) | 361.68 | |
|      | 5/30 | — | — | 15 | 18.084 | 271.26 | 5 | 18.084 | 90.42 | EI |
|      |      |    |    |    |         | $729.59 |    |        |        | |

---

*Computations*:

(a)  $\dfrac{(10 \times \$15) + (20 \times \$20)}{30} = \$18.333$

(b)  $\dfrac{(5 \times \$18.333) + (15 \times \$18)}{20} = \$18.084$

(c) **FIFO.**  The solution is the same as for Problem 3.1(c).

(d) **LIFO**

| | | Purchases | | | Issued | | | Balance | |
| | Date | Units | Unit Cost $ | Units | Unit Cost $ | Cost of Materials Issued | Units | Unit Cost $ | Total |
|---|---|---|---|---|---|---|---|---|---|
| (BI) | 5/1 | 10 | $15 | — | — | — | 10 | $15 | $150 |
| | 5/5 | 20 | 20 | — | — | — | 30 | (a) | 550 |
| | 5/15 | — | — | 15 | $20 | $300 | 15 | (b) | 250 |
| | 5/19 | — | — | 10 | (c) | 175 | 5 | 15 | 75 |
| | 5/24 | 15 | 18 | — | — | — | 20 | (d) | 345 |
| | 5/30 | — | — | 15 | 18 | 270 | 5 | 15 | $ 75  EI |
| | | | | | | $745 | | | |

*Computations:*

(a)  $(10 \times \$15) + (20 \times \$20) = \$550$

(b)  $(10 \times \$15) + (5 \times \$20) = \$250$

(c)  $(5 \times \$20) + (5 \times \$15) = \$175$

(d)  $(5 \times \$15) + (15 \times \$18) = \$345$

**3.3**  The Rainy Day Pool Company is preparing for the upcoming season.  The following data relate to the company's inventory of pool liners for the month of March:

(BI)  3/1   1,000 liners at $100 ea.

3/4   Purchased 1,500 at $90 ea.

3/10  Issued 1,200 liners

3/16  Issued 800 liners

3/20  Purchased 2,000 liners at $75 ea.

3/25  Issued 1,000 liners

3/28  Issued 900 liners

3/30  Purchased 1,000 liners at $110 ea.

(a)  Prepare the journal entries to record these transactions under both a periodic and a perpetual inventory system.  The company uses the LIFO method to value its ending inventory.

(b)  Compute the cost of materials issued and ending inventory under both periodic and perpetual inventory systems.

**SOLUTION**

(a)

| **Periodic Inventory System** | | | **Perpetual Inventory System** | | |
|---|---|---|---|---|---|
| 3/4 | Purchases   135,000 | | 3/4 | Materials | 135,000 | |
| | Cash | 135,000 | | Cash | 135,000 |
| 3/10 | No entry | | 3/10 | Work in Process | 108,000 | |
| | | | | Materials (1,200 × $90) | 108,000 |
| 3/16 | No entry | | 3/16 | Work in Process | 77,000 | |
| | | | | Materials (300 × $90) | 77,000 |
| | | | | + (500 × $100) | |
| 3/20 | Purchases   150,000 | | 3/20 | Materials | 150,000 | |
| | Cash | 150,000 | | Cash | 150,000 |

| Periodic Inventory System | | | Perpetual Inventory System | | |
|---|---|---|---|---|---|
| 3/25 | No entry | | 3/25 | Work in Process | 75,000 |
| | | | | Materials (1,000 × $75) | 75,000 |
| 3/28 | No entry | | 3/28 | Work in Process | 67,500 |
| | | | | Materials (900 × $75) | 67,500 |
| 3/30 | Purchases | 110,000 | 3/30 | Materials | 110,000 |
| | Cash | 110,000 | | Cash | 110,000 |

(b)   Periodic Inventory System

| Date | Units | Unit Cost ($) | Cost of Materials Issued |
|---|---|---|---|
| 3/30 | 1,000 | $110 | $110,000 |
| 3/20 | 2,000 | 75 | 150,000 |
| 3/4 | 900 | 90 | 81,000 |
| | 3,900 | | $341,000 |

Ending inventory:

| | Date | Units | Unit Cost ($) | Total |
|---|---|---|---|---|
| (BI) | 3/1 | 1,000 | $100 | $100,000 |
| | 3/4 | 600 | 90 | 54,000 |
| | | 1,600 | | $154,000 |

Perpetual Inventory System

| | | Purchases | | | Issued | | | Balance | |
|---|---|---|---|---|---|---|---|---|---|
| | Date | Units | Unit Cost $ | Units | Unit Cost $ | Cost of Materials Issued | Units | Unit Cost $ | Total |
| (BI) | 3/1 | 1,000 | $100 | — | — | — | 1,000 | $100 | $100,000 |
| | 3/4 | 1,500 | 90 | — | — | — | 2,500 | (a) | 235,000 |
| | 3/10 | — | — | 1,200 | $90 | $108,000 | 1,300 | (b) | 127,000 |
| | 3/16 | — | — | 800 | (c) | 77,000 | 500 | 100 | 50,000 |
| | 3/20 | 2,000 | 75 | — | — | — | 2,500 | (d) | 200,000 |
| | 3/25 | — | — | 1,000 | 75 | 75,000 | 1,500 | (e) | 125,000 |
| | 3/28 | — | — | 900 | 75 | 67,500 | 600 | (f) | 57,500 |
| | 3/30 | 1,000 | 110 | — | — | — | 1,600 | (g) | $167,500  EI |
| | | | | | | $327,500 | | | |

---

*Computations*:

(a)   (1,000 × $100) + (1,500 × $90) = $235,000

(b)   (1,000 × $100) + (300 × $90) = $127,000

(c)   (500 × $100) + (300 × $90) = $77,000

(d)   (500 × $100) + (2,000 × $75) = $200,000

(e)   (500 × $100) + (1,000 × $75) = $125,000

(f)   (500 × $100) + (100 × $75) = $57,500

(g)   (500 × $100) + (100 × $75) + (1,000 × $110) = $167,500

**3.4**   R.S.V.P., Inc. employs a periodic inventory system. Using the following information, compute the purchases and ending materials inventory for the month. Beginning materials inventory: $3,000; materials available for use: $10,000; cost of materials issued: $8,500.

**SOLUTION**

If we let $X$ = Purchases and $Y$ = Ending materials inventory, then

| | | |
|---|---|---|
| Materials inventory (begin.) | $ 3,000 | |
| + Purchases | + $X$ | $X = \$7,000$ |
| Materials available for use | $10,000 | |
| − Materials inventory (end.) | − $Y$ | $Y = \$1,500$ |
| Cost of materials issued | $ 8,500 | |

**3.5** The Effervescent Soda Company shows the following transactions in inventory of soda bottles (direct materials) for January 19X2. The company uses FIFO to value its cost of materials issued and ending inventory.

Ending materials inventory, Dec. 31, 19X1:　4,000 bottles @ $0.75 ea.

19X2
1/2　Purchased 2,850 bottles @ $0.80 ea.
1/6　Purchased 1,300 bottles @ $0.85 ea.
1/12　Issued 2,000 bottles
1/19　Issued 2,200 bottles
1/24　Purchased 3,500 bottles @ $0.75 ea.
1/30　Issued 1,450 bottles

(a) Using the following T accounts, post these transactions under both a periodic and perpetual inventory system. Assume work in process has no beginning balance.

| Materials Inventory | Purchases | Work in Process |
|---|---|---|
| | | |

(b) What would be the ending materials inventory on Jan. 31, 19X2 under each system?

**SOLUTION**

(a) Periodic Inventory System

| Materials Inventory | | Purchases | | Work in Process | |
|---|---|---|---|---|---|
| 1/1　3,000 | | 1/2　2,280 | | | |
| | | 1/6　1,105 | | | |
| | | 1/24　2,625 | | | |
| 1/31　4,690 | | 1/31　6,010 | | 1/31　4,320 | |

*Note*: 1/12, 1/19, and 1/30 are issuances of materials and are not posted during the month under a periodic inventory system.

Perpetual Inventory System

| Materials Inventory | | | | | Purchases | | Work in Process | | | |
|---|---|---|---|---|---|---|---|---|---|---|
| 1/1 | 3,000 | 1/12 | 1,500 (a) | | | | 1/12 | 1,500 | | |
| 1/2 | 2,280 | 1/19 | 1,660 (b) | | | | 1/19 | 1,660 | | |
| 1/6 | 1,105 | 1/30 | 1,160 (c) | | | | 1/30 | 1,160 | | |
| 1/24 | 2,625 | | | | | | | | | |
| 1/31 | 4,690 | | | | | 0 | 1/31 | 4,320 | | |

*Computations*:

(a)  $2,000 \times \$0.75 = \$1,500$

(b)  $(2,000 \times \$0.75) + (200 \times \$0.80) = \$1,660$

(c)  $1,450 \times \$0.80 = \$1,160$

*Note*: Regardless of whether a periodic or perpetual inventory system is used, the ending inventory of one period becomes the beginning inventory of the next period.

(b)  Periodic Inventory System

Let $X$ = Ending materials inventory.

| | | |
|---|---|---|
| Materials inventory (begin.) | $3,000 | |
| + Purchases | + 6,010 | |
| Materials available for use | $9,010 | |
| − Materials inventory (end.) | − X | $X = \$4,690$ |
| Cost of materials issued | $4,320* | |

* Cost of materials issued

| | | |
|---|---|---|
| 1/12 | $2,000 \times \$0.75$ | $= \$1,500$ |
| 1/19 | $(2,000 \times \$0.75) + (200 \times \$0.80)$ | $= \$1,660$ |
| 1/30 | $1,450 \times \$0.80$ | $= \$1,160$ |
| | | $\$4,320$ |

Perpetual Inventory System

Ending inventory here can be read directly from the materials inventory account by finding the balance after the period's entries are made.

### Materials Inventory

| 1/1 | 3,000 | 1/12 | 1,500 |
|---|---|---|---|
| 1/2 | 2,280 | 1/19 | 1,660 |
| 1/6 | 1,105 | 1/30 | 1,160 |
| 1/24 | 2,625 | | 4,320 |
| | 9,010 | | |
| 1/31 | 4,690 | | |

*Note*: This problem highlights the differences between a periodic and a perpetual inventory system. The calculations required to determine the ending inventory and cost of materials issued under the periodic system are not necessary under a perpetual system because *all* transactions flow through the accounts.

**3.6**    Prepare the necessary journal entries under both a periodic and a perpetual inventory system for the transactions given in Problem 3.5.

**SOLUTION**

| Periodic Inventory System | | | | Perpetual Inventory System | | | |
|---|---|---|---|---|---|---|---|
| 1/2 | Purchases | 2,280 | | 1/2 | Materials | 2,280 | |
| | Cash | | 2,280 | | Cash | | 2,280 |
| 1/6 | Purchases | 1,105 | | 1/6 | Materials | 1,105 | |
| | Cash | | 1,105 | | Cash | | 1,105 |
| 1/12 | No entry | | | 1/12 | Work in Process | 1,500 | |
| 1/19 | No entry | | | | Materials | | 1,500 |
| 1/24 | Purchases | 2,625 | | 1/19 | Work in Process | 1,660 | |
| | Cash | | 2,625 | | Materials | | 1,660 |
| 1/30 | No entry | | | 1/24 | Materials | 2,625 | |
| | | | | | Cash | | 2,625 |
| | | | | 1/30 | Work in Process | 1,160 | |
| | | | | | Materials | | 1,160 |

**3.7** The following information relates to the ending inventory of the Four Seasons Coat Company:

| Materials | Quantity | Cost per Unit | Replacement Cost |
|---|---|---|---|
| Sleeves | 50 | $2.00 | $1.95 |
| Collars | 32 | 1.50 | 1.60 |
| Linings | 25 | 2.50 | 2.25 |
| Belts | 41 | 1.75 | 1.80 |

(a) Compute the ending inventory before any LCM adjustment. Apply the LCM rule to the inventory (b) as a whole and (c) on an item-by-item basis.

**SOLUTION**

(a)  Before LCM adjustment

| Materials | Quantity | | Cost per Unit | | Total Cost |
|---|---|---|---|---|---|
| Sleeves | 50 | × | 2.00 | = | $100.00 |
| Collars | 32 | × | 1.50 | = | 48.00 |
| Linings | 25 | × | 2.50 | = | 62.50 |
| Belts | 41 | × | 1.75 | = | 71.75 |
| | | | | | $282.25 EI |

(b)  LCM applied to inventory in total

| Materials | Quantity | | Replacement Cost | | Total Replacement Cost |
|---|---|---|---|---|---|
| Sleeves | 50 | × | $1.95 | = | $ 97.50 |
| Collars | 32 | × | 1.60 | = | 51.20 |
| Linings | 25 | × | 2.25 | = | 56.25 |
| Belts | 41 | × | 1.80 | = | 73.80 |
| | | | | | $278.75 |

| | |
|---|---|
| Ending inventory before LCM adjustment | $282.25 |
| Ending inventory after LCM adjustment | 278.75 |
| Loss (to be entered in Cost of Goods Manufactured) | $  3.50 |

(c)    LCM applied to inventory item-by-item

| Materials | Quantity | | Lower of Cost or Replacement Cost | | Total |
|---|---|---|---|---|---|
| Sleeves | 50 | × | $1.95 | = | $ 97.50 |
| Collars | 32 | × | 1.50 | = | 48.00 |
| Linings | 25 | × | 2.25 | = | 56.25 |
| Belts | 41 | × | 1.75 | = | 71.75 |
| | | | | | $273.50 |

| | |
|---|---|
| Ending inventory before LCM adjustment | $282.25 |
| Ending inventory after LCM adjustment | 273.50 |
| Loss (to be entered in Cost of Goods Manufactured) | $  8.75 |

# Chapter 4

# Costing and Control of Labor

## 4.1 CHARACTERISTICS OF LABOR

Labor is the physical and/or mental effort expended to manufacture products. *Labor cost* is the price paid for using human resources. Labor cost may be either direct or indirect.

*Direct Labor.* The three characteristics of direct labor are: (1) it is easily traced to the product; (2) it is a major cost of producing the product, and (3) it can be identified directly with production of the product.

*Indirect Labor.* This includes all other labor costs related to production (e.g. salary of plant supervisor). Like indirect materials, this is considered a factory overhead cost.

## 4.2 LABOR COSTS

Labor costs usually represent a significant cost of production and are steadily increasing in proportion to other costs. Much of the increase is due to fringe benefits such as vacations, insurance, bonuses, etc., included in an employee's compensation. The single major component of employee compensation is usually the wage or salary.

*Wages* are payments made on an hourly, daily, or piecework basis, whereas *salaries* are fixed payments for managerial services. Other terms necessary for any discussion of labor costs are best defined by equations, as follows:

$$\textit{Gross earnings} = \text{Regular wages} + \text{Overtime premium}$$
$$\textit{Regular wage} = \textit{Total} \text{ hours worked (including overtime)} \times \textit{Regular} \text{ hourly rate}$$
$$\textit{Overtime premium} = \text{Overtime hours worked} \times \text{Extra hourly compensation for overtime}$$

## 4.3 OVERTIME AND SHIFT PREMIUM

**Overtime Premium**

The additional compensation paid for overtime is separated from regular wages and charged to factory overhead. The effect of this is to charge all units produced with the same rate of labor (regular rate).

**EXAMPLE 1**

An employee worked 45 hours this week. His regular wage is $5.00 per hour, and he is paid time and a half for overtime hours (i.e. hours beyond 40 per week).

Regular wage = $5.00/hr

Overtime wage = $7.50/hr

Overtime premium = $2.50/hr

| Periodic Cost Accumulation | | | Perpetual Cost Accumulation | | |
|---|---|---|---|---|---|
| Direct Labor* | 225.00 | | Work in Process* | 225.00 | |
| Overtime Premium— | | | Factory Overhead Control— | | |
| Factory Overhead** | 12.50 | | Overtime Premium** | 12.50 | |
| Payroll | | 237.50 | Payroll | | 237.50 |

\* 45 hours × $5.00

\*\* 5 hours × $2.50

*Note:* As with direct materials, direct labor is charged to work in process as incurred under a perpetual cost accumulation system. All additional compensation (above regular wage rates) is charged to *one* account, called Factory Overhead Control. When a periodic cost accumulation system is used, work in process is *not* charged until the end of the period. Here additional accounts are necessary in the general ledger. An account called Direct Labor is charged with regular wages. All premium and nonproductive pay is charged to *individual* factory overhead accounts (e.g. Overtime premium—factory overhead).

## Shift Premium or Differential

Often an above normal wage is paid for undesirable shifts (e.g. night shifts). Like the overhead premium, this *extra* portion is charged to factory overhead.

## EXAMPLE 2

Employees who work days are paid $5.00 per hour. Those who work nights are paid $5.50 per hour. All employees work 40 hours per week. Record the weekly wages for one night employee.

$$\text{Regular wage} = \$5.00/\text{hour}$$
$$\text{Night wage} = \$5.50/\text{hour}$$
$$\text{Shift premium} = \$0.50/\text{hour}$$

| Periodic Cost Accumulation | | | Perpetual Cost Accumulation | | |
|---|---|---|---|---|---|
| Direct Labor* | 200 | | Work in Process* | 200 | |
| Shift Premium— | | | Factory Overhead Control— | | |
| Factory Overhead** | 20 | | Shift Premium** | 20 | |
| Payroll | | 220 | Payroll | | 220 |

\* 40 hours × $5.00

\*\* 40 hours × $0.50

*Note:* By charging the "premium" portion of payroll to factory overhead, the cost is spread over all units produced.

## 4.4  BONUS

A bonus is additional compensation generally given in recognition of exceptional productivity. Bonuses may be a set amount, a percentage of profits, or a percentage of an employee's salary. Theoretically, a bonus is a direct cost of production. However, because the purpose of cost accumulation is the establishment of a standard unit cost, bonuses are charged to factory overhead. Ideally, a bonus should be charged to a liability each week the eligible employee works. In practice, due to the nature of bonuses this can rarely be done, so a single entry at the end of the period is made.

## EXAMPLE 3

Employees are entitled to receive a bonus equal to 0.5% of ABC Company's yearly profits. The company has determined its profit for the year to be $50,000. Record one employee's bonus if the employee's weekly pay is $200. For the purposes of this example, we will assume that we know the results of the year's operations ahead of time, so that we can show this as a weekly entry made in conjunction with the weekly payroll.

| Periodic Cost Accumulation | | | Perpetual Cost Accumulation | | |
|---|---|---|---|---|---|
| Direct Labor | 200.00 | | Work in Process | 200.00 | |
| Bonuses—Factory Overhead* | 4.81 | | Factory Overhead Control—Bonuses* | 4.81 | |
| Bonuses Payable | | 4.81 | Bonuses Payable | | 4.81 |
| Payroll | | 200.00 | Payroll | | 200.00 |

---

\* \$50,000 × 0.5% = \$250.00

   \$250 ÷ 52 weeks = \$4.808/week

## 4.5  VACATION AND HOLIDAY PAY

After a certain length of service, an employee generally receives paid vacations and holidays.  Compensation of this sort is called nonproductive pay because an employee is receiving wages while making no contribution to output.  Vacation and holiday pay is charged to factory overhead.  Unlike bonuses, this pay is based on company policy and is therefore known in advance.  As a result, we are able to charge each week of service equally with a portion of vacation pay (as is desirable, but usually impractical, with bonuses).

### EXAMPLE 4

Marlene has worked for the Long Life Battery Company for five years and is therefore entitled to two weeks' paid vacation.  Her weekly pay is \$500.  Make the entry to accrue Marlene's vacation pay for the week; assume she is not on vacation now.

       Total vacation pay: \$500 per week × 2 weeks = \$1,000

       Weeks over which vacation pay is to be accrued: 52 weeks − 2-week vacation = 50 weeks

       Weekly accrual: \$1,000 ÷ 50 weeks = \$20 per week

| Periodic Cost Accumulation | | | Perpetual Cost Accumulation | | |
|---|---|---|---|---|---|
| Direct Labor | 500 | | Work in Process | 500 | |
| Vacation Pay— | | | Factory Overhead Control— | | |
| Factory Overhead | 20 | | Vacation Pay | 20 | |
| Vacation Pay Payable | | 20 | Vacation Pay Payable | | 20 |
| Payroll | | 500 | Payroll | | 500 |

Some major points to remember about paid holidays and vacations are:

(1)  Like vacations, the number of company paid holidays is subject to policy and known in advance.  These two are often combined in one account called Vacation and Holiday Pay and accrued together.

(2)  Vacations are often taken in the summer, so any necessary corrections in the accruals can be spread over the remainder of the year.  In reality, employees leave or are hired or terminated, so adjustments are continually required.  Many companies charge off vacation and holiday pay monthly to reduce the number of entries.

(3)  For salaried employees, vacation and holiday pay is charged to the period when the absence occurs rather than being accrued.

## 4.6  PENSIONS

Pension accounting is a separate field in itself due to the complex nature and enormous expense of pension plans.  Actuaries, experts in life expectancies, determine a company's pension costs through a series of complicated formulas. To arrive at a cost for a pension plan the following factors must be considered:

(1) Number of employees retiring each year
(2) Amount of benefits paid to each retired employee
(3) Length of time that benefits will be paid
(4) Amount of income earned from pension fund investments
(5) Amount of administrative expenses
(6) Benefits for employees who leave before retirement age

After pension costs have been established, those costs associated with production employees are debited to factory overhead.

## 4.7   FRINGE COSTS

Wages and salaries plus any fringe benefits constitute the employer's payroll expense. Vacation pay and pension plans are only two of a number of employee benefits. Other common fringe costs are listed below.

(1) *Social Security Tax (FICA).* Employees *and* employers contribute *equal* percentages based on employee wages.
(2) *Federal Unemployment Tax (FUT).* This tax is paid *only* by employers as a percentage of employee wages.
(3) *State Unemployment Tax (SUT).* This tax is also a percentage based on employee wages and generally is fully paid by the employer.
(4) *State Workmen's Compensation.* Again, a percentage based on employee wages is contributed by the employer. Rates vary depending on occupational hazards.
(5) There are also a variety of optional plans an employer may provide, such as health or life insurance. Often the cost of these plans is shared by the employee.

The majority of companies treat the expenses of fringe costs as charges to factory overhead.

### Incentive Plans

Some companies adopt incentive plans to spur increases in production. Employees are not penalized for producing less than the specified amount but are paid extra for producing more. Wages paid but not earned on a piecework basis are charged to factory overhead.

### EXAMPLE 5

Muffler Ltd. manufactures scarves. The average salary is $200 per week. To increase production the company adopted an incentive plan. The piecework rate per scarf is $1.00. Any employee who produces fewer than 200 scarves per week will still receive his or her original pay. Production above this amount will earn the employee $1.00 for each additional scarf. One week after the plan was implemented, the following data were collected.

| Employee | Scarves Produced | Wages Paid |
|----------|------------------|------------|
| Bob      | 200              | $200       |
| Carol    | 215              | 215        |
| Ted      | 190              | 200        |
| Alice    | 205              | 205        |

Bob:   200 scarves × $1 per unit = $200    No adjustment necessary

Carol: 215 scarves × $1 per unit = $215    Entire amount is direct labor

Ted:   190 scarves × $1 per unit = $190    $\begin{cases} \$190 \text{ is direct labor} \\ \$10 \text{ is charged to factory overhead} \end{cases}$

Alice: 205 scarves × $1 per unit = $205    Entire amount is direct labor

Provided a unit is produced for each wage increment, the entire amount is considered direct labor. When an employee is paid for *more* than he or she actually produces, the difference is charged to factory overhead to avoid distorting the unit cost.

*Note*: Since in theory no single unit is any more expensive to produce than any other, all additional compensation above regular wage rates and all nonproductive pay are charged to factory overhead. This is then distributed over all units produced.

## 4.8  ACCOUNTING FOR LABOR

Three activities are involved in accounting for labor: (1) timekeeping, (2) computation of total payroll, and (3) allocation of payroll cost.

(1) *Timekeeping.* In a manufacturing concern, two forms of timekeeping are commonly used.
   (a) *Time card.* This is used for punching a time clock to record all hours spent at work.
   (b) *Labor job ticket.* This is a record prepared by an employee showing how the hours at work were spent (i.e. jobs that were worked on and hours spent on each). Any time *not* allocated to a particular job is charged to factory overhead.

(2) *Computing Total Payroll.* The function of determining each employee's pay, taking the appropriate deductions, and issuing the pay checks is generally done by the payroll department.

(3) *Allocating Payroll Costs.* This function is generally performed by the cost accounting department. The total payroll expense, including fringe costs, is allocated to particular jobs or departments. The *entire* payroll cost must be allocated.

### Journalizing Payroll

Once the preceding three steps have been completed, the payroll is entered into a journal. The entries required differ depending on whether a perpetual or periodic cost accumulation system is being used. With a perpetual system, direct materials and direct labor are charged to work in process as incurred, so that only an allocation of factory overhead is required to arrive at a unit cost. With a periodic system, labor data are accumulated in various accounts and a more extensive allocation process is required, along with a physical count of materials inventory, to determine the cost of production for the period. In either case, payroll is computed for each pay period, with employer payroll expenses generally being calculated and journalized only once each month.

**EXAMPLE 6**

| | |
|---|---|
| Direct labor | $20,000 |
| Indirect labor | 10,000 |
| Administrative salaries | 15,000 |
| Clerical salaries | 5,000 |
| Gross payroll | $50,000 |

FICA taxes: 6.07% each paid by both employer and employee

Federal Unemployment Tax (FUT): 0.70%

State Unemployment Tax (SUT): 2.70%

Pension Plan provided by the employer: 0.50%

Federal and State Withholding: 20%

Health Insurance: 1.50% paid by both employer and employee

*Procedure:*

(1) Calculate the dollar amount of all deductions and classify them as paid by employer, employee, or both.

| Deduction | Amount | Paid by |
|---|---|---|
| FICA | $50,000 × 6.07% = $3,035 | Both |
| FUT | $50,000 × 0.70% = $350 | Employer |
| SUT | $50,000 × 2.7% = $1,350 | Employer |
| Pension | $50,000 × 0.50% = $250 | Employer |
| Withholding | $50,000 × 20% = $10,000 | Employee |
| Health Insurance | $50,000 × 1.5% = $750 | Both |

(2) Record the payroll. The payable amount is composed of the gross payroll less those deductions paid by employees.

**Periodic Cost Accumulation**

| | | |
|---|---|---|
| Payroll | 50,000 | |
| Accrued Payroll Payable* | | 36,215 |
| FICA Tax Payable | | 3,035 |
| Fed. & State Income Tax Withheld | | 10,000 |
| Health Insurance | | 750 |

**Perpetual Cost Accumulation**

Same entry

\* This is the amount that will actually be paid out to employees in their checks. The other deductions represent liabilities to the firm.

(3) Distribute the payroll.

**Periodic Cost Accumulation**

| | | |
|---|---|---|
| Admin. Salaries Expense | 15,000 | |
| Cler. Salaries Expense | 5,000 | |
| Direct Labor | 20,000 | |
| Indirect Labor—Factory Overhead | 10,000 | |
| Payroll | | 50,000 |

**Perpetual Cost Accumulation**

| | | |
|---|---|---|
| Admin. Salaries Expense | 15,000 | |
| Cler. Salaries Expense | 5,000 | |
| Work in Process | 20,000 | |
| Factory Overhead Control | 10,000 | |
| Payroll | | 50,000 |

(4) Dispose of the amount payable (once the payroll is paid). The gross amount is *never* the amount due in checks.

**Periodic Cost Accumulation**

| | | |
|---|---|---|
| Accrued Payroll Payable | 36,215 | |
| Cash | | 36,215 |

**Perpetual Cost Accumulation**

Same entry

(5)  Enter and allocate the employer's payroll expenses.

| Periodic Cost Accumulation | | | Perpetual Cost Accumulation |
|---|---|---|---|
| *Admin. Salaries Expense** | 1,720.50 | | |
| *Cler. Salaries Expense*** | 573.50 | | |
| *Employer's Payroll Expense—* | | | |
| *Factory Overhead**** | 3,441.00 | | *Same entry (except that the* |
| *FICA Payable* | | 3,035 | *factory overhead control* |
| *FUT Payable* | | 350 | *account is used)* |
| *SUT Payable* | | 1,350 | |
| *Pension Payable* | | 250 | |
| *Health Insurance Payable* | | 750 | |

* FICA:     $15,000 × 6.07% = $  910.50
  FUT:      $15,000 × 0.70% =    105.00
  SUT:      $15,000 × 2.7%  =    405.00
  Pension:  $15,000 × 0.50% =     75.00
  Health:   $15,000 × 1.5%  =    225.00
                              $1,720.50

** FICA:     $5,000 × 6.07% = $  303.50
   FUT:      $5,000 × 0.70% =     35.00
   SUT:      $5,000 × 2.7%  =    135.00
   Pension:  $5,000 × 0.50% =     25.00
   Health:   $5,000 × 1.5%  =     75.00
                             $  573.50

*** Direct and indirect labor fringes both go to factory overhead:
   FICA:     $30,000 × 6.07% = $1,821.00
   FUT:      $30,000 × 0.70% =    210.00
   SUT:      $30,000 × 2.7%  =    810.00
   Pension:  $30,000 × 0.50% =    150.00
   Health:   $30,000 × 1.5%  =    450.00
                              $3,441.00

## 4.9  LEARNING CURVE

The production of new products or a change in the manufacturing process introduces a learning factor.  To aid in competent managerial decision making, a learning curve is employed.  Studies have demonstrated that output will increase by a constant percentage as a process becomes more familiar to employees.

(1)  During the learning stage, *each time the number of units produced doubles* the cumulative average time to produce one unit will decrease by a specified percentage.  The decrease is a percentage of the cumulative average time to produce one unit before the doubling occurred.

(2)  The constant stage is characterized by a leveling off in the increase in output per hour.  This occurs when the workers have become familiar with the production process and are performing at their peak efficiency.  The process has become routine when this stage appears.

**EXAMPLE 7**

Speedway Motor Parts has introduced a new process to manufacture carburetors. The engineers project a 90% learning curve will be evident until workers become familiar with the new techniques. The first five units produced under the new process will each take 4 hours, and labor cost is $5.00 per hour. Compute the average labor hours needed and the output per hour up to the fortieth unit. Also compute the labor cost per unit for each cumulative unit of production.

| Cumulative Units of Production | Cumulative Average Time per Unit (hr) | Total Time Needed (hr) | Output per Hour | Labor Cost per Unit |
|---|---|---|---|---|
| 5 | 4 | 20 (a) | 0.25 (b) | $20.00 (c) |
| 10 | 3.6 (4 × 90%) | 36 (a) | 0.28 (b) | 18.00 (c) |
| 20 | 3.24 (3.6 × 90%) | 64.8 (a) | 0.31 (b) | 16.20 (c) |
| 40 | 2.92 (3.24 × 90%) | 116.8 (a) | 0.34 (b) | 14.60 (c) |

*Computations:*

(a)  20 = 5 units × 4 hours; 36 = 10 units × 3.6 hours;
     64.8 = 20 units × 3.24 hours; 116.8 = 40 units × 2.92 hours.

(b)  0.25 = 5 units ÷ 20 hours; 0.28 = 10 units ÷ 36 hours;
     0.31 = 20 units ÷ 64.8 hours; 0.34 = 40 units ÷ 116.8 hours.

(c)  $20.00 = (20 hours ÷ 5 units) × $5/hour; $18.00 = (36 hours ÷ 10 units) × $5/hour;
     $16.20 = (64.8 hours ÷ 20 units) × $5/hour; $14.60 = (116.8 hours ÷ 40 units) × $5/hour.

# *Summary*

(1)  The three characteristics of direct labor are _____ , _____ , and _____ .

(2)  Direct labor is charged to the _____ account under a perpetual cost accumulation system and to the _____ account under a periodic system.

(3)  Overtime premium and shift premium are different items, but they are handled in the same way in the accounts.   (a) True, (b) false.

(4)  Under a perpetual system, all direct labor hours are charged to work in process at the regular wage rate.   (a) True, (b) false.

(5)  Bonuses are charged to (a) direct labor, (b) work in process, (c) factory overhead, (d) indirect labor.

(6)  Often bonuses (a) can't be computed until the end of a period, (b) distort unit cost, (c) are used to reward high productivity, (d) are paid in advance.

(7)  Ideally, bonuses should be (a) incorporated into an employee's regular salary, (b) not paid at all, (c) given to all employees, (d) accrued over the productive period to which they relate.

(8)  When determining the weekly accrual for vacation pay, the number of weeks the employee is absent is disregarded.   (a) True, (b) false.

(9)  Correction of the accruals provided to account for vacation pay is relatively common.   (a) True, (b) false.

(10) A company generally uses the services of an _____ to determine its pension costs. Once determined, pension costs are periodically _____ to factory overhead.

(11) _____ is a fringe cost that is mandatory and is contributed to equally by both the employer and the employee.

(12) Which of the following would be considered nonproductive pay? (a) Pension pay, (b) overtime premium, (c) vacation pay, (d) bonuses, (e) holiday pay.

(13) Under an incentive plan, a piecework price *must* be applied to all units produced. (a) True, (b) false.

(14) When an incentive plan is being used and an employee produces more than the specified number of units, the additional labor cost is considered to be direct labor. (a) True, (b) false.

(15) All payroll costs are allocated to the appropriate departments except (a) pension costs, (b) indirect labor, (c) administrative salaries, (d) state unemployment tax, (e) none of the above.

(16) When the constant stage has been reached on a learning curve, (a) more units are being produced, but the cost of each is higher; (b) there is a distinct inverse relationship between output per hour and labor cost per unit; (c) further improvement in productivity is impossible; (d) it is time to alter the production process.

*Answers:* (1) easily traced to the product, a major cost of production, can be identified directly with production of the product; (2) work-in-process, direct labor; (3) *a*; (4) *a*; (5) *c*; (6) *a* and *c*; (7) *d*; (8) *b*; (9) *a*; (10) actuary, debited; (11) Social Security tax; (12) *c* and *e*; (13) *a*; (14) *a*; (15) *e*; (16) *b*.

# Solved Problems

**4.1**    Dippin' Donuts has six bakers and a bakery supervisor on each of its two shifts. Bakers working from 8 a.m.–5 p.m. (with 1-hour break) are paid $6.00 per hour. Bakers working the 10 p.m.–7 a.m. shift (with 1-hour break) are paid $6.75 per hour. The supervisors are paid a salary of $300 per week. Due to the large volume of business, two of the daytime bakers worked until 8 p.m. three evenings this week; they both received time and a half for the extra hours worked. Prepare journal entries to distribute the weekly payroll under both periodic and perpetual cost accumulation systems.

**SOLUTION**

*Day Shift*

Wages:                    $6/hour × 40 hours/week = $240/week for each baker
                    6 bakers × $240/week = $1,440/week for all bakers (direct labor)

Overtime:            ($6/hour × 3 hours/evening) × 2 bakers = $36/evening × 3 evenings
                                        = $108 (direct labor)

Overtime premium:   ($3/hour × 3 hours/evening) × 2 bakers = $18/evening × 3 evenings
                                        = $54 (overtime premium)

*Night Shift*

Wages:                    $6/hour × 40 hours/week = $240/week for each baker
                    6 bakers × $240/week = $1,440/week for all bakers (direct labor)

Shift premium:           $0.75/hour × 40 hours/week = $30/week for each baker
                    6 bakers × $30/week = $180/week for all bakers (shift premium)

*Supervisors*

Salary:        $300/week × 2 supervisors = $600/week, both supervisors (indirect labor)

*Distribution*

|  | Days | Nights |  |
|---|---|---|---|
| Direct labor: | ($1,440 + $108) + | $1,440 | = $2,988 |
| Overtime premium: | $54 | | |
| Shift premium: | $180 | | |
| Indirect labor: | $600 | | |

| **Periodic Cost Accumulation** | | **Perpetual Cost Accumulation** | | |
|---|---|---|---|---|
| *Direct Labor* | 2,988 | *Work in Process* | 2,988 | |
| *Indirect Labor—* | | *Factory Overhead* | | |
| *Factory Overhead* | 600 | *Control* | 834 | |
| *Overtime Premium—* | | *Payroll* | | 3,822 |
| *Factory Overhead* | 54 | | | |
| *Shift Premium—* | | | | |
| *Factory Overhead* | 180 | | | |
| *Payroll* | 3,822 | | | |

Shift premium, overtime premium, and indirect labor are all elements of factory overhead. Under a perpetual system, these are all posted to one control account. A *control account* is a master balance for a subsidiary ledger. The reason the factory overhead control account appears with subtitles in this chapter (e.g. Factory overhead control—shift premium) is to denote the account in the *subsidiary ledger* in which the entry is made. It does not mean that separate factory overhead control accounts appear in the general ledger.

**4.2**    The Lion's Den fur coat factory has a bonus plan with the following structure:

(*a*)   The fur cleaners (direct labor) receive one week's salary as a bonus at year end. There are 20 workers in this category; each earns $273 per week.

(*b*)   The tailors (direct labor) are paid 5% of their yearly salary as a bonus at year end. The company has 10 tailors, each making $350 per week.

(*c*)   The representatives, who sell the coats to retailers, receive 1% of the company's profits as a bonus at year end. There are 10 representatives, each earning $300 per week, and the 1% is split evenly among them. (*Hint:* These employees are not factory labor, so their payroll data require separate accounts.) The company projects $1 million in profits this year.

Prepare separate journal entries to accrue the bonuses each week for each of the above categories of employees and distribute the weekly payroll in the same entry. Assume the company uses a periodic cost accumulation system.

**SOLUTION**

(a)              Direct Labor ($273 × 20)        5,460.00
                 Bonuses—Factory Overhead*        105.00
                     Bonuses Payable                              105.00
                     Payroll                                     5,460.00

$$* \quad \frac{\$273/year}{52\ weeks/year} = \$5.25/week \times 20\ fur\ cleaners = \$105.00$$

(b)              Direct Labor ($350 × 10)        3,500.00
                 Bonuses—Factory Overhead*        175.00
                     Bonuses payable                             175.00
                     Payroll                                     3,500.00

\* $350/week × 5% = $17.50/week × 10 tailors = $175.00

(c)              Sales Salaries Expense ($300 × 10)    3,000.00
                 Sales Bonuses*                         192.30
                     Bonuses Payable                                 192.30
                     Payroll                                        3,000.00

$$* \quad \frac{\$1,000,000/year \times 1\%}{52\ weeks/year} = \$192.30/week\ for\ all\ 10\ representatives$$

**4.3**    The Billings Industrial Supply Corporation has the following vacation policy:

| 1 to 3 years of service: | 1 week paid vacation |
| 4 to 7 years of service: | 2 weeks paid vacation |
| 8 to 10 years of service: | 3 weeks paid vacation |
| Over 10 years of service: | 4 weeks paid vacation |

Examination of the payroll data on the company's 10 assembly line workers revealed the following:

| Name | Years of Service | Weekly Salary |
|------|------------------|---------------|
| J. Adams | 5 | $210 |
| O. White | 10 | 355 |
| A. McFinny | 6 | 250 |
| F. Vasquez | 8 | 300 |
| R. Rubin | 12 | 390 |
| E. Cheshire | 1/2 | 150 |
| K. Quentin | 4 | 190 |
| D. Mancini | 2 | 175 |
| L. Johnson | 15 | 425 |
| Y. Flynn | 1 | 160 |

(a)  Determine the weekly accrual for each employee.
(b)  Prepare the journal entry to distribute the payroll and accrue the vacation pay under a perpetual cost accumulation system.

## SOLUTION

(a)

| Name | Weeks of Vacation | Total Vacation Pay | Weekly Accrual* |
|---|---|---|---|
| J. Adams | 2 | $ 420 | $ 8.40 |
| O. White | 3 | 1,065 | 21.73 |
| A. McFinny | 2 | 500 | 10.00 |
| F. Vasquez | 3 | 900 | 18.37 |
| R. Rubin | 4 | 1,560 | 32.50 |
| E. Cheshire | 0 | 0 | 0 |
| K. Quentin | 2 | 380 | 7.60 |
| D. Mancini | 1 | 175 | 3.43 |
| L. Johnson | 4 | 1,700 | 35.42 |
| Y. Flynn | 1 | 160 | 3.14 |
| | | | $140.59 |

* Total vacation pay/[52 weeks − week(s) of vacation due]

(b)

| | | |
|---|---|---|
| Work in Process | 2,605.00 | |
| Factory Overhead Control—Vacation Pay | 140.59 | |
| Vacation Pay Payable | | 140.59 |
| Payroll | | 2,605.00 |

**4.4** Management at Easy Listening, Inc., a manufacturer of cassette tapes, believes production can be improved if an incentive plan is implemented. Under the plan workers are to be paid $0.30 per tape produced with a minimum guaranteed salary of $150 per week. The data collected after the first week of implementation are as follows:

| Employee | Units Produced |
|---|---|
| Jones | 485 |
| Allen | 500 |
| Webster | 520 |
| Simms | 536 |
| Taylor | 419 |
| Rollins | 511 |

(a) Compute each employee's gross wages.
(b) Prepare the journal entry to distribute the payroll under a perpetual cost accumulation system.

## SOLUTION

(a)

| Employee | Units Produced | Piecework Wage | Gross Wages |
|---|---|---|---|
| Jones | 485 | 485 × $.30 = $145.50 | $150.00 |
| Allen | 500 | 500 × .30 = 150.00 | 150.00 |
| Webster | 520 | 520 × .30 = 156.00 | 156.00 |
| Simms | 536 | 536 × .30 = 160.80 | 160.80 |
| Taylor | 419 | 419 × .30 = 125.70 | 150.00 |
| Rollins | 511 | 511 × .30 = 153.30 | 153.30 |
| | | $891.30 | $920.10 |

(b)
| | | |
|---|---|---|
| Work in Process | 891.30 | |
| Factory Overhead Control* | 28.80 | |
| Payroll | | 920.10 |

---

\* $920.10 − $891.30 = $28.80 (paid, but not earned on a piecework basis)

**4.5** Payroll is being prepared at Morgan Manufacturing, Inc. Examination of the labor job tickets for the week ending August 20 produced the following data:

| | | Labor Hours | |
|---|---|---|---|
| Employee | Hourly Wage | Direct | Indirect |
| Howard | $4.50 | 32 | 8 |
| Peabody | 5.25 | 38 | 2 |
| Lancer | 4.25 | 29 | 11 |
| Cahill | 4.30 | 40 | 0 |
| Barnes | 5.05 | 34 | 6 |
| Williams | 4.75 | 39 | 1 |
| Thomas | 4.90 | 28 | 12 |
| Greene | 5.15 | 36 | 4 |

| | |
|---|---|
| Total FICA (employee) | $102.24 |
| Total FICA (employer) | 102.24 |
| Total Federal and State Income Tax | 350.26 |
| Union Dues | 115.00 |
| Federal Unemployment Tax (FUT) | 10.68 |
| State Unemployment Tax (SUT) | 41.20 |

Prepare journal entries for a periodic cost accumulation system to (a) record payroll, (b) distribute payroll, (c) enter the payment of payroll, and (d) record the employer's payroll taxes.

**SOLUTION**

| | | Payroll | | | | | |
|---|---|---|---|---|---|---|---|
| Employee | Hourly Wage | Direct Labor | | Indirect Labor | | Total | |
| Howard | $4.50 | (32 hr) | $ 144.00 | (8 hr) | $ 36.00 | $ 180.00 | |
| Peabody | 5.25 | (38 hr) | 199.50 | (2 hr) | 10.50 | 210.00 | |
| Lancer | 4.25 | (29 hr) | 123.25 | (11 hr) | 46.75 | 170.00 | |
| Cahill | 4.30 | (40 hr) | 172.00 | (0) | 0 | 172.00 | |
| Barnes | 5.05 | (34 hr) | 171.70 | (6 hr) | 30.30 | 202.00 | |
| Williams | 4.75 | (39 hr) | 185.25 | (1 hr) | 4.75 | 190.00 | |
| Thomas | 4.90 | (28 hr) | 137.20 | (12 hr) | 58.80 | 196.00 | |
| Greene | 5.15 | (36 hr) | 185.40 | (4 hr) | 20.60 | 206.00 | |
| | | | $1,318.30 | | $207.70 | $1,526.00 | |

(a)
| | | |
|---|---|---|
| Payroll | 1,526.00 | |
| Accrued Payroll Payable | | 958.50 |
| FICA Payable | | 102.24 |
| Federal & State Withholding Income Tax Payable | | 350.26 |
| Union Dues | | 115.00 |

| | | | |
|---|---|---|---|
| (b) | Direct Labor | 1,318.30 | |
| | Indirect Labor—Factory Overhead | 207.70 | |
| | Payroll | | 1,526.00 |
| (c) | Accrued Payroll Payable | 958.50 | |
| | Cash | | 958.50 |
| (d) | Employer's Payroll Expense—Factory Overhead | 154.12 | |
| | FICA Payable | | 102.24 |
| | FUT Payable | | 10.68 |
| | SUT Payable | | 41.20 |

**4.6**    You are a bookkeeper for Candy Canes, Inc., for which the payroll data are:

| | |
|---|---:|
| Direct Labor | $25,000 |
| Indirect Labor | 10,000 |
| Administrative Salaries | 18,000 |
| Clerical Salaries | 9,000 |
| Gross Payroll | $62,000 |

FICA: $4,154 each for employer and employee ($2,345 Direct & Indirect; $1,206 Administrative Salaries; $603 Clerical Salaries)

FUT: 0.70%

SUT: 2.70%

Pension plan provided by employer: 0.75%

Health insurance paid by employees: 3.0%

Federal and state withholding income tax: 20%

Prepare journal entries for a perpetual cost accumulation system to (a) record payroll, (b) distribute payroll, (c) enter payment of payroll, and (d) record the employer's payroll taxes.

**SOLUTION**

**Schedule of Deductions**

| | Wages | FICA | Income Tax | FUT | SUT | Pension Plan | Health Insurance |
|---|---|---|---|---|---|---|---|
| Direct & Indirect Labor | $35,000 | $2,345 | $ 7,000 | $245 | $ 945 | $262.50 | $1,050 |
| Admin. Salaries | 18,000 | 1,206 | 3,600 | 126 | 486 | 135.00 | 540 |
| Clerical Salaries | 9,000 | 603 | 1,800 | 63 | 243 | 67.50 | 270 |
| Total | $62,000 | $4,154 | $12,400 | $434 | $1,674 | $465.00 | $1,860 |
| Paid by | | Both | Employee | Employer | Employer | Employer | Employee |

| | | | |
|---|---|---|---|
| (a) | Payroll | 62,000 | |
| | Accrued Payroll Payable | | 43,586 |
| | FICA Payable | | 4,154 |
| | Federal & State Income Tax Withheld | | 12,400 |
| | Health Insurance | | 1,860 |
| (b) | Work in Process | 25,000 | |
| | Factory Overhead Control— | | |
| | Indirect Labor | 10,000 | |
| | Administrative Salaries Expense | 18,000 | |
| | Clerical Salaries Expense | 9,000 | |
| | Payroll | | 62,000 |
| (c) | Accrued Payroll Payable | 43,586 | |
| | Cash | | 43,586 |

(d)　　　　　　　*Factory Overhead Control—*

| | | |
|---|---|---|
| *Employer's Payroll Expenses** | 3,797.50 | |
| *Administrative Salaries Expense** | 1,953.00 | |
| *Clerical Salaries Expense** | 976.50 | |
| *FICA Payable* | | 4,154.00 |
| *FUT Payable* | | 434.00 |
| *SUT Payable* | | 1,674.00 |
| *Pension Plan Payable* | | 465.00 |

\* FICA, FUT, SUT, Pension

**4.7** Detecto-Thief, a burglar alarm company, is implementing a new technique to install circuitry panels in its alarm units. The engineers consulted project an 80% learning curve until workers master the new methods. The technique requires 5 hours for installation of the first unit and labor cost is $6.00 per hour. Compute the average labor hours needed, output per hour up to the eightieth unit (start with 5 units), and the labor cost per unit for each cumulative unit of production. (Round to the nearest tenth.)

**SOLUTION**

| Cumulative Units of Production | Cumulative Average Time per Unit | Total Time Needed | Output per Hour | Labor Cost per Unit |
|---|---|---|---|---|
| 5 | 5 | 25 (a) | 0.20 (b) | $30.00 (c) |
| 10 | 4 (5 × 80%) | 40 (a) | 0.25 (b) | 24.00 (c) |
| 20 | 3.2 (4 × 80%) | 64 (a) | 0.31 (b) | 19.20 (c) |
| 40 | 2.6 (3.2 × 80%) | 104 (a) | 0.38 (b) | 15.60 (c) |
| 80 | 2.1 (2.6 × 80%) | 168 (a) | 0.48 (b) | 12.60 (c) |

*Computations:*

(a) 25 = 5 units × 5 hours; 40 = 10 units × 4 hours; 64 = 20 units × 3.2 hours; 104 = 40 units × 2.6 hours; 168 = 80 units × 2.1 hours.

(b) 0.20 = 5 units ÷ 25 hours; 0.25 = 10 units ÷ 40 hours; 0.31 = 20 units ÷ 64 hours; 0.38 = 40 units ÷ 104 hours; 0.48 = 80 units ÷ 168 hours.

(c) $30.00 = (25 hours ÷ 5 units) × $6/hour; $24.00 = (40 hours ÷ 10 units) × $6/hour; $19.20 = (64 hours ÷ 20 units) × $6/hour; $15.60 = (104 hours ÷ 40 units) × $6/hour; $12.60 = (168 hours ÷ 80 units) × $6/hour.

# Chapter 5

# Factory Overhead
# and the Factory Ledger

## 5.1 FACTORY OVERHEAD DEFINED

The cost of direct labor and direct materials can easily be identified and charged to specific jobs. All other costs, i.e. the costs of indirect materials, indirect labor and other factory expenses which cannot be identified with or charged directly to specific jobs, are called *factory overhead*. These *indirect* costs are categorized as described below.

*Variable Costs.* Costs that vary in direct proportion to production volume are called variable costs. If 20 gallons of glue are needed to produce 100,000 units and 40 gallons of glue are needed for the production of 200,000 units, glue will be considered a variable cost.

*Fixed Costs.* Costs that do not vary in proportion to production volume within a relevant range are called fixed overhead. Rent is one example. Whether 100 or 1,000 units are produced, the rent for the use of a factory remains the same.

At the same time, fixed overhead *per unit* varies with production. If rent were $10,000 a year and 100,000 units were produced in a year, each unit would cost $0.10. If 200,000 units were produced in a year, each unit would cost only $0.05.

*Semivariable Costs.* Costs that will change, but *not in direct proportion* to production volume. An example of this would be purchase orders. If 50 pads of purchase orders are required to buy the materials necessary to produce 100,000 units but only 60 pads are needed to buy enough materials to produce 200,000 units, then the cost of the pads is a semivariable cost.

## 5.2 APPLIED FACTORY OVERHEAD

An estimate of the next period's factory overhead costs is made which is then divided by a base such as labor hours, machine hours, etc. and expressed as a predetermined rate. This predetermined rate helps management in measuring unit costs. If no predetermined rate is used, management would have to wait until the end of the period to know the amount of factory overhead costs. Thus, it would be more difficult to quote selling prices to customers since costs would be less exact.

## 5.3 BASE TO BE USED

The base used to compute the predetermined overhead rate should be closely related to functions represented by the overhead cost being applied. Note that the base, like the total overhead costs, is an estimate of the future period's production quantity or cost. The five bases generally used to calculate the factory overhead rate are described below.

***Units of Production.*** This method is considered the most efficient means of applying factory overhead.  The equation is

$$\frac{\text{Estimated factory overhead}}{\text{Estimated units of production}} = \text{Overhead rate per unit}$$

**EXAMPLE 1**

Based on the units of production method, if 20,000 units are to be manufactured and the estimated factory overhead for the period is $100,000, the factory overhead rate would be $5 per unit ($100,000 ÷ 20,000).

***Materials Cost.*** This method uses estimated total direct materials cost as a basis, and the rate is expressed as a percentage.  The equation is

$$\frac{\text{Estimated factory overhead}}{\text{Estimated materials cost}} \times 100 = \begin{array}{l}\text{Percentage of overhead} \\ \text{per direct materials cost}\end{array}$$

**EXAMPLE 2**

Suppose that estimated materials cost is $50,000 and estimated factory overhead for the period is $100,000. Using materials cost as the base, the factory overhead rate is computed as follows.

$$\frac{\$100,000}{\$50,000} \times 100 = 200\% \text{ of direct materials cost}$$

***Direct Labor Cost.*** This basis is widely used because of the high degree of correlation found in most cases between labor cost and factory overhead.  The following equation is used:

$$\frac{\text{Estimated factory overhead}}{\text{Estimated direct labor cost}} \times 100 = \text{Percentage of direct labor cost}$$

**EXAMPLE 3**

Based on direct labor hours, an estimated direct labor cost of $400,000 and an estimated factory overhead per period of $100,000 would result in an overhead rate of 25% of direct labor cost, since

$$\frac{\$100,000}{\$400,000} \times 100 = 25\%$$

***Direct Labor Hours.*** Where labor rates vary widely, direct labor hours may be more suitable than direct labor cost as a basis.  The equation in this case is

$$\frac{\text{Estimated factory overhead}}{\text{Estimated direct labor hours}} = \text{Rate per direct labor hour}$$

**EXAMPLE 4**

If direct labor hours are estimated at 8,000 and estimated factory overhead per period is $100,000, the factory overhead rate based on direct labor hours is calculated as follows:

$$\frac{\$100,000}{8,000} = \$12.50 \text{ per direct labor hour}$$

***Machine Hours.*** Where production is largely by machine an appropriate basis would be the time required by a machine or group of machines to perform production operations.  The base used is total machine hours estimated for the period.  The equation is

$$\frac{\text{Estimated factory overhead}}{\text{Estimated machine hours}} = \text{Rate per machine hour}$$

**EXAMPLE 5**

Assume that estimated machine hours equal 10,000 and estimated factory overhead per period is $100,000. The factory overhead rate based on machine hours would be calculated as follows:

$$\frac{\$100,000}{10,000} = \$10 \text{ per machine hour}$$

In summary, the reader should note that in the above five methods the numerator is always the estimated factory overhead cost. The denominator changes with each method.

Note also that when costs or dollars are used as a base, a percentage rate is developed and therefore the fraction is multiplied by 100. When units or hours are used as a base, a dollar rate is developed.

## 5.4   ACTIVITY LEVEL TO BE USED

*Normal or Long-run Capacity.* This concept assumes a stable rate or capacity level of production over a period of time long enough to even out high and low levels of production. Therefore, the expected or estimated capacity used each period to compute overhead rates does not change.

*Expected Actual or Short-run Capacity.* The capacity expected for the next period may be used as a base to determine an overhead rate. Therefore, overhead rates may vary each period depending on estimated changes in capacity levels, whereas the overhead rates based on normal capacity will remain constant even if expected actual capacity fluctuates.

*Which Activity Level to Use.* The use of normal capacity will result in a uniform cost per unit for different periods (assuming all other factors are constant), whereas the use of expected actual capacity may result in varying unit costs for different periods (if expected actual capacity changes). Therefore, the use of normal capacity is preferred because it eliminates the possible manipulation of unit costs by changing production levels. Expected actual capacity is generally used only when the normal production activity is difficult to determine.

## 5.5   JOURNALIZING FACTORY OVERHEAD

The journal entries to record factory overhead costs will depend on the cost accumulation system used and the amount of information desired by management. Actual factory overhead costs are basically recorded the same way under both periodic and perpetual systems (debit factory overhead control and credit either cash, vouchers payable, accumulated depreciation, etc.). When a perpetual cost accumulation system is used both actual and applied factory overhead costs are commonly recorded, whereas in a periodic cost accumulation system, only actual costs are recorded. The remaining examples in this chapter are presented on the assumption that a perpetual cost accumulation system is in use.

As was previously stated, actual overhead costs incurred during a period are debited to a factory overhead control account. Ideally, the balance in the factory overhead control account should equal the amount of overhead applied for the period. This rarely occurs in actual situations because of the difficulty in accurately estimating the extent of involvement of various factors (see Section 5.6). Only applied (not actual) factory overhead is charged to work in process.

The applied factory overhead account is closed out to the factory overhead control account at the end of the period. The factory overhead control account debit balance and the applied factory overhead account credit balance are compared to arrive at a net debit or credit balance. Some companies do not use a separate factory overhead applied account; instead they credit factory overhead control for overhead applied.

## EXAMPLE 6

Assume the following account balances:

| Factory Overhead Control | | | |
|---|---|---|---|
| 1/5 | 7,000 | | |
| 1/8 | 9,000 | | |
| 1/12 | 10,000 | | |
| 1/28 | 6,000 | | |

| Work in Process, Factory Overhead | | | |
|---|---|---|---|
| 1/15 | 15,000 | | |
| 1/31 | 25,000 | | |

| Vouchers Payable | | | |
|---|---|---|---|
| | | 1/5 | 7,000 |
| | | 1/8 | 9,000 |
| | | 1/12 | 10,000 |
| | | 1/28 | 6,000 |

| Applied Factory Overhead | | | |
|---|---|---|---|
| | | 1/15 | 15,000 |
| | | 1/31 | 25,000 |

The entries to record rent of $8,000 payable on January 29, 19X5 and to close out the factory overhead control and applied accounts are

| | | | |
|---|---|---|---|
| January 29 | *Factory Overhead Control, Rent* | *8,000* | |
| | *Vouchers Payable* | | *8,000* |
| January 31 | *Applied Factory Overhead* | *40,000* | |
| | *Factory Overhead Control* | | *40,000* |

The entries are posted to the accounts as follows:

| Factory Overhead Control | | | |
|---|---|---|---|
| 1/5 | 7,000 | 1/31 | 40,000 |
| 1/8 | 9,000 | | |
| 1/12 | 10,000 | | |
| 1/28 | 6,000 | | |
| 1/29 | 8,000 | | |
| | 40,000 | | 40,000 |

| Work in Process, Factory Overhead | | | |
|---|---|---|---|
| 1/15 | 15,000 | | |
| 1/31 | 25,000 | | |

| Vouchers Payable | | | |
|---|---|---|---|
| | | 1/5 | 7,000 |
| | | 1/8 | 9,000 |
| | | 1/12 | 10,000 |
| | | 1/28 | 6,000 |
| | | 1/29 | 8,000 |

| Applied Factory Overhead | | | |
|---|---|---|---|
| 1/31 | 40,000 | 1/15 | 15,000 |
| | | 1/31 | 25,000 |
| | 40,000 | | 40,000 |

## 5.6 OVER- OR UNDERAPPLIED OVERHEAD

The balance in the factory overhead control account will usually not equal the balance in the applied factory overhead account because of incorrect estimates of one or more of the following:

(1) Estimated factory overhead cost for the period

(2) Estimated production (did not equal normal capacity)

(3) Labor or machine hour efficiency

### EXAMPLE 7

Assume direct labor hours are used to apply factory overhead. The following formula would be used:

$$\frac{\text{Estimated factory overhead cost}}{\text{Estimated direct labor hours}} = \text{Rate per direct labor hour}$$

If either of the above two estimates are incorrect, the resulting rate per direct labor hour would be incorrect.

### EXAMPLE 8

Assume that the normal amount of time to complete a job is 100 direct labor hours and that factory overhead is $5 per direct labor hour (applied on the basis of direct labor hours). If a specific job took 105 direct labor hours (the 5 extra hours due to labor inefficiency), overhead would be overapplied by $25 (5 extra hours × $5 per direct labor hour).

When overhead is over- or underapplied, either of the following two methods are acceptable to account for the difference in closing the account:

(1) *To Cost of Goods Sold and Ending Inventories (if difference is significant)*
    The over- or underapplied overhead may be debited or credited to cost of goods sold and ending inventories. This would change cost per unit.

(2) *To Cost of Goods Sold (if difference is insignificant)*
    The over- or underapplied overhead may be debited or credited to cost of goods sold. This has no effect on unit cost and treats the entire variance as a period cost.

### EXAMPLE 9

Assume the following data:

| | |
|---|---|
| Underapplied overhead | $12,000 |
| Goods sold | 80,000 units (80%) |
| Goods in ending inventory | 20,000 units (20%) |

The journal entries to close the applied overhead account according to the two acceptable methods are shown below.

(1) To Cost of Goods Sold and Inventory:

| | | |
|---|---|---|
| *Cost of Goods Sold* | | |
| ($12,000 × 80%) | *9,600* | |
| *Ending Inventory* | | |
| ($12,000 × 20%) | *2,400* | |
| *Factory Overhead Control* | | *12,000* |

(2)  To Cost of Goods Sold:

$$
\begin{array}{lrr}
\textit{Cost of Goods Sold} & 12,000 & \\
\quad \textit{Factory Overhead Control} & & 12,000 \\
\end{array}
$$

## 5.7  ALLOCATION OF SERVICE DEPARTMENT COSTS TO PRODUCING DEPARTMENTS

There are two basic types of factory departments in a manufacturing company: producing departments and service departments. A producing department is where the conversion or production takes place. A service department (e.g. personnel or maintenance) provides support to the producing departments. Since the producing departments are directly benefited by service departments, the expenses of a service department should be allocated to the appropriate producing departments (as part of factory overhead costs). One of the following methods may be used to allocate service department costs to producing departments:

(1)  Direct method
(2)  Step method
(3)  Algebraic method

### Direct Method

This is the most common method of allocating service department costs to producing departments because of its mathematical simplicity and ease of application. It involves allocation of service department costs directly to producing departments and ignores any services provided by one service department to another.

### EXAMPLE 10

Assume the following data for R. Mirador Rattan Industries:

**Service Departments:**

| | |
|---|---|
| Dept. N, Maintenance | $12,000 |
| Dept. I, Cafeteria | 5,500 |

**Producing Departments:**

| | |
|---|---|
| Dept. C, Machinery | 42,000 |
| Dept. K, Assembly | 78,700 |

The cost of the maintenance department is allocated to the producing departments based on the number of square feet; the cost of the cafeteria department is allocated based on the number of employees.

| Department | Direct Labor Hours | Square Feet | Number of Employees |
|---|---|---|---|
| N, Maintenance | — | 250 | 15 |
| I, Cafeteria | — | 900 | 12 |
| C, Machinery | 4,500 | 2,250 | 35 |
| K, Assembly | 20,000 | 5,700 | 150 |
| Total | 24,500 | 9,100 | 212 |

The service departments' costs allocation under the direct method is shown below:

**Allocation of Costs**
**Direct Method**

| | Service Departments | | Producing Departments | |
|---|---|---|---|---|
| | N, Maintenance | I, Cafeteria | C, Machinery | K, Assembly |
| Total Cost | $12,000 | $5,500 | $42,000 | $78,700 |
| Allocated to Producing Depts. C and K | ⟨12,000⟩ (c) | | 3,396 (a) | 8,604 (b) |
| | | ⟨5,500⟩ (f) | 1,041 (d) | 4,459 (e) |
| Balance after Allocation | 0 | 0 | $46,437 | $91,763 |
| Factory Overhead Rates | | | $10.319 (g) | $ 4.588 (h) |

*Computations*:

Allocation of Department N, Maintenance:

$$\frac{\text{Total cost}}{\text{Total square feet—Departments C and K}} = \text{Allocation rate}$$

$$\frac{\$12,000}{7,950 \text{ sq ft}} = \$1.50943/\text{sq ft}$$

|  |  | | Square Feet × Rate/Sq ft | | |
|---|---|---|---|---|---|
| (a) | To Dept. C, Machinery | $ 3,396 | = | 2,250 | × $1.50943 |
| (b) | To Dept. K, Assembly | 8,604 | = | 5,700 | × $1.50943 |
| (c) | Total | $12,000 | | | |

Allocation of Department I, Assembly:

$$\frac{\text{Total cost}}{\text{Total number of employees—Departments C and K}} = \text{Allocation rate}$$

$$\frac{\$5,500}{185 \text{ employees}} = \$29.72973/\text{employee}$$

|  |  | | Number of Employees × Rate/Employee | | |
|---|---|---|---|---|---|
| (d) | To Dept. C, Machinery | $1,041 | = | 35 | × $29.72973 |
| (e) | To Dept. K, Assembly | 4,459 | = | 150 | × $29.72973 |
| (f) | Total | $5,500 | | | |

Factory overhead rates (based on direct labor hours) for producing departments:

|  |  | | | Total Cost After Allocation | ÷ | Direct Labor Hours |
|---|---|---|---|---|---|---|
| (g) | For Dept. C, Machinery | $10.319 | = | $46,437 | ÷ | 4,500 |
| (h) | For Dept. K, Assembly | $4.588 | = | $91,763 | ÷ | 20,000 |

## Step Method

This method is more accurate than the direct method because it takes into consideration the services provided to other service departments. The allocation of service department costs is performed by a series of steps:

(1) The costs of the service department that provides services to the greatest number of other service departments are usually allocated first.

(2) The costs of the service department that provides services to the next greatest number of service departments are then allocated. Any costs added to this department from step 1 are included. Note that under this method, the costs of subsequent service departments will not be allocated to the preceding service departments; thus any reciprocal services among service departments are ignored.

(3) The sequence outlined above is continued, step by step, until all the service department costs have been allocated to producing departments.

## EXAMPLE 11

Using the same data as in Example 10, assume that the cost of the maintenance department is allocated first. The allocation of service department costs under the step method is as follows:

*Allocation of Costs*
*Step Method*

|  | Service Departments | | Producing Departments | |
|---|---|---|---|---|
|  | N, Maintenance | I, Cafeteria | C, Machinery | K, Assembly |
| Total Cost | $12,000 | $5,500 | $42,000 | $78,700 |
| Allocated to Service Dept. I and Producing Depts. C and K | ⟨12,000⟩ | 1,220 (a) | 3,051 (b) | 7,729 (c) |
| Subtotal |  | $6,720 | $45,051 | $86,429 |
| Allocated to Producing Depts. C and K |  | ⟨6,720⟩ | 1,271 (d) | 5,449 (e) |
| Balance after Allocation | 0 | 0 | $46,322 | $91,878 |
| Factory Overhead Rates |  |  | $10.293 (f) | $4.594 (g) |

*Computations:*

Allocation of Department N, Maintenance:

$$\frac{\text{Total cost}}{\text{Square feet—Departments I, C, and K}} = \frac{\$12,000}{8,850} = \$1.35593/\text{sq ft}$$

|  |  |  | Square Feet × Rate/Sq ft | |
|---|---|---|---|---|
| (a) | To Dept. I, Cafeteria | $ 1,220 = | 900 | × $1.35593 |
| (b) | To Dept. C, Machinery | 3,051 = | 2,250 | × $1.35593 |
| (c) | To Dept. K, Assembly | 7,729 = | 5,700 | × $1.35593 |
|  | Total | $12,000 |  |  |

Allocation of Department I, Cafeteria:

$$\frac{\text{Total cost}}{\text{Total number of employees—Departments C and K}} = \frac{\$6,720}{185} = \$36.32432/\text{employee}$$

|  |  |  | Number of Employees | × | Rate/Employee |
|---|---|---|---|---|---|
| (d) | To Dept. C, Machinery | $1,271 = | 35 | × | $36.32432 |
| (e) | To Dept. K, Assembly | 5,449 = | 150 | × | $36.32432 |
|  | Total | $6,720 |  |  |  |

Factory overhead rates (based on direct labor hours) for producing departments:

|  |  |  | Total Cost After Allocation | ÷ | Direct Labor Hours |
|---|---|---|---|---|---|
| (f) | For Dept. C, Machinery | $10.293 = | $46,322 | ÷ | 4,500 |
| (g) | For Dept. K, Assembly | $4.594 = | $91,878 | ÷ | 20,000 |

## Algebraic Method

This is the most accurate of the three methods because it considers any reciprocal services provided among the service departments. With the algebraic method, simultaneous equations are used to allocate service department costs to service departments and producing departments. The number of simultaneous equations is proportional to the number of service departments. The use of a computer facilitates the computations when many service departments exist.

**EXAMPLE 12**

In addition to the data from Example 10, assume the following:

|  | Services Provided by | |
|---|---|---|
|  | Department N | Department I |
| **Service Departments:** |  |  |
| Dept. N, Maintenance | — | 10% |
| Dept. I, Cafeteria | 15% | — |
| **Producing Departments:** |  |  |
| Dept. C, Machinery | 25% | 20% |
| Dept. K, Assembly | 60% | 70% |
| Total | 100% | 100% |

Using the algebraic method and the above percentages, the allocation of service department costs to the producing departments is computed as follows:

The cost to be allocated by Department N, Maintenance: $N = \$12,000 + 0.10I$

The cost to be allocated by Department I, Cafeteria: $I = \$5,500 + 0.15N$

By substituting the above value for $I$ (i.e. $\$5,500 + 0.15N$) for the unknown $I$ in the first equation, we can solve for $N$:

$$N = \$12,000 + 0.10(\$5,500 + 0.15N)$$
$$N = \$12,000 + \$550 + 0.015N$$
$$N - 0.015N = \$12,000 + \$550$$
$$0.985N = \$12,550$$
$$N = \$12,741$$

By inserting the above value for $N$ in the equation for Department I, we can calculate the cost for Department I as follows:

$$I = \$5,500 + 0.15N$$
$$= \$5,500 + 0.15(\$12,741) = \$5,500 + \$1,911 = \$7,411$$

*Allocation of Costs*
*Algebraic Method*

|  | Service Departments | | Producing Departments | |
|---|---|---|---|---|
|  | **N,**<br>**Maintenance** | **I,**<br>**Cafeteria** | **C,**<br>**Machinery** | **K,**<br>**Assembly** |
| Total Cost | $12,000 | $5,500 | $42,000 | $78,700 |
| Allocated to Service Dept. I<br>and Producing Depts. C and K | ⟨12,741⟩ | 1,911 (a) | 3,185 (b) | 7,645 (c) |
| Allocated to Service Dept. N<br>and Producing Depts. C and K | 741 (d) | ⟨7,411⟩ | 1,482 (e) | 5,188 (f) |
| Balance after Allocation | 0 | 0 | $46,667 | $91,533 |
| Factory Overhead Rates |  |  | $10.370 (g) | $4.577 (h) |

---

*Computations*:

Allocation of Department N, Maintenance:

|  |  |  | Amount of Service<br>Received | × | Total<br>Cost |
|---|---|---|---|---|---|
| (a) | To Dept. I, Cafeteria | $ 1,911 = | 15% | × | $12,741 |
| (b) | To Dept. C, Machinery | 3,185 = | 25% | × | $12,741 |
| (c) | To Dept. K, Assembly | 7,645 = | 60% | × | $12,741 |
|  | Total | $12,741 |  |  |  |

Allocation of Department I, Cafeteria:

|  |  |  | Amount of Service<br>Received | × | Total<br>Cost |
|---|---|---|---|---|---|
| (d) | To Dept. N, Maintenance | $ 741 = | 10% | × | $7,411 |
| (e) | To Dept. C, Machinery | 1,482 = | 20% | × | $7,411 |
| (f) | To Dept. K, Assembly | 5,188 = | 70% | × | $7,411 |
|  | Total | $7,411 |  |  |  |

Factory overhead rates (based on direct labor hours) for producing departments:

|  |  |  | Total Cost After<br>Allocation | ÷ | Direct Labor<br>Hours |
|---|---|---|---|---|---|
| (g) | For Dept. C, Machinery | $10.370 = | $46,667 | ÷ | 4,500 |
| (h) | For Dept. K, Assembly | $4.577 = | $91,533 | ÷ | 20,000 |

## 5.8  THE FACTORY LEDGER

It is often practical for a manufacturing concern to include a factory ledger in its accounting system.   Generally, this procedure is used when manufacturing operations are far from the main office, or when the nature of such operations requires a great number of accounts.

**Table 5-1**

| Transaction | General Journal | Factory Journal |
|---|---|---|
| 1. Factory material purchased on account | Dr. Factory Ledger<br>Cr. Accounts Payable | Dr. Materials<br>Cr. General Ledger |
| 2. Materials put into process | No entry | Dr. Work in Process, Materials<br>Dr. Factory Overhead (Indirect Materials)<br>Cr. Materials |
| 3. Payment of payroll | Dr. Factory Ledger<br>Cr. FICA Taxes Payable<br>Cr. Federal Withholding Taxes Payable<br>Cr. Payroll Accrued<br>Dr. Payroll Accrued<br>Cr. Cash | Dr. Payroll<br>Cr. General Ledger |
| 4. Distribution of payroll | No entry | Dr. Work in Process<br>Dr. Factory Overhead (Indirect Labor)<br>Cr. Payroll |
| 5. Employer's share of payroll | Dr. Factory Ledger<br>Cr. FICA Taxes Payable<br>Cr. State Unemployment Taxes Payable<br>Cr. Federal Unemployment Taxes Payable | Dr. Factory Overhead<br>Cr. General Ledger |
| 6. Factory expenses | Dr. Factory Ledger<br>Cr. Allowance for Depreciation of Factory Equipment<br>Cr. Rent Payable | Dr. Factory Overhead<br>Cr. General Ledger |
| 7. Apply overhead | No entry | Dr. Work in Process, Factory Overhead<br>Cr. Applied Factory Overhead |
| 8. Record finished goods | No entry | Dr. Finished Goods<br>Cr. Work in Process, Materials<br>Cr. Work in Process, Labor<br>Cr. Work in Process, Factory Overhead |
| 9. Record sale of goods on account | Dr. Accounts Receivable<br>Cr. Sales<br>Dr. Cost of Goods Sold<br>Cr. Factory Ledger | Dr. General Ledger<br>Cr. Finished Goods |

In such cases, the data related *only* to manufacturing operations (i.e. the data needed to compile cost of goods manufactured and cost of goods sold) are posted to accounts in the Factory Ledger. Typically, these include Stores (Materials), Work in Process, Payroll (factory only), Manufacturing Overhead, and Finished Goods. A control account, General Ledger, is also included on the factory books.

Most firms maintain cash and other factory assets on the general office records. Thus, the General Ledger includes such accounts as Sales, Cost of Goods Sold, Factory Equipment, Accumulated Depreciation (depreciation expense for the period kept in the factory journal), and Liabilities. It also includes the control account, Factory Ledger.

Entries relating to the General Ledger and Factory Ledger are first recorded in the general journal and factory journal, as shown in Table 5-1. Note that the control accounts Factory Ledger and General Ledger are reciprocal in nature (i.e. a debit to one is an automatic credit to the other, and vice versa). They are used whenever a transaction affects both journals, should always equal each other, and cancel out for statement purposes. In essence, they permit each ledger to be self-balancing.

## EXAMPLE 13

The J. Prendergast Cadillac Company uses a general journal and a factory journal. The following transactions were completed during January and February:

January
 1: Purchased $20,000 of materials to be used in the factory and $5,000 of supplies for use in the home office.
 8: Placed $15,000 of materials into process.
15: Prepared and paid factory and office payroll for the first two weeks of January:

| | | |
|---|---|---|
| Factory payroll | | |
| Direct labor | $5,000 | |
| Indirect labor | 3,000 | $8,000 |
| Office payroll | | 2,000 |
| FICA taxes | | 500 |
| Federal withholding | | 1,400 |

16: Recorded employer's share of payroll taxes:

| | |
|---|---|
| FICA taxes | $ 500 |
| State unemployment | 50 |
| Federal unemployment | 200 |

19: Paid rent of $1,200 for factory.

31: Recorded depreciation on factory equipment of $350.

31: Applied factory overhead, 40% of direct labor

February
 2: Recorded finished goods of $10,000.

 4: Sold finished goods costing $7,000 for $11,000.

These transactions were recorded in the appropriate journals as follows:

| Transaction | | General Journal | Factory Journal |
|---|---|---|---|
| Jan. 1 | Factory Ledger | 20,000 | |
| | Office Supplies | 5,000 | |
| | Accounts Payable | 25,000 | |
| | Materials | | 20,000 |
| | General Ledger | | 20,000 |
| Jan. 8 | Work in Process | | 15,000 |
| | Materials | | 15,000 |

| Transaction | | General Journal | Factory Journal |
|---|---|---|---|

| | | | | |
|---|---|---|---|---|
| Jan. 15 | Factory Ledger | 8,000 | | |
| | Office Payroll | 2,000 | | |
| |   FICA Taxes Payable | | 500 | |
| |   Federal Withholding | | | |
| |     Taxes Payable | | 1,400 | |
| |   Accrued Payroll | | 8,100 | |
| | Accrued Payroll | 8,000 | | |
| |   Cash | | 8,000 | |
| | Factory Payroll | | | 8,000 |
| |   General Ledger | | | 8,000 |
| | Selling and Administrative | | | |
| |   Expenses | 2,000 | | |
| |   Office Payroll | | 2,000 | |
| | Work in Process | | | 5,000 |
| | Factory Overhead | | | |
| |   (Indirect Labor) | | | 3,000 |
| |   Factory Payroll | | | 8,000 |
| Jan. 16 | Factory Ledger | | | |
| |   ($750 × 8/10) | 600 | | |
| | Office Payroll Taxes | | | |
| |   ($750 × 8/10) | 150 | | |
| |   FICA Taxes Payable | | 500 | |
| |   State Unemployment | | | |
| |     Taxes Payable | | 50 | |
| |   Federal Unemployment | | | |
| |     Taxes Payable | | 200 | |
| | Factory Overhead | | | 600 |
| |   General Ledger | | | 600 |
| Jan. 19 | Factory Ledger | 1,200 | | |
| |   Cash | | 1,200 | |
| | Factory Overhead | | | 1,200 |
| |   General Ledger | | | 1,200 |
| Jan. 31 | Factory Ledger | 350 | | |
| | Accumulated Depreciation, | | | |
| |   Equipment | | 350 | |
| | Factory Overhead | | | 350 |
| |   General Ledger | | | 350 |
| Jan. 31 | Work in Process | | | |
| |   (5,000 × 40%) | | | 2,000 |
| |   Applied Factory Overhead | | | 2,000 |
| Feb. 2 | Finished Goods | | | 10,000 |
| |   Work in Process | | | 10,000 |
| Feb. 4 | Accounts Receivable | 11,000 | | |
| |   Sales | | 11,000 | |
| | General Ledger | | | 7,000 |
| |   Finished Goods | | | 7,000 |
| | Cost of Goods Sold | | | 7,000 |
| |   Factory Ledger | | | 7,000 |

# Summary

(1) Expenses incurred during production, other than direct materials and direct labor, are called _____ factory expenses; those charged to production on an estimated basis are called _____ factory expenses.

(2) The per unit expense of the _____ portion of factory overhead varies with the volume of production while the _____ portion remains the same with volume.

(3) The activity level which smooths out the highs and lows of production is called _____ capacity.

(4) The difference between actual factory overhead and applied factory overhead is referred to as the _____ overhead.

(5) Factory overhead includes all production costs other than direct materials, direct labor, and depreciation.   (a) True, (b) false.

(6) Examples of factory overhead expenses are: salaries of plant manager and department heads, indirect labor, and depreciation.   (a) True, (b) false.

(7) The principal bases used for applying factory overhead are: units of production, materials cost, direct labor cost, direct labor hours, and machine hours.   (a) True, (b) false.

(8) Where direct labor rates vary widely, direct labor cost would be more suitable than direct labor hours in applying factory overhead.   (a) True, (b) false.

(9) Factory overhead should be applied on the basis of: (a) direct labor hours, (b) direct labor cost, (c) relationship to costs incurred, (d) direct machine hours.

(10) When the factory overhead control account has an ending debit balance, factory overhead was (a) overapplied, (b) underapplied, (c) fixed, (d) variable.

(11) When goods are shipped to a customer, the factory ledger entry is a debit to General Ledger and a credit to Finished Goods.   (a) True, (b) false.

(12) With reference to item (11), the entry in the general ledger is a debit to Accounts Receivable and a credit to Sales at retail price, and a debit to Cost of Goods Sold and a credit to Finished Goods at cost.   (a) True, (b) false.

(13) When Factory X ships finished goods to Factory Y, the entry on the seller's books is a debit to Factory Ledger Y and a credit to Finished Goods.   (a) True, (b) false.

*Answers:*   (1) actual, applied; (2) fixed, variable; (3) normal; (4) over- or underapplied; (5) *b*; (6) *a*; (7) *a*; (8) *b*; (9) *c*; (10) *b*; (11) *a*; (12) *b*; (13) *a.*

# Solved Problems

**5.1**     **Factory Overhead Rates.**    The Myriad Corporation estimates the following for the next period:

| | |
|---|---:|
| Factory overhead | $250,000 |
| Units produced | 50,000 |
| Materials cost of units produced | $500,000 |

Production will require 50,000 labor hours at an estimated direct labor cost of $100,000. The machine is estimated to run about 40,000 hours.

Determine the factory overhead rate to be used in applying factory overhead to production on each of the following bases: (*a*) units of production, (*b*) direct labor cost, (*c*) materials cost, (*d*) direct labor hours, and (*e*) machine hours.

**SOLUTION**

(*a*)   Units of production

$$\frac{\text{Estimated factory overhead}}{\text{Estimated units of production}} = \frac{\$250,000}{50,000} = \$5 \text{ overhead per unit}$$

(*b*)   Direct labor cost

$$\frac{\text{Estimated factory overhead}}{\text{Estimated direct labor cost}} \times 100 = \frac{\$250,000}{\$100,000} \times 100 = 250\% \text{ of direct labor cost}$$

(*c*)   Materials cost

$$\frac{\text{Estimated factory overhead}}{\text{Estimated materials cost}} \times 100 = \frac{\$250,000}{\$500,000} \times 100 = 50\% \text{ of direct materials cost}$$

(*d*)   Direct labor hours

$$\frac{\text{Estimated factory overhead}}{\text{Estimated direct labor hours}} = \frac{\$250,000}{50,000} = \$5 \text{ per direct labor hour}$$

(*e*)   Machine hours

$$\frac{\text{Estimated factory overhead}}{\text{Estimated machine hours}} = \frac{\$250,000}{40,000} = \$6.25 \text{ per machine hour}$$

**5.2**     **Factory Overhead: Journal Entries.**    Mint Airlines has factory overhead to be allocated. It maintains a work-in-process account and an overhead control account. The amounts are:

| | | |
|---|---|---:|
| July 3: | Indirect material | $ 500 |
| July 5: | Indirect labor | 1,000 |
| July 10: | Other expenses | 3,000 |

4,000 direct labor hours were worked during the month. Overhead is applied at a rate of $1.10 per direct labor hour.

Prepare the journal entries for factory overhead. Assume a perpetual cost accumulation system.

**SOLUTION**

| | | | |
|---|---|---:|---:|
| July 3 | *Factory Overhead Control, Indirect Material* | 500 | |
| | *Vouchers Payable* | | 500 |

| | | |
|---|---|---|
| July  5   *Factory Overhead Control, Indirect Labor* | *1,000* | |
|              *Vouchers Payable* | | *1,000* |
| July 10   *Factory Overhead Control, Other Expenses* | *3,000* | |
|              *Various Credits* | | *3,000* |
| July 31   *Work in Process, Factory Overhead Account* | | |
|              *($1.10 × 4,000)* | *4,400* | |
|              *Factory Overhead Applied* | | *4,400* |

**5.3     Factory Overhead Applied to Jobs.**   The Simplex Manufacturing Company is an average size firm with the following costs incurred during August 19X8.

### Actual Factory Overhead

| | |
|---|---|
| Indirect materials | $6,000 |
| Indirect labor | 8,000 |
| Salaries (supervisors) | 6,000 |
| Depreciation, Building | 2,000 |
| Depreciation, Equipment | 6,000 |
| Fuel, Factory | 1,000 |
| Insurance on building | 500 |
| Amortization of patents | 3,000 |

During the month the company completed three jobs.  The following data have been collected for these jobs:

| | Job 101 | Job 102 | Job 103 |
|---|---|---|---|
| Materials cost | $ 4,000 | $7,000 | $2,000 |
| Direct labor cost | $12,000 | $8,000 | $6,000 |
| Direct labor hours | 8,000 | 6,000 | 2,000 |
| Machine hours | 2,500 | 1,500 | 1,000 |

Compute the cost of each job, charging factory overhead on the basis of (a) direct labor cost and (b) machine hours.

### SOLUTION

| Actual Factory Overhead | Direct Labor Cost | Machine Hours |
|---|---|---|
| $ 6,000 | $12,000 | 2,500 |
| 8,000 | 8,000 | 1,500 |
| 6,000 | 6,000 | 1,000 |
| 2,000 | $26,000 | 5,000 |
| 6,000 | | |
| 1,000 | | |
| 500 | | |
| 3,000 | | |
| $32,500 | | |

(a) $\dfrac{\$32,500}{26,000} \times 100 = 125\%$ of direct labor cost

|  | Job 101 | Job 102 | Job 103 |
|---|---|---|---|
| Materials cost | $ 4,000 | $ 7,000 | $ 2,000 |
| Direct labor cost | 12,000 | 8,000 | 6,000 |
| Factory overhead* | 15,000 | 10,000 | 7,500 |
| Cost of job | $31,000 | $25,000 | $15,500 |

* Factory overhead is computed as follows:
Job 101, 12,000 × 1.25; Job 102, 8,000 × 1.25; Job 103, 6,000 × 1.25.

(b) $\dfrac{\$32,500}{5,000} = \$6.50$ per machine hour

|  | Job 101 | Job 102 | Job 103 |
|---|---|---|---|
| Materials cost | $ 4,000 | $ 7,000 | $ 2,000 |
| Direct labor cost | 12,000 | 8,000 | 6,000 |
| Factory overhead* | 16,250 | 9,750 | 6,500 |
| Cost of job | $32,250 | $24,750 | $14,500 |

* Factory overhead is computed as follows:
Job 101, 2,500 × $6.50; Job 102, 1,500 × $6.50; Job 103, 1,000 × $6.50.

**5.4    Factory Overhead Rates.**    Factory overhead for Melville Manufacturing Company has been estimated for July 19X1 as follows:

| Fixed overhead | $20,000 |
|---|---|
| Variable overhead | 50,000 |
| Direct labor hours | 25,000 |

Production for the month was 75% of the budget.   Actual factory overhead was $60,000.

Compute (a) the total overhead rate, showing fixed and variable portions, and (b) the number of actual direct labor hours.

**SOLUTION**

(a)

| Fixed rate | = $20,000 ÷ 25,000 = $ .80 |
|---|---|
| Variable rate | = $50,000 ÷ 25,000 = $2.00 |
| Total overhead rate = | $2.80 |

(b) Actual direct hours = 75% × 25,000 hours = 18,750

**5.5    Over- and Underapplied Overhead.**    The Overbrook Company manufactures widgets using a job order cost system with a predetermined overhead rate based on direct labor hours.  For the year ended June 30, 19X8, there were 200,000 direct labor hours used at the established rate of $1.75 per direct labor hour.  Actual factory overhead for the period amounted to $360,000.  Overbrook Company uses a perpetual cost accumulation system.

Prepare journal entries to (a) record the total factory overhead costs to be applied to jobs, (b) close out the applied overhead to the factory overhead control account, (c) accumulate total actual factory overhead, and (d) close out the underapplied overhead balance to cost of goods sold.

**SOLUTION**

| | | | |
|---|---|---|---|
| (a) | Work in Process | 350,000 | |
| | Factory Overhead Applied (200,000 × $1.75) | | 350,000 |
| (b) | Factory Overhead Applied | 350,000 | |
| | Factory Overhead Control | | 350,000 |
| (c) | Factory Overhead Control | 360,000 | |
| | Materials, Payroll and Other Payables | | 360,000 |
| (d) | Cost of Goods Sold | 10,000 | |
| | Factory Overhead Control | | 10,000 |

**5.6** **Factory Overhead Entries.** The Wilson Company assembles and sells one product, the Speedy Blender. The costs per unit are: materials, $15; labor, $17. Production for year 19X8 is estimated to be 20,000 units; estimated factory overhead is: indirect labor, $22,000; indirect materials, $16,000; depreciation, $7,000; light and power, $5,000; miscellaneous, $10,000. Wilson Company uses a perpetual cost accumulation system.

Completed production for year 19X8 was 18,000 units and actual factory overhead cost was $56,500. There were no beginning or ending work in process inventories.

Prepare (a) the journal entries for materials, labor and overhead, and (b) the entry to close out over- or underapplied factory overhead.

**SOLUTION**

| | | | |
|---|---|---|---|
| (a) | Work in Process | 270,000 | |
| | Materials (18,000 × $15) | | 270,000 |
| | Work in Process | 306,000 | |
| | Payroll (18,000 × $17) | | 306,000 |
| | Work in Process | 54,000 | |
| | Factory Overhead Applied (18,000 × $3*) | | 54,000 |
| | Factory Overhead Applied | 54,000 | |
| | Factory Overhead Control | | 54,000 |
| | Factory Overhead Control | 56,500 | |
| | Payroll, Materials and Other Payables | | 56,500 |

* ($22,000 + $16,000 + $7,000 + $5,000 + $10,000) ÷ 20,000 = $3

| | | | |
|---|---|---|---|
| (b) | Cost of Goods Sold | 2,500 | |
| | Factory Overhead Control ($56,500 − $54,000) | | 2,500 |

*Note:* The underapplied overhead could have been charged to Income Summary if the variation was considered a managerial rather than an assembly cost.

**5.7** **Closing Entries.** For the month of August, the Pam and Sam Manufacturing Company estimated that factory overhead cost would be $15,500. At August 31, 19X8, the factory overhead control account had a balance of $16,700. The applied factory overhead account had a balance of $16,000. Factory overhead is applied on the basis of direct labor hours.

Prepare journal entries to close the factory overhead balances and set up the over- or underapplied factory overhead account. Assume a perpetual cost accumulation system.

**SOLUTION**

| | | |
|---|---|---|
| Applied Factory Overhead | 16,000 | |
| Factory Overhead Control | | 16,000 |
| Underapplied Factory Overhead | 700 | |
| Factory Overhead Control | | 700 |

**5.8    Factory Overhead: Service Departments' Costs Allocation.**  The Val Aur Company has two service departments and two production departments.

| Service Departments: | Total Cost |
|---|---|
| Dept. N, Factory Administration | $12,900 |
| Dept. J, Building and Grounds | 10,500 |
| **Producing Departments:** | |
| Dept. G, Machinery | 41,600 |
| Dept. P, Assembly | 38,000 |

*Additional Information:*

| Department | Estimated Total Labor Hours | Square Footage |
|---|---|---|
| N, Factory Administration | 2,900 | 1,200 |
| J, Building and Grounds | 1,100 | 1,500 |
| G, Machinery | 2,000 | 1,900 |
| P, Assembly | 1,600 | 3,200 |
| | 7,600 | 7,800 |

The costs of factory administration are allocated based on estimated labor hours; building and grounds costs are allocated based on square footage. The producing departments use machine hours, with 30,000 for machinery and 22,800 for assembly.

Allocate the costs of the service departments to the producing departments by using the following: (*a*) Direct Method, (*b*) Step Method (allocate the costs of factory administration first), and (*c*) Algebraic Method. Include the factory overhead rates for each producing department.

**SOLUTION**

(*a*)

*Allocation of Costs*
*Direct Method*

| | Service Departments | | Producing Departments | |
|---|---|---|---|---|
| | N, Factory Admin. | J, Bldg. and Grounds | G, Machinery | P, Assembly |
| Total Cost | $12,900 | $10,500 | $41,600 | $38,000 |
| Allocate to Producing Depts. G and P | ⟨12,900⟩ | | 7,167 (a) | 5,733 (b) |
| | | ⟨10,500⟩ | 3,912 (c) | 6,588 (d) |
| Balance after Allocation | 0 | 0 | $52,679 | $50,321 |
| Factory Overhead Rates | | | $1.75597 (e) | $2.20706 (f) |

*Computations:*

Allocation of Department N, Factory Administration:

$$\frac{\text{Total cost}}{\text{Total estimated labor hours—Departments G and P}} = \frac{\$12,900}{3,600} = \$3.58333/\text{labor hour}$$

Labor Hours × Rate/Labor Hour

| | | | |
|---|---|---|---|
| (a) | To Dept. G, Machinery | $ 7,167 = | 2,000 × $3.58333 |
| (b) | To Dept. P, Assembly | 5,733 = | 1,600 × $3.58333 |
| | Total | $12,900 | |

Allocation of Department J, Building and Grounds:

$$\frac{\text{Total cost}}{\text{Total square feet—Departments G and P}} = \frac{\$10,500}{5,100} = \$2.05882/\text{sq ft}$$

|  |  |  |  | Square Feet × Rate/Sq ft |
|---|---|---|---|---|
| (c) | To Dept. G, Machinery | $ 3,912 | = | 1,900 × $2.05882 |
| (d) | To Dept. P, Assembly | 6,588 | = | 3,200 × $2.05882 |
|  | Total | $10,500 |  |  |

Factory overhead rates (based on machine hours) for producing departments:

|  |  |  |  | Total Cost After Allocation ÷ Machine Hours |
|---|---|---|---|---|
| (e) | For Dept. G, Machinery | $1.75597 | = | $52,679 ÷ 30,000 |
| (f) | For Dept. P, Assembly | $2.20706 | = | $50,321 ÷ 22,800 |

(b)

**Allocation of Costs**
**Step Method**

|  | Service Departments | | Producing Departments | |
|---|---|---|---|---|
|  | N, Factory Admin. | J, Bldg. and Grounds | G, Machinery | P, Assembly |
| Total Cost | $12,900 | $10,500 | $41,600 | $38,000 |
| Allocated to Service Dept. J and Producing Depts. G and P | ⟨12,900⟩ | 3,019 (a) | 5,489 (b) | 4,392 (c) |
| Subtotal |  | $13,519 | $47,089 | $42,392 |
| Allocated to Producing Depts. G and P |  | ⟨13,519⟩ | 5,036 (d) | 8,483 (e) |
| Balance after Allocation | 0 | 0 | $52,125 | $50,875 |
| Factory Overhead Rates |  |  | $1.737 (f) | $2.231 (g) |

*Computations:*

Allocation of Department N, Factory Administration:

$$\frac{\text{Total cost}}{\text{Total estimated labor hours—Departments J, G, and P}} = \frac{\$12,900}{4,700} = \$2.74468/\text{labor hour}$$

|  |  |  |  | Labor Hours × Rate/Labor Hour |
|---|---|---|---|---|
| (a) | To Dept. J, Building and Grounds | $ 3,019 | = | 1,100 × $2.74468 |
| (b) | To Dept. G, Machinery | 5,489 | = | 2,000 × $2.74468 |
| (c) | To Dept. P, Assembly | 4,392 | = | 1,600 × $2.74468 |
|  | Total | $12,900 |  |  |

*Note:* The cost allocated to Department P, Assembly includes the corrected rounding difference.

Allocation of Department J, Buildings and Grounds:

$$\frac{\text{Total cost}}{\text{Total square feet—Departments G and P}} = \frac{\$13,519}{5,100} = \$2.65078/\text{sq ft}$$

|  |  | Square Feet | × | Rate/Sq ft |
|---|---|---|---|---|
| (d) To Dept. G, Machinery | $ 5,036 = | 1,900 | × | $2.65078 |
| (e) To Dept. P, Assembly | 8,483 = | 3,200 | × | $2.65078 |
| Total | $13,519 |  |  |  |

Factory overhead rates (based on machine hours) for producing departments:

|  |  | Total Cost after Allocation | ÷ | Direct Labor Hours |
|---|---|---|---|---|
| (f) For Dept. G, Machinery | $1.737 = | $52,125 | ÷ | 30,000 |
| (g) For Dept. P, Assembly | $2.231 = | $50,875 | ÷ | 22,800 |

(c)

| Department | Services Provided by | |
|---|---|---|
|  | **Factory Administration (Labor Hours)** | **Buildings and Grounds (Square Feet)** |
| N, Factory Administration | — | 1,200 |
| J, Building and Grounds | 1,100 | — |
| G, Machinery | 2,000 | 1,900 |
| P, Assembly | 1,600 | 3,200 |
| Total | 4,700 | 6,300 |

Let $N$ = Total cost of factory administration and $J$ = Total cost of building and grounds. The cost to be allocated to each department is then

$$N = \$12,900 + \frac{1,200}{6,300} J \quad \text{and} \quad J = \$10,500 + \frac{1,100}{4,700} N$$

By substitution we get

$$N = \$12,900 + \frac{1,200}{6,300} \left( \$10,500 + \frac{1,100}{4,700} N \right)$$
$$N = \$12,900 + \$2,000 + 0.04458N$$
$$0.95542N = \$14,900$$
$$N = \$15,595$$

By inserting the value for $N$ in the equation for Department J, we get

$$J = \$10,500 + \frac{1,100}{4,700} (\$15,595) = \$10,500 + \$3,650 = \$14,150$$

*Allocation of Costs*
*Algebraic Method*

|  | Service Departments | | Producing Departments | |
|---|---|---|---|---|
|  | **N, Factory Admin.** | **J, Bldg. and Grounds** | **G, Machinery** | **P, Assembly** |
| Total Cost | $12,900 | $10,500 | $41,600 | $38,000 |
| Allocated to Service Dept. J and Producing Depts. G and P | ⟨15,595⟩ | 3,650 (a) | 6,636 (b) | 5,309 (c) |
| Allocated to Service Dept. N and Producing Depts. G and P | 2,695 (d) | ⟨14,150⟩ | 4,268 (e) | 7,187 (f) |
| Balance after Allocation | 0 | 0 | $52,504 | $50,496 |
| Factory Overhead Rates |  |  | $1.750 (g) | $2.215 (h) |

*Computations:*

Allocation of Department N, Factory Administration:

|  |  |  | $\frac{\text{Proportionate}}{\text{Labor Hours}} \times$ Total Cost |
|---|---|---|---|
| (a) To Dept. J, Building and Grounds | $ 3,650 | = | $(1,100 \div 4,700) \times$ $15,595 |
| (b) To Dept. G, Machinery | 6,636 | = | $(2,000 \div 4,700) \times$ $15,595 |
| (c) To Dept. P, Assembly | 5,309 | = | $(1,600 \div 4,700) \times$ $15,595 |
| Total | $15,595 | | |

Allocation of Department J, Building and Grounds:

|  |  |  | $\frac{\text{Proportionate}}{\text{Square Feet}} \times$ Total Cost |
|---|---|---|---|
| (d) To Dept. N, Factory Administration | $ 2,695 | = | $(1,200 \div 6,300) \times$ $14,150 |
| (e) To Dept. G, Machinery | 4,268 | = | $(1,900 \div 6,300) \times$ $14,150 |
| (f) To Dept. P, Assembly | 7,187 | = | $(3,200 \div 6,300) \times$ $14,150 |
| Total | $14,150 | | |

*Note:* The cost allocated to Department G, Machinery includes corrected rounding difference.

Factory overhead rates (based on machine hours) for producing departments

|  |  |  | $\frac{\text{Total Cost After}}{\text{Allocation}} \div$ Machine Hours |  |
|---|---|---|---|---|
| (g) For Dept. G, Machinery | $1.750 | = | $52,504 | ÷ 30,000 |
| (h) For Dept. P, Assembly | $2.215 | = | $50,496 | ÷ 22,800 |

**5.9 Overhead Distribution—Service Departments.** Jing's BMX Incorporated has two service departments and three producing departments.

| **Service Departments:** | **Total Cost** |
|---|---|
| Dept. 1, Maintenance | $25,000 |
| Dept. 2, Storeroom | 18,000 |
| **Producing Departments:** | |
| Dept. 70, Machinery | 60,000 |
| Dept. 71, Assembly | 89,200 |
| Dept. 72, Packaging | 43,600 |

*Additional Information:*

| Departments | **Services Provided by Department 1** | **Number of Requisitions** |
|---|---|---|
| 1, Maintenance | — | 400 |
| 2, Storeroom | 14% | — |
| 70, Machinery | 32% | 3,500 |
| 71, Assembly | 26% | 6,000 |
| 72, Packaging | 28% | 4,100 |
| Total | 100% | 14,000 |

The costs of Department 1 are allocated on the basis of percent of services rendered, while the costs of Department 2 are allocated on the basis of the number of requisitions.

Using the (a) Direct Method, (b) Step Method (Department 1 costs are allocated first), and (c) Algebraic Method, distribute the service departments' costs to the producing departments and compute the factory overhead rates based on direct labor hours: 20,000 for Department 70; 36,000 for Department 71; and 18,000 for Department 72.

**SOLUTION**

(a)

### Allocation of Costs
### Direct Method

|  | Service Departments | | Producing Departments | | |
|---|---|---|---|---|---|
|  | **1,<br>Maintenance** | **2,<br>Storeroom** | **70,<br>Machinery** | **71,<br>Assembly** | **72,<br>Packaging** |
| Total Cost | $25,000 | $18,000 | $60,000 | $89,200 | $43,600 |
| Allocated to Producing<br>Depts. 70, 71, and 72 | ⟨25,000⟩ |  | 9,302 (a) | 7,558 (b) | 8,140 (c) |
|  |  | ⟨18,000⟩ | 4,632 (d) | 7,941 (e) | 5,427 (f) |
| Balance after Allocation | 0 | 0 | $73,934 | $104,699 | $57,167 |
| Factory Overhead Rates |  |  | $3.696 (g) | $2.908 (h) | $3.175 (i) |

*Computations:*

Allocation of Department 1, Maintenance:

|  |  |  |  | Proportionate<br>Amount of<br>Service Received | × Total Cost |
|---|---|---|---|---|---|
| (a) | To Dept. 70, Machinery | $ 9,302 | = | (32% ÷ 86%) | × $25,000 |
| (b) | To Dept. 71, Assembly | 7,558 | = | (26% ÷ 86%) | × $25,000 |
| (c) | To Dept. 72, Packaging | 8,140 | = | (28% ÷ 86%) | × $25,000 |
|  | Total | $25,000 |  |  |  |

*Note:* Under the Direct Method, services provided by one service department to another are ignored. Hence, the total percentage of cost to be distributed among the producing departments in this problem is 100% − 14% = 86%.

Allocation of Department 2, Storeroom:

$$\frac{\text{Total cost}}{\text{Total number of requisitions—Departments 70, 71, 72}} = \frac{\$18,000}{13,600} = \$1.32353/\text{requisition}$$

|  |  |  |  | Number of<br>Requisitions | × Rate/Requisition |
|---|---|---|---|---|---|
| (d) | To Dept. 70, Machinery | $ 4,632 | = | 3,500 | × $1.32353 |
| (e) | To Dept. 71, Assembly | 7,941 | = | 6,000 | × $1.32353 |
| (f) | To Dept. 72, Packaging | 5,427 | = | 4,100 | × $1.32353 |
|  | Total | $18,000 |  |  |  |

*Note:* The cost allocated to Department 72, Packaging includes corrected rounding difference.

Factory overhead rates (based on direct labor hours) for producing departments:

|  |  |  |  | Total Cost After<br>Allocation | ÷ | Direct Labor<br>Hours |
|---|---|---|---|---|---|---|
| (g) | For Dept. 70, Machinery | $3.696 | = | $ 73,934 | ÷ | 20,000 |
| (h) | For Dept. 71, Assembly | $2.908 | = | $104,699 | ÷ | 36,000 |
| (i) | For Dept. 72, Packaging | $3.175 | = | $ 57,167 | ÷ | 18,000 |

(b)

*Allocation of Costs*
*Step Method*

| | Service Departments | | Producing Departments | | |
|---|---|---|---|---|---|
| | 1,<br>Maintenance | 2,<br>Storeroom | 70,<br>Machinery | 71,<br>Assembly | 72,<br>Packaging |
| Total Cost | $25,000 | $18,000 | $60,000 | $ 89,200 | $43,600 |
| Allocated to Service Dept. 2<br>and Producing Depts.<br>70, 71, and 72 | ⟨25,000⟩ | 3,500 (a) | 8,000 (b) | 6,500 (c) | 7,000 (d) |
| Subtotal | | $21,500 | $68,000 | $ 95,700 | $50,600 |
| Allocated to Producing<br>Depts. 70, 71, and 72 | | ⟨21,500⟩ | 5,533 (e) | 9,485 (f) | 6,482 (g) |
| Balance after Allocation | 0 | 0 | $73,533 | $105,185 | $57,082 |
| Factory Overhead Rates | | | $3.676 (h) | $2.921 (i) | $3.171 (j) |

*Computations:*

Allocation of Department 1, Maintenance:

| | | | | Amount of Service<br>Received | × Total Cost |
|---|---|---|---|---|---|
| (a) | To Dept. 2, Storeroom | $ 3,500 | = | 14% | × $25,000 |
| (b) | To Dept. 70, Machinery | 8,000 | = | 32% | × $25,000 |
| (c) | To Dept. 71, Assembly | 6,500 | = | 26% | × $25,000 |
| (d) | To Dept. 72, Packaging | 7,000 | = | 28% | × $25,000 |
| | Total | $25,000 | | | |

Allocation of Department 2, Storeroom:

$$\frac{\text{Total cost}}{\text{Total number of requisitions—Departments 70, 71 and 72}} = \frac{\$21,500}{13,600} = \$1.58088/\text{requisition}$$

| | | | | Number of<br>Requisitions | × Rate/Requisition |
|---|---|---|---|---|---|
| (e) | To Dept. 70, Machinery | $ 5,533 | = | 3,500 | × $1.58088 |
| (f) | To Dept. 71, Assembly | 9,485 | = | 6,000 | × $1.58088 |
| (g) | To Dept. 72, Packaging | 6,482 | = | 4,100 | × $1.58088 |
| | Total | $21,500 | | | |

Factory overhead rates (based on direct labor hours) for producing departments:

| | | | | Total Cost after<br>Allocation | ÷ | Direct Labor<br>Hours |
|---|---|---|---|---|---|---|
| (h) | For Dept. 70, Machinery | $3.676 | = | $ 73,533 | ÷ | 20,000 |
| (i) | For Dept. 71, Assembly | $2.921 | = | $105,185 | ÷ | 36,000 |
| (j) | For Dept. 72, Packaging | $3.171 | = | $ 57,082 | ÷ | 18,000 |

(c) **Allocation of Costs, Algebraic Method.** Let $M$ = Total cost of maintenance and $S$ = Total cost of storeroom. Then

$$M = \$25,000 + \frac{400}{14,000}\, S \quad \text{and} \quad S = \$18,000 + 0.14M$$

By substitution, we get

$$M = \$25,000 + \frac{400}{14,000} (\$18,000 + 0.14M)$$
$$= \$25,000 + \$514 + 0.004M$$
$$0.996\ M = \$25,514$$
$$M = \$25,616$$

By inserting the value for $M$ in the equation for the cost to be allocated to $S$, we get

$$S = \$18,000 + 0.14M$$
$$= \$18,000 + 0.14(\$25,616) = \$18,000 + \$3,586 = \$21,586$$

| | Service Departments | | Producing Departments | | |
|---|---|---|---|---|---|
| | 1, Maintenance | 2, Storeroom | 70, Machinery | 71, Assembly | 72, Packaging |
| Total Cost | $25,000 | $18,000 | $60,000 | $ 89,200 | $43,600 |
| Allocated to Service Dept. 2 and Producing Depts. 70, 71, and 72 | ⟨25,616⟩ | 3,586 (a) | 8,197 (b) | 6,660 (c) | 7,173 (d) |
| Allocated to Service Dept. 1 and Producing Depts. 70, 71, and 72 | 617 (e) | ⟨21,586⟩ | 5,397 (f) | 9,251 (g) | 6,322 (h) |
| Balance after Allocation (includes rounding difference) | $ 1 | 0 | $73,594 | $105,111 | $57,095 |
| Factory Overhead Rates | | | $3.679 (i) | $2.919 (j) | $3.171 (k) |

*Computations:*

Allocation of Department 1, Maintenance:

| | | | Amount of Service Received | × Total Cost |
|---|---|---|---|---|
| (a) | To Dept. 2, Storeroom | $ 3,586 | 14% | × $25,616 |
| (b) | To Dept. 71, Machinery | 8,197 | 32% | × $25,616 |
| (c) | To Dept. 71, Assembly | 6,660 | 26% | × $25,616 |
| (d) | To Dept. 72, Packaging | 7,173 | 28% | × $25,616 |
| | Total | $25,616 | | |

*Note:* The cost allocated to Department 72, Packaging includes corrected rounding difference.

Allocation of Department 2, Storeroom:

| | | | | Proportionate Number of Requisitions | × Total Cost |
|---|---|---|---|---|---|
| (e) | To Dept. 1, Maintenance | $ 617 | = | (400 ÷ 14,000) × | $21,586 |
| (f) | To Dept. 70, Machinery | 5,397 | = | (3,500 ÷ 14,000) × | $21,586 |
| (g) | To Dept. 71, Assembly | 9,251 | = | (6,000 ÷ 14,000) × | $21,586 |
| (h) | To Dept. 72, Packaging | 6,322 | = | (4,100 ÷ 14,000) × | $21,586 |
| | Total (includes rounding difference) | $21,587 | | | |

Factory overhead rates (based on direct labor hours) for producing departments:

|  |  |  |  | Total Cost After Allocation | ÷ | Direct Labor Hours |
|---|---|---|---|---|---|---|
| (i) | For Dept. 70, Machinery | $3.679 | = | $ 73,594 | ÷ | 20,000 |
| (j) | For Dept. 71, Assembly | $2.919 | = | $105,111 | ÷ | 36,000 |
| (k) | For Dept. 72, Packaging | $3.171 | = | $ 57,095 | ÷ | 18,000 |

**5.10    Factory Ledger Entries.** The Kaufman Corporation maintains general offices in Pittsburgh, Pennsylvania, and two factories in New York State—one in Syracuse and the other in Buffalo. A separate set of books is kept at each location.

The factory books showed the following debits on April 1:

|  | **Syracuse** | **Buffalo** |
|---|---|---|
| Materials | $27,000 | $25,000 |
| Work in Process | 15,500 | 17,000 |
| Finished Goods | 8,000 | 11,000 |

During the month, the following transactions were completed:

|  |  | **Syracuse** | **Buffalo** |
|---|---|---|---|
| (1) | Materials purchased | $30,000 | $25,000 |
| (2) | Materials requisitioned: |  |  |
|  | Direct materials | 32,000 | 30,000 |
|  | Indirect materials | 8,000 | 5,000 |
| (3) | Materials returned to suppliers | 450 | 550 |
| (4) | Sundry factory overhead expenses | 20,000 | 15,000 |

(5)    Payrolls vouchered (FICA tax of $2,164.50 and federal income tax of 10% to be deducted)

|  | **Syracuse** | **Buffalo** |
|---|---|---|
| Direct labor (@ $3 per hour) | 15,000 | 12,000 |
| Indirect labor | 3,000 | 2,000 |
| Sales salaries | 2,800 |  |
| Office salaries | 2,200 |  |

(6)    Suppliers paid (2% discount taken)

(7)    Payrolls issued, and employer's payroll recorded. The state unemployment insurance rate is 1%, the federal unemployment insurance rate is 0.5% and the employer's FICA tax is $2,164.50.

(8)    Applied factory overhead to production at $5 per direct labor hour.

(9)    Completed goods valued at 75% of total work in process costs.

(10)    Shipped finished goods amounting to $105,000—$55,000 from the Syracuse plant and $50,000 from the Buffalo plant. (The gross profit on these shipments is 20% of the sales price.)

Prepare journal entries to record these transactions (a) on the factory books and (b) on the general office books. Use one work in process account for each plant. Note that the liability for payrolls and payroll taxes is maintained on the general office books.

## SOLUTION

(a)  **Factory Books**

|  |  | Syracuse Plant | | Buffalo Plant | |
|---|---|---|---|---|---|
| (1) | *Materials* | 30,000 |  | 25,000 |  |
|  | *General Ledger* |  | 30,000 |  | 25,000 |
| (2) | *Work in Process* | 32,000 |  | 30,000 |  |
|  | *Factory Overhead Control* | 8,000 |  | 5,000 |  |
|  | *Materials* |  | 40,000 |  | 35,000 |
| (3) | *General Ledger* | 450 |  | 550 |  |
|  | *Materials* |  | 450 |  | 550 |
| (4) | *Factory Overhead Control* | 20,000 |  | 15,000 |  |
|  | *General Ledger* |  | 20,000 |  | 15,000 |
| (5) | *Payroll* | 18,000 |  | 14,000 |  |
|  | *General Ledger* |  | 18,000 |  | 14,000 |
|  | *Work in Process* | 15,000 |  | 12,000 |  |
|  | *Factory Overhead Control* | 3,000 |  | 2,000 |  |
|  | *Payroll* |  | 18,000 |  | 14,000 |
| (6) | No entry |  |  |  |  |
| (7) | *Factory Overhead Control* | 1,323 |  | 1,029 |  |
|  | *General Ledger* |  | 1,323 |  | 1,029 |
| (8) | *Work in Process* | 25,000 |  | 20,000 |  |
|  | *Factory Overhead Applied* |  | 25,000 |  | 20,000 |
| (9) | *Finished Goods** | 65,625 |  | 59,250 |  |
|  | *Work in Process* |  | 65,625 |  | 59,250 |
| (10) | *General Ledger* | 55,000 |  | 50,000 |  |
|  | *Finished Goods* |  | 55,000 |  | 50,000 |

————————————

*Computations:*

|  | Syracuse | Buffalo |
|---|---|---|
| Work in process |  |  |
| Inventory, April 1 | $15,500 | $17,000 |
| Direct materials | 32,000 | 30,000 |
| Direct labor | 15,000 | 12,000 |
| Factory overhead | 25,000 | 20,000 |
| Total work in process cost | $87,500 | $79,000 |
| Transferred to finished goods (75%) | $65,625 | $59,250 |

(b)  **General Office Books**

| (1) | *Factory Ledger, Syracuse* | 30,000.00 |  |
|---|---|---|---|
|  | *Factory Ledger, Buffalo* | 25,000.00 |  |
|  | *Vouchers Payable* |  | 55,000.00 |
| (2) | No entry |  |  |

| | | | |
|---|---|---|---|
| (3) | Vouchers Payable | 1,000.00 | |
| | Factory Ledger, Syracuse | | 450.00 |
| | Factory Ledger, Buffalo | | 550.00 |
| (4) | Factory Ledger, Syracuse | 20,000.00 | |
| | Factory Ledger, Buffalo | 15,000.00 | |
| | Sundry Credits | | 35,000.00 |
| (5) | Factory Ledger, Syracuse | 18,000.00 | |
| | Factory Ledger, Buffalo | 14,000.00 | |
| | Payroll—Marketing and Admin. | 5,000.00 | |
| | Federal Income Tax Withheld | | 3,700.00 |
| | FICA Tax Payable | | 2,164.50 |
| | Accrued Payroll | | 31,135.50 |
| | Marketing Expenses Control | 2,800.00 | |
| | Administrative Expenses Control | 2,200.00 | |
| | Payroll—Marketing and Admin. | | 5,000.00 |
| (6) | Vouchers Payable | 54,000.00 | |
| | Cash | | 52,920.00 |
| | Discount on Purchases | | 1,080.00 |
| (7) | Accrued Payroll | 31,135.50 | |
| | Vouchers Payable | | 31,135.50 |
| | Vouchers Payable | 31,135.50 | |
| | Cash | | 31,135.50 |
| | Factory Ledger, Syracuse* | 1,323.00 | |
| | Factory Ledger, Buffalo | 1,029.00 | |
| | Marketing Expenses Control | 205.80 | |
| | Administrative Expenses Control | 161.70 | |
| | FICA Tax Payable | | 2,164.50 |
| | State Unemployment Insurance Tax Payable | | 370.00 |
| | Federal Unemployment Insurance Tax Payable | | 185.00 |
| (8) | No entry | | |
| (9) | No entry | | |
| (10) | Cost of Goods Sold | 105,000.00 | |
| | Factory Ledger, Syracuse | | 55,000.00 |
| | Factory Ledger, Buffalo | | 50,000.00 |
| | Accounts Receivable | 131,250.00 | |
| | Sales | | 131,250.00 |

*Computations:

| Payroll Taxes | Syracuse | Buffalo | Sales | Office |
|---|---|---|---|---|
| FICA | $1,053.00 | $ 819.00 | $163.80 | $128.70 |
| State Unemployment Tax | 180.00 | 140.00 | 28.00 | 22.00 |
| Federal Unemployment Tax | 90.00 | 70.00 | 14.00 | 11.00 |
| Totals | $1,323.00 | $1,029.00 | $205.80 | $161.70 |

**5.11    Trial Balances, Ledger Accounts.** The Reinhardt Manufacturing Company employs both general and factory ledgers in its cost accounting system. Selected accounts showed the following balances at December 31, 19X2, after the books were closed.

| | | | |
|---|---|---|---|
| Cash | $10,000 | Vouchers Payable | $15,000 |
| Accounts Receivable | 20,000 | Accrued Payroll | 2,500 |
| Materials | 10,000 | Capital Stock | 47,000 |
| Work in Process | 5,000 | Retained Earnings | 20,500 |
| Finished Goods | 10,000 | Factory Ledger | 25,000 |
| Machinery | 30,000 | General Ledger | 25,000 |

The following transactions were completed during the first month of 19X3:

(1)   Materials purchased: $90,000.

(2)   Materials used in production: direct, $85,000; indirect, $10,000.

(3)   Work in process completed and transferred to finished goods: $175,000.

(4)   Factory overhead applied: 75% of the direct labor cost.

(5)   Sundry factory overhead: $20,000.

(6)   Labor costs incurred: direct labor, $50,000; indirect labor, $10,000; sales salaries, $5,000; administrative salaries, $5,000. Accrued Payroll is credited for total gross wages. The employer's payroll tax cost is applied on the basis of labor costs incurred. The state and federal unemployment insurance tax rates are 1.7% and 0.5%, respectively, and the employer's FICA tax is $4,095.00.

(7)   Sales and administrative expenses for the month: $30,000. This cost was shared equally by the two departments and credited to Vouchers Payable.

(8)   Payrolls paid, $50,000. Ten percent of wages paid was withheld for income taxes, and $2,925 for FICA taxes.

(9)   All but $15,000 of the finished goods were sold, terms 2/10, n/60, at a 25% markup above production cost.

(10)  Accounts Receivable collected: 75%, less 2% discount.

(11)  In addition to the payrolls issued, the check register showed voucher payments totalling $100,000.

(a)   Prepare trial balances of the general ledger and factory ledger as of January 1, 19X3.

(b)   Open general ledger and factory ledger accounts as of January 1, and post the month's transactions.

(c)   Prepare trial balances of the general ledger and factory ledger as of January 31, 19X3.

**SOLUTION**

(a)

*The Reinhart Manufacturing Company*
*Trial Balance of General Ledger*
*January 1, 19X3*

| | | |
|---|---|---|
| Cash | $10,000 | |
| Accounts Receivable | 20,000 | |
| Machinery | 30,000 | |
| Vouchers Payable | | $15,000 |
| Accrued Payroll | | 2,500 |
| Capital Stock | | 47,000 |
| Retained Earnings | | 20,500 |
| Factory Ledger | 25,000 | |
| | $85,000 | $85,000 |

*The Reinhart Manufacturing Company*
*Trial Balance of Factory Ledger*
*January 1, 19X3*

| | | |
|---|---|---|
| Materials | $10,000 | |
| Work in Process | 5,000 | |
| Finished Goods | 10,000 | |
| General Ledger | | $25,000 |
| | $25,000 | $25,000 |

(b)

## GENERAL LEDGER

### Cash

| | | | | | |
|---|---|---|---|---|---|
| 1/1 | Bal. | 10,000.00 | (8) | | 42,075.00 |
| (10) | | 170,887.50 | (11) | | 100,000.00 |
| | | 180,887.50 | Bal. | | 38,812.50 |
| 1/31 | Bal. | 38,812.50 | | | 180,887.50 |

### Cost of Goods Sold

| | |
|---|---|
| (9) 170,000 | |

### Machinery

| | | |
|---|---|---|
| 1/1 | Bal. | 30,000 |

### Accrued Payroll

| | | | | | |
|---|---|---|---|---|---|
| (8) | | 50,000 | 1/1 | Bal. | 2,500 |
| Bal. | | 22,500 | (6) | | 70,000 |
| | | 72,500 | | | 72,500 |
| | | | 1/31 | Bal. | 22,500 |

### Discount on Sales

| | |
|---|---|
| (10) 3,487.50 | |

### Income Tax Withheld

| | |
|---|---|
| | (8) 5,000 |

### Accounts Receivable

| | | | | | |
|---|---|---|---|---|---|
| 1/1 | Bal. | 20,000 | (10) | | 174,375 |
| (9) | | 212,500 | Bal. | | 58,125 |
| | | 232,500 | | | 232,500 |
| 1/31 | Bal. | 58,125 | | | |

### State Unemployment Tax Payable

| | |
|---|---|
| | (6) 1,190.00 |

### Payroll—Marketing and Admin.

| | |
|---|---|
| (6) 10,000 | (6) 10,000 |

### Sales

| | |
|---|---|
| | (9) 212,500 |

### Retained Earnings

| | |
|---|---|
| | (1/1) Bal. 20,500 |

### Federal Unemployment Tax Payable

| | |
|---|---|
| | (6) 350.00 |

### Capital Stock

| | |
|---|---|
| | 1/1 Bal. 47,000.00 |

### FICA Tax Payable

| | |
|---|---|
| | (6) 4,095.00 |
| | (8) 2,925.00 |

### Vouchers Payable

| | | | | | |
|---|---|---|---|---|---|
| (8) | | 42,075.00 | 1/1 | Bal. | 15,000.00 |
| (11) | | 100,000.00 | | (1) | 90,000.00 |
| Bal. | | 55,000.00 | | (5) | 20,000.00 |
| | | 197,075.00 | | (7) | 30,000.00 |
| | | | | (8) | 42,075.00 |
| | | | | | 197,075.00 |
| | | | 1/31 | Bal. | 55,000.00 |

## GENERAL LEDGER (Continued)

| Marketing Expenses Control | | Factory Ledger | |
|---|---|---|---|
| (6)   5,000.00 | | 1/1   Bal.   25,000.00 | (9) 170,000.00 |
| (6)      402.50* | | (1)   90,000.00 | Bal.   29,830.00 |
| (7) 15,000.00 | | (5)   20,000.00 | 199,830.00 |
| | | (6)   60,000.00 | |
| **Administrative Expenses Control** | | (6)    4,830.00 | |
| (6)   5,000.00 | | 199,830.00 | |
| (6)      402.50* | | 1/31  Bal.   29,830.00 | |
| (7) 15,000.00 | | | |

## FACTORY LEDGER

| Materials | | Finished Goods | |
|---|---|---|---|
| 1/1   Bal.   10,000 | (2)   95,000 | 1/1   Bal.   10,000 | (9) 170,000 |
| (1)   90,000 | Bal.   5,000 | (3) 175,000 | 15,000 |
| 100,000 | 100,000 | 185,000 | 185,000 |
| 1/31  Bal.   5,000 | | 1/31  Bal.   15,000 | |

| Work in Process | | Factory Overhead Control | |
|---|---|---|---|
| 1/1   Bal.   5,000 | (3) 175,000 | (2)   10,000 | (4)   37,500 |
| (2)   85,000 | Bal.   2,500 | (5)   20,000 | Bal.   7,330 |
| (4)   37,500 | 177,500 | (6)   10,000 | 44,830 |
| (6)   50,000 | | (6)    4,830* | |
| 177,500 | | 1/31  Bal.   7,330 | |
| 1/31  Bal.   2,500 | | | |

| General Ledger | |
|---|---|
| (9) 170,000 | 1/1   Bal.   25,000 |
| Bal.   29,830 | (1)   90,000 |
| 199,830 | (5)   20,000 |
| | (6)   60,000 |
| | (6)    4,830* |
| | 199,830 |
| | 1/31  Bal.   29,830 |

* Computations:

| Payroll Taxes | Factory | Sales | Administrative | Total |
|---|---|---|---|---|
| FICA | $3,510.00 | $292.50 | $292.50 | $4,095.00 |
| State Unemployment Insurance Tax | 1,020.00 | 85.00 | 85.00 | 1,190.00 |
| Federal Unemployment Insurance Tax | 300.00 | 25.00 | 25.00 | 350.00 |
| | $4,830.00 | $402.50 | $402.50 | $5,635.00 |

(c)
### The Reinhardt Manufacturing Company
### Trial Balance of General Ledger
### January 31, 19X3

|  | Debit | Credit |
|---|---|---|
| Cash | $ 38,812.50 | |
| Accounts Receivable | 58,125.00 | |
| Machinery | 30,000.00 | |
| Sales | | $212,500.00 |
| Accrued Payroll | | 22,500.00 |
| Vouchers Payable | | 55,000.00 |
| Income Tax Withheld | | 5,000.00 |
| FICA Tax Payable | | 7,020.00 |
| State Unemployment Insurance Tax Payable | | 1,190.00 |
| Federal Unemployment Insurance Tax Payable | | 350.00 |
| Cost of Goods Sold | 170,000.00 | |
| Retained Earnings | | 20,500.00 |
| Marketing Expenses Control | 20,402.50 | |
| Administrative Expenses Control | 20,402.50 | |
| Discount on Sales | 3,487.50 | |
| Capital Stock | | 47,000.00 |
| Factory Ledger | 29,830.00 | |
| | $371,060.00 | $371,060.00 |

### The Reinhardt Manufacturing Company
### Trial Balance of Factory Ledger
### January 31, 19X3

|  | Debit | Credit |
|---|---|---|
| Materials | $ 5,000 | |
| Work in Process | 2,500 | |
| Finished Goods | 15,000 | |
| Factory Overhead Control | 7,330 | |
| General Ledger | | $29,830 |
| | $29,830 | $29,830 |

# Chapter 6

# Job Order Costs

## 6.1 JOB ORDER COST SYSTEM

The job order cost system is most suitable where the products differ in types of material and work performed. Thus, each product is custom made according to the customer's specifications and the price quoted is closely tied to estimated cost. Examples of types of companies which might use job order costing are printing companies and shipbuilding firms.

Under a job order cost system, the three basic elements of cost—direct material, direct labor and factory overhead—are accumulated according to assigned job numbers. The unit cost for each job is obtained by dividing the total units for the job into the total cost. Selling and administrative costs are *not* considered part of the cost of the job and are shown separately on the cost sheet and income statement.

In order for a job order cost system to function properly, it must be possible to identify each job physically and segregate its related costs. Each individual order or batch is assigned a job number. Material requisitions, labor costs and other charges carry the particular job number, and a cost sheet is used to summarize the applicable job costs. The profit or loss can be computed for each job and the unit cost can be computed for purposes of inventory costing.

## EXAMPLE 1

Power Manufacturing Corporation uses a job order cost system to cost out its production. During 19X1, the specified costs were incurred on the following open jobs:

| Direct Materials | | | Direct Labor | | |
|---|---|---|---|---|---|
| Job # | Cost | | Job # | Hours | Cost |
| H 702 | $16,872 | | L 1670 | 200 | $ 800 |
| G 901 | 10,980 | | J 1901 | 3,000 | 9,600 |
| B 168 | 5,670 | | H 702 | 500 | 1,575 |
| | | | G 901 | 600 | 1,200 |
| | | | B 168 | 90 | 180 |

### Factory Overhead

Applied at $2.00 per direct labor hour.

### Jobs in Process—Beginning

| Job # | Materials | Labor | Factory Overhead | Total |
|---|---|---|---|---|
| L 1670 | $1,500 | $6,000 | $8,000 | $15,500 |
| J 1901 | 5,000 | 8,000 | 4,000 | 17,000 |

### Sales

| Job # | Selling Price |
|---|---|
| L 1690 | $ 18,000 |
| J 1901 | 45,000 |
| H 702 | 28,000 |
| G 901 | 25,000 |
| | $116,000 |

**Jobs Completed during the Year:** #L 1670, #J 1901, #H 702, #G 901

**Selling and Administrative Expenses:** $25,510

Computed below are (1) the cost of completed jobs, (2) the ending work in process, and (3) the net income for the year.

(1) *Cost of Completed Jobs*

| Job # | Opening W.I.P. | Direct Materials | Direct Labor | Factory Overhead | Total Cost |
|---|---|---|---|---|---|
| L 1670 | $15,500 | | $ 800 | $ 400 | $16,700 |
| J 1901 | 17,000 | | 9,600 | 6,000 | 32,600 |
| H 702 | | $16,872 | 1,575 | 1,000 | 19,447 |
| G 901 | | 10,980 | 1,200 | 1,200 | 13,380 |
| | $32,500 | $27,852 | $13,175 | $8,600 | $82,127 |

(2) *Work in Process—Ending*

| Job # | Opening W.I.P. | Direct Materials | Direct Labor | Factory Overhead | Total Cost |
|---|---|---|---|---|---|
| B 168 | 0 | $5,670 | $180 | $180 | $6,030 |

(3) *Net Income*

| | |
|---|---|
| *Sales* | $116,000 |
| *Cost of Sales* | 82,127 |
| *Gross Profit* | $ 33,873 |
| *Selling and Administrative Expenses* | 25,510 |
| *Net Income* | $ 8,363 |

## 6.2 JOURNAL ENTRIES FOR JOB ORDER COST SYSTEM

The appropriate journal entries for a job order cost system are illustrated in Examples 2 and 3.

## EXAMPLE 2

Sloane Manufacturing Company uses a job order cost system and compiled the following data for 19X1:

| | |
|---|---:|
| Materials and Supplies Purchased | $242,000 |
| Direct Material Used | 190,000 |
| Supplies Used | 20,000 |
| Direct Labor | 150,000 |
| Other Labor | 35,000 |
| Utility Costs for Year | 65,000 |
| Miscellaneous Overhead | 40,000 |
| Depreciation, Equipment | 22,000 |
| Depreciation, Buildings | 8,000 |
| Applied Factory Overhead (20% of direct labor costs) | |
| Cost of Goods Completed (material, $170,000; labor, $130,000) | 326,000 |
| Sales | 500,000 |
| Cost of Goods Sold | 326,000 |
| Selling and Administrative Expenses | 110,000 |

Shown below are (1) the appropriate journal entries and (2) the computation of net income.

### (1) *Journal Entries*

| | | |
|---|---:|---:|
| Stores Control | 242,000 | |
|     *Vouchers Payable* | | 242,000 |
|   *To record purchase of materials.* | | |
| | | |
| Work in Process, Direct Material | 190,000 | |
| Factory Overhead Control, Indirect Material | 20,000 | |
|     *Stores Control* | | 210,000 |
|   *To record placing material into process.* | | |
| | | |
| Work in Process, Direct Labor | 150,000 | |
| Factory Overhead Control, Indirect Labor | 35,000 | |
|     *Accrued Payroll* | | 185,000 |
|   *To record factory payroll earned.* | | |
| | | |
| Accrued Payroll | 185,000 | |
|     *Cash* | | 185,000 |
|   *To record payment of payroll.* | | |
| | | |
| Factory Overhead Control | 135,000 | |
|     *Vouchers Payable* | | 105,000 |
|     *Depreciation, Equipment* | | 22,000 |
|     *Depreciation, Building* | | 8,000 |
|   *To record factory overhead.* | | |
| | | |
| Work in Process, Factory Overhead | 30,000 | |
|     *Factory Overhead Applied* | | 30,000 |
|   *To record applied overhead.* | | |
| | | |
| Finished Goods | 326,000 | |
|     *Work in Process, Material* | | 170,000 |
|     *Work in Process, Direct Labor* | | 130,000 |
|     *Work in Process, Factory Overhead* | | 26,000 |
|   *To record transfer of completed goods.* | | |
| | | |
| Cost of Sales | 326,000 | |
|     *Finished Goods* | | 326,000 |
|   *To record cost of sales.* | | |

|                              |           |         |
|------------------------------|-----------|---------|
| Accounts Receivable          | 500,000   |         |
| Sales                        |           | 500,000 |
| To record sales.             |           |         |
| Selling and Administrative Expenses | 110,000 |   |
| Vouchers Payable             |           | 110,000 |
| To record selling and administrative expenses. |  |  |

(2)  **Net Income**

|                                     |           |
|-------------------------------------|-----------|
| Sales                               | $500,000  |
| Cost of Sales                       | 326,000   |
| Gross Profit                        | $174,000  |
| Selling and Administrative Expenses | 110,000   |
| Net Income                          | $ 64,000  |

## EXAMPLE 3

The Powerproducts Manufacturing Company had the following data for the month ending April 19X2:

(1)  Material purchased: $40,000

(2)  Material put into process:

| Direct material   | $30,000 |
|-------------------|---------|
| Indirect material | 6,000   |
| Material used     | $36,000 |

(3)  Material sent back to storeroom:

| Direct material   | $  800 |
|-------------------|--------|
| Indirect material | 200    |
| Total returned    | $1,000 |

(4)  Payroll for period: $38,600

(5)  Breakdown of the payroll was as follows:

| Direct labor           | 60%  |
|------------------------|------|
| Indirect labor         | 15%  |
| Selling salaries       | 10%  |
| Administrative salaries | 15% |
|                        | 100% |

(6)  Actual factory overhead costs incurred amounted to $10,500, excluding the above, but including $3,000 for depreciation of machinery and equipment.

(7)  Factory overhead is applied to production at 60% of direct labor cost.

(8)  Cost sheets for completed work show the following:

| Material         | $24,000 |
|------------------|---------|
| Labor            | 19,500  |
| Factory overhead | 11,700  |
| Total            | $55,200 |

(9)  Sales of completed items amounted to $85,000.

The journal entries for these transactions are given below.

| (1) | Stores Control | 40,000 | |
| | Vouchers Payable | | 40,000 |
| (2) | Work in Process, Direct Material | 30,000 | |
| | Factory Overhead Control, Indirect Material | 6,000 | |
| | Stores Control | | 36,000 |
| (3) | Stores Control | 1,000 | |
| | Work in Process, Direct Material | | 800 |
| | Factory Overhead Control, Indirect Material | | 200 |
| (4) | Payroll | 38,600 | |
| | Accrued Payroll | | 38,600 |
| (5) | Work in Process, Direct Labor | 23,160 | |
| | Factory Overhead Control, Indirect Labor | 5,790 | |
| | Selling Expense | 3,860 | |
| | Administrative Expense | 5,790 | |
| | Payroll | | 38,600 |
| (6) | Factory Overhead Control | 10,500 | |
| | Accumulated for Depreciation | | 3,000 |
| | Vouchers Payable | | 7,500 |
| (7) | Work in Process, Factory Overhead | 13,896 | |
| | Factory Overhead Applied | | |
| | ($23,160 × 60%) | | 13,896 |
| (8) | Finished Goods Inventory | 55,200 | |
| | Work in Process, Direct Material | | 24,000 |
| | Work in Process, Direct Labor | | 19,500 |
| | Work in Process, Factory Overhead | | 11,700 |
| (9) | Accounts Receivable | 85,000 | |
| | Sales | | 85,000 |

## 6.3  JOB ORDER COST SHEET

This form is used to summarize the materials, labor and overhead charged to a particular job. The form varies according to the needs of the particular company. Where the record may be handled a great deal, the company may have the form printed on heavier material, and it may be a cost card and filed in a cabinet rather than in a book.

The material cost and labor cost may be obtained from material and labor summaries or may be recorded directly from material requisitions and time tickets. Factory overhead is applied on the basis of a predetermined rate. The rate may be based on direct labor hours, direct labor cost, machine hours, total cost or other recognized basis. Where there are two or more departments, it is usually desirable to have separate overhead rates for each department, or separate bases may be used. For example, overhead may be applied in Department A on the basis of machine hours and in Department B on the basis of direct labor hours.

In order to have additional information for the particular job readily available, many companies provide a summary on the cost sheet that includes the selling price as well as estimated selling and administrative expenses so that the estimated profit can be shown.

### EXAMPLE 4

The Pompano Company received an order from the Bayville Company on July 13, 19X1 for 1,000 coffee pots, model #6. The price is $0.75 each and delivery is promised in three months. Job No. 1201 was assigned to the order.

*Materials.*  Materials costs for the job, obtained from materials requisitions, are as follows:

| | | |
| --- | --- | --- |
| Department A: | August 5, 500 bases at $0.08 | $40.00 |
| | August 10, 500 bases at $0.09 | 45.00 |

Department B: September 8, 600 handles at $0.03      $18.00
September 20, 400 handles at $0.05      20.00

*Direct labor.*   Labor costs obtained from time tickets are as follows:

Department A: August 15, Forming, 12 hours at $3.00      $36.00
August 20, Polishing, 10 hours at $3.20      32.00
Department B: September 12, Assembly, 14 hours at $4.00      56.00
September 25, Assembly, 13 hours at $4.50      58.50

*Factory overhead.*   Overhead is applied when the job is completed or at the end of a period for jobs in process. The predetermined overhead rate is based on direct labor hours for each department as follows: Department A, $5.00 per hour; Department B, $5.25 per hour.

*Other data.*   The company expects a *gross profit* of about 25% on each job in order to cover selling and administrative expenses and to provide a reasonable profit.   Therefore, the factory costs as computed should be about 75% of the selling price.   Thus, $557.25 ÷ 0.75 = $743.00, which is rounded off to $750.

Selling and Administrative Expenses are based on 10% of selling price ($750 × 10% = $75.00).   Profit of about 15% is required to allow for income taxes of nearly 50% and for miscellaneous losses.   The *net profit* shown on the income statement would then be about a 7½% return on sales.   The unit cost for monthly accounting purposes is $0.557.

The completed Job Cost Sheet for Job No. 1201 is shown in Fig. 6-1.

## POMPANO COMPANY
### Job Order Cost Sheet

Customer:  Bayville Company     Job No:  1201
Date Ordered:  July 13, 19X1     Product:  Copper Pot #6
Date Completed:  October 13, 19X1     Quantity:  1,000

**Materials**

| Date | Description | Quantity | Cost | Amount |
|---|---|---|---|---|
| 8/5 | Bases, Dept. A | 500 | $.08 | $ 40.00 |
| 8/10 | Bases, Dept. A | 500 | .09 | 45.00 |
| 9/8 | Handles, Dept. B | 600 | .03 | 18.00 |
| 9/20 | Handles, Dept. B | 400 | .05 | 20.00 |
| | | | Total | $123.00 |

**Overhead**

| Month | Dept. | Hours | Rate | Amount |
|---|---|---|---|---|
| Aug. | A | 22 | $5.00 | $110.00 |
| Sept. | B | 27 | 5.25 | 141.75 |
| | | | Total | $251.75 |

**Summary**

| | | |
|---|---|---|
| Selling price | | $750.00 |
| Factory Costs | | |
| Materials | $123.00 | |
| Labor | 182.50 | |
| Overhead | 251.75 | |
| (Unit cost: $0.557) | | 557.25 |
| Gross Profit (25.7%) | | $192.25 |
| Selling & Admin. (10%) | | 75.00 |
| Profit (15.7%) | | $117.75 |

**Labor**

| Date | Description | Hours | Rate | Amount |
|---|---|---|---|---|
| 8/15 | Forming, Dept. A | 12 | $3.00 | $ 36.00 |
| 8/20 | Polishing, Dept. A | 10 | 3.20 | 32.00 |
| 9/12 | Assembly, Dept. B | 14 | 4.00 | 56.00 |
| 9/25 | Assembly, Dept. B | 13 | 4.50 | 58.50 |
| | | | Total | $182.50 |

**Fig. 6-1**

## Summary

(1) Costs are accumulated by jobs under the _____ _____ _____ system and by process or department under the _____ _____ system.

(2) Where the product or order is custom made the _____ _____ _____ system is most suitable.

(3) The unit cost for a job is computed by dividing the total cost by the total _____ for the job.

(4) Under the job order cost system each job is assigned an identifying job _____.

(5) The job order cost system is most suitable for a large volume steel mill.  (a) True, (b) false.

(6) Factory overhead cost applied to a job is usually based on a predetermined rate.  (a) True, (b) false.

(7) Materials and labor applied to a job are usually actual charges.  (a) True, (b) false.

(8) The Job Order Cost Sheet may be used for estimating profit on the job.  (a) True, (b) false.

(9) The Job Order Cost Sheet used by some companies also provides for showing the selling price, selling and administrative expenses, and net profit.  (a) True, (b) false.

*Answers:*  (1) job order cost, process cost; (2) job order cost; (3) units; (4) number; (5) b; (6) a; (7) a; (8) b; (9) a.

## Solved Problems

**6.1**  **Journal Entries.** The J. Nelson Company maintains its cost records under the job order system.  Selected cost data pertaining to the jobs for the month of July, 19X1 are as follows:

Work in Process, July 1, 19X1                                                  $35,000
Transactions for July:
(1) Raw materials purchased                                                    45,000
(2) Materials issued (indirect, $5,000)                                        35,000
(3) Payroll (indirect, $10,000)                                                50,000
(4) Factory overhead, actual                                                   60,000
(5) Factory overhead is applied to production at 120% of direct labor.
(6) Jobs with a cost of $110,000 were completed in July.
(7) Jobs costing $140,000 were shipped out and billed at a markup of 25% on cost.

(a) Prepare the general journal entries for the above transactions using the voucher system.
(b) Compute the work in process amount at July 31, 19X1.

## SOLUTION

(*a*)   General Journal Entries

| | | | |
|---|---|---:|---:|
| (1) | Materials | 45,000 | |
| | Vouchers Payable | | 45,000 |
| (2) | Work in Process—Direct Material | 30,000 | |
| | Factory Overhead Control—Indirect Material | 5,000 | |
| | Materials Inventory | | 35,000 |
| (3) | Payroll | 50,000 | |
| | Accrued Payroll | | 50,000 |
| | Work in Process—Direct Labor | 40,000 | |
| | Factory Overhead Control—Indirect Labor | 10,000 | |
| | Payroll | | 50,000 |
| (4) | Factory Overhead Control | 60,000 | |
| | Vouchers Payable and Accruals | | 60,000 |
| (5) | Work in Process—Factory Overhead | 48,000 | |
| | Factory Overhead Applied | | 48,000 |
| | Factory Overhead Applied | 48,000 | |
| | Factory Overhead Control | | 48,000 |
| (6) | Finished Goods | 110,000 | |
| | Work in Process | | 110,000 |
| (7) | Cost of Goods Sold | 140,000 | |
| | Finished Goods | | 140,000 |
| (8) | Accounts Receivable | 175,000 | |
| | Sales | | 175,000 |

(*b*)   Work in Process Inventory, July 31, 19X1

### Work in Process

| | | | | |
|---|---:|---|---|---:|
| Balance 7/1 | 35,000 | | Completed in July | 110,000 |
| Materials, July | 30,000 | | Balance 7/31 | 43,000 |
| Labor, July | 40,000 | | | |
| Overhead, July | 48,000 | | | |
| | 153,000 | | | 153,000 |
| Balance 7/31 | 43,000 | | | |

**6.2   Journal Entries.**  The Binderman Manufacturing Company uses a factory journal and a general journal to record cost data.

The following transactions were recorded for August, 19X2.

(1)   Materials purchased: $35,000 for the factory and $8,000 for the office.

(2)   Freight paid on materials shipped to factory, $385.

(3)   Materials put into process: Direct, $22,000; factory supplies, $3,000.

(4)   Purchased factory equipment:

| | |
|---|---:|
| List price | $10,000 |
| Trade discount | 20% |
| Cash discount | 5% |
| Transportation costs | $100 |

(5)   Payroll for period:

| | |
|---|---|
| Direct labor | $60,000 |
| Indirect labor | 15,000 |
| Office payroll | 25,000 |
| FICA tax | 7,000 |
| Federal withholding tax | 18,000 |

(6)   Employers portion of payroll:

| | |
|---|---|
| FICA tax | $7,000 |
| Federal unemployment | 4,000 |

(7)   Depreciation: Office equipment, $7,500; factory equipment, $14,000.

(8)   Overhead applied at 50% of direct labor cost.

(9)   Goods finished were $80,000 for the period.

(10)  Sold goods costing $80,000 for $90,000.

Prepare the journal entries required for the above transactions.

## SOLUTION

| | | General Journal | | Factory Journal | |
|---|---|---|---|---|---|
| (1) | *Factory Ledger* | 35,000 | | | |
| | *Office Supplies* | 8,000 | | | |
| | *Accounts Payable* | | 43,000 | | |
| | *Materials* | | | 35,000 | |
| | *General Ledger* | | | | 35,000 |
| (2) | *Factory Ledger* | 385 | | | |
| | *Accounts Payable* | | 385 | | |
| | *Materials or Freight-in* | | | 385 | |
| | *General Ledger* | | | | 385 |
| (3) | *Work in Process—Direct Materials* | | | 22,000 | |
| | *Factory Overhead—Indirect Materials* | | | 3,000 | |
| | *Materials* | | | | 25,000 |
| (4) | *Equipment* | 7,700 | | | |
| | *Accounts Payable* | | 7,700 | | |
| | ($10,000 − 20% − 5% + $100 = $7,700) | | | | |
| (5) | *Factory Ledger* | 75,000 | | | |
| | *Office Payroll* | 25,000 | | | |
| | *FICA Taxes Payable* | | 7,000 | | |
| | *Federal Withholding Taxes Payable* | | 18,000 | | |
| | *Accrued Payroll* | | 75,000 | | |
| | *Accrued Payroll* | 75,000 | | | |
| | *Cash* | | 75,000 | | |
| | *Factory Payroll* | | | 75,000 | |
| | *General Ledger* | | | | 75,000 |
| | *Selling and Administrative Expenses* | 25,000 | | | |
| | *Office Payroll* | | 25,000 | | |
| | *Work in Process—Direct Labor* | | | 60,000 | |
| | *Factory Overhead, Indirect Labor* | | | 15,000 | |
| | *Factory Payroll* | | | | 75,000 |

| | | | | | |
|---|---|---|---|---|---|
| (6) | Factory Ledger | | | | |
| | [(75,000/100,000) × 11,000] | 8,250 | | | |
| | Office Payroll Taxes | | | | |
| | [(25,000/100,000) × 11,000] | 2,750 | | | |
| | FICA Taxes Payable | | 7,000 | | |
| | Federal Unemployment Taxes Payable | | 4,000 | | |
| | Factory Overhead | | | 8,250 | |
| | General Ledger | | | | 8,250 |
| (7) | Factory Ledger | 14,000 | | | |
| | Depreciation Expense, Office Equipment | 7,500 | | | |
| | Accumulated Depreciation, Factory Equipment | | 14,000 | | |
| | Accumulated Depreciation, Office Equipment | | 7,500 | | |
| | Factory Overhead | | | 14,000 | |
| | General Ledger | | | | 14,000 |
| (8) | Work in Process—Factory Overhead (50% × 60,000) | | | 30,000 | |
| | Applied Factory Overhead | | | | 30,000 |
| (9) | Finished Goods | | | 80,000 | |
| | Work in Process | | | | 80,000 |
| (10) | Accounts Receivable | 90,000 | | | |
| | Sales | | 90,000 | | |
| | General Ledger | | | 80,000 | |
| | Finished Goods | | | | 80,000 |
| | Cost of Goods Sold | 80,000 | | | |
| | Factory Ledger | | 80,000 | | |

**6.3    Journal Entries.** The Harvey and Marty Manufacturing Company is a partnership engaged in producing electronic components on special order. At the end of July 19X5, the work in process consisted of Jobs 701 and 702 as follows:

### Cost Summary

| Item | Total | Job 701 | Job 702 |
|---|---|---|---|
| Materials | $30,000 | $10,000 | $20,000 |
| Labor | 9,000 | 5,000 | 4,000 |
| Overhead | 6,500 | 4,500 | 2,000 |
| | $45,500 | $19,500 | $26,000 |

Prepare journal entries to record (a) the liability for costs and (b) the application of costs to work in process.

**SOLUTION**

(a)  **Incurrence of Costs**

| | | |
|---|---|---|
| Materials | 30,000 | |
| Accounts Payable | | 30,000 |
| Payroll | 9,000 | |
| Accrued Payroll, Taxes, Etc. | | 9,000 |
| Factory Overhead | 6,500 | |
| Accounts Payable, Accruals, Etc. | | 6,500 |

(b)  **Application to Work in Process**

| | | |
|---|---|---|
| Work in Process—Materials, Job 701 | 10,000 | |
| Work in Process—Materials, Job 702 | 20,000 | |
| Materials | | 30,000 |

| Work in Process—Labor, Job 701 | 5,000 | |
| Work in Process—Labor, Job 702 | 4,000 | |
| Payroll | | 9,000 |
| Work in Process—Overhead, Job 701 | 4,500 | |
| Work in Process—Overhead, Job 702 | 2,000 | |
| Overhead—Applied | | 6,500 |

**6.4    Factory Ledger Entries.** The Carson Company completed the following transactions during the month of October, 19X7:

Oct.  3: Materials requisitioned: direct, $2,000; indirect, $1,000.

4: Raw materials purchased: $10,000.   Terms: 2/10, n/30.

7: Weekly factory payroll of $1,000 was allocated as follows: direct labor, $940; maintenance, $60. Income taxes were $90, FICA taxes were $45. The factory received $865 in cash for payroll distribution.

10: Completed factory job with following costs: direct labor, $480; materials, $225; factory overhead, 75% of direct labor.

12: Shipped completed job to customer per instructions of home office: billing, $1,150.

13: Home office vouchered and paid miscellaneous factory overhead, $400.

Make the necessary journal entries on the company's home office books and factory books.

## SOLUTION

### General Ledger

Oct.  3 No entry

| 4 Factory Ledger | 10,000 | |
| Vouchers Payable | | 10,000 |
| 7 Factory Ledger | 1,000 | |
| Fed. Inc. Taxes Pay. | | 90 |
| FICA Taxes Pay. | | 45 |
| Accrued Payroll | | 865 |

10 No entry

| 12 Cost of Goods Sold | 1,065 | |
| Factory Ledger | | 1,065 |
| Accounts Receivable | 1,150 | |
| Sales | | 1,150 |
| 13 Factory Ledger | 400 | |
| Vouchers Payable | | 400 |
| Vouchers Payable | 400 | |
| Cash | | 400 |

### Factory Ledger

| Oct.  3 Work in Process— | | |
| Direct Material | 2,000 | |
| Factory Overhead Control— | | |
| Indirect Material | 1,000 | |
| Materials | | 3,000 |
| 4 Materials | 10,000 | |
| General Ledger | | 10,000 |
| 7 Payroll | 1,000 | |
| General Ledger | | 1,000 |
| Work in Process— | | |
| Direct Labor | 940 | |
| Factory Overhead Control— | | |
| Indirect Labor | 60 | |
| Payroll | | 1,000 |
| 10 Work in Process— | | |
| Factory Overhead | 360 | |
| Factory Overhead Applied | | 360 |
| Finished Goods | 1,065 | |
| Work in Process | | 1,065 |
| 12 General Ledger | 1,065 | |
| Finished Goods | | 1,065 |
| 13 Factory Overhead Control | 400 | |
| General Ledger | | 400 |

**6.5    Factory Overhead Rate.** The J. M. Cain Company shows the following costs for 19X1.

| | |
|---|---|
| Materials used | $250,000 |
| Direct labor | 200,000 |
| Actual overhead | 250,000 |
| Work in process (ending) | 90,000 |

Compute (a) the predetermined rate to be used for the following year based on direct labor, and (b) the other components of work in process if materials are 40% of total cost.

**SOLUTION**

(a)  **Overhead Rate**

$$\frac{\text{Overhead}}{\text{Direct labor}} = \frac{\$250,000}{\$200,000} = 125\%, \text{ or } 1.25$$

(b)  **Components of Inventory**

| | |
|---|---|
| Materials ($90,000 × 0.40) | $36,000 |
| Labor* | 24,000 |
| Overhead* | 30,000 |
| Work in Process Total | $90,000 |

---

* Given a total work in process inventory of $90,000 and materials cost of $36,000, the remaining $54,000 is allocated between labor and overhead as follows:

Labor: $54,000 ÷ 2.25 (1.00 + 1.25) = $24,000
Overhead: $24,000 × 1.25 = $30,000

**6.6    Factory Overhead Rates.** The Tableau Manufacturing Company has been in business for one month. At the end of the month the company had the following account balances on its books:

| | |
|---|---|
| Materials used | $ 5,000 |
| Direct labor | 10,000 |
| Indirect labor | 3,000 |
| Indirect materials | 2,000 |
| Labor fringe costs | 1,000 |
| Supervisor's salary | 1,000 |
| Depreciation of machinery | 2,000 |
| Miscellaneous factory overhead | 1,000 |
| Heat and light | 500 |
| Insurance on plant | 1,500 |

The company processed two jobs during the month with costs as follows:

| | Job 101 | Job 102 |
|---|---|---|
| Materials cost | $3,000 | $2,000 |
| Direct labor cost | 6,000 | 4,000 |
| Direct labor hours | 4,000 | 3,000 |
| Machine hours | 2,000 | 1,000 |

The company does not use a predetermined rate for factory overhead.  The rate is computed at the end of each month.

In terms of both direct labor hours and machine hours, compute (a) the overhead rates for the month, (b) the overhead cost of each job, and (c) the total cost for each job.

**SOLUTION**

(a)  The overhead rates for the month are as follows:

$$\frac{\text{Overhead costs}}{\text{Total direct labor hours}} = \frac{\$12,000}{7,000} = \$1.71$$

$$\frac{\text{Overhead costs}}{\text{Total machine hours}} = \frac{\$12,000}{3,000} = \$4.00$$

(b)  Overhead charged to jobs is as follows.  For Job 101:

Overhead rate × direct labor hours = \$1.71 × 4,000 = \$6,840
Overhead rate × machine hours = \$4.00 × 2,000 = \$8,000

For Job 102:

Overhead rate × direct labor hours = \$1.71 × 3,000 = \$5,130
Overhead rate × machine hours = \$4.00 × 1,000 = \$4,000

(c)  Total cost

|                        | Job 101 | | Job 102 | |
| --- | --- | --- | --- | --- |
| **Component Costs**    | **Direct Labor Hours** | **Machine Hours** | **Direct Labor Hours** | **Machine Hours** |
| Direct materials       | $ 3,000  | $ 3,000  | $ 2,000  | $ 2,000  |
| Direct labor           | 6,000    | 6,000    | 4,000    | 4,000    |
| Factory overhead       | 6,840    | 8,000    | 5,130    | 4,000    |
| Total cost             | $15,840  | $17,000  | $11,130  | $10,000  |

**6.7    Predetermined Rates.**  The K. M. Hill Company has the following cost data for the year 19X5.

| Description | Production Department | Finishing Department |
| --- | --- | --- |
| Materials used    | $50,000 | $20,000 |
| Direct labor cost | $80,000 | $60,000 |
| Overhead (actual) | $96,000 | $40,000 |
| Machine hours     |         | 2,000   |

Compute (a) the overhead rates to be used for 19X6 based on direct labor cost for the Production Department and machine hours for the Finishing Department and (b) the total overhead to be applied to Job No. 408, which had $3,000 direct labor cost in the Production Department and 250 machine hours in the Finishing Department.

**SOLUTION**

(a)  **Overhead Rates.**  Production Department, based on direct labor cost:

$$\frac{\text{Overhead cost}}{\text{Direct labor cost}} = \frac{\$96,000}{\$80,000} = 120\%, \text{ or } 1.2$$

Finishing Department, based on machine hours:

$$\frac{\text{Overhead cost}}{\text{Machine hours}} = \frac{\$40,000}{2,000} = \$20 \text{ per machine hour}$$

(b)  **Overhead Applied to Job. No. 408.**

| | |
|---|---|
| Direct labor cost ($3,000 × 120%) | $3,600 |
| Machine hours (250 × $20) | 5,000 |
| Overhead applied | $8,600 |

**6.8  Factory Overhead Applied.** The Liebman Manufacturing Company produces expensive furniture only on order. Two orders were started and completed during August. There was no other production. Overhead is applied at $4.00 per direct labor hour. Cost information for the month was as follows:

| | Job 201 | Job 202 |
|---|---|---|
| Direct materials | $11,500 | $ 8,500 |
| Direct labor | | |
| Cost | $10,500 | $ 4,500 |
| Hours | 3,500 | 1,500 |
| Factory overhead | | |
| Indirect materials | $10,000 | $ 5,000 |
| Other factory overhead | 3,000 | 1,800 |
| Total | $13,000 | $ 6,800 |
| Selling price | $40,000 | $23,000 |

Compute (a) the overapplied or underapplied overhead and (b) the gross profit on each job.

**SOLUTION**

(a)  **Factory Overhead Applied**

| Cost Components | Total | Job 201 | Job 202 |
|---|---|---|---|
| Indirect materials | $15,000 | $10,000 | $5,000 |
| Other overhead | 4,800 | 3,000 | 1,800 |
| Total overhead (actual) | $19,800 | $13,000 | $6,800 |
| Overhead applied | 20,000 | 14,000 | 6,000 |
| (Overapplied) Underapplied | $ (200) | $(1,000) | $ 800 |

(b)  **Gross Profit**

| | Job 201 | Job 202 |
|---|---|---|
| Selling price | $40,000 | $23,000 |
| Product costs | | |
| Direct material | 11,500 | 8,500 |
| Direct labor | 10,500 | 4,500 |
| Factory overhead | 13,000 | 6,800 |
| Total cost | $35,000 | $19,800 |
| Gross profit | $ 5,000 | $ 3,200 |

**6.9    Flow of Costs—T Accounts.**  The Riverside Company uses a job order system for costing.  The total debits and credits in selected accounts at December 31, 19X5 are:

| Accounts | Debits | Credits |
|---|---|---|
| Materials | $ 40,000 | $20,000 |
| Work in process | 105,000 | 75,000 |
| Finished goods | 120,000 | 90,000 |
| Materials purchases | (a)  25,000 | |
| Direct labor | (b)  30,000 | |
| Factory overhead control | (c)  40,000 | |
| Factory overhead applied | | (d)  36,000 |
| Cost of goods sold | 94,000 | |

The total debits in an inventory account include the beginning inventory amount.

(a)   Compute the beginning inventory balances using T accounts.

(b)   Prepare closing entries and post them to the T accounts.

**SOLUTION**

(a)   Materials Inventory, at beginning: $15,000

Total debits ($40,000) − purchases ($25,000) = $15,000

Work in Process, at beginning: $19,000

Total debits ($105,000) − material, labor, and overhead ($86,000) = $19,000

Finished Goods, at beginning: $45,000

Total debits ($120,000) − completed goods ($75,000) = $45,000

**Materials Inventory**

| | | | |
|---|---|---|---|
| 1/1 Inv. | 15,000 | (1) | 20,000 |
| (a) Purchases | 25,000 | | 20,000 |
| | 40,000 | | 40,000 |
| 12/31 Inv. | 20,000 | | |

**Work in Process**

| | | | |
|---|---|---|---|
| 1/1 Inv. | 19,000 | | |
| (1) Materials | 20,000 | | |
| (b) Labor | 30,000 | (2) | 75,000 |
| (d) Overhead | 36,000 | | 30,000 |
| | 105,000 | | 105,000 |
| 12/31 Inv. | 30,000 | | |

**Finished Goods**

| | | | |
|---|---|---|---|
| 1/1 Inv. | 45,000 | (3) | 90,000 |
| (2) | 75,000 | | 30,000 |
| | 120,000 | | 120,000 |
| 12/31 Inv. | 30,000 | | |

**Cost of Goods Sold**

| | | |
|---|---|---|
| (3) | 90,000 | |
| (4) | 4,000 | |
| | 94,000 | |

**Factory Overhead Control**

| | | | |
|---|---|---|---|
| (c) | 40,000 | (4) | 40,000 |

**Factory Overhead Applied**

| | | | |
|---|---|---|---|
| (4) | 36,000 | (d) | 36,000 |

(b)   **Closing entries**

| | | | |
|---|---|---|---|
| (1) | Work in Process | 20,000 | |
| | Materials | | 20,000 |
| (2) | Finished Goods | 75,000 | |
| | Work in Process | | 75,000 |
| (3) | Cost of Goods Sold | 90,000 | |
| | Finished Goods | | 90,000 |
| (4) | Factory Overhead Applied | 36,000 | |
| | Cost of Goods Sold | 4,000 | |
| | Factory Overhead Control | | 40,000 |

**6.10** **Cost of Goods Sold Statement.** The Golden Shaft Corporation uses the job order cost system to cost its customized products. At December 31, 19X5, its accounts showed the following balances for the month:

|  | November 30 | December 31 |
|---|---|---|
| Materials inventory | $10,500 | $ 5,500 |
| Work in process | 2,000 | 1,000 |
| Finished goods | 12,500 | 15,000 |
| Materials purchased |  | 20,000 |
| Direct labor |  | 3,150 |
| Indirect labor (2% of direct) |  | 63 |
| Electricity |  | 600 |
| Heat |  | 210 |
| Insurance |  | 240 |
| Depreciation, factory |  | 180 |
| Factory supplies |  | 330 |
| Maintenance |  | 270 |

Prepare a Statement of Cost of Goods Sold.

**SOLUTION**

*Golden Shaft Corporation*
*Statement of Cost of Goods Sold*
*for the month of December, 19X5*

| | | |
|---|---|---|
| Raw Materials | | |
| Inventory at 11/30 | $10,500 | |
| Purchases | 20,000 | |
| Materials Available | $30,500 | |
| Less: Inventory at 12/31 | 5,500 | |
| Raw Materials Used | | $25,000 |
| Direct Labor | | 3,150 |
| Factory Overhead | | |
| Indirect Labor | $   63 | |
| Electricity | 600 | |
| Heat | 210 | |
| Insurance | 240 | |
| Depreciation, factory | 180 | |
| Maintenance | 270 | |
| Factory Supplies | 330 | 1,893 |
| Total Manufacturing Costs | | $30,043 |
| Work in Process Decrease | | |
| Inventory at 11/30 | $ 2,000 | |
| Inventory at 12/31 | 1,000 | 1,000 |
| Cost of Goods Manufactured | | $31,043 |
| Finished Goods Increase | | |
| Inventory at 12/31 | $15,000 | |
| Inventory at 11/30 | 12,500 | (2,500) |
| Cost of Goods Sold | | $28,543 |

**6.11    Profit on Jobs.**   The Green Engineering Company produces specialized machine parts according to customer specifications.   At January 1, 19X1, the following jobs were in process:

| Components | Job #20 | Job #28 | Job #48 |
|---|---|---|---|
| Material | $4,000 | $ 8,000 | $3,300 |
| Labor | 2,000 | 4,000 | 2,200 |
| Overhead | 1,000 | 2,000 | 1,100 |
| Totals | $7,000 | $14,000 | $6,600 |

*Additional costs to complete:*

Material: $20,000, allocated as follows: Job #20, 40%; Job #28, 40%; and Job #48, 20%.

Labor: $4,000 per job.

Overhead: 20% of labor.

*Unit selling prices:* Job #20, $2.20; Job #28, $2.50; Job #48, $1.80.

(*a*) Prepare the journal entry to record transfer of Job #20 from Work in Process to Finished Goods.   (*b*) Assuming the total unit cost for each job is $2.00, calculate the number of units completed on each job.   (*c*) Compute the profit or loss on each job.

## SOLUTION

Before any entries can be prepared or unit costs computed, it is necessary to determine the total cost for each job, as follows.

| Job #20 | January 1 | Additional | Total |
|---|---|---|---|
| Material | $ 4,000 | $ 8,000 | $12,000 |
| Labor | 2,000 | 4,000 | 6,000 |
| Overhead | 1,000 | 800 | 1,800 |
| Total | $ 7,000 | $12,800 | $19,800 |

| Job #28 | January 1 | Additional | Total |
|---|---|---|---|
| Material | $ 8,000 | $ 8,000 | $16,000 |
| Labor | 4,000 | 4,000 | 8,000 |
| Overhead | 2,000 | 800 | 2,800 |
| Total | $14,000 | $12,800 | $26,800 |

| Job #48 | January 1 | Additional | Total |
|---|---|---|---|
| Material | $ 3,300 | $ 4,000 | $ 7,300 |
| Labor | 2,200 | 4,000 | 6,200 |
| Overhead | 1,100 | 800 | 1,900 |
| Total | $ 6,600 | $ 8,800 | $15,400 |

(*a*)   **Journal Entry (Job #20)**

| | | |
|---|---|---|
| *Finished Goods* | *19,800* | |
| *Work in Process, Material—Job #20* | | *12,000* |
| *Work in Process, Labor—Job #20* | | *6,000* |
| *Work in Process, Overhead—Job #20* | | *1,800* |

(b)   **Units Completed**

|  | Total Cost | | Unit Cost | | Total Units |
|---|---|---|---|---|---|
| Job #20 | $19,800 | ÷ | $2.00 | = | 9,900 |
| Job #28 | 26,800 | ÷ | 2.00 | = | 13,400 |
| Job #48 | 15,400 | ÷ | 2.00 | = | 7,700 |
| Totals | $62,000 | | | | 31,000 |

(c)   **Profit or Loss on Each Job**

| | Units | Unit Price Selling | Cost | Selling Price | Total Cost | Profit (Loss) |
|---|---|---|---|---|---|---|
| Job #20 | 9,900 | $2.20 | $2.00 | $21,780 | $19,800 | $1,980 |
| Job #28 | 13,400 | 2.50 | 2.00 | 33,500 | 26,800 | 6,700 |
| Job #48 | 7,700 | 1.80 | 2.00 | 13,860 | 15,400 | (1,540) |
| Totals | | | | $69,140 | $62,000 | $7,140 |

**6.12    Price Quotations.** The McGinn Manufacturing Company has received requests from a customer for quotations on two machines to be built to specifications. Following are the estimated cost data on each machine.

| | Machine 1 | Machine 2 |
|---|---|---|
| Material | | |
| Material required | $350.00 | $550.00 |
| Parts to be purchased | 115.00 | 175.00 |

| | Number of Hours | | Hourly Rates | |
|---|---|---|---|---|
| Labor and overhead | Machine 1 | Machine 2 | Labor | Overhead |
| Dept. A | 9 | 12 | $2.50 | $2.50 |
| Dept. B | 12 | 25 | 2.80 | 2.20 |
| Dept. C | 8 | 16 | 2.75 | 1.75 |
| Dept. D | 60 | 90 | 2.20 | 1.90 |
| Dept. E | 0 | 18 | 2.20 | .90 |

*Other Expenses and Profit.* The allowance for selling and administrative expenses and profit is 25%, based on sales. Estimated spoilage is 8% of direct labor and materials cost.

Prepare the estimated bid price for each machine. Round to the nearest dollar.

**SOLUTION**

| | Machine 1 | Machine 2 |
|---|---|---|
| Materials cost | | |
| Material required | $350.00 | $550.00 |
| Parts to be purchased | 115.00 | 175.00 |
| Total materials cost | $465.00 | $725.00 |

| | Labor | Overhead | Labor | Overhead |
|---|---|---|---|---|
| Labor and overhead cost | | | | |
| Dept. A | $ 22.50 | $ 22.50 | $ 30.00 | $ 30.00 |
| Dept. B | 33.60 | 26.40 | 70.00 | 55.00 |
| Dept. C | 22.00 | 14.00 | 44.00 | 28.00 |
| Dept. D | 132.00 | 114.00 | 198.00 | 171.00 |
| Dept. E | 0 | 0 | 39.60 | 16.20 |
| Total labor and overhead | $210.10 | $176.90 | $381.60 | $300.20 |

|                                      | Machine 1 | Machine 2 |            |
|--------------------------------------|-----------|-----------|------------|
| Summary                              |           |           |            |
| Materials cost                       | $  465.00 | $  725.00 |            |
| Direct labor cost                    | 210.10    | 381.60    |            |
| Factory overhead                     | 176.90    | 300.20    |            |
| Spoilage allowance*                  | 54.01     | 88.53     |            |
| Manufacturing cost (75%)             | $  906.01 | $1,495.33 |            |
| Selling, admin., and profit (25%)**  | 302.00    | 498.44    |            |
| Computed price                       | $1,208.01 | $1,993.77 | (rounded)  |
| Quoted price (rounded)               | $1,208.00 | $1,994.00 |            |

*Computations*

|              | **Machine 1**                       | **Machine 2**                          |
|--------------|-------------------------------------|----------------------------------------|
| * Spoilage:  | 0.08($465.00 + 210.10) = $54.01     | 0.08($725.00 + 381.60) = $88.53        |

** The allowance for selling and administrative expenses and profit can also be calculated as a percentage of manufacturing costs. In this case, the selling price (100%) less other expenses and profit (25%) results in manufacturing costs of 75%. Other expenses and profit (25%) divided by manufacturing costs (75%) equals $\frac{1}{3}$. Applied to the two machines,

|                                          | Machine 1 | Machine 2  |
|------------------------------------------|-----------|------------|
| Manufacturing costs                      | $906.01   | $1,495.33  |
| Other expenses and profit ($\frac{1}{3}$)| $302.00   | $  498.44  |

# Chapter 7

# Process Costs I

## 7.1 INTRODUCTION

Under a process cost system costs are accumulated according to each department, cost center or process. The average unit cost for a day, week or year is obtained by dividing the department cost by the number of units (tons, gallons, etc.) produced during the particular period.

The process cost system is used where products are manufactured under mass production methods or by continuous processing. Industries using process costs are paper, steel, chemicals, and textiles. Assembly-type processes such as automobiles, washing machines, and electric appliances would also use process costs.

## 7.2 ACCUMULATION OF COSTS

In a process cost system procedures must be developed to:

(1) Accumulate materials, labor, and factory overhead by departments.

(2) Determine the unit cost for each department.

(3) Transfer costs from one department to the next.

(4) Assign costs to work in process.

For simplicity, this discussion of cost accumulation will refer to departments rather than cost centers or processes. Note, however, that there may be two or more processes performed in one department (and therefore, more than one cost center in a department). In such cases, costs may vary significantly between cost centers, so it is desirable in practice to accumulate costs according to cost center or process rather than by department.

The accumulation of costs on the books is described below.

(1) *Materials Costs.* In a process cost system the number of requisitions or charges for materials is far less than in a job order cost system, since charges are made to departments rather than to individual jobs. In some industries the type and quantity of materials may be specified by formulas or engineering specifications. Where there is continuous use of the same materials, the usage each day or week is obtained from consumption reports rather than individual requisitions. The journal entry for charging materials would be

> Work in Process, Materials, Department A    10,500
>
> Materials                                         10,500

Some companies use a slightly different version of the entry as follows:

> Materials in Process—Department A    10,500
>
> Stores                                   10,500

(2) *Labor Costs.* The detail of accumulating labor costs by departments is also less than

accumulating the same costs by individual jobs under the job order cost system. Labor costs to departments may be summarized in the payroll distribution entry as follows:

| | | |
|---|---|---|
| Work in Process, Labor—Department A | 6,000 | |
| Work in Process, Labor—Department B | 2,000 | |
| Payroll | | 8,000 |

The entry may also be written as

| | | |
|---|---|---|
| Labor in Process—Department A | 6,000 | |
| Labor in Process—Department B | 2,000 | |
| Payroll | | 8,000 |

(3) *Factory Overhead Costs.* There is a greater difference between job order costing and process costing with respect to factory overhead than with material or labor costs. Generally, production is more stable for process costing from month to month, since products are made for stock rather than to order. The entry charging overhead is

| | | |
|---|---|---|
| Work in Process, Factory Overhead—Department A | 9,000 | |
| Work in Process, Factory Overhead—Department B | 4,000 | |
| Factory Overhead Control | | 13,000 |

An alternative entry is

| | | |
|---|---|---|
| Overhead in Process—Department A | 9,000 | |
| Overhead in Process—Department B | 4,000 | |
| Factory Overhead | | 13,000 |

Where factory overhead costs accumulate fairly evenly throughout the year, or at a reasonably normal rate each month, many companies apply actual overhead to costs. However, substantial fluctuation in production between months can distort the overhead charged to production. Thus, a predetermined rate based on a year's operation is frequently used to eliminate the difficulties of allocating overhead based on month-to-month volumes of production.

## 7.3   DEPARTMENTAL TRANSFERS

Process costing ordinarily is used where products require a number of different production operations which are performed in two or more departments or cost centers. For example, the first operation may be performed in Department A, such as a machining or mixing process. After completion the units are transferred to Department B, for an assembly or refining process. When this is completed, the units are transferred to finished goods.

### EXAMPLE 1

The Sunshine Company manufactures Product X, which requires processing in Departments A and B. During July 19X1, 5,000 units were placed in production and completed during the month. The costs were as follows: materials, $10,000; direct labor, $9,000; and factory overhead, $6,000. The computations are

#### Work in Process—Department A

| | Total Cost | Unit Cost |
|---|---|---|
| Materials placed in production | $10,000 | $2.00 |
| Direct labor | 9,000 | 1.80 |
| Factory overhead | 6,000 | 1.20 |
| Total cost | $25,000 | $5.00 |

The unit cost in each case is found by dividing the total cost by the number of units produced. When the process in Department A is completed, the 5,000 units are transferred to Department B.

## 7.4  FLOW OF UNITS

The flow of units (in terms of quantity) through a process cost system can be summarized by the following equation:

Units in process at beginning + Units started in process or transferred in
= Units transferred out + Units completed and on hand + Units still in process

When any four terms in the equation are known, the missing component can be computed from the equation. Note that all the components are not necessarily present in each situation (i.e. there may not always be units in process at the beginning of the period or units completed and still on hand at the end of the period).

### EXAMPLE 2

Assume that the Bickerman Company had 1,500 units in work in process at the beginning of the month, put 5,000 units into process and had 1,000 units in work in process at the end of the month. All units completed were transferred out to Department B. The number of units transferred is computed as follows:

|        |                               |
|--------|-------------------------------|
| 1,500  | Units in process at beginning |
| 5,000  | Units started in process      |
| 6,500  | Units available               |
| 1,000  | Units still in process        |
| 5,500  | Units transferred to Department B |

## 7.5  EQUIVALENT UNITS OF PRODUCTION

Rarely are all units placed in production during the month completed and sent to the next department by the end of the month. In most cases there will be beginning and ending inventories of work in process at different stages of completion for each month.

To allocate costs when inventories of partially finished goods are involved, all units (beginning inventory, goods transferred, ending inventory) must be expressed in terms of completed units. This is done by means of a common denominator, known as *equivalent units of production* or *equivalent production*. By using the equivalent production figure, the unit cost for the month would include the cost of completing any work in process at the beginning of the month and the cost to date of work in process at the end of the period.

Two separate equivalent production computations are usually needed, one for materials and another for conversion costs, since the degree of completion for each is rarely the same.

There are two principal methods for costing work in process inventories: *average costing* and *first-in, first-out* (FIFO) *costing*. There are minor differences in cost report format or procedure; the major difference relates to the way in which the work-in-process inventories are treated.

*Average Costing.* Under this method, also known as weighted-average costing, the opening work-in-process inventory costs are *merged* with the costs of the new period and a new average cost is obtained. Thus, there is only one average cost for goods completed.

Equivalent units under average costing may be computed as follows:

Units Completed (Transferred out plus still on hand) + [Ending Work in Process
× Degree of Completion (%)]

This method is based on the assumption that *all* the beginning work in process was started and completed during the current period.

**EXAMPLE 3**

The following data relate to the activities of Department A during the month of May:

|  | Units |
|---|---|
| Beginning work in process | |
| (100% complete as to materials, | |
| 70% complete as to conversion costs) | 8,000 |
| Goods started in process | 86,000 |
| Units transferred to Dept. B | 80,000 |
| Units completed and on hand | 4,000 |
| Ending work in process | |
| (100% complete as to materials, | |
| 60% complete as to conversion costs) | 10,000 |

Equivalent production in Department A for the month, using average costing, is computed as follows.

|  | Materials | Conversion Costs |
|---|---|---|
| Units completed | | |
| Transferred to Dept. B | 80,000 | 80,000 |
| Completed and on hand | 4,000 | 4,000 |
| Ending inventory units, amount completed: | | |
| Materials (100%) | 10,000 | |
| Conversion costs (60%) | | 6,000 |
| Equivalent production | 94,000 | 90,000 |

This method adds the portion of beginning work in process that was completed in the previous month to the current month's production. The result is that the portion of beginning work in process completed during the previous period is counted twice, in this case once as last April's ending work in process and again as May's beginning work in process.

**FIFO Costing.** Under this method, the opening work in process inventory costs are *separated* from additional costs applied in the new period. Thus, there are two unit costs for the period: (1) opening work in process units completed and (2) units started and finished in the same period.

Under FIFO, the beginning work in process is assumed to be completed and transferred first. The ending work in process is then assumed to be from the goods put into production during the period. Thus, ending work in process is calculated from current period unit costs according to degree of completion.

Equivalent units under FIFO Costing may be computed as follows:

Units Completed (Transferred out plus still on hand)
  − Opening Work in Process (regardless of stage of completion)
  + Amount needed to complete Beginning Work in Process
  + Amount completed in Ending Work in Process

**EXAMPLE 4**

Using the same data as in Example 3, we compute the equivalent production for Department A under the FIFO method as follows.

|  | Units | |
|---|---|---|
|  | **Materials** | **Conversion Costs** |
| Units Completed | | |
| Transferred to Dept. B | 80,000 | 80,000 |
| Completed and on hand | 4,000 | 4,000 |
| Less: Beginning work in process | ⟨8,000⟩ | ⟨8,000⟩ |
| Started and completed this period | 76,000 | 76,000 |
| | | |
| Completion of Beginning Inventory Units | | |
| Materials (0%) | 0 | |
| Conversion costs (30%) | | 2,400 |
| | 76,000 | 78,400 |
| | | |
| Ending Inventory Units, Amount Completed | | |
| Materials (100%) | 10,000 | |
| Conversion costs (60%) | | 6,000 |
| Equivalent production | 86,000 | 84,400 |

Equivalent production under FIFO may also be computed by subtracting the portion of beginning work in process that was completed during the previous month from equivalent production under average costing.

|  | Units | |
|---|---|---|
|  | **Materials** | **Conversion Costs** |
| Equivalent production, average costing (from Example 3) | 94,000 | 90,000 |
| Less: Beginning work in process (portion completed last month) | | |
| Materials (100%) | ⟨8,000⟩ | |
| Conversion costs (70%) | | ⟨5,600⟩ |
| Equivalent production, FIFO costing | 86,000 | 84,400 |

The FIFO method is superior to the average method in that it corrects the double count resulting from the carry-over of the previous month's work in process. Even with this inherent inaccuracy in the average method, it is still commonly used in business because the double count usually represents an insignificant portion of the total units produced.

## 7.6  COST OF PRODUCTION REPORT

The Cost of Production Report shows all costs chargeable to a department or cost center for the period. Since its principal objective is the control of costs, detailed data relating to total and unit costs must be provided. Typically, the cost breakdown is made by cost elements for each department (or cost center). This report is also a good source for summary journal entries at the end of the month.

The cost of production report generally contains four sections:

*Quantities.* This section accounts for the physical flow of *units* into and out of a department.

*Equivalent Production.* This section shows the sum of: (1) units still in process, restated in terms of completed units, and (2) total units actually completed. Section 7.5 illustrated the computation of equivalent units of production under both average costing and FIFO costing.

*Costs to Account For.* This section accounts for the *incurrence* of costs that were: (1) *in process* at the beginning of the period, (2) *transferred in* from previous departments, and (3) *added* by the department.

*Costs Accounted For.* This section accounts for the *disposition* of costs charged to the department. Were the costs: (1) *transferred out* to another department or to finished goods? (2) *completed* and on *hand*? (3) *still in process* at end of the period? It should be noted that the total of the *Costs to Account For* must equal the total of the *Costs Accounted For*.

The Cost of Production report may be greatly detailed (i.e. item by item) or may show only totals, depending on the needs of the business and the desire of management. In our presentation we will show the breakdown according to cost elements in each of the cost categories.

## EXAMPLE 5

The Vogel Manufacturing Corporation uses the first-in, first-out method of process costing. The following data relate to the operations of Department A during the month of July, 19X1:

### Production (in units)

| | |
|---|---|
| Beginning work in process (100% complete as to materials; 66⅔% complete as to conversion costs) | 1,500 |
| Started in process | 5,000 |
| Transferred to Dept. B | 5,500 |
| Ending work in process (100% complete as to materials; 60% complete as to conversion costs) | 1,000 |

| Costs in Beginning Inventory | | | Costs Added during the Month | |
|---|---|---|---|---|
| Materials | $1,680 | 1.12 | Materials | $10,000 |
| Labor | 1,400 | .93 | Labor | 8,500 |
| Overhead | 1,120 | .75 | Overhead | 6,800 |
| | | 2.8 | | |

The July Cost of Production Report for Department A is shown below.

*The Vogel Manufacturing Corporation*
*Cost of Production Report, Department A*
*FIFO Cost Method*
*for the month of July, 19X1*

### Quantities

| | | |
|---|---|---|
| Units in Process at Beginning (all materials; ⅔ conversion costs) | 1,500 | |
| Units Started in Process | 5,000 | 6,500 |
| Units Transferred to Next Department | 5,500 | |
| Units Still in Process (all materials; ⅗ labor and overhead) | 1,000 | 6,500 |

### Equivalent Production

| | Materials | Conversion Costs |
|---|---|---|
| Transferred to next department | 5,500 | 5,500 |
| — Beginning inventory (total) | 1,500 | 1,500 |
| | 4,000 | 4,000 |
| + Amount needed to complete beginning inventory (⅓) | 0 | 500 |
| | 4,000 | 4,500 |
| + Ending inventory | 1,000 | 600 |
| Equivalent production | 5,000 | 5,100 |

|                                                              | Total Cost | Unit Cost |     |
|--------------------------------------------------------------|-----------|-----------|-----|
| **Costs to Account For**                                     |           |           |     |
| Work in Process, Beginning Balance $(1,500 \times 2.8) =$    | $ 4,200   |           |     |
| Costs Added during Month                                     |           |           |     |
|     Materials                            | $10,000   | $2.000    | (a) |
|     Labor                                | 8,500     | 1.667     | (b) |
|     Factory Overhead                     | 6,800     | 1.333     | (c) |
| Total Costs Added                                            | $25,300   | $5.000    |     |
| Total Costs to Account For                                   | $29,500   |           |     |

|                                                              | Total Cost |     |
|--------------------------------------------------------------|-----------|-----|
| **Costs Accounted For**                                      |           |     |
| Transferred to Next Department                               |           |     |
| From Beginning Inventory (1,500 units)                       |           |     |
|     Inventory Value                      | $ 4,200   |     |
|     Labor Added (1,500 × $1.667 × $\frac{1}{3}$) | 833 |  |
|     Factory Overhead Added (1,500 × $1.333 × $\frac{1}{3}$) | 667 | |
| Total Cost, Beginning Units                                  | $ 5,700   |     |
| From Current Production                                       |           |     |
|     Units Started and Completed (4,000 units × $5.00) | 20,000 | |
| Total Cost                                                   | $25,700   |     |
| Work in Process, Ending ($\frac{2}{3}$ complete)             |           |     |
|     Materials (1,000 × $2.00)            | 2,000     |     |
|     Processing Costs (1,000 × $3.00 × $\frac{2}{3}$) | 1,800 | |
| Total Costs Accounted For                                    | $29,500   |     |

**Computations**

*Unit costs:*

(a)   Materials: $10,000/5,000 = $2.000

(b)   Labor: $8,500/5,100 = $1.666

(c)   Overhead: $6,800/5,100 = $1.333

## EXAMPLE 6

If the Vogel Manufacturing Corporation had used the average costing method instead of FIFO, its cost of production report for the month of July would have appeared as shown below. The data are the same as in Example 5.

*The Vogel Manufacturing Corporation*
*Cost of Production Report, Department A*
*Average Costing Method*
*for the month of July, 19X1*

| **Quantities**                                    |       |       |
|---------------------------------------------------|-------|-------|
| Units in Process at Beginning                     |       |       |
|   (all materials: $\frac{2}{3}$ conversion costs) | 1,500 |       |
| Units Started in Process                          | 5,000 | 6,500 |
| Units Transferred to Next Department              | 5,500 |       |
| Units Still in Process                            |       |       |
|   (all materials: $\frac{2}{3}$ conversion costs) | 1,000 | 6,500 |

**Equivalent Production**

|  | Materials | Conversion Costs |
|---|---|---|
| Transferred to next department | 5,500 | 5,500 |
| Ending work in process |  |  |
|   Materials (100%) | 1,000 |  |
|   Conversion costs (60%) |  | 600 |
| Equivalent production | 6,500 | 6,100 |

|  | Total Cost | Unit Cost |  |
|---|---|---|---|
| **Costs to Account For** |  |  |  |
| Work in Process, Beginning Inventory |  |  |  |
|   Materials | $ 1,680 |  |  |
|   Labor | 1,400 |  |  |
|   Overhead | 1,120 |  |  |
| Costs Added during Period |  |  |  |
|   Materials | 10,000 | $1.79692 | (a) |
|   Labor | 8,500 | 1.62295 | (b) |
|   Overhead | 6,800 | 1.29836 | (c) |
| Total Costs to Account For | $29,500 | $4.71823 |  |

| **Costs Accounted For** |  |  |
|---|---|---|
| Transferred to Next Department |  |  |
|   (5,500 × $4.71823) |  | $25,950 |
| Work in Process, Ending Inventory |  |  |
|   Materials (1,000 × $1.79692) | $1,797 |  |
|   Labor (1,000 × $1.62295 × $\frac{3}{5}$) | 974 |  |
|   Overhead (1,000 × $1.29836 × $\frac{3}{5}$) | 779 | 3,550 |
| Total Costs Accounted For |  | $29,500 |

**Computations**

*Unit costs:*

(a)  Materials: ($1,680 + $10,000)/6,500 = $1.79692

(b)  Labor: ($1,400 + $8,500)/6,100 = $1.62295

(c)  Overhead: ($1,120 + $6,800)/6,100 = $1.29836

## 7.7  SCHEDULE OF COMPLETED GOODS

Another type of report often prepared to provide further information, particularly when FIFO is used, is the Schedule of Completed Goods.

## EXAMPLE 7

A Schedule of Completed Goods for the data in Example 5 is shown below for FIFO.

*The Vogel Manufacturing Corporation*
*Schedule of Completed Goods, Department A*
*for the month of July, 19X1*

|  | Units | Total Cost | Unit Cost |
|---|---|---|---|
| **Beginning Work in Process** | | | |
| ($\frac{2}{3}$ completed) | | | |
| Balance, July 1 | | $ 4,200 | |
| Added During July | | | |
| Direct Labor ($8,500 ÷ 5,100 × 500) | | 833 | |
| Factory Overhead ($6,800 ÷ 5,100 × 500) | | 667 | |
| | 1,500 | $ 5,700 | $3.80 |
| **Started and Completed during Period** | | | |
| Put into Process | 5,000 | $25,300 | |
| Less: Applied to Beginning Work in Process, (500 × $3.00) | | (1,500) | |
| Ending Work in Process | 1,000 | (3,800) | |
| | 4,000 | $20,000 | $5.00 |
| Total Completed Goods | 5,500 | $25,700 | $4.67 |

## 7.8  JOURNAL ENTRIES

Two sets of journal entries are needed to record the information developed in the Cost of Production Report.

(1)  *Entry for Costs to Account For.*  The following entry is needed to record the costs put into process in the current period:

| | | |
|---|---|---|
| *Work in Process, Department I* | *xx* | |
| *Materials* | | *xx* |
| *Payroll* | | *xx* |
| *Factory Overhead Control* | | *xx* |

(2)  *Entry for Costs Accounted For.*  The following entry is needed to record the costs transferred out:

| | | |
|---|---|---|
| *Work in Process, Department II* | *xx* | |
| *Work in Process, Department I* | | *xx* |

## EXAMPLE 8

Continuing with the Vogel Manufacturing Corporation data in Examples 5 and 6, the journal entry to record costs put into the process in Department A is as follows, whether average costing or FIFO is used:

| | | |
|---|---|---|
| *Work in Process, Department A* | *25,300* | |
| *Materials* | | *10,000* |
| *Labor* | | *8,500* |
| *Factory Overhead Control* | | *6,800* |

Under FIFO, the entry to record transfer of costs to Department B is

| | | |
|---|---|---|
| *Work in Process, Department B* | *25,700* | |
| *Work in Process, Department A* | | *25,700* |

When average costing is used, the entry to record the transfer is

*Work in Process, Department B*     25,950
*Work in Process, Department A*           25,950

# *Summary*

(1) Costs are accumulated by department, cost center or process in a _____ system.

(2) The unit cost for a department is computed by dividing the total cost by _____.

(3) The counterpart in the process cost system of the job order cost sheet is the _____.

(4) The journal entry for materials used during a period is a debit to _____ and a credit to _____.

(5) The process cost system is suitable for a large paper manufacturing plant. (*a*) True, (*b*) false.

(6) Process costing is ordinarily used where all the operations are performed in one department. (*a*) True, (*b*) false.

(7) The number of requisitions for materials is greater in a process cost system than in a job order cost system. (*a*) True, (*b*) false.

(8) For process costing, individual production reports for departments or processes are preferred to one report for the entire plant. (*a*) True, (*b*) false.

(9) Materials may not be put into process (*a*) at the beginning of an operation, (*b*) continuously, (*c*) at the end of the operation, (*d*) in the shipping department.

(10) Process cost systems are especially suitable for (*a*) custom production, (*b*) standard costs, (*c*) FIFO, (*d*) LIFO.

(11) In process costing, costs follow: (*a*) price rises, (*b*) price declines, (*c*) product flow, (*d*) finished goods.

*Answers:* (1) process cost; (2) the equivalent units; (3) cost of production report; (4) work in process (dept.), materials; (5) *a*; (6) *b*; (7) *b*; (8) *a*; (9) *d*; (10) *b*; (11) *c*.

# Solved Problems

**7.1** **Flow of Units; Quantity Schedules.** The Katz Supply Company manufactures door knobs. The products pass through two departments. Department A had 5,500 door knobs in process on July 1, and 2,500 in process on July 31. During the month, 6,000 door knobs were transferred to Department B for further processing. There were no completed units on hand at the end of the month.

(a) Compute the number of door knobs started in process during July and (b) prepare a quantity schedule for Department A.

**SOLUTION**

(a)  Let $x$ = the number of units started in process.

$$5,500 + x = 6,000 + 0 + 2,500$$
$$x = 8,500 - 5,500$$
$$x = 3,000$$

See Section 7.4.

(b)  **Quantity schedule**

| | | |
|---|---:|---:|
| Units in process at beginning of period | 5,500 | |
| Units started in process | 3,000 | 8,500 |
| | | |
| Units transferred to next department | 6,000 | |
| Units still in process at end of period | 2,500 | 8,500 |

**7.2** **Flow of Units; Quantity Schedules.** The Meyer Manufacturing Company manufactures woolen mittens that require processing in two departments, A and B. During the month of October, Department A completed 10,500 mittens, of which 8,000 were transferred to Department B. There were 500 mittens in process in Department A and 300 in Department B on October 1. During the month, 15,000 additional mittens were started in production in Department A; no additional units were added by Department B. All 7,000 mittens completed during the month were transferred from Department B to the finished goods storeroom. The remaining units for Departments A and B were still in process on October 31.

For each department (a) compute the number of units still in process on October 31, and (b) prepare a quantity schedule.

**SOLUTION**

(a) Let $x$ = the number of units still in process.

| Department A | Department B |
|---|---|
| $500 + 15,000 + 0 = 8,000 + 2,500 + x$ | $300 + 0 + 8,000 = 7,000 + 0 + x$ |
| $15,500 = 10,500 + x$ | $8,300 = 7,000 + x$ |
| $5,000 = x$ | $1,300 = x$ |

(b) **Quantity Schedules**

| | | | |
|---|---|---:|---:|
| **Department A:** | Units in process at beginning | 500 | |
| | Units started in process | 15,000 | 15,500 |
| | | | |
| | Units transferred to next dept. | 8,000 | |
| | Units completed and on hand | 2,500 | |
| | Units still in process | 5,000 | 15,500 |

| | | | |
|---|---|---|---|
| **Department B:** | Units in process at beginning | 300 | |
| | Units from preceding dept. | 8,000 | 8,300 |
| | Units transferred to next dept. | 7,000 | |
| | Units still in process | 1,300 | 8,300 |

**7.3**    **Equivalent Production—Average Costing.**   The following information is available for the Blutter Manufacturing Company:

| | **Units** | |
|---|---|---|
| Work in process, January 1 | | |
| (75% complete as to materials and conversion costs) | 4,000 | |
| Units started in process | 46,000 | 50,000 |
| Units transferred out | 36,000 | |
| Units completed and on hand | 8,000 | |
| Units still in process | | |
| (all materials; $33\frac{1}{3}$% conversion costs) | 6,000 | 50,000 |

Compute the equivalent units for the Blutter Manufacturing Company using the average costing method.

**SOLUTION**

| | **Materials** | **Conversion Costs** |
|---|---|---|
| Units completed | | |
| Transferred to next department | 36,000 | 36,000 |
| Still on hand | 8,000 | 8,000 |
| Work in process | | |
| Materials (6,000 × 100%) | 6,000 | |
| Conversion costs (6,000 × $33\frac{1}{3}$%) | | 2,000 |
| Equivalent production | 50,000 | 46,000 |

**7.4**    **Equivalent Production—FIFO.**   Using the data in Problem 7.3, compute the equivalent units under the FIFO method.

**SOLUTION**

| | **Materials** | **Conversion Costs** |
|---|---|---|
| Units completed | | |
| Transferred out | 36,000 | 36,000 |
| Still on hand | 8,000 | 8,000 |
| Less: Beginning work in process | ⟨4,000⟩ | ⟨4,000⟩ |
| | 40,000 | 40,000 |
| Add: Amount needed to complete beginning work in process | | |
| Materials and conversion costs ($\frac{1}{4}$ × 4,000) | 1,000 | 1,000 |
| | 41,000 | 41,000 |
| Add: Amount completed in ending work in process | | |
| Materials (6,000 × 100%) | 6,000 | |
| Conversion costs (6,000 × $\frac{1}{3}$) | | 2,000 |
| Equivalent production | 47,000 | 43,000 |

**7.5    Equivalent Production—Average Costing.**  The Bobal Manufacturing Company operates two processing departments, A and B, in the manufacture of light bulbs.  Units completed in Department B are transferred to the finished goods storeroom.  The following data are available for the month of July:

|  | **Department A** | **Department B** |
|---|---|---|
| Units from preceding department | 0 | 25,000 |
| Units started in process | 50,000 | 5,000 |
| Units in process, beginning inventory | 3,500 | 2,000 |
| Units completed and transferred to next dept. | 25,000 |  |
| Units in process, ending inventory |  | 10,000 |
| (There were no units completed and on hand.) |  |  |
| Stages of completion of inventories: |  |  |
| Beginning (materials, labor, and overhead) | 2/3 | 1/4 |
| Ending: Materials | all | all |
| Labor and overhead | 2/3 | 1/3 |

Compute equivalent production under the average costing for (a) Department A and (b) Department B.

**SOLUTION**

(a)   Department A

|  | **Materials** | **Conversion Costs** |
|---|---|---|
| Units completed | 25,000 | 25,000 |
| Ending work in process |  |  |
| Materials | 28,500* |  |
| Conversion costs (28,500 × $\frac{2}{3}$) |  | 19,000 |
| Equivalent production | 53,500 | 44,000 |

* Computation of ending work in process inventory (x):
$$3,500 + 0 + 50,000 = 25,000 + x$$
$$28,500 = x$$

(b)   Department B

|  | **Materials** | **Conversion Costs** |
|---|---|---|
| Units completed* | 22,000 | 22,000 |
| Ending work in process |  |  |
| Materials | 10,000 |  |
| Conversion costs (10,000 × $\frac{1}{3}$) |  | 3,333 |
| Equivalent production | 32,000 | 25,333 |

* Computation of units completed (x):
$$2,000 + 25,000 + 5,000 = x + 10,000$$
$$22,000 = x$$

**7.6    Equivalent Production—FIFO.**  Using the data presented in Problem 7.5, compute the equivalent units of production under the FIFO method for Departments A and B.

**SOLUTION**

| | Department A | | Department B | |
|---|---|---|---|---|
| | Materials | Conversion Costs | Materials | Conversion Costs |
| Units completed | 25,000 | 25,000 | 22,000 | 22,000 |
| Less: Beginning work in process | (3,500) | (3,500) | (2,000) | (2,000) |
| | 21,500 | 21,500 | 20,000 | 20,000 |
| Add: Completion of beginning work in process inventory | 1,167 | 1,167 | 1,500 | 1,500 |
| | 22,667 | 22,667 | 21,500 | 21,500 |
| Add: Ending work in process inventory | 28,500 | 19,000 | 10,000 | 3,333 |
| Equivalent production | 51,167 | 41,667 | 31,500 | 24,833 |

*Note:* All amounts in the following problems have been rounded off to the nearest dollar.

**7.7**    **Cost of Production Report: Average Costing.** Prepare a cost of production report for the Elko Corporation, which uses a process cost system to account for the manufacture of mousetraps. All production is done in one department; the average costing method is used. The following information is available:

**Units**

| | |
|---|---:|
| Beginning work in process | |
|     (100% complete for materials, 75% complete for conversion costs) | 10,000 |
| Started in process during the period | 70,000 |
| Transferred to finished goods | 65,000 |
| Completed and still on hand | 2,000 |
| Ending work in process | |
|     (100% complete for materials, 40% complete for conversion costs) | 13,000 |

**Costs**

| | | |
|---|---:|---:|
| Beginning work in process: | | |
|     Materials | $2,000 | |
|     Labor | 3,000 | |
|     Factory Overhead | 1,000 | $6,000 |
| Added during the period: | | |
|     Materials | $ 50,000 | |
|     Labor | 170,000 | |
|     Factory Overhead | 80,000 | $300,000 |

**SOLUTION**

*Elko Corporation*
*Cost of Production Report*
*Average Costing Method*

**Quantities**

| | | |
|---|---:|---:|
| Units in Process at Beginning (all materials; | | |
| 75% conversion costs) | 10,000 | |
| Units Started in Process | 70,000 | 80,000 |
| | | |
| Units Transferred to Finished Goods | 65,000 | |
| Units Completed and On Hand | 2,000 | |
| Units Still in Process (all materials; | | |
| 40% conversion costs) | 13,000 | 80,000 |

| **Equivalent Production** | **Materials** | **Conversion Costs** |
|---|---:|---:|
| Units completed | | |
| Transferred to finished goods | 65,000 | 65,000 |
| Still on hand | 2,000 | 2,000 |
| Work in process, ending inventory | | |
| Materials | 13,000 | |
| Conversion costs (13,000 × 40%) | | 5,200 |
| Equivalent production | 80,000 | 72,200 |

| **Costs to Account For** | **Total Cost** | **Unit Cost** |
|---|---:|---:|
| Work in Process, Beginning Inventory | | |
| Materials | $ 2,000 | |
| Labor | 3,000 | |
| Factory Overhead | 1,000 | |
| Costs Added during the Period | | |
| Materials | 50,000 | $ .65000 |
| Labor | 170,000 | 2.39612 |
| Factory Overhead | 80,000 | 1.12188 |
| Total Costs to Account For | $306,000 | $4.16800 |

**Costs Accounted For**

| | | |
|---|---:|---:|
| Transferred to Finished Goods | | |
| (65,000 × $4.168) | | $270,920 |
| Completed and On Hand (2,000 × $4.168) | | 8,336 |
| Work in Process, Ending Inventory | | |
| Materials (13,000 × $0.65) | $ 8,450 | |
| Labor (13,000 × 0.40 × $2.39612) | 12,460 | |
| Factory Overhead (13,000 × 0.40 × $1.12188) | 5,834 | 26,744 |
| Total Costs Accounted For | | $306,000 |

**Computations**

*Unit costs:*   Materials: ($50,000 + $2,000)/80,000 = $0.6500
                   Labor: $173,000/72,200 = $2.39612
                   Overhead: $81,000/72,200 = $1.12188

**7.8**     **Cost of Production Report: FIFO.**   Recompute Problem 7.7 under FIFO costing.

**SOLUTION**

*Elko Corporation*
*Cost of Production Report*
*FIFO Cost Method*

**Quantities**

| | | |
|---|---:|---:|
| Units in Process at Beginning (all materials, | | |
| conversion costs 75% complete) | 10,000 | |
| Units Started in Process | 70,000 | 80,000 |
| | | |
| Units Transferred to Finished Goods | 65,000 | |
| Units Completed and On Hand | 2,000 | |
| Units Still in Process (all materials, | | |
| conversion costs 40% complete) | 13,000 | 80,000 |

| **Equivalent Production** | **Materials** | **Conversion Costs** |
|---|---:|---:|
| Transferred out and still on hand | 67,000 | 67,000 |
| Less: Beginning inventory (total) | (10,000) | (10,000) |
| Started and finished this period | 57,000 | 57,000 |
| Amount needed to complete beginning work in process | | |
| Materials | 0 | |
| Conversion costs (25%) | | 2,500 |
| | 57,000 | 59,500 |
| Amount completed in ending work in process | | |
| Materials (100%) | 13,000 | |
| Conversion costs (40%) | | 5,200 |
| Equivalent production | 70,000 | 64,700 |

| **Cost to Be Accounted For** | **Total Cost** | **Unit Cost** |
|---|---:|---:|
| Work in Process, Beginning Inventory | $ 6,000 | |
| Cost Added by Department | | |
| Materials | $ 50,000 | $ .71429 |
| Labor | 170,000 | 2.62751 |
| Overhead | 80,000 | 1.23648 |
| Total Cost Added | $300,000 | $4.57828 |
| Total Cost to Be Accounted For | $306,000 | |

**Cost Accounted For**

Transferred to Finished Goods

From Beginning Inventory

| | | | |
|---|---|---|---|
| Inventory Cost | $6,000 | | |
| Labor Added (10,000 × 0.25 × $2.62751) | 6,569 | | |
| Overhead Added (10,000 × 0.25 × $1.23648) | 3,091 | $ 15,660 | |

From Current Production

| | | | |
|---|---|---|---|
| Units Started and Finished (55,000 × $4.57828) | | 251,805 | $267,465 |

| | | | |
|---|---|---|---|
| Completed and On Hand (2,000 × $4.57828) | | | 9,156 |

Work in Process, Ending Inventory

| | | | |
|---|---|---|---|
| Materials (13,000 × $0.71429) | | $ 9,286 | |
| Labor (13,000 × 0.40 × $2.62751) | | 13,663 | |
| Overhead (13,000 × 0.40 × $1.23648) | | 6,430 | 29,379 |
| Total Cost Accounted For | | | $306,000 |

**Computations**

*Unit costs*

Materials:  $50,000/70,000 = $0.71429

Labor:  $170,000/64,700 = $2.62751

Overhead:  $80,000/64,700 = $1.23648

**7.9  Cost of Production Report: Average Costing.**  Nan Corporation manufactures typewriters and uses a process cost system to account for the costs.  Production is done in two departments and the average costing method is used.  The following information is available for you to prepare a cost of production report (*a*) for Dept. 1 and (*b*) for Dept. 2.

| Units | Dept. 1 | Dept. 2 |
|---|---|---|
| Beginning work in process | | |
| Dept. 1: | | |
| All materials; 20% complete for conversion costs | 6,000 | |
| Dept. 2: | | |
| All materials; 70% complete for conversion costs | | 8,000 |
| Started in process during the period | 45,000 | — |
| Received in from Dept. 1 | — | 42,000 |
| Transferred to finished goods | — | 44,000 |
| Completed and still on hand | — | 1,000 |
| Ending work in process | | |
| Dept. 1: | | |
| All materials; 75% complete for conversion costs | 9,000 | |
| Dept. 2: | | |
| All materials; 40% complete for conversion costs | | 5,000 |

| Costs | Dept. 1 | Dept. 2 |
|---|---|---|
| **Beginning work in process** | | |
| From preceding department | $ 0 | $57,720 |
| Materials | 8,000 | 0 |
| Labor | 5,000 | 18,000 |
| Overhead | 3,000 | 8,000 |
| | $16,000 | $83,720 |
| **Added during the period** | | |
| Materials | $200,000 | $ 0 |
| Labor | 100,000 | 150,000 |
| Overhead | 90,000 | 120,000 |
| | $390,000 | $270,000 |

## SOLUTION

(a)

*Nan Corporation*
*Cost of Production Report, Dept. 1*
*Average Costing Method*

**Quantities**

| | | |
|---|---|---|
| Units in Process at Beginning (all materials, 20% conversion costs) | 6,000 | |
| Units Started in Process | 45,000 | 51,000 |
| Units Transferred to Dept. 2 | 42,000 | |
| Units Still in Process (all materials, 75% conversion costs) | 9,000 | 51,000 |

| Equivalent Production | Materials | Conversion Costs |
|---|---|---|
| Units completed | 42,000 | 42,000 |
| Work in process, ending inventory | | |
| Materials | 9,000 | |
| Conversion costs (9,000 × 75%) | | 6,750 |
| Equivalent production | 51,000 | 48,750 |

| Cost to Be Accounted For | Total Cost | Unit Cost |
|---|---|---|
| Work in Process, Beginning Inventory | | |
| Materials | $ 8,000 | |
| Labor | 5,000 | |
| Overhead | 3,000 | |
| Cost Added during the Period | | |
| Materials | $200,000 | $4.07843 |
| Labor | 100,000 | 2.15385 |
| Overhead | 90,000 | 1.90769 |
| Total Costs to Account For | $406,000 | $8.13997 |

**Costs Accounted For**

Transferred to Next Dept.

(42,000 × $8.13997)                                                                      $341,879

Work in Process, Ending Inventory

Materials (9,000 × $4.07843)                                      $ 36,706

Labor (9,000 × 0.75 × $2.15385)                                   14,538

Overhead (9,000 × 0.75 × $1.90769)                               12,877                64,121

Total Costs Accounted For                                                               $406,000

**Computations**

*Unit costs:*  Materials: $208,000/51,000 = $4.07843

Labor: $105,000/48,750 = $2.15385

Overhead: $93,000/48,750 = $1.90769

(b)

**Nan Corporation**
**Cost of Production Report, Dept. 2**
**Average Costing Method**

**Quantities**

| | | |
|---|---:|---:|
| Units in Process at Beginning (all materials, 70% conversion costs) | 8,000 | |
| Received from Previous Department | 42,000 | 50,000 |
| | | |
| Units Transferred to Finished Goods | 44,000 | |
| Units Completed and Still On Hand | 1,000 | |
| Units Still in Process (all materials, 40% conversion costs) | 5,000 | 50,000 |

**Equivalent Production** (Conversion Costs only)

| | |
|---|---:|
| Units completed | |
| Transferred to finished goods | 44,000 |
| Still on hand | 1,000 |
| Work in process, ending inventory (5,000 × 40%) | 2,000 |
| Equivalent production | 47,000 |

| Costs to Be Accounted For | | Total Cost | Unit Cost |
|---|---:|---:|---:|
| Cost from Preceding Department | | | |
| Work in Process, Beginning Inventory | 8,000 | $ 57,720 | $ 7.21500 |
| Transferred In during the Period | 42,000 | 341,879 | |
| Total | 50,000 | $399,599 | $ 7.99198 |
| Cost Added by Department | | | |
| Work in Process, Beginning Inventory | | | |
| Labor | | $ 18,000 | |
| Overhead | | 8,000 | |
| Cost Added during the Period | | | |
| Labor | | 150,000 | 3.57447 |
| Overhead | | 120,000 | 2.72340 |
| Total Cost Added | | $296,000 | $ 6.29787 |
| Total Costs to Be Accounted For | | $695,599 | $14.28985 |

**Costs Accounted For**

Transferred to Finished Goods

    (44,000 × $14.28985)                               $628,753

Units Completed and On Hand

    (1,000 × $14.28985)                                14,290

Work in Process, Ending Inventory

  Cost from Previous Dept.

| | | |
|---|---:|---:|
| (5,000 × $7.99198) | $39,960 | |
| Labor (5,000 × 0.40 × $3.57447) | 7,149 | |
| Overhead (5,000 × 0.40 × $2.72340) | 5,447 | 52,556 |
| Total Costs Accounted For | | $695,599 |

**Computations**

*From preceding dept.:*    Unit costs:    $57,720/8,000 = $7.21500

                                         ($57,720 + $341,879)/50,000 = $7.99198

*Added during period (conversion costs only):*

    Unit costs:    Labor: ($150,000 + $18,000)/47,000 = $3.57447

                        Overhead: ($120,000 + $8,000)/47,000 = $2.72340

**7.10**     **Cost of Production Report: FIFO.**    Recompute Problem 7.9 under FIFO costing.

**SOLUTION**

(a)                                *Nan Corporation*

                     *Cost of Production Report, Dept. 1*

                           *FIFO Method*

**Quantities**

| | | |
|---|---:|---:|
| Units in Process at Beginning (all materials, 20% conversion costs) | 6,000 | |
| Units Started in Process | 45,000 | 51,000 |
| Units Transferred to Dept. 2 | 42,000 | |
| Units Still in Process (all materials, 75% conversion costs) | 9,000 | 51,000 |

| Equivalent Production | Materials | Conversion Costs |
|---|---:|---:|
| Transferred out | 42,000 | 42,000 |
| Less: Beginning inventory (total) | (6,000) | (6,000) |
| Started and finished this period | 36,000 | 36,000 |
| Add: Work added to beginning inventory (materials, 0; conversion costs, 80%) | 0 | 4,800 |
| Add: Units completed in ending inventory (materials, 100%; conversion costs, 75%) | 9,000 | 6,750 |
| Equivalent production | 45,000 | 47,550 |

| Costs to Be Accounted For | Total Cost | Unit Cost |
|---|---|---|
| Work in Process, Beginning Inventory | $ 16,000 | |
| Cost Added by Department | | |
| Materials | 200,000 | $4.44444 |
| Labor | 100,000 | 2.10305 |
| Overhead | 90,000 | 1.89274 |
| Total Cost Added | $390,000 | $8.44023 |
| Total Costs to Be Accounted For | $406,000 | |

**Costs Accounted For**

Transferred to Next Department
From Beginning Inventory

| | | | |
|---|---|---|---|
| Inventory Cost | $16,000 | | |
| Labor Added | | | |
| (6,000 × 0.80 × $2.10305) | 10,095 | | |
| Overhead Added | | | |
| (6,000 × 0.80 × $1.89274) | 9,085 | $ 35,180 | |
| From Current Production | | | |
| Units Started and Finished (36,000 × $8.44023) | | 303,848 | $339,028 |
| Work in Process, Ending Inventory | | | |
| Materials (9,000 × $4.44444) | | $ 40,000 | |
| Labor (9,000 × 0.75 × $2.10305) | | 14,196 | |
| Overhead (9,000 × 0.75 × $1.89274) | | 12,776 | 66,972 |
| Total Costs Accounted For | | | $406,000 |

**Computations**

*Unit costs:*  Materials: $200,000/45,000 = $4.44444

Labor: $100,000/47,550 = $2.10305

Overhead: $90,000/47,550 = $1.89274

(b)

*Nan Corporation*
*Cost of Production Report, Dept. 2*
*FIFO Method*

**Quantities**

| | | |
|---|---|---|
| Units in Process at Beginning (all materials, 70% conversion costs) | 8,000 | |
| Units Received from Depart. 1 | 42,000 | 50,000 |
| Units Transferred to Finished Goods | 44,000 | |
| Units Completed and Still On Hand | 1,000 | |
| Units Still in Process (all materials, 40% conversion costs) | 5,000 | 50,000 |

**Equivalent Production** (Conversion Costs Only)

| | |
|---|---|
| Transferred out and still on hand | 45,000 |
| Less:  Beginning inventory | (8,000) |
| Started and finished | 37,000 |
| Add:  Work to complete beginning inventory (30% × 8,000) | 2,400 |
| Add:  Units completed in ending inventory (40% × 5,000) | 2,000 |
| Equivalent production | 41,400 |

| Costs to Be Accounted For | | Total Cost | Unit Cost |
|---|---|---|---|
| Work in Process, Beginning Inventory | | $ 83,720 | |
| Cost from Preceding Department | | | |
|   Transferred In during the Month (42,000) | | $339,028 | $ 8.07210 |
| Cost Added by Department: | | | |
|   Labor | | $150,000 | $ 3.62319 |
|   Overhead | | 120,000 | 2.89855 |
| Total Cost Added | | $270,000 | $ 6.52174 |
| Total Cost to Be Accounted For | | $692,748 | $14.59384 |

| Costs Accounted For | | | |
|---|---|---|---|
| Transferred to Next Department | | | |
|   From Beginning Inventory: | | | |
|     Inventory Cost | $83,720 | | |
|     Labor Added | | | |
|       (8,000 × 0.30 × $3.62319) | 8,696 | | |
|   Overhead Added | | | |
|       (8,000 × 0.30 × $2.89855) | 6,956 | $ 99,372 | |
|   From Current Production | | | |
|     Units Started and Finished (36,000 × $14.59384) | | 525,378 | $624,750 |
|     Units Completed and Still On Hand | | | |
|       (1,000 × $14.59384) | | | 14,594 |
| Work in Process, Ending Inventory | | | |
|   Cost from Preceding Department | | | |
|     (5,000 × $8.07210) | | $ 40,361 | |
|   Labor (5,000 × 0.40 × $3.62319) | | 7,246 | |
|   Overhead (5,000 × 0.40 × $2.89855) | | 5,797 | 53,404 |
| Total Costs Accounted For | | | $692,748 |

**Computations**

*Unit costs:*  Labor: $150,000/41,400 = $3.62319

             Overhead: $120,000/41,400 = $2.89855

*Current production units:*  44,000  Transferred to next department

                     (8,000)  From beginning inventory

                     36,000  Started and completed this period

**7.11    Cost of Production Report: Average Costing.**  The Mintz Corporation manufactures seven-inch rulers in three departments: Mixing, Shaping and Finishing.  A process cost system is used to account for the goods manufactured.  The following information is available:

| Units | Departments | | |
|---|---|---|---|
| | **Mixing** | **Shaping** | **Finishing** |
| Beginning work in process | | | |
| *Mixing Dept.:* All materials,<br>    30% complete for conversion costs | 10,000 | | |
| *Shaping Dept.:* All materials,<br>    60% complete for conversion costs | | 18,000 | |
| *Finishing Dept.·* All materials,<br>    45% complete for conversion costs | | | 5,000 |
| Started in process during the period | 90,000 | | |
| Transferred out | — | — | — |
| Completed and still on hand | 4,000 | 2,000 | 6,000 |
| Ending work in process | | | |
| *Mixing Dept.:* All materials,<br>    75% complete for conversion costs | 7,000 | | |
| *Shaping Dept.:* All materials,<br>    35% complete for conversion costs | | 8,000 | |
| *Finishing Dept.:* All materials,<br>    70% complete for conversion costs | | | 9,000 |

| Costs | **Mixing** | **Shaping** | **Finishing** |
|---|---|---|---|
| Beginning work in process | | | |
| Materials | $15,000 | — | — |
| From preceding department | | $ 9,620 | $11,630 |
| Labor | 8,075 | 13,954 | 6,531 |
| Overhead | 10,215 | 9,792 | 4,650 |
| Total | $33,290 | $33,366 | $22,811 |
| | | | |
| Added during the period | | | |
| Materials | $195,000 | — | — |
| Labor | 100,000 | $40,000 | $ 60,000 |
| Overhead | 90,000 | 35,000 | 45,000 |
| Total | $385,000 | $75,000 | $105,000 |

Using the average costing method, prepare a Cost of Production Report for (a) the Mixing Department, (b) the Shaping Department and (c) the Finishing Department.

## SOLUTION

(a)

*Mintz Corporation*
*Cost of Production Report, Mixing Department*
*Average Costing Method*

**Quantities**

| | | |
|---|---|---|
| Units in Process at Beginning (all materials,<br>    30% conversion costs) | 10,000 | |
| Units Started in Process | 90,000 | 100,000 |

| Units Transferred to Next Department (100,000 − 4,000 − 7,000) | 89,000 | |
|---|---|---|
| Units Completed and Still On Hand | 4,000 | |
| Units Still in Process (all materials, 75% conversion costs) | 7,000 | 100,000 |

| Equivalent Production | Materials | Conversion Costs |
|---|---|---|
| Units completed | | |
| Transferred to next dept. | 89,000 | 89,000 |
| Still on hand | 4,000 | 4,000 |
| Work in process, ending inventory | | |
| Materials | 7,000 | |
| Conversion costs (7,000 × 75%) | | 5,250 |
| Equivalent production | 100,000 | 98,250 |

| Costs to Be Accounted For | Total Cost | Unit Cost |
|---|---|---|
| Cost Added by Department | | |
| Work in Process, Beginning Inventory | | |
| Materials | $ 15,000 | |
| Labor | 8,075 | |
| Overhead | 10,215 | |
| Cost Added during the Period | | |
| Materials | 195,000 | $ 2.10 |
| Labor | 100,000 | 1.10 |
| Overhead | 90,000 | 1.02 |
| Total Costs to Be Accounted For | $418,290 | $ 4.22 |

| Costs Accounted For | | |
|---|---|---|
| Transferred to Next Department (89,000 × $4.22) | | $375,580 |
| Completed and On Hand (4,000 × $4.22) | | 16,880 |
| Work in Process, Ending Inventory | | |
| Materials (7,000 × $2.10) | $ 14,700 | |
| Labor (7,000 × 0.75 × $1.10) | 5,775 | |
| Overhead (7,000 × 0.75 × $1.02) | 5,355 | 25,830 |
| Total Costs Accounted For | | $418,290 |

**Computations**

*Unit costs:* Materials: ($15,000 + $195,000) ÷ 100,000 = $2.10
Labor: ($8,075 + $100,000) ÷ 98,250 = $1.10
Overhead: ($10,215 + $90,000) ÷ 98,250 = $1.02

(b)

*Mintz Corporation*
*Cost of Production Report, Shaping Department*
*Average Costing Method*

**Quantities**

| Units in Process at Beginning (all materials, 60% conversion costs) | 18,000 | |
|---|---|---|
| Units Transferred from Previous Department | 89,000 | 107,000 |

| | | |
|---|---|---|
| Units Transferred to Next Department | 97,000 | |
| Units Completed and Still On Hand | 2,000 | |
| Units Still in Process (all materials, 35% conversion costs) | 8,000 | 107,000 |

**Equivalent Production** (Conversion Costs Only)

| | |
|---|---|
| Units completed | |
|   Transferred to next dept. | 97,000 |
|   Still on hand | 2,000 |
| Work in process, ending inventory (8,000 × 35%) | 2,800 |
| Equivalent production | 101,800 |

| Costs to Be Accounted For | | Total Cost | Unit Cost |
|---|---|---|---|
| Cost from Preceding Department | | | |
|   Work in Process, Beginning Inventory | 18,000 | $ 9,620 | $0.5344 |
|   Transferred In during Period | 89,000 | 375,580 | |
|   Total Cost from Preceding Department | 107,000 | $385,200 | $3.6000 |
| | | | |
| Cost Added by Department | | | |
|   Work in Process, Beginning Inventory | | | |
|     Labor | | $ 13,954 | |
|     Overhead | | 9,792 | |
|   Cost Added during the Period | | | |
|     Labor | | 40,000 | $0.5300 |
|     Overhead | | 35,000 | 0.4400 |
|   Total Cost Added by Department | | $ 98,746 | $0.9700 |
| Total Cost to Be Accounted For | | $483,946 | $4.5700 |

| Costs Accounted For | | |
|---|---|---|
| Transferred to Finishing Department (97,000 × $4.57) | | $443,290 |
| Completed and On Hand (2,000 × $4.57) | | 9,140 |
| Work in Process, Ending Inventory | | |
|   Cost from Preceding Department (8,000 × $3.60) | $ 28,800 | |
|   Labor (8,000 × 0.35 × $0.53) | 1,484 | |
|   Overhead (8,000 × 0.35 × $0.44) | 1,232 | 31,516 |
| Total Costs Accounted For | | $483,946 |

**Computations**

*Unit costs:*  Labor: ($13,954 + $40,000) ÷ 101,800 = $0.53

           Overhead: ($9,792 + $35,000) ÷ 101,800 = $0.44

(c)

*Mintz Corporation*
*Cost of Production Report, Finishing Department*
*Average Costing Method*

**Quantities**

| | | |
|---|---|---|
| Units in Process at Beginning (all materials, 45% conversion costs) | 5,000 | |
| Units Transferred from Previous Department | 97,000 | 102,000 |

| | | |
|---|---|---|
| Units Transferred Out | 87,000 | |
| Units Completed and Still On Hand | 6,000 | |
| Units Still in Process (all materials, 70% conversion costs) | 9,000 | 102,000 |

**Equivalent Production** (Conversion Costs Only)

| | |
|---|---|
| Units completed | |
| Transferred to finished goods | 87,000 |
| Still on hand | 6,000 |
| Work in process, ending inventory (9,000 × 70%) | 6,300 |
| Equivalent production | 99,300 |

| Costs to Be Accounted For | | Total Cost | Unit Cost |
|---|---|---|---|
| Cost from Preceding Department | | | |
| Work in Process, Beginning Inventory | 5,000 | $ 11,630 | $ 2.326 |
| Transferred In during Period | 97,000 | 443,290 | |
| Total Cost from Preceding Department | 102,000 | $454,920 | $ 4.460 |
| Cost Added by Department | | | |
| Work in Process, Beginning Inventory | | | |
| Labor | | $ 6,531 | |
| Overhead | | 4,650 | |
| Cost Added during the Period | | | |
| Labor | | 60,000 | 0.670 |
| Overhead | | 45,000 | 0.500 |
| Total Cost Added by Department | | $116,181 | 1.170 |
| Total Cost to Be Accounted For | | $571,101 | $ 5.630 |

**Costs Accounted For**

| | | |
|---|---|---|
| Transferred to Finished Goods (87,000 × $5.63) | | $489,810 |
| Completed and On Hand (6,000 × $5.63) | | 33,780 |
| Work in Process, Ending Inventory | | |
| Cost from Preceding Department (9,000 × $4.46) | $ 40,140 | |
| Labor (9,000 × 0.70 × $0.67) | 4,221 | |
| Overhead (9,000 × 0.70 × $0.50) | 3,150 | 47,511 |
| Total Costs Accounted For | | $571,101 |

**Computations**

*Unit costs:*   Labor: $66,531 ÷ 99,300 = $0.67
                Overhead: $49,650 ÷ 99,300 = $0.50

**7.12    Cost of Production Report: FIFO.** Recompute Problem 7.11 using FIFO.

**SOLUTION**

(a)

*Mintz Corporation*
*Cost of Production Report, Mixing Department*
*FIFO Method*

**Quantities**

| | | |
|---|---:|---:|
| Units in Process at Beginning (all materials, 30% conversion costs) | 10,000 | |
| Units Started in Process | 90,000 | 100,000 |
| | | |
| Units Transferred to Next Department | 89,000 | |
| Units Completed and On Hand | 4,000 | |
| Units Still in Process (all materials, 75% conversion costs) | 7,000 | 100,000 |

| **Equivalent Production** | **Materials** | **Conversion Costs** |
|---|---:|---:|
| Completed units (transferred out and still on hand) | 93,000 | 93,000 |
| Less:  Beginning inventory | (10,000) | (10,000) |
| Started and finished this period | 83,000 | 83,000 |
| Add:  Work added to beginning inventory (materials 0; conversion costs 70%) | — | 7,000 |
| Add:  Units completed in ending inventory (materials, 100%; conversion costs, 75%) | 7,000 | 5,250 |
| | 90,000 | 95,250 |

| **Costs to Be Accounted For** | **Total Cost** | **Unit Cost** |
|---|---:|---:|
| Work in Process, Beginning Inventory | $ 33,290 | |
| Cost Added by Department | | |
| Materials | $195,000 | $2.166667 |
| Labor | 100,000 | 1.049869 |
| Overhead | 90,000 | .944881 |
| Total Cost Added | $385,000 | $4.161417 |
| Costs to Be Accounted For | $418,290 | |

**Costs Accounted For**

| | | |
|---|---:|---:|
| Transferred to Next Department | | |
| From Beginning Inventory | | |
|   Inventory Cost | $33,290 | |
|   Labor Added (10,000 × 0.70 × $1.049869) | 7,349 | |
|   Overhead Added (7,000 × $0.944881) | 6,614 | $ 47,253 |
| From Current Production | | |
|   Started and Finished (79,000 × $4.161417) | 328,752 | $ 376,005 |
| Completed and On Hand (4,000 × $4.161417) | | 16,646 |
| Work in Process, Ending Inventory | | |
|   Materials (7,000 × $2.166667) | $ 15,167 | |
|   Labor (7,000 × 0.75 × $1.049869) | 5,512 | |
|   Overhead (7,000 × 0.75 × $0.944881) | 4,960 | 25,639 |
| Total Costs Accounted for | | $ 418,290 |

**Computations**

*Unit costs:*

Materials: $195,000 ÷ 90,000 = $2.166667

Labor: $100,000 ÷ 95,250 = $1.049869

Overhead: $90,000 ÷ 95,250 = $0.944881

(b)

*Mintz Corporation*
**Cost of Production Report, Shaping Department**
*FIFO Method*

**Quantities**

| | | |
|---|---|---|
| Units in Process at Beginning (all materials, 60% conversion costs) | 18,000 | |
| Units Transferred from Preceding Department | 89,000 | 107,000 |
| | | |
| Units Transferred to Next Department | 97,000 | |
| Units Completed and On Hand | 2,000 | |
| Units Still in Process (all materials, 35% conversion costs) | 8,000 | 107,000 |

**Equivalent Production** (Conversion Costs Only)

| | |
|---|---|
| Units completed (transferred out and still on hand) | 99,000 |
| Less: Beginning inventory | (18,000) |
| Started and finished this period | 81,000 |
| Add: Work to complete beginning inventory (18,000 × 0.40) | 7,200 |
| Add: Units completed in ending inventory (8,000 × 0.35) | 2,800 |
| | 91,000 |

| Costs to Be Accounted For | Total Cost | Unit Cost |
|---|---|---|
| Work in Process, Beginning Inventory | $ 33,366 | |
| | | |
| Cost from Preceding Department | | |
| Transferred In during Month (89,000) | $376,005 | $4.22477 |
| | | |
| Cost Added by Department | | |
| Labor | $ 40,000 | $0.43956 |
| Overhead | 35,000 | 0.38462 |
| Total Cost Added | $ 75,000 | $0.82418 |
| Total Costs to Be Accounted For | $484,371 | $5.04895 |

**Costs Accounted For**

| | | | |
|---|---|---|---|
| Transferred to Next Department | | | |
| From Beginning Inventory | | | |
| Inventory Cost | $33,366 | | |
| Labor Added | | | |
| (18,000 × 0.40 × $0.43956) | 3,165 | | |
| Overhead Added | | | |
| (18,000 × 0.40 × $0.38462) | 2,769 | $ 39,300 | |
| | | | |
| From Current Production | | | |
| Started and Finished (79,000 × $5.04895) | | 398,867 | $438,167 |

| Units Completed and On Hand | | |
|---|---|---|
| (2,000 × $5.04895) | | $ 10,098 |
| Work in Process, Ending Inventory | | |
| Cost from Preceding Department | | |
| (8,000 × $4.22477) | $ 33,798 | |
| Labor (8,000 × 0.35 × $0.43956) | 1,231 | |
| Overhead (8,000 × 0.35 × $0.38462) | 1,077 | 36,106 |
| Total Costs Accounted For | | $484,371 |

### Computations

*Unit costs:*   Labor: $40,000 ÷ 91,000 = $0.43956

Overhead: $35,000 ÷ 91,000 = $0.38462

(c)

**Mintz Corporation**
**Cost of Production Report, Finishing Department**
**FIFO Method**

### Quantities

| | | |
|---|---|---|
| Units in Process at Beginning | | |
| (all materials; 45% conversion costs) | 5,000 | |
| Units Transferred from Preceding Department | 97,000 | 102,000 |
| | | |
| Units Transferred Out | 87,000 | |
| Units Completed and On Hand | 6,000 | |
| Units Still in Process | | |
| (all materials, 70% conversion costs) | 9,000 | 102,000 |

### Equivalent Production (Conversion Costs Only)

| | |
|---|---|
| Completed units (transferred out and still on hand) | 93,000 |
| Less: Beginning inventory | (5,000) |
| | 88,000 |
| Add: Work added to beginning inventory (5,000 × 0.55) | 2,750 |
| Add: Work completed on ending inventory (9,000 × 0.70) | 6,300 |
| | 97,050 |

| Costs to Be Accounted For | Total Cost | Unit Cost |
|---|---|---|
| Work in Process, Beginning Inventory | $ 22,811 | |
| Cost from Preceding Department | | |
| Transferred In during Month (97,000) | $438,167 | $4.51718 |
| Cost Added by Department | | |
| Labor | $ 60,000 | $ .61824 |
| Overhead | 45,000 | .46368 |
| Total Cost Added | $105,000 | $1.08192 |
| Total Costs to Be Accounted For | $565,978 | $5.59910 |

**Costs Accounted For**

Transferred to Finished Goods

From Beginning Inventory

| | | |
|---|---|---|
| Inventory Cost | $22,811 | |
| Labor Added (5,000 × 0.55 × $0.61824) | 1,700 | |
| Overhead Added (5,000 × 0.55 × $0.46368) | 1,275 | $ 25,786 |

From Current Production

| | | |
|---|---|---|
| Started and Finished (82,000 × $5.59910) | 459,126 | $484,912 |

| | | |
|---|---|---|
| Units Completed and On Hand (6,000 × $5.59910) | | 33,595 |
| Work in Process, Ending Inventory | | |
| Cost from Preceding Department (9,000 × $4.51718) | $ 40,655 | |
| Labor (9,000 × 0.70 × $0.61824) | 3,895 | |
| Overhead (9,000 × 0.70 × $0.46368) | 2,921 | 47,471 |
| Total Costs Accounted For | | $565,978 |

**Computations**

*Unit Costs:*

Labor: $60,000 ÷ 97,050 = $0.61824

Overhead: $45,000 ÷ 97,050 = $0.46368

**• 7.13  Cost of Production Report: Average Costing, FIFO.**  Margie Corporation manufactures toy plastic frogs and uses a process cost system to account for the costs.  Production is done in two departments with the average costing method being used in the first department and the FIFO cost method in the second.  The following information is available for you to prepare a cost of production report for (*a*) Department 1 and (*b*) Department 2.

| Units | Dept. 1 | Dept. 2 |
|---|---|---|
| Beginning work in process | | |
| Dept. 1: All materials, | | |
| 40% complete for conversion costs | 7,000 | |
| Dept. 2: All materials, | | |
| 80% complete for conversion costs | | 4,000 |
| Started in process during the period | 80,000 | |
| Received from Dept. 1 | — | 74,000 |
| Transferred to finished goods | — | 70,000 |
| Completed and still on hand | — | 5,000 |
| Ending work in process | | |
| Dept. 1: All materials, | | |
| 90% complete for conversion costs | 13,000 | |
| Dept. 2: All materials, | | |
| 25% complete for conversion costs | | 3,000 |

| Costs | Dept. 1 | Dept. 2 |
|---|---|---|
| Beginning work in process | | |
| Materials | $ 11,000 | $ 0 |
| Labor | 2,000 | 5,000 |
| Overhead | 7,000 | 6,000 |
| | $ 20,000 | $ 11,000 |
| | | |
| Added during the period | | |
| Materials | $300,000 | $ 0 |
| Labor | 150,000 | 90,000 |
| Overhead | 200,000 | 130,000 |
| | $650,000 | $220,000 |

## SOLUTION

(a)

*Margie Corporation*
*Cost of Production Report, Department 1*
*Average Costing Method*

**Quantities**

| | | |
|---|---|---|
| Units in Process at Beginning (all materials, 40% conversion costs) | 7,000 | |
| Units Started in Process | 80,000 | 87,000 |
| Units Transferred to Department 2 | 74,000 | |
| Units Still in Process (all materials, 90% conversion costs) | 13,000 | 87,000 |

| Equivalent Production | Materials | Conversion Costs |
|---|---|---|
| Units completed | 74,000 | 74,000 |
| Work in process, ending inventory | | |
| Materials | 13,000 | |
| Conversion costs (13,000 × 90%) | | 11,700 |
| Equivalent production | 87,000 | 85,700 |

| Costs to Be Accounted For | Total Cost | Unit Cost |
|---|---|---|
| Costs Added by Department | | |
| Work in Process, Beginning Inventory | | |
| Materials | $ 11,000 | |
| Labor | 2,000 | |
| Overhead | 7,000 | |
| Costs Added during the Period | | |
| Materials | 300,000 | $3.574712 |
| Labor | 150,000 | 1.773628 |
| Overhead | 200,000 | 2.415402 |
| Total Costs to Be Accounted For | $670,000 | $7.763742 |

**Costs Accounted For**

| | | |
|---|---:|---:|
| Transferred to Next Department (74,000 × $7.763742) | | $ 574,517 |
| Work in Process, Ending Inventory | | |
| Materials (13,000 × $3.574712) | $ 46,471 | |
| Labor (13,000 × 90% × $1.773628) | 20,752 | |
| Overhead (13,000 × 90% × $2.415402) | 28,260 | 95,483 |
| Total Costs Accounted For | | $ 670,000 |

**Computations**

*Unit Costs:*  Materials: ($11,000 + $300,000) ÷ 87,000 = $3.574712
Labor: ($2,000 + $150,000) ÷ 85,700 = $1.773628
Overhead: ($7,000 + $200,000) ÷ 85,700 = $2.415402

(b)

*Margie Corporation*
*Cost of Production Report, Department 2*
*FIFO Method*

**Quantities**

| | | |
|---|---:|---:|
| Units in Process at Beginning (all materials, 80% conversion costs) | 4,000 | |
| Units Received from Preceding Department | 74,000 | 78,000 |
| Units Transferred to Finished Goods | 70,000 | |
| Units Still On Hand | 5,000 | |
| Units Still in Process (all materials; 25% conversion costs) | 3,000 | 78,000 |

**Equivalent Production** (Conversion Costs Only)

| | |
|---|---:|
| Completed units (transferred out and still on hand) | 75,000 |
| Less: Beginning inventory | (4,000) |
| Units started and completed | 71,000 |
| Add: Work added to beginning inventory (4,000 × 20%) | 800 |
| Add: Work completed on ending inventory (3,000 × 25%) | 750 |
| Equivalent production | 72,550 |

| Costs to Be Accounted For | Total Cost | Unit Cost |
|---|---:|---:|
| Work in Process, Beginning Inventory | $ 11,000 | |
| Costs from Preceding Department | | |
| Transferred In from Dept. 1 (74,000) | $574,517 | $ 7.763742 |
| Costs Added During the Period | | |
| Labor | $ 90,000 | $ 1.240524 |
| Overhead | 130,000 | 1.791867 |
| Total Costs Added | $220,000 | $ 3.032391 |
| Total Costs to Be Accounted For | $805,517 | $10.796133 |

**Costs Accounted For**

| | | |
|---|---:|---:|
| Transferred to Next Department | | |
| From Beginning Inventory | | |
| Inventory Cost | $11,000 | |
| Labor Added (20% × 4,000 × $1.240524) | 992 | |
| Overhead Added (20% × 4,000 × $1.791867) | 1,434 | $ 13,426 |

From Current Production
 Units Started and Finished
  (66,000 × $10.796133)        712,545  $ 725,971
 Completed and On Hand (5,000 × $10.796133)       53,981
Work in Process, Ending Inventory
 Adjusted Cost from Preceding Department
  (3,000 × $7.763742)         $ 23,291
 Labor (3,000 × 25% × $1.240524)      930
 Overhead (3,000 × 25% × $1.791867)    1,344   25,565
Total Costs Accounted For           $ 805,517

**Computations**
*Unit Costs:* Labor: $90,000 ÷ 72,550 = $1.240524
     Overhead: $130,000 ÷ 72,550 = $1.791867

# Chapter 8

# Process Costs II

## 8.1 INTRODUCTION

The basic procedures associated with process cost accumulation were described in Chapter 7. This chapter elaborates on that discussion by presenting specific methods for treating the various components in a process cost system.

## 8.2 ADDITIONAL MATERIALS

While in many cases all materials are introduced at the beginning of the process, it is sometimes necessary to include additional materials in departments subsequent to the first. In such instances, there are two possible effects on units and related costs:

(1) The number of final units *remains the same while the unit cost increases*. In this case, the treatment of the additional materials cost is identical to that for the inclusion of all materials in the first department (i.e. it is included in "Cost Added by Department"; that total is divided by the appropriate equivalent units figure to derive the periodic unit cost).

(2) The number of final units *increases* while unit cost *decreases*. When this occurs, an adjustment of the preceding department's unit cost becomes necessary, because the same total cost will be allocated over a greater number of units.

### EXAMPLE 1

Assume the following information for Department 2:

| | |
|---|---|
| Costs transferred in from Dept. 1 | $50,000 |
| Units transferred in from Dept. 1 | 20,000 |
| Additional units put into process in Dept. 2 | 5,000 |

The preceding department's unit cost to be used in Department 2 is computed as follows:

$50,000 (cost transferred in) ÷ 25,000 units = $2 per unit

## 8.3 SPOILED UNITS (GOODS)

Goods that do not meet production standards and are either sold for their salvage value or discarded are called spoiled goods. When spoiled goods are discovered, they are immediately taken out of production and no further work is performed on them. The amount of spoilage for a period can be considered either normal or abnormal.

*Normal.* Spoilage that results from an efficient production process is called normal spoilage. It is the unavoidable cost of producing good units.

*Abnormal.* Spoilage that exceeds what is considered normal for a particular production process is called abnormal spoilage. It is controllable and results from inefficient operations.

## 8.4  FLOW OF UNITS—QUANTITIES

The equation presented in Section 7.4 for the flow of units must now be modified to provide for the addition of materials after the first department and the possibility of spoiled units, as follows:

(1) When materials are added after the first department and *increase the* number of units for the department, they are accounted for in a separate category captioned "Additional Units Put into Process" on the left side of the equation.

(2) If units are spoiled during production, they are accounted for on the right side of the equation under the caption "Spoiled units."   The complete equation is

$$
\left.
\begin{aligned}
&\text{Units in process at beginning} \\
+\ &\text{Units started in process or} \\
&\quad\text{transferred in} \\
+\ &\text{Additional units put into process}
\end{aligned}
\right\}
=
\left\{
\begin{aligned}
&\text{Units transferred out} \\
+\ &\text{Units still on hand} \\
+\ &\text{Units still in process} \\
+\ &\text{Spoiled units}
\end{aligned}
\right.
$$

(3) A breakdown between abnormal and normal is not necessary because only units are being accounted for.

## EXAMPLE 2

Assume the following information for the Abel Corporation:

|  | Units | |
|---|---|---|
|  | **Dept. 1** | **Dept. 2** |
| Beginning work in process | 10,000 | 15,000 |
| Started in process | 40,000 | — |
| Transferred in from Dept. 1 | — | 42,000 |
| Additional units added to production | — | 5,000 |
| Units transferred out | 42,000 | ? |
| Spoiled units | 2,000 | 7,000 |
| Units still on hand | 5,000 | 2,000 |
| Units still in process | 1,000 | 0 |

The quantity schedules for the above data should be prepared as follows:

### Department 1

| | | |
|---|---|---|
| Units in process at beginning | 10,000 | |
| Units started in process | 40,000 | 50,000 |
| | | |
| Units transferred out | 42,000 | |
| Units still on hand | 5,000 | |
| Spoiled units | 2,000 | |
| Units still in process | 1,000 | 50,000 |

### Department 2

| | | |
|---|---|---|
| Units in process at beginning | 15,000 | |
| Units transferred in from Dept. 1 | 42,000 | |
| Additional units started in production | 5,000 | 62,000 |

|  |  |  |
|---|---|---|
| Units transferred out | 53,000* | |
| Units still on hand | 2,000 | |
| Spoiled units | 7,000 | 62,000 |

*Computation of units transferred out:*

|  |  |  |
|---|---|---|
| Total to account for | | 62,000 |
| Less: Units still on hand | 2,000 | |
| Spoiled units | 7,000 | 9,000 |
| Units transferred out | | 53,000 |

## 8.5　SPOILED (LOST) UNIT COMPUTATIONS—FIRST DEPARTMENT

Spoiled units in a process cost system may be handled using either of the following methods.

### Method 1

This method is commonly referred to as the "theory of neglect" because spoiled units are considered as *never* having been put into production, regardless of the amount of work performed on them. Since spoiled units are ignored in the computation of equivalent units, costs for the period are divided by fewer equivalent units, which increases the cost per unit. Cost allocation to goods completed and goods still in process is computed using the higher unit cost, so that spoilage costs are automatically spread over all good units.

The advantage of this method is its simplicity. The main disadvantage is that it is inaccurate if work-in-process inventories exist or if materials, conversion costs, and spoilage costs are not incurred evenly throughout the production process. In addition, units that are still in process are charged with spoilage costs irrespective of whether they have been inspected.

### Method 2

Spoiled units are considered to be part of production and are included in the computation of equivalent production up to the point at which they are removed from production (usually at the quality control inspection point).

For example, if 500 spoiled units are removed 60% of the way through production and both materials and conversion costs are added evenly throughout the production process, equivalent production would include 300 spoiled units (from $500 \times 60\%$) in addition to the good units. The cost of spoiled units is calculated separately and is allocated to both work in process and completed units or, if work in process has not yet reached the inspection point, to completed units only.

### EXAMPLE 3

Assume the following for GPB Corporation:

(1)　Materials are added at the beginning of the process.

(2)　Conversion costs are added evenly.

(3)　Inspection takes place when goods are 40% complete.

|  | Units |
|---|---|
| Beginning work in process (all materials; 25% complete as to conversion costs) | 7,000 |
| Received from preceding department | 18,000 |
| Transferred to finished goods | 19,000 |

Ending work in process (all materials;
     60% complete as to conversion costs)     4,000

Spoiled units
    Normal                                1,000
    Abnormal                            1,000

*Method 1.* Spoiled units are ignored for computation (theory of neglect). Under the FIFO method, the equivalent production schedule is as follows:

| Equivalent Production | Materials | Conversion Costs |
|---|---|---|
| Units completed and transferred | 19,000 | 19,000 |
| Less: Beginning work in process | ⟨7,000⟩ | ⟨7,000⟩ |
| Units started and completed | 12,000 | 12,000 |
| Add: Work needed to complete beginning work in process | | |
|     Materials | 0 | |
|     Conversion costs (7,000 × 75%) | | 5,250 |
| Add: Ending work in process | | |
|     Materials | 4,000 | |
|     Conversion costs (4,000 × 60%) | | 2,400 |
| Equivalent production | 16,000 | 19,650 |

*Method 2.* Spoiled units are included in the computation of equivalent units. Under the FIFO method, the equivalent production schedule is as follows:

| Equivalent Production | Materials | Conversion Costs |
|---|---|---|
| Units completed and transferred | 19,000 | 19,000 |
| Less: Beginning work in process | ⟨7,000⟩ | ⟨7,000⟩ |
| Units started and completed | 12,000 | 12,000 |
| Add: Work needed to complete beginning work in process | | |
|     Materials | 0 | |
|     Conversion costs (7,000 × 75%) | | 5,250 |
| Add: Ending work in process | | |
|     Materials | 4,000 | |
|     Conversion costs (4,000 × 60%) | | 2,400 |
| Add: Spoiled units | | |
|     Materials (100% complete) | 2,000 | |
|     Conversion costs [2,000 × 40% (the point of inspection)] | | 800 |
| Equivalent production | 18,000 | 20,450 |

## EXAMPLE 4

For the following data, assume materials are added at the beginning of the process and conversion costs are incurred evenly throughout the period. Spoilage up to 500 units is considered normal for the production process.

**Units**

| | |
|---|---:|
| Work in process, January 1 | |
|     (100% complete as to materials; | |
|         80% complete as to labor and overhead) | 1,500 |
| Put into process in January | 9,000 |
| Total | 10,500 |
| | |
| Transferred to finished goods | 8,000 |
| Work in process, December 31 | |
|     (100% complete as to materials; | |
|         50% complete as to labor and overhead) | 2,000 |
| Spoiled units (lost at beginning; | |
|     materials cost included) | 500 |
| Total | 10,500 |

**Costs to Be Accounted For**

| | | |
|---|---:|---:|
| Work in Process, January 1 | | |
|     Materials | $ 1,000 | |
|     Labor | 1,400 | |
|     Overhead | 600 | $ 3,000 |
| Current Costs | | |
|     Materials | $11,000 | |
|     Labor | 8,500 | |
|     Overhead | 4,800 | 24,300 |
| Total | | $27,300 |

Under the cost accounting system used, costs incurred on spoiled units are absorbed by the remaining units (theory of neglect). Quality control inspection takes place at the end of production. Discovery of the 500 spoiled units occurred on the assembly line, before the inspection point; no spoiled units were discovered at the inspection point.

The respective cost of production reports under the (a) average method and (b) FIFO method are as follows.

(a)
### Cost of Production Report
### Average Costing Method

**Quantities**

| | | |
|---|---:|---:|
| Work in Process, January 1 | 1,500 | |
| Units Started in Process | 9,000 | 10,500 |
| | | |
| Units Transferred to Finished Goods | 8,000 | |
| Work in Process, December 31 | 2,000 | |
| Spoiled Units | 500 | 10,500 |

| Equivalent Production | Materials | Conversion Costs |
|---|---:|---:|
| Units completed and transferred | 8,000 | 8,000 |
| Work in process, December 31 | | |
|     Materials (100% × 2,000) | 2,000 | |
|     Conversion costs (50% × 2,000) | | 1,000 |
| Equivalent production | 10,000 | 9,000 |

| Costs to Account For | Total Cost | Unit Cost |
|---|---|---|
| Costs Added by Department: | | |
| Work in Process, January 1 | | |
|    Materials | $ 1,000 | |
|    Labor | 1,400 | |
|    Overhead | 600 | |
| Costs Added during the Period | | |
|    Materials | 11,000 | $1.20 (a) |
|    Labor | 8,500 | 1.10 (b) |
|    Overhead | 4,800 | 0.60 (c) |
| Total Costs to Account For | $27,300 | $2.90 |

| Costs Accounted For | | |
|---|---|---|
| Transferred to Finished Goods | | |
|    (8,000 × $2.90) | | $23,200 |
| Work in Process, December 31 | | |
|    Materials (2,000 × $1.20) | $ 2,400 | |
|    Labor (2,000 × 50% × $1.10) | 1,100 | |
|    Overhead (2,000 × 50% × $0.60) | 600 | 4,100 |
| Total Costs Accounted For | | $27,300 |

**Computations**

(a)   Materials: ($1,000 + $11,000) ÷ 10,000 = $1.20

(b)   Labor: ($1,400 + $8,500) ÷ 9,000 = $1.10

(c)   Overhead: ($600 + $4,800) ÷ 9,000 = $0.60

(b)

*Cost of Production Report*
*FIFO Method*

**Quantities**

| | | |
|---|---|---|
| Work in Process, January 1 | 1,500 | |
| Units Started in Process | 9,000 | 10,500 |
| | | |
| Units Transferred to Finished Goods | 8,000 | |
| Work in Process, December 31 | 2,000 | |
| Spoiled Units | 500 | 10,500 |

| Equivalent Production | Materials | Conversion Costs |
|---|---|---|
| Units completed and transferred | 8,000 | 8,000 |
| Less: Work in process, January 1 | ⟨1,500⟩ | ⟨1,500⟩ |
| Units started and completed | 6,500 | 6,500 |
| Amount needed to complete beginning work in process | | |
|    Conversion costs (1,500 × 20%) | | 300 |
| Work in process, December 31 | | |
|    Materials (100% × 2,000) | 2,000 | |
|    Conversion costs (50% × 2,000) | | 1,000 |
| Equivalent production | 8,500 | 7,800 |

| Costs to Account For | Total Cost | Unit Cost |
|---|---|---|
| Work in Process, January 1 | $ 3,000 | |
| Cost Added during the Period | | |
| Materials | $11,000 | $1.29412 (a) |
| Labor | 8,500 | 1.08974 (b) |
| Overhead | 4,800 | 0.61538 (c) |
| Total Costs Added | $24,300 | $2.99924 |
| Total Costs to Account For | $27,300 | |

| Costs Accounted For | | |
|---|---|---|
| Transferred to Finished Goods | | |
| From Work in Process, January 1 | | |
| Inventory Cost | $3,000 | |
| Labor (1,500 × 20% × $1.08974) | 327 | |
| Overhead (1,500 × 20% × $0.61538) | 185 | $ 3,512 |
| From Current Production (6,500 × $2.99924) | | 19,495 |
| Total Transferred | | $23,007 |
| Work in Process, December 31 | | |
| Materials (2,000 × $1.29412) | $2,588 | |
| Labor (2,000 × 50% × $1.08974) | 1,090 | |
| Overhead (2,000 × 50% × $0.61538) | 615 | 4,293 |
| Total Costs Accounted For | | $27,300 |

**Computations**

(a)  Materials: ($11,000 ÷ 8,500) = $1.29412

(b)  Labor: ($8,500 ÷ 7,800) = $1.08974

(c)  Overhead: ($4,800 ÷ 7,800) = $0.61538

## EXAMPLE 5

With reference to the data in Example 4, if spoiled units are considered to be part of production, Method 2 is used to prepare the cost of production report under the (a) average method and (b) FIFO method as follows:

(a)

*Cost of Production Report*
*Average Costing Method*

| Quantities | | |
|---|---|---|
| Work in Process, January 1 | 1,500 | |
| Units Started in Process | 9,000 | 10,500 |
| Units Transferred to Finished Goods | 8,000 | |
| Work in Process, December 31 | 2,000 | |
| Spoiled Units | 500 | 10,500 |

| Equivalent Production | Materials | Conversion Costs |
|---|---|---|
| Units completed and transferred | 8,000 | 8,000 |
| Work in process, December 31 | | |
| Materials (2,000 × 100%) | 2,000 | |
| Conversion costs (2,000 × 50%) | | 1,000 |
| Spoiled units | 500 | |
| Equivalent production | 10,500 | 9,000 |

| Costs to Account For | Total Cost | Unit Cost |
|---|---|---|
| Costs Added by Department | | |
| Work in Process, January 1 | | |
| Materials | $ 1,000 | |
| Labor | 1,400 | |
| Overhead | 600 | |
| Costs Added during Period | | |
| Materials | 11,000 | $1.14286 (a) |
| Labor | 8,500 | 1.10000 (b) |
| Overhead | 4,800 | 0.60000 (c) |
| Total Costs to Account For | $27,300 | $2.84286 |

| Costs Accounted For | | |
|---|---|---|
| Transferred to Finished Goods | | |
| (8,000 × $2.84286) | $22,743 | |
| Normal Spoilage | 571 (d) | $23,314 |
| Work in Process, December 31 | | |
| Materials (2,000 × $1.14286) | $ 2,286 | |
| Labor (2,000 × 50% × $1.10000) | 1,100 | |
| Overhead (2,000 × 50% × $0.60000) | 600 | 3,986 |
| Total Costs Accounted For | | $27,300 |

**Computations**

(a)  Materials: ($1,000 + $11,000) ÷ 10,500 = $1.14286

(b)  Labor: ($1,400 + $8,500) ÷ 9,000 = $1.10000

(c)  Overhead: ($600 + $4,800) ÷ 9,000 = $0.60000

(d)  Spoilage: 500 × $1.14286 = $571

(b)
*Cost of Production Report*
*FIFO Method*

**Quantities**

| | | |
|---|---|---|
| Work in Process, January 1 | 1,500 | |
| Units Started in Process | 9,000 | 10,500 |
| Units Transferred to Finished Goods | 8,000 | |
| Work in Process, December 31 | 2,000 | |
| Spoiled Units | 500 | 10,500 |

Do we have to Memorize a Cost of Prod. Report?



| t Production | Materials | Conversion Costs |
|---|---|---|
| npleted and transferred | 8,000 | 8,000 |
| rk in process, January 1 | ⟨1,500⟩ | ⟨1,500⟩ |
| Units started and completed | 6,500 | 6,500 |
| Amount needed to complete beginning work in process | | |
| Conversion costs (1,500 × 20%) | | 300 |
| Work in process, December 31 | | |
| Materials (2,000 × 100%) | 2,000 | |
| Conversion costs (2,000 × 50%) | | 1,000 |
| Spoiled units | 500 | |
| Equivalent production | 9,000 | 7,800 |

| Costs to Account For | Total Cost | Unit Cost |
|---|---|---|
| Work in Process, January 1 | $ 3,000 | |
| Costs Added during the Period | | |
| Materials | $11,000 | $1.22222 (a) |
| Labor | 8,500 | 1.08974 (b) |
| Overhead | 4,800 | 0.61538 (c) |
| Total Costs Added | $24,300 | $2.92734 |
| Total Costs to Account For | $27,300 | |

| Costs Accounted For | | |
|---|---|---|
| Transferred to Finished Goods | | |
| From Work in Process, January 1 | | |
| Inventory Cost | $ 3,000 | |
| Labor (1,500 × 20% × $1.08974) | 327 | |
| Overhead (1,500 × 20% × $0.61538) | 185 | $ 3,512 |
| From Current Production (6,500 × $2.92734) | $19,028 | |
| Normal Spoilage | 611 (d) | 19,639 |
| Total Transferred | | $23,151 |
| Work in Process, December 31 | | |
| Materials (2,000 × $1.22222) | $ 2,444 | |
| Labor (2,000 × 50% × $1.08974) | 1,090 | |
| Overhead (2,000 × 50% × $0.61538) | 615 | 4,149 |
| Total Costs Accounted For | | $27,300 |

**Computations**

(a) Materials: ($11,000 ÷ 9,000) = $1.22222

(b) Labor: ($8,500 ÷ 7,800) = $1.08974

(c) Overhead: ($4,800 ÷ 7,800) = $0.61538

(d) Spoilage: 500 × $1.22222 = $611

## 8.6 SPOILED (LOST) UNIT COMPUTATIONS—AFTER FIRST DEPARTMENT

### Method 1 (Theory of Neglect)

Units spoiled *after* the first department cannot be completely ignored because they have costs assigned to them from preceding department(s). A spoiled unit cost must be computed for the costs attributed to the units by preceding departments.

$$\text{Total spoilage cost} = \text{Spoiled units} \times \text{Transferred-in unit costs}$$
$$\text{Spoiled unit cost} = \text{Total spoilage cost} \div \text{Remaining good units}$$

The spoiled unit cost is added to the unit cost of producing good units for the period. The result spreads the loss over the remaining good units.

## Method 2

As in Method 1, transferred-in costs of the spoiled units are included to determine the spoilage cost. However, an *additional* amount of spoilage cost must be calculated as follows:

$$\begin{array}{l}\text{Equivalent units spoiled}\\\text{(based on degree of completion}\\\text{when spoiled units are removed}\\\text{from production)}\end{array} \times \begin{array}{l}\text{Unit cost (in department in which}\\\text{spoilage occurred) of materials}\\\text{and/or conversion costs}\end{array}$$

Both methods treat costs from preceding departments in basically the same way. However, Method 2 is preferred because it includes costs added to the spoiled units (by the department in which the spoilage occurred) while Method 1 does not.

## EXAMPLE 6

Assume the following for Pauled Company:

|                        | Dept. 1       | Dept. 2        |
|------------------------|---------------|----------------|
| Spoiled units          | 2,000         | 1,000          |
| Addition of costs      |               |                |
|   Materials            | Beginning     |                |
|   Conversion costs     | Evenly        | Evenly         |
| Transferred-out costs  | $300,000      | $550,000       |
| Transferred-out units  | 20,500        | 26,000         |
| Unit costs, added:     |               |                |
|   Materials            | $3.75         |                |
|   Labor                | $7.70         | $3.20          |
|   Overhead             | $1.50         | $1.75          |
| ↘Point of inspection   | End of process | 60% of process |

The computation of total spoilage costs under the preferred method—Method 2—is as follows.
Spoilage costs for Department 1 are

$$\begin{array}{lr}\text{Materials: } (2,000 \times 100\%) \times \$3.75 = & \$\ 7,500 \\ \text{Labor: } \quad (2,000 \times 100\%) \times \$7.70 = & 15,400 \\ \text{Overhead: } (2,000 \times 100\%) \times \$1.50 = & \underline{3,000} \\ \text{Total spoilage cost} \hspace{2.5cm} = & \underline{\$25,900}\end{array}$$

or

$$\text{Total spoilage cost} = 2,000 \times \$12.95 = \$25,900$$

since inspection is at the end of the process.
Spoilage costs for Department 2 are

$$\begin{array}{lr}\text{Transferred-in spoilage costs} & \\ \quad [1,000 \times (\$300,000 \div 20,500)] & \$14,634 \\ \text{Added by department} & \\ \quad \text{Labor } (1,000 \times 60\%) \times \$3.20 & 1,920 \\ \quad \text{Overhead } (1,000 \times 60\%) \times 1.75 & \underline{1,050} \\ \text{Total spoilage cost} & \underline{\$17,604}\end{array}$$

## Allocation of Spoilage Costs

One of the primary advantages of Method 2 is that it permits us to allocate spoilage costs to normal and abnormal spoilage on the costs accounted for schedule. Abnormal spoilage costs are a period cost and should be removed from the work-in-process account and listed separately. Normal spoilage costs, on the other hand, are included in the cost of producing good units. Spoilage costs are allocated between normal and abnormal spoilage by using either of the following methods. (The methods differ in technique only and will therefore result in identical answers.)

*Method 1.* The cost associated with each type of spoilage is based on a ratio of type of spoilage to total spoilage (in units).

$$\text{Normal spoilage cost} = \text{Total spoilage cost} \times \frac{\text{Normal spoiled units}}{\text{Total spoiled units}}$$

$$\text{Abnormal spoilage cost} = \text{Total spoilage cost} \times \frac{\text{Abnormal spoiled units}}{\text{Total spoiled units}}$$

*Method 2.* Total spoilage cost can also be allocated by using the spoilage unit cost. The equations are as follows:

$$\text{Spoilage unit cost} = \text{Total spoilage cost} \div \text{Total spoiled units}$$

$$\text{Normal spoilage cost} = \text{Spoilage unit cost} \times \text{Normal spoiled units}$$

$$\text{Abnormal spoilage cost} = \text{Spoilage unit cost} \times \text{Abnormal spoiled units}$$

## Further Allocation of Normal Spoilage Cost

Normal spoilage costs may have to be allocated between work-in-process units and/or completed units. Under FIFO costing, an attempt should be made to identify any spoiled units from beginning work in process. (To simplify matters, we will assume in our example and solved problems that spoilage occurred only in units started and completed and/or in ending work in process.) Allocation to ending work in process is acceptable when ending work in process is at or beyond the inspection stage. The allocation of normal spoilage cost to all three areas is computed as follows.

$$\text{Total units} = \text{Beginning work-in-process units}$$
$$+ \text{ Started and completed units}$$
$$+ \text{ Ending work-in-process units}$$

To beginning work in process:

$$\text{Normal spoilage cost} \times \frac{\text{Beginning work-in-process units}}{\text{Total units}}$$

To units started and completed:

$$\text{Normal spoilage cost} \times \frac{\text{Units started and completed}}{\text{Total units}}$$

To ending work in process:

$$\text{Normal spoilage cost} \times \frac{\text{Ending work-in-process units}}{\text{Total units}}$$

## EXAMPLE 7

Assume the following for V&A Company:

| | |
|---|---|
| Total spoilage cost | $37,578 |
| Units | |
|    Units started and completed | 19,000 |
|    Work in process (all materials; | |
|       60% conversion costs) | 4,000 |
|    Spoilage (40% at inspection point) | |
|       Normal | 1,000 |
|       Abnormal | 1,000 |
|    Addition of costs | |
|       Materials | Beginning |
|       Conversion costs | Evenly |

The allocation of total spoilage cost to normal and abnormal spoilage is computed as follows:

*Method 1*

Normal spoilage cost:   $37,578 \times (1,000 \div 2,000) = \$18,789$

Abnormal spoilage cost: $37,578 \times (1,000 \div 2,000) = \$18,789$

*Method 2*

Spoilage unit cost:   $37,578 \div 2,000 = \$18.789$

Normal spoilage cost:   $18.789 \times 1,000 = \$18,789$

Abnormal spoilage cost: $18.789 \times 1,000 = \$18,789$

Further allocation of normal spoilage cost is as follows:

To completed units:   $18,789 \times (19,000 \div 23,000) = \$15,521$

To ending work in process: $18,789 \times (4,000 \div 23,000) = \$3,268$

# *Summary*

(1) Production completed and on hand in a processing department is considered as _____.

(2) Spoilage that occurs under efficient operating conditions and is ordinarily uncontrollable is called _____.

(3) Spoilage that occurs under inefficient operating conditions and is ordinarily controllable is called _____.

(4) The two methods of costing opening work in process inventory in continuous processing manufacturing are the _____ method and the _____ method.

(5) When materials are added in a department after the first department the number of units may increase or the unit cost may increase.   (a) True, (b) false.

(6) When FIFO costing is used, the opening work in process inventory is broken down into its components, as in average costing.   (a) True, (b) false.

(7) When average costing is used, the opening inventory costs are (a) kept separate from the costs for the new period, (b) added to the costs of the new period, (c) subtracted from the costs of the new period, (d) taken as a percentage of cost of the new period.

(8) When FIFO costing is used, the opening inventory costs are (a) kept separate from the costs of the new period, (b) added to the new costs, (c) subtracted from the new costs, (d) averaged with other costs to arrive at total cost.

(9) A disadvantage of FIFO costing is that (a) the first units produced cannot be distinguished from later production, (b) several unit costs are used at the same time, (c) the units have to be kept separate, (d) the shipping costs are higher.

(10) When materials are added in a department after the first and the volume of production is increased, the unit costs for the preceding department are (a) increased, (b) unchanged, (c) decreased, (d) not applicable.

*Answers:* (1) Finished goods inventory; (2) normal spoilage; (3) abnormal spoilage; (4) average costing, FIFO; (5) *a*; (6) *b*; (7) *b*; (8) *a*; (9) *b*; (10) *c*.

# Solved Problems

**8.1   Unit Costs.** The Slavin Corporation uses a process cost system. On the basis of the following data, compute the preceding department's unit cost to be used in Department B.

| | |
|---|---|
| Costs transferred in from Dept. A | $180,000 |
| Units transferred in from Dept. A | 35,000 |
| Additional units put into process in Dept. B | 10,000 |

**SOLUTION**

$180,000 (costs transferred in) ÷ 45,000 (units) = $4.00 per unit

**8.2   Adjusted Unit Costs.** Using Method 1, compute the adjusted unit cost in Department 4 for the Chaykin Corporation, which uses a process cost system. The following information is available:

| | |
|---|---|
| Transferred-in cost from Dept. 3 | $850,000 |
| Quantity received from Dept. 3 | 93,000 |
| Additional units put into process in Dept. 4 | 12,000 |
| Units spoiled during production in Dept. 4 | 5,000 |

**SOLUTION**

12,000 (units added) − 5,000 (spoiled units) = 7,000 Net additional units

$$\frac{\$850,000}{93,000 + 7,000} = \$8.50 \text{ Adjusted unit cost}$$

**8.3   Quantity Schedule.** G.D.F. Incorporated manufactures a product in two departments, Department A and Department B. The plant manager's report for August 19X1 states that 600,000 units were in process at beginning in Department A. Of this amount, 150,000 were spoiled in production and 360,000 were completed and transferred to Department B. For the balance in process at the end of the month, all materials had been added, but only one-third of the labor and factory overhead had been applied.

In Department B, 90,000 units were added and 390,000 units were completed and transferred to finished goods.

Prepare a quantity schedule for the two departments.

## SOLUTION

*G.D.F. Incorporated*
*Quantity Schedule*
*for the month of August, 19X1*

|                                | **Department A** |          | **Department B** |          |
| ------------------------------ | ---------------- | -------- | ---------------- | -------- |
| **Quantities**                 |                  |          |                  |          |
| In Process at Beginning        | 600,000          | 600,000  |                  |          |
|                                |                  |          |                  |          |
| Started in Process             |                  |          | 90,000           |          |
| Received from Preceding Dept.  |                  |          | 360,000          | 450,000  |
|                                |                  |          |                  |          |
| Transferred to Next Dept.      | 360,000          |          |                  |          |
| Transferred to Finished Goods  |                  |          | 390,000          |          |
| Completed and On Hand          | —                |          | —                |          |
| Still in Process               | 90,000           |          | 60,000           |          |
|                                |                  |          |                  |          |
| Spoiled Units                  | 150,000          | 600,000  |                  | 450,000  |

**8.4    Cost of Production Report: Average Costs.**  The Benson Plastic Company produces plastic containers in three departments: mixing, molding, and finishing.  In the first month of operation a report from the Mixing Department showed the following:

| Units started in process          |         | 100,000 |
| --------------------------------- | ------- | ------- |
| Units transferred to next department | 88,000 |         |
| Units still in process            | 9,000   |         |
| Spoiled units                     | 3,000   | 100,000 |

Costs for the first month were: materials, $36,860; labor, $50,875; factory overhead, $46,930.  The portion of work in process completed was: materials, 100%; labor, 50%; and factory overhead, 25%.

For the second month, the quantity schedule showed that 95,000 units were started in process, 90,000 units were transferred to the next department, 11,000 units were still in process (100% complete as to material, 50% complete as to labor and factory overhead), and 3,000 units were spoiled in process.  The costs added during the period were: materials, $36,980; labor, $51,005; and factory overhead, $50,400.

Inspection for spoiled units occurs at the end of the process; 1,500 units are considered normal spoilage.

Using average costing and both methods of accounting for spoilage, prepare a Cost of Production Report for the Mixing Department for (a) the first month and (b) the second month.

**SOLUTION**

(*a*)  *Method 1:* Spoiled units ignored in calculation of equivalent production.

*Benson Plastic Company*
*Mixing Department*
*Cost of Production Report*
*First Month*

**Quantities**

| | | |
|---|---:|---:|
| Units Started in Process | | 100,000 |
| | | |
| Units Transferred to Next Department | 88,000 | |
| Units Still in Process (all materials; 1/2 labor; 1/4 factory overhead) | 9,000 | |
| Spoiled Units | 3,000 | 100,000 |

| **Equivalent Production** | **Materials** | **Labor** | **Overhead** |
|---|---:|---:|---:|
| Units completed | 88,000 | 88,000 | 88,000 |
| Still in process, ending | | | |
|   Materials | 9,000 | | |
|   Labor (9,000 × 50%) | | 4,500 | |
|   Overhead (9,000 × 25%) | | | 2,250 |
| Equivalent production | 97,000 | 92,500 | 90,250 |

| **Costs to Be Accounted For** | **Total Cost** | **Unit Cost** |
|---|---:|---:|
| Cost Added by Department | | |
|   Materials | $ 36,860 | $0.38 |
|   Labor | 50,875 | 0.55 |
|   Factory Overhead | 46,930 | 0.52 |
| Total Costs to Be Accounted For | $134,665 | $ 1.45 |

| **Costs Accounted For** | | |
|---|---:|---:|
| Transferred to Next Department | | |
|   (88,000 × $1.45) | | $127,600 |
| Work in Process, Ending Inventory | | |
|   Materials (9,000 × $0.38) | $ 3,420 | |
|   Labor (9,000 × 1/2 × $0.55) | 2,475 | |
|   Factory Overhead (9,000 × 1/4 × $0.52) | 1,170 | 7,065 |
| Total Costs Accounted For | | $134.665 |

**Computations**

*Unit costs:*  Materials: $36,860 ÷ 97,000 = $0.38
           Labor: $50,875 ÷ 92,500 = $0.55
           Overhead: $46,930 ÷ 90,250 = $0.52

*Method 2:* Spoiled units included in computation of equivalent production.

**Benson Plastic Company**
**Mixing Department**
**Cost of Production Report**
**First Month**

**Quantities**

| | | |
|---|---|---|
| Units Started in Process | | 100,000 |
| | | |
| Units Transferred to Next Department | 88,000 | |
| Units Still in Process | 9,000 | |
| Spoiled Units | 3,000 | 100,000 |

| Equivalent Production | Materials | Labor | Factory Overhead |
|---|---|---|---|
| Units completed | 88,000 | 88,000 | 88,000 |
| Work in process, ending | | | |
| Materials | 9,000 | | |
| Labor (9,000 × 50%) | | 4,500 | |
| Factory overhead (9,000 × 25%) | | | 2,250 |
| Spoiled units (inspection at end of process) | 3,000 | 3,000 | 3,000 |
| Equivalent production | 100,000 | 95,500 | 93,250 |

| Costs to Be Accounted For | Total Cost | Unit Cost |
|---|---|---|
| Cost Added by Department | | |
| Materials | $ 36,860 | $0.36860 |
| Labor | 50,875 | 0.53272 |
| Factory Overhead | 46,930 | 0.50327 |
| Total Costs to Be Accounted For | $134,665 | $1.40459 |

**Costs Accounted For**

| | | |
|---|---|---|
| Transferred to Next Department | | |
| Completed (88,000 × $1.40459) | $123,604 | |
| Normal Spoilage (1,500 × $1.40459) | 2,107 | $125,711 |
| Work in Process, Ending Inventory | | |
| Materials (9,000 × $0.36860) | $ 3,317 | |
| Labor (9,000 × 50% × $0.53272) | 2,397 | |
| Factory Overhead (9,000 × 25% × $0.50327) | 1,132 | 6,846 |
| Abnormal Spoilage (1,500 × $1.40459) | | 2,107 |
| Add Rounding Difference | | 1 |
| Total Costs Accounted For | | $134,665 |

**Computations**

*Unit costs:* Materials: $36,860 ÷ 100,000 = $0.36860

Labor: $50,875 ÷ 95,500 = $0.53272

Factory Overhead: $46,930 ÷ 93,250 = $0.50327

(b)  *Method 1:* Spoiled units ignored in calculation of equivalent production.

**Benson Plastic Company**
**Mixing Department**
**Cost of Production Report**
**Second Month**

**Quantities**

| | | |
|---|---|---|
| Units in Process at Beginning | 9,000 | |
| Units Started in Process | 95,000 | 104,000 |
| | | |
| Units Transferred to Next Department | 90,000 | |
| Units Still in Process | | |
| (all materials; 1/2 labor and factory overhead) | 11,000 | |
| Spoiled Units | 3,000 | 104,000 |

| **Equivalent Production** | **Materials** | **Conversion Costs** |
|---|---|---|
| Units completed | 90,000 | 90,000 |
| Still in process, ending | | |
| Materials | 11,000 | |
| Conversion costs (11,000 × 1/2) | | 5,500 |
| Equivalent production | 101,000 | 95,500 |

| **Costs to Be Accounted For** | **Total Cost** | **Unit Cost** |
|---|---|---|
| Cost Added by Department | | |
| Work in Process, Beginning Inventory | | |
| Materials | $  3,420 | |
| Labor | 2,475 | |
| Factory Overhead | 1,170 | |
| Costs Added during Period | | |
| Materials | 36,980 | $0.40 |
| Labor | 51,005 | 0.56 |
| Factory Overhead | 50,400 | 0.54 |
| Total Costs to Be Accounted For | $145,450 | $1.50 |

**Costs Accounted For**

| | | |
|---|---|---|
| Transferred to Next Department | | |
| (90,000 × $1.50) | | $135,000 |
| Work in Process, Ending Inventory | | |
| Materials (11,000 × $0.40) | $ 4,400 | |
| Labor (11,000 × 1/2 × $0.56) | 3,080 | |
| Factory Overhead (11,000 × 1/2 × $0.54) | 2,970 | 10,450 |
| Total Costs Accounted For | | $145,450 |

**Computations**

*Unit costs:*  Materials: ($3,420 + $36,980) ÷ 101,000 = $0.40
              Labor: ($2,475 + $51,005) ÷ 95,500 = $0.56
              Factory overhead: ($1,170 + $50,400) ÷ 95,500 = $0.54

*Method 2:* Spoiled units included in computation of equivalent production.

***Benson Plastic Company***
***Mixing Department***
***Cost of Production Report***
***Second Month***

**Quantities**

| | | |
|---|---|---|
| Units in Process at Beginning | 9,000 | |
| Units Started in Process | 95,000 | 104,000 |
| | | |
| Units Transferred to Next Department | 90,000 | |
| Units Still in Process | 11,000 | |
| Spoiled Units | 3,000 | 104,000 |

| **Equivalent Production** | **Materials** | **Conversion Costs** |
|---|---|---|
| Units completed | 90,000 | 90,000 |
| Work in process, ending | | |
| Materials | 11,000 | |
| Conversion costs (11,000 × 50%) | | 5,500 |
| Spoiled units (inspection at end of process) | 3,000 | 3,000 |
| Equivalent production | 104,000 | 98,500 |

**Costs to Be Accounted For**

| | | |
|---|---|---|
| Costs Added by Department | | |
| Work in Process, Beginning Inventory | | |
| Materials | $ 3,317 | |
| Labor | 2,397 | |
| Factory Overhead | 1,132 | |
| Costs Added during Period | | |
| Materials | 36,980 | $0.38747 |
| Labor | 51,005 | 0.54215 |
| Factory Overhead | 50,400 | 0.52317 |
| Total Costs to Be Accounted For | $145,231 | $1.45279 |

**Costs Accounted For**

| | | |
|---|---|---|
| Transferred to Next Department | | |
| Completed (90,000 × $1.45279) | $130,751 | |
| Normal Spoilage (1,500 × $1.45279) | 2,179 | $132,930 |
| Work in Process, Ending Inventory | | |
| Materials (11,000 × $0.38747) | $ 4,262 | |
| Labor (11,000 × 50% × $0.54215) | 2,982 | |
| Factory Overhead (11,000 × 50% × $0.52317) | 2,877 | 10,121 |
| Abnormal Spoilage (1,500 × $1.45279) | | 2,179 |
| Add Rounding Difference | | 1 |
| Total Costs Accounted For | | $145,231 |

**Computations**

*Unit costs:*   Materials: ($3,317 + $36,980) ÷ 104,000 = $0.38747

Labor: ($2,397 + $51,005) ÷ 98,500 = $0.54215

Factory Overhead: ($1,132 + $50,400) ÷ 98,500 = $0.52317

**8.5    Cost of Production Report: Average Costs.**    Carstairs, Incorporated produces one item in two departments, A and B.    As units proceed through both sections, materials are added to create additional units.

Cost information for the month of September 19X2 is as follows:

| Cost Component | Dept. A | Dept. B |
|---|---|---|
| Materials | $45,000 | $33,750 |
| Labor | 19,500 | 20,700 |
| Overhead | 3,900 | 10,350 |

At the beginning of the month, 150,000 units were put into production in Department A.    Of these, 37,500 were spoiled in production and 22,500 were still in process at the end of the period.    The units in process at the end were 100% complete as to materials and $33\frac{1}{3}$% complete as to labor and overhead.    Materials were added in the beginning of the process; conversion costs were added evenly.    The inspection point is at 25% of the process; 20,000 units are considered normal spoilage.

In Department B, 22,500 units were added to the units already transferred in from Department A.    Department B sent 97,500 units to finished goods inventory during the month.    The units still in process at the end of the period were 100% complete as to materials and 40% complete as to labor and overhead.

Using both methods of accounting for spoilage and average costs, prepare a Cost of Production Report for September 19X2 for (a) Department A and (b) Department B.

**SOLUTION**

(a)    *Method 1:* Spoiled units ignored.

*Carstairs, Incorporated*
*Cost of Production Report, Department A*
*for the month of September, 19X2*

**Quantity Schedule**

| | | |
|---|---|---|
| Put into Production | 150,000 | 150,000 |
| | | |
| Transferred to Department B | 90,000 | |
| Units Still in Process | 22,500 | |
| Spoiled Units | 37,500 | 150,000 |

| **Equivalent Production** | **Materials** | **Conversion Costs** |
|---|---|---|
| Units completed | 90,000 | 90,000 |
| Work in process, ending | | |
| Materials | 22,500 | |
| Conversion costs (22,500 × $33\frac{1}{3}$%) | | 7,500 |
| Equivalent production | 112,500 | 97,500 |

| **Costs to Account For** | **Total Cost** | **Unit Cost** |
|---|---|---|
| Cost Added by Department A | | |
| Materials | $45,000 | $0.40 |
| Labor | 19,500 | 0.20 |
| Overhead | 3,900 | 0.04 |
| Total Costs to Account For | $68,400 | $0.64 |

**Costs Accounted For**

| | | |
|---|---|---|
| Transferred to Department B (90,000 × $0.64) | | $57,600 |
| Work in Process, Ending Inventory | | |
| Materials (22,500 × 100% × $0.40) | $9,000 | |
| Labor (22,500 × 1/3 × $0.20) | 1,500 | |
| Overhead (22,500 × 1/3 × $0.04) | 300 | 10,800 |
| Total Costs Accounted For | | $68,400 |

**Computations**

*Unit costs:*  Materials: $45,000 ÷ 112,500 = $0.40
Labor: $19,500 ÷ 97,500 = $0.20
Overhead: $3,900 ÷ 97,500 = $0.04

*Method 2:* Spoiled units included.

*Carstairs, Incorporated*
*Cost of Production Report Department A*
*for the month of September, 19X2*

**Quantities**

| | |
|---|---|
| Put into Production | 150,000 |

| | | |
|---|---|---|
| Transferred to Department B | 90,000 | |
| Units Still in Process | 22,500 | |
| Spoiled Units | 37,500 | 150,000 |

| **Equivalent Production** | **Materials** | **Conversion Costs** |
|---|---|---|
| Units completed | 90,000 | 90,000 |
| Work in process, ending | | |
| Materials | 22,500 | |
| Conversion costs (22,500 × $33\frac{1}{3}$%) | | 7,500 |
| Spoiled units | | |
| Materials | 37,500 | |
| Conversion costs [37,500 × 25% (point of inspection)] | | 9,375 |
| Equivalent production | 150,000 | 106,875 |

| **Costs to Account For** | **Total Cost** | **Unit Cost** |
|---|---|---|
| Costs Added by Department A | | |
| Materials | $45,000.00 | $0.30000 |
| Labor | 19,500.00 | 0.18247 |
| Overhead | 3,900.00 | 0.03649 |
| Total Costs to Account For | $68,400.00 | $0.51896 |

**Costs Accounted For**

| | | |
|---|---|---|
| Transferred to Department B | | |
| Completed (90,000 × $0.51896) | $46,706.00 | |
| Normal Spoilage | 5,676.00 | $52,382.00 |

Work in Process, Ending Inventory

| | | |
|---|---|---|
| Materials (22,500 × $0.30000) | $ 6,750.00 | |
| Labor (22,500 × $0.18247 × $33\frac{1}{3}$%) | 1,369.00 | |
| Overhead (22,500 × $0.03649 × $33\frac{1}{3}$%) | 274.00 | |
| Normal Spoilage | 1,419.00 | 9,812.00 |
| Abnormal Spoilage | | 6,208.00 |
| Less Rounding Difference | | ⟨2.00⟩ |
| Total Costs Accounted For | | $68,400.00 |

**Computations**

*Unit costs:*  Materials: $45,000 ÷ 150,000 = $0.30000

Labor: $9,500 ÷ 106,875 = $0.18247

Overhead: $3,900 ÷ 106,875 = $0.03649

*Spoilage*  (37,500 units):

| | |
|---|---|
| Materials: 37,500 × $0.30000 | $11,250.00 |
| Labor: 37,500 × $0.18247 × 25% | 1,711.00 |
| Overhead: 37,500 × $0.03649 × 25% | 342.00 |
| Total Spoilage | $13,303.00 |

Allocated to Abnormal: (17,500 ÷ 37,500) × $13,303 = $6,208.00

Allocated to Normal: (20,000 ÷ 37,500) × $13,303  = $7,095.00

Further Allocated Normal Spoilage to:

Units Transferred to Department B:

(90,000 ÷ 112,500) × $7,095 = $5,676.00

Work in Process, Ending:

(22,500 ÷ 112,500) × $7,095 = $1,419.00

(b)  *Method 1:* Spoiled units ignored.

*Carstairs, Incorporated*
*Cost of Production Report, Department B*
*for the month of September, 19X2*

**Quantity Schedule**

| | | |
|---|---|---|
| Received from Department A | 90,000 | |
| Additional Units Put into Process | 22,500 | 112,500 |
| | | |
| Transferred to Finished Goods | 97,500 | |
| Units Still in Process | 15,000 | 112,500 |

| **Equivalent Production** | **Materials** | **Conversion Costs** |
|---|---|---|
| Units completed | 97,500 | 97,500 |
| Work in process, ending | | |
| Materials | 15,000 | |
| Conversion costs (15,000 × 40%) | | 6,000 |
| Equivalent production | 112,500 | 103,500 |

| Costs to Account For | Total Cost | Unit Cost |
|---|---|---|
| Transferred In during Period | $ 57,600 | $0.64 |
| | | |
| Cost Added by Department B | | |
|   Materials | $ 33,750 | $0.30 |
|   Labor | 20,700 | 0.20 |
|   Overhead | 10,350 | 0.10 |
| Total Cost Added | $ 64,800 | $ .60 |
| Adjusted Unit Cost of Units Transferred | | |
|     In from Department A | | 0.512 |
| Total Costs to Account For | $122,400 | $1.112 |

| Costs Accounted For | | |
|---|---|---|
| Transferred to Finished Goods (97,500 × $1.112) | | $108,420 |
| Work in Process, Ending Inventory | | |
|   Cost from Department A (15,000 × $0.512) | $7,680 | |
|   Materials (15,000 × 100% × $0.30) | 4,500 | |
|   Labor (15,000 × 40% × $0.20) | 1,200 | |
|   Overhead (15,000 × 40% × $0.10) | 600 | 13,980 |
| Total Costs Accounted For | | $122,400 |

**Computations**

*Unit costs:*    Materials: $33,750 ÷ 112,500 = $0.30

               Labor: $20,700 ÷ 103,500 = $0.20

               Overhead: $10,350 ÷ 103,500 = $0.10

*Adjustment of Department A's unit cost:* $57,600 ÷ 112,500 = $0.512

*Method 2:* Spoiled units included.

*Carstairs, Incorporated*
*Cost of Production Report, Department B*
*for the month of September, 19X2*

**Quantities**

| | | |
|---|---|---|
| Received from Department A | 90,000 | |
| Additional Units Put into Process | 22,500 | 112,500 |
| | | |
| Transferred to Finished Goods | 97,500 | |
| Units Still in Process | 15,000 | 112,500 |

| Equivalent Production | Materials | Conversion Costs |
|---|---|---|
| Units completed | 97,500 | 97,500 |
| Work in process, ending | | |
|   Materials | 15,000 | |
|   Conversion costs (15,000 × 40%) | | 6,000 |
| Equivalent production | 112,500 | 103,500 |

| Costs to Account For | Total Cost | Unit Cost |
|---|---|---|
| Transferred in during Period | $ 52,382.00 | $0.58202 |
| Cost Added by Department B | | |
|   Materials | $ 33,750.00 | 0.30000 |
|   Labor | 20,700.00 | 0.20000 |
|   Overhead | 10,350.00 | 0.10000 |
|     Total Cost Added | $ 64,800.00 | 0.60000 |
| Adjusted Unit Costs Transferred in from Department A | | 0.46562 |
| Total Costs to Account For | $117,182.00 | $1.06562 |

| Costs Accounted For | | |
|---|---|---|
| Transferred to Finished Goods (97,500 × $1.06562) | | $103,898.00 |
| Work in Process, Ending Inventory | | |
|   Cost from Department A (15,000 × $0.46562) | $6,984.00 | |
|   Materials (15,000 × $0.30) | 4,500.00 | |
|   Labor (15,000 × $0.20 × 40%) | 1,200.00 | |
|   Overhead (15,000 × $0.10 × 40%) | 600.00 | 13,284.00 |
| Total Costs Accounted For | | $117,182.00 |

**Computations**

Unit costs:   Materials: $33,750 ÷ 112,500 = $0.30000

Labor: $20,700 ÷ 103,500 = $0.20000

Overhead: $10,350 ÷ 103,500 = $0.10000

Adjustment of Department A's Unit Cost: $52,382 ÷ 112,500 = $0.46562

**8.6**   **Cost of Production Report: FIFO.**   Company B has three departments: mixing, refining and finishing.   Its January 19X3 ending work in process inventory details are given below:

| Cost Details | Mixing (all materials; 1/2 labor and overhead) | Refining (1/3 labor and overhead) | Finishing (1/4 labor and overhead) |
|---|---|---|---|
| Units in process | 8,000 | 6,000 | 4,000 |
| Work in process, beginning | $6,200 | $8,000 | $18,750 |

For the month of February 19X3, the following information is available:

| Units | Mixing | Refining | Finishing |
|---|---|---|---|
| Started in process | 50,000 | | |
| Transferred to next department | 50,000 | 49,000 | 46,000 |
| Completed and on hand | 4,000 | | |
| Still in process | 3,000 | 6,000 | 6,000 |
| | (All materials; 2/3 labor and overhead) | (1/2 labor and overhead) | (1/3 labor and overhead) |

| | Mixing | Refining | Finishing |
|---|---|---|---|
| Spoiled Units | 1,000 | 1,000 | 1,000 |
| Normal<br>Abnormal | 100 %<br>0% | 50%<br>50% | 100%<br>0% |
| Costs added to department | | | |
| Materials | $20,000 | $ — | $ — |
| Labor | 25,000 | 35,000 | 35,460 |
| Factory overhead | 22,000 | 30,000 | 22,650 |

Additional information:

(1)  Materials are added in the beginning of production

(2)  Conversion costs are added evenly in each of the three departments.

(3)  Inspection stages: Mixing and Refining, end of the process; Finishing, 25% of the process.

Using FIFO costing, prepare a Cost of Production Report under (a) Method 1 (spoiled units ignored for computation of equivalent production) and (b) Method 2 (spoiled units included for computation of equivalent production) for the Mixing, Refining, and Finishing departments for the month of February, 19X3.

## SOLUTION

(a)  Method 1.

***Company B***
***Mixing Department***
***Cost of Production Report***
***for the month of February, 19X3***

**Quantities**

| | | |
|---|---|---|
| In Process at Beginning (all materials, 1/2 labor and overhead) | 8,000 | |
| Started in Process | 50,000 | 58,000 |
| | | |
| Transferred to Next Department | 50,000 | |
| Completed and On Hand | 4,000 | |
| Still in Process (all materials; 2/3 labor and overhead) | 3,000 | |
| Spoiled Units | 1,000 | 58,000 |

| **Equivalent Production** | **Materials** | **Conversion Costs** |
|---|---|---|
| Units completed and transferred | 50,000 | 50,000 |
| Less: Beginning work in process | ⟨8,000⟩ | ⟨8,000⟩ |
| Units started, completed and transferred | 42,000 | 42,000 |
| Add: Work needed to complete beginning work in process | | |
| Materials | 0 | |
| Conversion costs (8,000 × 1/2) | | 4,000 |

| | | |
|---|---|---|
| Add: Units completed and still on hand | 4,000 | 4,000 |
| Add: Work in process, ending | | |
|     Materials | 3,000 | |
|     Conversion costs (3,000 × 2/3) | | 2,000 |
| Equivalent production | 49,000 | 52,000 |

| Costs to Account For | Total Cost | Unit Cost |
|---|---|---|
| Work in Process, Beginning | $ 6,200 | |
| Cost Added by Department | | |
|   Materials | $20,000 | $0.408163 |
|   Labor | 25,000 | 0.480769 |
|   Factory Overhead | 22,000 | 0.423077 |
| Total Cost Added | $67,000 | $1.312009 |
| Total Costs to Account For | $73,200 | |

**Costs Accounted For**

| | | | |
|---|---|---|---|
| Transferred to Next Department | | | |
|   From Beginning Inventory | | | |
|     Inventory Value | $6,200 | | |
|     Labor Added (8,000 × 1/2 × $0.480679) | 1,923 | | |
|     Factory Overhead Added (8,000 × 1/2 × $0.423077) | 1,692 | $ 9,815 | |
|   From Current Production | | | |
|     Units Started and Finished (42,000 × $1.312009) | | 55,104 | $64,919 |
|   Completed and On Hand (4,000 × $1.312009) | | | 5,248 |
| Work in Process, Ending Inventory | | | |
|   Materials (3,000 × $0.408163) | | $ 1,225 | |
|   Labor (3,000 × 2/3 × $0.480769) | | 962 | |
|   Factory Overhead (3,000 × 2/3 × $0.423077) | | 846 | 3,033 |
| Total Costs Accounted For | | | $73,200 |

**Computations**

*Unit costs:*    Materials: $20,000 ÷ 49,000 = $0.408163
               Labor: $25,000 ÷ 52,000 = $0.480769
               Factory overhead: $22,000 ÷ 52,000 = $0.423077

***Company B***
***Refining Department***
***Cost of Production Report***
***for the month of February, 19X3***

**Quantities**

| | | |
|---|---|---|
| In Process at Beginning (1/3 labor and factory overhead) | 6,000 | |
| Received from Preceding Department | 50,000 | 56,000 |
| | | |
| Transferred to Next Department | 49,000 | |
| Still in Process (1/2 labor and factory overhead) | 6,000 | |
| Spoiled Units | 1,000 | 56,000 |

**Equivalent Production** (Conversion Costs Only)

| | |
|---|---:|
| Units completed and transferred | 49,000 |
| Less: Beginning work in process | ⟨6,000⟩ |
| Units started and completed | 43,000 |
| Add: Work needed to complete beginning work in process (6,000 × 2/3) | 4,000 |
| Add: Work in process, ending (6,000 × 1/2) | 3,000 |
| Equivalent production | 50,000 |

| Costs to Be Accounted For | Total Cost | Unit Cost |
|---|---:|---:|
| Work in Process, Beginning | $ 8,000 | |
| Cost from Preceding Department | | |
| Transferred In (50,000) | $ 64,919 | $1.29838 |
| Cost Added by Department | | |
| Labor | $ 35,000 | $0.70000 |
| Factory Overhead | 30,000 | 0.60000 |
| Total Cost Added | $ 65,000 | $1.30000 |
| Adjustment for Spoiled Units | | 0.02649 |
| Total Costs to Be Accounted For | $137,919 | $2.62487 |

**Costs Accounted For**

| | | |
|---|---:|---:|
| Transferred to Next Department | | |
| From Beginning Inventory | | |
| Inventory Value | $8,000 | |
| Labor Added (6,000 × 2/3 × $0.70) | 2,800 | |
| Factory Overhead (6,000 × 2/3 × $0.60) | 2,400 | $ 13,200 |
| From Current Production | | |
| Units Started and Finished (43,000 × $2.62487) | | 112,870 | $126,070 |
| Work in Process, Ending Inventory | | |
| Adjusted Cost from Preceding Department [6,000 × ($1.29838 + $0.02649)] | | $ 7,949 |
| Labor (6,000 × 1/2 × $0.70) | | 2,100 |
| Factory Overhead (6,000 × 1/2 × $0.60) | | 1,800 |
| Total Costs Accounted For | | 11,849 |
| | | $137,919 |

**Computations**

*Unit costs:*  Labor: $35,000 ÷ 50,000 = $0.70

Factory overhead: $30,000 ÷ 50,000 = $0.60

*Adjustment for spoiled units:*  1,000 × $1.29838 = $1,298; $1,298 ÷ 49,000 = $0.026490

*Company B*
*Finishing Department*
*Cost of Production Report*
*for the month of February, 19X3*

**Quantities**

| | | |
|---|---:|---:|
| In Process at Beginning (1/4 labor and factory overhead) | 4,000 | |
| Received from Preceding Department | 49,000 | 53,000 |
| | | |
| Transferred to Finished Goods Storeroom | 46,000 | |
| Still in Process (1/3 labor and factory overhead) | 6,000 | |
| Spoiled Units | 1,000 | 53,000 |

**Equivalent Production** (Conversion Costs Only)

| | |
|---|---:|
| Units completed and transferred | 46,000 |
| Less: Beginning work in process | ⟨4,000⟩ |
| Units started and completed | 42,000 |
| Add: Work needed to complete beginning work in process (4,000 × 3/4) | 3,000 |
| Add: Work in process, ending (6,000 × 1/3) | 2,000 |
| Equivalent production | 47,000 |

| **Costs to Be Accounted For** | **Total Cost** | **Unit Cost** |
|---|---:|---:|
| Work in Process, Beginning | $ 18,750 | |
| Cost from Preceding Department | | |
| Transferred In during Month (49,000) | $126,070 | $2.572857 |
| Cost Added by Department | | |
| Labor | $ 35,460 | $0.754468 |
| Factory Overhead | 22,650 | 0.481915 |
| Total Cost Added | $ 58,110 | $1.236383 |
| Adjustment for Spoiled Units | | 0.053604 |
| Total Costs to Be Accounted For | $202,930 | $3.862844 |

**Costs Accounted For**

| | | | |
|---|---:|---:|---:|
| Transferred to Next Department | | | |
| From Beginning Inventory | | | |
| Inventory Value | $18,750 | | |
| Labor Added (4,000 × 3/4 × $0.754468) | 2,263 | | |
| Factory Overhead (4,000 × 3/4 × $0.481915) | 1,446 | $ 22,459 | |
| From Current Production | | | |
| Units Started and Finished (42,000 × $3.862844) | | 162,239 | $184,698 |
| Work in Process, Ending Inventory | | | |
| Adjusted Cost from Preceding Department [6,000 × ($2.572857 + $0.053604)] | | $ 15,759 | |
| Labor (6,000 × 1/3 × $0.754468) | | 1,509 | |
| Factory Overhead (6,000 × 1/3 × $0.481915) | | 964 | 18,232 |
| Total Costs Accounted For | | | $202,930 |

**Computations**

*Unit costs:*   Labor: $35,460 ÷ 47,000 = $0.754468

Factory overhead: $22,650 ÷ 47,000 = $0.481915

*Adjustment for spoiled units:*   1,000 × $2.572857 = $2,573; $2,573 ÷ 48,000 = $0.053604

(b)　*Method 2.*

***Company B***
***Mixing Department***
***Cost of Production Report***
*for the month of February, 19X3*

**Quantities**

| | | |
|---|---:|---:|
| In Process at Beginning | 8,000 | |
| Started in Process | 50,000 | 58,000 |
| | | |
| Transferred to Next Department | 50,000 | |
| Completed and on Hand | 4,000 | |
| Still in Process | 3,000 | |
| Spoiled Units | 1,000 | 58,000 |

| **Equivalent Production** | **Materials** | **Conversion Costs** |
|---|---:|---:|
| Units completed and transferred | 50,000 | 50,000 |
| Less: Beginning work in process | 8,000 | 8,000 |
| Units started, completed and transferred | 42,000 | 42,000 |
| Add: Work needed to complete beginning work in process | | |
| Materials | 0 | |
| Conversion costs (8,000 × 1/2) | | 4,000 |
| Add: Units completed and still on hand | 4,000 | 4,000 |
| Add: Work in process, ending | | |
| Materials | 3,000 | |
| Conversion costs (3,000 × 2/3) | | 2,000 |
| Add: Spoiled units (inspection at end of process) | 1,000 | 1,000 |
| Equivalent production | 50,000 | 53,000 |

| **Costs to Account For** | **Total Cost** | **Unit Cost** |
|---|---:|---:|
| Work in Process, Beginning | $ 6,200.00 | |
| Cost Added by Department | | |
| Materials | $20,000.00 | $0.40000 |
| Labor | 25,000.00 | 0.47170 |
| Factory Overhead | 22,000.00 | 0.41509 |
| Total Costs Added | $67,000.00 | $1.28679 |
| Total Costs to Account For | $73,200.00 | |

| **Costs Accounted For** | | |
|---|---:|---:|
| Transferred to Next Department | | |
| From Beginning Inventory | | |
| Inventory Value | $ 6,200.00 | |
| Labor Added (8,000 × 1/2 × $0.47170) | 1,887.00 | |
| Factory Overhead (8,000 × 1/2 × $0.41509) | 1,660.00 | $ 9,747.00 |
| From Current Production | | |
| Units Started and Finished (42,000 × $1.28679) | $54,045.00 | |
| Normal Spoilage | 1,175.00 | 55,220.00 |
| Total Transferred | | $64,967.00 |

| | | |
|---|---:|---:|
| Completed and on Hand (4,000 × $1.28679) | $ 5,147.00 | |
| Add: Portion of Normal Spoilage | 112.00 | 5,259.00 |
| Work in Process, Ending Inventory | | |
|   Materials (3,000 × $0.40000) | $ 1,200.00 | |
|   Labor (3,000 × 2/3 × $0.47170) | 943.00 | |
|   Factory Overhead (3,000 × 2/3 × $0.41509) | 830.00 | 2,973.00 |
| Add: Rounding Difference | | 1.00 |
| Total Costs Accounted For | | $73,200.00 |

**Computations**

*Unit costs:*  Materials: $20,000 ÷ 50,000 = $0.40000

               Labor: $25,000 ÷ 53,000 = $0.47170

               Factory Overhead: $22,000 ÷ 53,000 = $0.41509

*Spoilage*  (1,000 units, all normal): 1,000 × $1.28679 = $1,287

$$\text{Allocated to Units Started, Finished and Transferred: } \$1,287 \times \frac{42,000}{46,000} = \$1,175$$

$$\text{Allocated to Units Completed and on Hand: } \$1,287 \times \frac{4,000}{46,000} = \$112$$

*Company B*
*Refining Department*
*Cost of Production Report*
*for the month of February, 19X3*

**Quantities**

| | | |
|---|---:|---:|
| In Process at Beginning | 6,000 | |
| Received from Preceding Department | 50,000 | 56,000 |
| | | |
| Transferred to Next Department | 49,000 | |
| Still in Process | 6,000 | |
| Spoiled Units | 1,000 | 56,000 |

**Equivalent Production** (Conversion Costs Only)

| | |
|---|---:|
| Units completed and transferred | 49,000 |
| Less: Beginning work in process | ⟨6,000⟩ |
| Units started and completed | 43,000 |
| Add: Work needed to complete beginning | |
|       work in process (6,000 × 2/3) | 4,000 |
| Add: Work in process, ending (6,000 × 1/2) | 3,000 |
| Add: Spoiled units (inspection at end of process) | 1,000 |
| Equivalent production | 51,000 |

| **Costs to Be Accounted For** | **Total Cost** | **Unit Cost** |
|---|---:|---:|
| Work in Process, Beginning | $ 8,000.00 | |
| Cost from Preceding Department | | |
|     Transferred-in (50,000 units) | $ 64,967.00 | $1.29934 |
| Costs Added by Department | | |
|   Labor | $ 35,000.00 | $0.68627 |
|   Factory Overhead | 30,000.00 | 0.58824 |
|     Total Cost Added | $ 65,000.00 | $1.27451 |
| Total Costs to Be Accounted For | $137,967.00 | $2.57385 |

**Costs Accounted For**

Transferred to Next Department:

  From Beginning Inventory:

| | | |
|---|---:|---:|
| Inventory Value | $ 8,000.00 | |
| Labor Added (6,000 × 2/3 × $0.68627) | 2.745.00 | |
| Factory Overhead (6,000 × 2/3 × $0.58824) | 2,353.00 | $ 13,098.00 |

  From Current Production

| | | |
|---|---:|---:|
| Units Started and Finished (43,000 × $2.57385) | $110,676.00 | |
| Normal Spoilage (500 × $2.57385) | 1,287.00 | 111,963.00 |
| Total Transferred | | $125,061.00 |

Work in Process, Ending Inventory

| | | |
|---|---:|---:|
| From Preceding Department (6,000 × $1.29934) | $ 7,796.00 | |
| Labor (6,000 × 1/2 × $0.68627) | 2,059.00 | |
| Factory Overhead (6,000 × 1/2 × $0.58824) | 1,765.00 | 11,620.00 |
| Abnormal Spoilage (500 × $2.57385) | | 1,287.00 |
| Less: Rounding Difference | | ⟨1.00⟩ |
| Total Costs Accounted For | | $137,967.00 |

**Computations**

*Unit costs:*  Labor: $35,000 ÷ 51,000 = $0.68627

               Overhead: $30,000 ÷ 51,000 = $0.58824

*Company B*
*Finishing Department*
*Cost of Production Report*
*for the month of February, 19X3*

**Quantities**

| | | |
|---|---:|---:|
| In Process at Beginning | 4,000 | |
| Received from Preceding Department | 49,000 | 53,000 |
| | | |
| Transferred to Finished Goods | 46,000 | |
| Still in Process | 6,000 | |
| Spoiled Units | 1,000 | 53,000 |

**Equivalent Production** (Conversion Costs Only)

| | |
|---|---:|
| Units Completed and Transferred | 46,000 |
| Less: Beginning Work in Process | ⟨4,000⟩ |
| Units Started and Completed | 42,000 |
| Add: Work Needed to Complete Beginning | |
|        Work in Process (4,000 × 3/4) | 3,000 |
| Add: Work in Process, Ending (6,000 × 1/3) | 2,000 |
| Add: Spoiled Units [1,000 × 25% (point of inspection)] | 250 |
| Equivalent Production | 47,250 |

| Costs to Be Accounted For | Total Cost | Unit Cost |
|---|---:|---:|
| Work in Process, Beginning | $ 18,750.00 | |
| Cost from Preceding Department | | |
|   Transferred-in (49,000 units) | $125,061.00 | $2.55227 |
| Cost Added by Department | | |
|   Labor | $ 35,460.00 | $0.75048 |
|   Factory Overhead | 22,650.00 | 0.47937 |
|     Total Costs Added | $ 58,110.00 | $1.22985 |
| Total Costs to Be Accounted For | $201,921.00 | $3.78212 |

**Costs Accounted For**

Transferred to Finished Goods

  From Beginning Inventory

    Inventory Value      $ 18,750.00

    Labor Added (4,000 × 3/4 × $0.75048)    2,251.00

    Factory Overhead (4,000 × 3/4 × $0.47937)   1,438.00    $ 22,439.00

  From Current Production

    Units Started and Finished (42,000 × $3.78212)   $158,849.00

    Normal Spoilage      2,530.00    161,379.00

      Total Transferred      $183,818.00

Work in Process, Ending Inventory

  From Preceding Department (6,000 × $2.55227)   $ 15,314.00

  Labor (6,000 × 1/3 × $0.75048)    1,501.00

  Factory Overhead (6,000 × 1/3 × $0.47937)   959.00

  Normal Spoilage      330.00    18,104.00

Less: Rounding Difference      ⟨1.00⟩

Total Costs Accounted For      $201,921.00

**Computations**

*Unit costs:*   Labor: $35,460 ÷ 47,250 = $0.75048

         Factory Overhead: $22,650 ÷ 47,250 = $0.47937

*Spoilage*   (1,000 units, all normal):

  From Preceding Department (1,000 × $2.55227)   $2,552.00

  Added during the Period

    Labor (1,000 × 25% × $0.75048)    188.00

    Overhead (1,000 × 25% × $0.47937)   120.00

    Total Spoilage      $2,860.00

  Allocated to Finished Goods:

    (46,000 ÷ 52,000) × $2,860 = $2,530.00

  Allocated to Work in Process, Ending:

    (6,000 ÷ 52,000) × $2,860 =   $330.00

**8.7**   **Cost of Production Report: Average Cost.** Company A has three departments: mixing, refining and finishing. The January 19X1 closing work-in-process inventory details are as follows:

| Cost Components | Mixing | Refining | Finishing |
|---|---|---|---|
| Units | 3,000 | 4,000 | 4,000 |
| Cost from previous department | — | $6,400 | $12,800 |
| Materials in process | $3,000 | — | — |
| Labor in process | 2,250 | 1,000 | 2,000 |
| Overhead in process | 1,400 | 800 | 1,500 |

For the month of February 19X1, the following information is available:

| Cost Components | Mixing | Refining | Finishing |
|---|---|---|---|
| Units started in process | 50,000 | — | — |
| Units transferred to next department | 45,000 | 44,000 | 41,000 |
| Units completed and on hand | 2,000 | | |
| Units still in process | 4,000 | 4,000 | 6,000 |
| Degree of completion, units in process | | | |
| Materials | all | — | — |
| Labor and overhead | 1/2 | 1/2 | 1/3 |
| Spoiled units | 2,000 | 1,000 | 1,000 |
| Normal | 50% | 75% | 100% |
| Abnormal | 50% | 25% | 0% |
| Costs added to department: | | | |
| Materials | $20,170 | — | — |
| Labor | 26,320 | $35,000 | $37,000 |
| Overhead | 21,640 | 30,000 | 22,000 |

Additional information:

(1)  Materials are added in the beginning of production.
(2)  Conversion costs are added evenly in each of the three departments.
(3)  Inspection stages: Mixing, 50% of the process; Refining, end of the process; Finishing, 30% of the process.

Using average costing, prepare a Cost of Production Report under (a) Method 1 (spoiled units ignored for computation of equivalent production) and (b) Method 2 (spoiled units included for computation of equivalent production) for the Mixing, Refining, and Finishing departments for the month of February, 19X1.

**SOLUTION**

(a)  *Method 1.*
*Company A*
*Mixing Department*
*Cost of Production Report*
*February, 19X1*

**Quantities**

| | | |
|---|---|---|
| Units in Process at Beginning | 3,000 | |
| Units Started in Process | 50,000 | 53,000 |
| Units Transferred to Next Department | 45,000 | |
| Units Completed and On Hand | 2,000 | |
| Units Still in Process (all material, 1/2 labor and overhead) | 4,000 | |
| Spoiled Units | 2,000 | 53,000 |

| Equivalent Production | Materials | Conversion Costs |
|---|---|---|
| Units completed | | |
| Transferred to next department (45,000) | | |
| Still on hand (2,000) | 47,000 | 47,000 |
| Still in process, ending | | |
| Materials | 4,000 | |
| Conversion costs (4,000 × 1/2) | | 2,000 |
| Equivalent production | 51,000 | 49,000 |

| Costs to Be Accounted For | Total Cost | Unit Cost |
|---|---|---|
| Cost Added by Department | | |
| Work in Process, Beginning Inventory | | |
| Materials | $ 3,000 | |
| Labor | 2,250 | |
| Overhead | 1,400 | |
| Cost Added during Period | | |
| Materials | 20,170 | $0.45431 |
| Labor | 26,320 | 0.58306 |
| Overhead | 21,640 | 0.47020 |
| Total Costs to Be Accounted For | $74,780 | $1.50757 |

| Costs Accounted For | | |
|---|---|---|
| Transferred to Next Department | | |
| (45,000 × $1.50757) | | $67,841 |
| Completed and On Hand | | |
| (2,000 × $1.50757) | | $3,015 |
| Work in Process, Ending Inventory | | |
| Materials (4,000 × $0.45431) | $1,817 | |
| Labor (4,000 × 1/2 × $0.58306) | 1,166 | |
| Overhead (4,000 × 1/2 × $0.47020) | 941 | 6,939 |
| Total Costs Accounted For | | $74,780 |

**Computations**

*Unit costs:*   Materials: ($3,000 + $20,170) ÷ 51,000 = $0.45431

Labor: ($2,250 + $26,320) ÷ 49,000 = $0.58306

Overhead: ($1,400 + $21,640) ÷ 49,000 = $0.47020

*Company A*
*Refining Department*
*Cost of Production Report*
*February, 19X1*

**Quantities**

| | | |
|---|---|---|
| Units in Process at Beginning | 4,000 | |
| Units Received from Preceding Department | 45,000 | 49,000 |
| | | |
| Units Transferred to Next Department | 44,000 | |
| Units Still in Process (1/2 labor and overhead) | 4,000 | |
| Spoiled Units | 1,000 | 49,000 |

**Equivalent Production** (Conversion Costs Only)

| | |
|---|---|
| Units completed | 44,000 |
| Still in process, ending (4,000 × 1/2) | 2,000 |
| Equivalent production | 46,000 |

| **Costs to Be Accounted For** | | **Total Cost** | **Unit Cost** |
|---|---|---|---|
| Cost from Preceding Department | | | |
| Work in Process, Beginning Inventory | (4,000) | $  6,400 | $1.60000 |
| Transferred In | (45,000) | 67,841 | 1.50758 |
| Total | (49,000) | $ 74,241 | $1.51512 |
| | | | |
| Cost Added by Department | | | |
| Work in Process, Beginning Inventory | | | |
| Labor | | $  1,000 | |
| Overhead | | 800 | |
| Cost Added during Period | | | |
| Labor | | 35,000 | $0.78261 |
| Overhead | | 30,000 | 0.66956 |
| Total Cost Added | | $ 66,800 | $1.45217 |
| Adjustment for Spoiled Units | | | 0.03156 |
| Total Costs to Be Accounted For | | $141,041 | $2,99885 |

| **Costs Accounted For** | | |
|---|---|---|
| Transferred to Next Department | | |
| (44,000 × $2.99885) | | $131,950 |
| Work in Process, Ending Inventory | | |
| Adjustment of Cost from Preceding | | |
| Department [4,000 × ($1.51512 + $0.03156)] | $6,187 | |
| Labor (4,000 × 1/2 × $0.78261) | 1,565 | |
| Overhead (4,000 × 1/2 × $0.66956) | 1,339 | 9,091 |
| Total Costs Accounted For | | $141,041 |

**Computations**

*Unit costs:*   Labor: ($1,000 + $35,000) ÷ 46,000 = $0.78261

Overhead: ($800 + $30,000) ÷ 46,000 = $0.66956

*Adjustment for spoiled units:*   1,000 × $1.51512 = $1,515; $1,515 ÷ 48,000 = $0.03156

*Company A*
*Finishing Department*
*Cost of Production Report*
*February, 19X1*

**Quantities**

| | | |
|---|---|---|
| Units in Process at Beginning | 4,000 | |
| Units Received from Preceding Department | 44,000 | 48,000 |
| | | |
| Units Transferred to Finished Goods Storeroom | 41,000 | |
| Units Still in Process (1/3 labor and overhead) | 6,000 | |
| Spoiled Units | 1,000 | 48,000 |

**Equivalent Production** (Conversion Costs Only)

| | | |
|---|---|---:|
| Units completed | | 41,000 |
| Still in process, ending (6,000 × 1/3) | | 2,000 |
| Equivalent production | | 43,000 |

| **Costs to Be Accounted For** | | **Total Cost** | **Unit Cost** |
|---|---|---:|---:|
| Cost from Preceding Department | | | |
|   Work in Process, Beginning Inventory | ( 4,000) | $ 12,800 | $3.20000 |
|   Transferred In | (44,000) | 131,950 | 2.99885 |
| Total | (48,000) | $144,750 | $3.01562 |
| | | | |
| Cost Added by Department | | | |
|   Work in Process, Beginning Inventory | | | |
|     Labor | | $ 2,000 | |
|     Overhead | | 1,500 | |
|   Cost Added during Period | | | |
|     Labor | | 37,000 | $0.90698 |
|     Overhead | | 22,000 | 0.54651 |
| Total Cost Added | | $ 62,500 | $1.45349 |
| Adjustment for Spoiled Units | | | 0.06417 |
| Total Costs to Be Accounted For | | $207,250 | $4.53328 |

**Costs Accounted For**

| | | |
|---|---:|---:|
| Transferred to Finished Goods | | |
|   (41,000 × $4.53328) | | $185,864 |
| Work in Process, Ending Inventory | | |
|   Adjusted Cost from Preceding | | |
|     Department [6,000 × ($3.01562 + $0.06417)] | $18,479 | |
|   Labor (6,000 × 1/3 × $0.90698) | 1,814 | |
|   Overhead (6,000 × 1/3 × $0.54651) | 1,093 | 21,386 |
| Total Costs Accounted For | | $207,250 |

**Computations**

*Unit costs:*   Labor: ($2,000 + $37,000) ÷ 43,000 = $0.90698

               Overhead: ($1,500 + $22,000) ÷ 43,000 = $0.54651

*Adjustment for lost units:*   1,000 × $3.01562 = $3,016; $3,016 ÷ 47,000 = $0.06417

(b)  *Method 2.*

***Company A***
***Mixing Department***
***Cost of Production Report***
***February, 19X1***

**Quantities**

| | | |
|---|---:|---:|
| Units in Process at Beginning | 3,000 | |
| Units Started in Process | 50,000 | 53,000 |
| | | |
| Units Transferred to Next Department | 45,000 | |
| Units Completed and on Hand | 2,000 | |
| Units Still in Process | 4,000 | |
| Spoiled Units | 2,000 | 53,000 |

| Equivalent Production | Materials | Conversion Costs |
|---|---|---|
| Units completed | | |
|   Transferred to next department | 45,000 | 45,000 |
|   Still on hand | 2,000 | 2,000 |
| Work in process, ending | | |
|   Materials | 4,000 | |
|   Conversion costs (4,000 × 1/2) | | 2,000 |
| Spoiled units | | |
|   Materials | 2,000 | |
|   Conversion costs [2,000 × 50% (point of inspection)] | | 1,000 |
| Equivalent production | 53,000 | 50,000 |

| Costs to Be Accounted For | Total Cost | Unit Cost |
|---|---|---|
| Costs Added by Department | | |
|   Work in Process, Beginning Inventory | | |
|     Materials | $ 3,000.00 | |
|     Labor | 2,250.00 | |
|     Overhead | 1,400.00 | |
|   Costs Added During Period | | |
|     Materials | 20,170.00 | $0.43717 |
|     Labor | 26,320.00 | 0.57140 |
|     Overhead | 21,640.00 | 0.46080 |
| Total Costs to Be Accounted For | $74,780.00 | $1.46937 |

**Costs Accounted For**

| | | |
|---|---|---|
| Transferred to Next Department | | |
|   Completed (45,000 × $1.46937) | $66,122.00 | |
|   Normal Spoilage | 841.00 | $66,963.00 |
| | | |
| Completed and on Hand (2,000 × $1.46937) | $ 2,939.00 | |
| Add: Portion of Normal Spoilage | 37.00 | 2,976.00 |
| Work in Process, Ending Inventory | | |
|   Materials (4,000 × $0.43717) | $ 1,749.00 | |
|   Labor (4,000 × 1/2 × $0.57140) | 1,143.00 | |
|   Overhead (4,000 × 1/2 × $0.46080) | 922.00 | |
|   Normal Spoilage | 75.00 | 3,889.00 |
| Abnormal Spoilage | | 953.00 |
| Less: Rounding Difference | | ⟨1.00⟩ |
| Total Costs Accounted For | | $74,780.00 |

**Computations**

*Unit costs:*  Materials: ($3,000 + $20,170) ÷ 53,000 = $0.43717

           Labor: ($2,250 + $26,230) ÷ 50,000 = $0.57140

           Overhead: ($1,400 + $21,640) ÷ 50,000 = $0.46080

*Spoilage*  (2,000 units):

| | |
|---|---|
|   Materials (2,000 × $0.43717) | $ 874.00 |
|   Labor (2,000 × 50% × $0.57140) | 571.00 |
|   Overhead (2,000 × 50% × $0.46080) | 461.00 |
|   Total Spoilage | $1,906.00 |

Allocate to Abnormal Spoilage: (1,000 ÷ 2,000) × $1,906 = $ 953.00

Allocate to Normal Spoilage: (1,000 ÷ 2,000) × $1,906 = $ 953.00

Further Allocated Normal To:

Transferred to Next Department: (45,000 ÷ 51,000) × $953 = $ 841.00

Still on Hand: (2,000 ÷ 51,000) × $953 = $ 37.00

Work in Process: (4,000 ÷ 51,000) × $953 = $ 75.00

## Company A
### Refining Department
### Cost of Production Report
### February, 19X1

**Quantities**

| | | |
|---|---:|---:|
| Units in Process at Beginning | 4,000 | |
| Units Received from Preceding Department | 45,000 | 49,000 |
| | | |
| Units Transferred to Next Department | 44,000 | |
| Units Still in Process | 4,000 | |
| Spoiled Units | 1,000 | 49,000 |

**Equivalent Production** (Conversion Costs Only)

| | |
|---|---:|
| Units completed | 44,000 |
| Work in process, ending (4,000 × 1/2) | 2,000 |
| Spoiled units (inspection at end of process) | 1,000 |
| Equivalent production | 47,000 |

| Costs to Be Accounted For | | Total Cost | Unit Cost |
|---|---|---:|---:|
| Cost from Preceding Department | | | |
| Work in Process, Beginning Inventory | (4,000) | $ 6,400.00 | $1.60000 |
| Transferred-in | (45,000) | 66,963.00 | $1.48807 |
| Total | (49,000) | $73,363.00 | $1.49720 |
| Costs Added by Department | | | |
| Work in Process, Beginning Inventory | | | |
| Labor | | $ 1,000.00 | |
| Overhead | | 800.00 | |
| Costs Added During the Period | | | |
| Labor | | 35,000.00 | $0.76596 |
| Overhead | | 30,000.00 | 0.65532 |
| Total Cost Added | | $ 66,800.00 | $1.42128 |
| Total Costs to Be Accounted For | | $140,163.00 | $2.91848 |

**Costs Accounted For**

| | | |
|---|---:|---:|
| Transferred to Next Department | | |
| Completed (44,000 × $2.91848) | $128,413.00 | |
| Normal Spoilage (750 × $2.91848) | 2,189.00 | $130,602.00 |

Work in Process, Ending Inventory
  Cost from Preceding Department
     (4,000 × $1.49720)                          5,989.00
  Labor (4,000 × 1/2 × $0.76596)            1,532.00
  Overhead (4,000 × 1/2 × $0.65532)     1,311.00        8,832.00
Abnormal Spoilage (250 × $2.91848)                730.00
Less: Rounding Difference                      ⟨1.00⟩
Total Costs Accounted For                   $140,164.00

**Computations**

*Unit costs:*  Labor: ($1,000 + $35,000) ÷ 47,000 = $0.76596
               Overhead: ($800 + $30,000) ÷ 47,000 = $0.65532

*Company A*
*Finishing Department*
*Cost of Production Report*
*February, 19X1*

**Quantities**

| | | |
|---|---:|---:|
| Units in Process Beginning | 4,000 | |
| Units Received from Preceding Department | 44,000 | 48,000 |
| | | |
| Units Transferred to Finished Goods | 41,000 | |
| Units Still in Process | 6,000 | |
| Spoiled Units | 1,000 | 48,000 |

**Equivalent Production** (Conversion Costs Only)

| | |
|---|---:|
| Units completed | 41,000 |
| Work in process, ending (6,000 × 1/3) | 2,000 |
| Spoiled units [1,000 × 30% (point of inspection)] | 300 |
| Equivalent production | 43,300 |

| Costs to Be Accounted For | | Total Cost | Unit Cost |
|---|---:|---:|---:|
| Costs from Preceding Department | | | |
|   Work in Process, Beginning Inventory | (4,000) | $ 12,800.00 | $3.20000 |
|   Transferred-in | (44,000) | 130,602.00 | $2.96823 |
|     Total | (48,000) | $143,402.00 | $2.98754 |
| Cost Added by Department | | | |
|   Work in Process, Beginning Inventory | | | |
|     Labor | | $ 2,000.00 | |
|     Overhead | | 1,500.00 | |
|   Cost Added during the Period | | | |
|     Labor | | 37,000.00 | $0.90069 |
|     Overhead | | 22,000.00 | 0.54273 |
|     Total Costs Added | | $ 62,500.00 | $1.44342 |
| Total Costs to Be Accounted For | | $205,902.00 | $4.43096 |

**Costs Accounted For**

| | | |
|---|---:|---:|
| Transferred to Finished Goods | | |
|   Completed (41,000 × $4.43096) | $181,669.00 | |
|   Normal Spoilage | 2,984.00 | $184,653.00 |

Work in Process, Ending Inventory

   Costs from Preceding Department

      (6,000 × $2.98754)                                       $ 17,925.00

      Labor (6,000 × 1/3 × $0.90069)                       1,801.00

      Overhead (6,000 × 1/3 × $0.54273)                1,085.00

      Normal Spoilage                                   437.00       21,248.00

  Add: Rounding Difference                                    1.00

  Total Costs Accounted For                               $205,902.00

### Computations

*Unit costs:*   Labor: ($2,000 + $37,000) ÷ 43,300 = $0.90069

                Overhead: ($1,500 + $22,000) ÷ 43,300 = $0.54273

*Spoilage*  (1,000 units, all normal):

        From Preceding Department (1,000 × $2.98754)   $2,988.00

        Added during the Period:

           Labor (1,000 × 30% × $0.90069)         270.00

           Overhead (1,000 × 30% × $0.54273)     163.00

        Total Spoilage                         $3,421.00

        Allocated Normal To:

           Transferred to Finished Goods:

                  (41,000 ÷ 47,000) × $3,421 = $2,984.00

           Work in Process:

                  (6,000 ÷ 47,000) × $3,421 = $   437.00

Problems 8.8 through 8.11 present a comprehensive exercise in the average cost method associated with process costing. A similar exercise is presented in Problems 8.12 through 8.15, using the first-in, first-out (FIFO) method. Both exercises relate to the operations of the same company, as described below.

The Hennessy Company developed and has successfully marketed a household cleaning agent for a number of years. The product is manufactured by continuous processing in four departments. The significant cost facts relating to each department are as follows:

### Department

| | |
|---|---|
| I | Materials first put into process (see Problem 8.8) |
| II | Beginning work in process from preceding department (see Problem 8.9) |
| III | Additional materials added (see Problem 8.10) |
| IV | Spoiled units during production (see Problem 8.11) |

**8.8**    **Average Cost: Materials First Put into Process.** Department I had a beginning work in process inventory of 2,000 units, consisting of: materials, $3,000; labor, $2,500; and factory overhead, $4,000. Costs added by the department during the month were: materials, $19,000; labor, $13,500; and factory overhead, $8,000. During the month, 20,000 units were started and 19,000 units were transferred out. The ending work in process inventory was 3,000 units, consisting of materials 100% complete and conversion costs $33\frac{1}{3}$% complete.

    Prepare a Cost of Production Report for the Hennessy Company, Department 1 for the month of July, 19X1, using the average cost method.

**SOLUTION**

*The Hennessy Company*
*Department I*
*Cost of Production Report*
*for the month of July, 19X1*

| Quantities | Physical Units | |
|---|---|---|
| Units to Account For | | |
| Work in Process, Beginning Inventory | 2,000 | |
| Started in Process | 20,000 | 22,000 |
| | | |
| Units Accounted For | | |
| Transferred Out | 19,000 | |
| Work in Process, Ending Inventory | 3,000 | 22,000 |

| Equivalent Production | Materials | Conversion Costs |
|---|---|---|
| Units completed | 19,000 | 19,000 |
| Work in process, ending | | |
| Materials | 3,000 | |
| Conversion costs $(3,000 \times 33\frac{1}{3}\%)$ | | 1,000 |
| Equivalent production | 22,000 | 20,000 |

| Costs to Account For | Total Cost | Unit Cost |
|---|---|---|
| Work in Process, Beginning Inventory | | |
| Materials | $ 3,000 | |
| Labor | 2,500 | |
| Factory Overhead | 4,000 | |
| Cost Added by Department | | |
| Materials | 19,000 | $1.00 (a) |
| Labor | 13,500 | 0.80 (b) |
| Factory Overhead | 8,000 | 0.60 (c) |
| Total Costs to Account For | $50,000 | $2.40 |

| Costs Accounted For | | |
|---|---|---|
| Transferred Out $(19,000 \times \$2.40)$ | $45,600 | |
| Work in Process, Ending Inventory | | |
| Materials $(3,000 \times \$1.00)$ | 3,000 | |
| Labor $(3,000 \times 33\frac{1}{3}\% \times \$0.80)$ | 800 | |
| Factory Overhead $(3,000 \times 33\frac{1}{3}\% \times \$0.60)$ | 600 | |
| Total Costs Accounted For | $50,000 | |

**Computations**

*Unit costs:*　(a)　Materials: $(\$3,000 + \$19,000) \div 22,000 = \$1.00$

　　　　　　　(b)　Labor: $(\$2,500 + \$13,500) = \$16,000 \div 20,000 = \$0.80$

　　　　　　　(c)　Factory overhead: $(\$4,000 + \$8,000) \div 20,000 = \$0.60$

**8.9**    **Average Costs: Beginning Work in Process from Preceding Department.**  In Department II of
the Hennessy Company, beginning work in process costs consist of two parts:

(1)  Materials plus conversion costs of Department I, and

(2)  Costs added by Department II.  No materials are added in this department.

Thus, Department II's beginning work in process inventory of 6,000 units had related
costs of $15,000 from Department I plus the following costs added by Department II in the
preceding month: labor, $2,000; factory overhead, $1,000.  Costs added by Department II
during the current month were: labor, $46,000; factory overhead, $23,000.  During the month
19,000 units with related costs of $45,600 were transferred in from Department I. There were
20,000 parts transferred out to Department III during the month.  The ending work in process inventory, was 5,000 units, 80% complete as to conversion costs.

Prepare a Cost of Production Report for Department II covering the month of July,
19X1, using average costs.

### SOLUTION

*The Hennessy Company*
*Department II*
*Cost of Production Report*
*for the month of July, 19X1*

| Quantities | | Physical Units | |
|---|---|---|---|
| Units to Account For | | | |
| Work in Process, Beginning Inventory | | 6,000 | |
| Transferred In from Department I | | 19,000 | 25,000 |
| | | | |
| Units Accounted For | | | |
| Transferred Out to Department III | | 20,000 | |
| Work in Process, Ending Inventory | | 5,000 | 25,000 |

| Equivalent Production (Conversion Costs Only) | | |
|---|---|---|
| Units completed | | 20,000 |
| Work in process, ending (5,000 × 80%) | | 4,000 |
| Equivalent production | | 24,000 |

| Costs to Account For | | Total Cost | Unit Cost |
|---|---|---|---|
| Costs from Department I | | | |
| Work in Process, Beginning | (6,000) | $ 15,000 | $2.500 |
| Transferred In during Month | (19,000) | 45,600 | 2.400 |
| Total | (25,000) | $ 60,600 | $2.424 (a) |
| Cost Added by Department | | | |
| Work in Process (added during last period) | | | |
| Labor | | $  2,000 | |
| Factory Overhead | | 1,000 | |
| Added during Current Period | | | |
| Labor | | 46,000 | $2.000 (b) |
| Factory Overhead | | 23,000 | 1.000 (c) |
| Total Costs to Account For | | $132,600 | $5.424 |

**Costs Accounted For**

Transferred to Department III
(20,000 × $5.424) .......................... $108,480

Work in Process, Ending Inventory
From Department I (5,000 × $2.424) ......... 12,120
Department II
Labor (5,000 × 80% × $2.00) ............ 8,000
Factory Overhead (5,000 × 80% × $1.00) .. 4,000

Total Costs Accounted For ................... $132,600

**Computations**

*Unit costs:*

(a)  Costs from Department I: $60,600 ÷ 25,000 = $2.424 (materials, $1.00; conversion costs, $1.424)

(b)  Labor: ($2,000 + $46,000) ÷ 24,000 = $2.00

(c)  Factory overhead: ($1,000 + $23,000) ÷ 24,000 = $1.00

**8.10**  **Average Costs: Materials Added in Subsequent Department.**  Department III of the Hennessy Company had no beginning work in process inventory in July.  Costs added by the department during the month were: materials, $25,000; labor, $12,000; and factory overhead, $6,000.  During the month, 20,000 units with related costs of $108,480 were transferred in from Department II, 22,000 units were transferred out to Department IV.  The ending work in process inventory was 3,000 units, 100% complete as to materials cost and $66\frac{2}{3}$% complete as to conversion costs.

Prepare a Cost of Production Report for Department III, using average costs.

**SOLUTION**

*The Hennessy Company*
*Department III*
*Cost of Production Report*
*for the month of July, 19X1*

| Quantities | Physical Units | |
|---|---|---|
| Units to Account For | | |
| Transferred In from Department II | 20,000 | |
| Additional Units Put into Process | 5,000 | 25,000 |
| | | |
| Units Accounted For | | |
| Transferred Out to Department IV | 22,000 | |
| Work in Process, Ending Inventory | 3,000 | 25,000 |

| Equivalent Production | Materials | Conversion Costs |
|---|---|---|
| Units completed | 22,000 | 22,000 |
| Work in process, ending | | |
| Materials | 3,000 | |
| Conversion costs (3,000 × $66\frac{2}{3}$%) | | 2,000 |
| Equivalent production | 25,000 | 24,000 |

| Costs to Account For | Total Cost | Unit Cost |
|---|---|---|
| Transferred In from Department II (20,000) | $108,480 | $5.4240 |
| Adjusted Unit Cost—Additional Units | $108,480 | $4.3392 (a) |
| Cost Added by Department | | |
| Materials | $ 25,000 | $1.0000 (b) |
| Labor | 12,000 | 0.5000 (c) |
| Factory Overhead | 6,000 | 0.2500 (d) |
| Total Cost Added | $ 43,000 | $1.7500 |
| Total Costs to Account For | $151,480 | $6.0892 |

| Costs Accounted For | | |
|---|---|---|
| Transferred to Department IV | | |
| (22,000 × $6.0892) | $133,962 | |
| Work in Process, Ending Inventory | | |
| Adjusted Cost, Preceding Department (3,000 × $4.3392) | 13,018 | |
| Materials (3,000 × $1.00) | 3,000 | |
| Labor (3,000 × 66⅔% × $0.50) | 1,000 | |
| Factory Overhead (3,000 × 66⅔% × $0.25) | 500 | |
| Total Costs Accounted For | $151,480 | |

**Computations**

*Unit costs:*

    (a)   Costs for Department II: $108,480 ÷ 25,000 = $4.3392

    (b)   Materials (additional): $25,000 ÷ 25,000 = $1.00

    (c)   Labor: $12,000 ÷ 24,000 = $0.50

    (d)   Factory overhead: $6,000 ÷ 24,000 = $0.25

**8.11**    **Average Costs: Spoiled Units during Production.** Department IV of the Hennessy Company had no beginning work in process inventory in July. Costs added by the department during the month were: labor, $38,000 and factory overhead, $9,500. During the month, 22,000 units with related costs of $133,962 were transferred in from Department III, and 18,000 units were transferred out to Finished Goods. The ending work in process inventory was 2,000 units, 100% complete as to materials and 50% complete as to conversion costs. There were 2,000 spoiled units during production in this department. Spoilage considered to be uncontrollable amounted to 1,500 units. Inspection occurs at 40% of the process. Conversion costs are added evenly.

    Prepare a cost of production report for Department IV, using average costing under (a) Method 1 and (b) Method 2 of accounting for spoiled units in equivalent production.

## SOLUTION

(a)   *Method 1:* Spoiled units ignored.

*The Hennessy Company*
*Department IV*
*Cost of Production Report*
*for the month of July, 19X1*

| Quantities | Physical Units | |
|---|---|---|
| Units to Account For | | |
| Transferred In from Department III | | 22,000 |
| | | |
| Units Accounted For | | |
| Transferred Out to Finished Goods | 18,000 | |
| Work in Process, Ending Inventory | 2,000 | |
| Spoiled Units | 2,000 | 22,000 |

| Equivalent Production (Conversion Costs Only) | | |
|---|---|---|
| Units completed | 18,000 | |
| Work in process, ending (2,000 × 50%) | 1,000 | |
| Equivalent production | 19,000 | |

| Costs to Account For | Total Cost | Unit Cost |
|---|---|---|
| Transferred In from Department III (22,000) | $133,962 | $6.08920 |
| | | |
| Cost Added by Department | | |
| Labor | $ 38,000 | $2.00000 (a) |
| Factory Overhead | 9,500 | 0.50000 (b) |
| | $ 47,500 | $2.50000 |
| Adjustment for Spoiled Units | | $0.60892 (c) |
| Total Costs to Account For | $181,462 | $9.19812 |

| Costs Accounted For | | |
|---|---|---|
| Transferred to Finished Goods (18,000 × $9.19812) | $165,566 | |
| Work in Process, Ending Inventory | | |
| Adjusted Cost, Preceding Department (2,000 × $6.69812) | 13,396 (d) | |
| Labor (2,000 × 50% × $2.00) | 2,000 | |
| Factory Overhead (2,000 × 50% × $0.50) | 500 | |
| Total Costs Accounted For | $181,462 | |

### Computations

*Unit costs:*

(a)   Labor: $38,000 ÷ 19,000 = $2.00

(b)   Factory overhead: $9,500 ÷ 19,000 = $0.50

(c)   Spoiled units

$$\frac{\$133,962}{22,000 - 2,000} = \$6.69810; \quad \$6.69810 - \$6.08918 = \$0.608920$$

or $\quad 2,000 \times \$6.08918 = \$12,178.36; \quad \dfrac{\$12,178.36}{22,000 - 2,000} = \$0.608918$

(d)   Adjusted cost: $6.08918 + $0.60892 = $6.69812

*Note:* The discrepancy between the two methods is due to rounding: $0.60892 is used in this solution.

(b)   *Method 2:* Spoiled units included.

*The Hennessy Company*
*Department IV*
*Cost of Production Report*
*for the month of July, 19X1*

| Quantities | Physical Units | |
|---|---:|---:|
| **Units to Account For** | | |
| Transferred In from Department III | | 22,000 |
| | | |
| **Units Accounted For** | | |
| Transferred Out to Finished Goods | 18,000 | |
| Work in Process, Ending Inventory | 2,000 | |
| Spoiled Units | 2,000 | 22,000 |

**Equivalent Production** (Conversion Costs Only)

| | | |
|---|---:|---|
| Units completed | 18,000 | |
| Work in process (2,000 × 50%) | 1,000 | |
| Spoiled units [2,000 × 40% (point of inspection)] | 800 | |
| Equivalent production | 19,800 | |

| Costs to Account For | Total Cost | Unit Cost |
|---|---:|---:|
| Transferred in from Department III (22,000 units) | $133,962.00 | $6.08920 |
| Cost Added by Department | | |
| Labor | $ 38,000.00 | $1.91919 |
| Factory Overhead | 9,500.00 | 0.47980 |
| Total Cost Added | $ 47,500.00 | $2.39899 |
| Total Costs to Account For | $181,462.00 | $8.48819 |

| Costs Accounted For | | |
|---|---:|---:|
| Transferred to Finished Goods | | |
| Completed (18,000 × $8.48819) | $152,787.00 | |
| Normal Spoilage | 9,516.00 | $162,303.00 |
| Work in Process, Ending Inventory | | |
| From Preceding Department (2,000 × $6.08920) | $ 12,178.00 | |
| Labor (2,000 × 50% × $1.91919) | 1,919.00 | |
| Factory Overhead (2,000 × 50% × $0.47980) | 480.00 | |
| Normal Spoilage | 1,057.00 | 15,634.00 |
| Abnormal Spoilage | | 3,524.00 |
| Add: Rounding Difference | | 1.00 |
| Total Costs Accounted For | | $181,462.00 |

**Computations**

*Unit costs:*   Labor: $38,000 ÷ 19,800 = $1.91919

Factory Overhead: $9,500 ÷ 19,800 = $0.47980

*Spoilage*   (2,000 units):

| | |
|---|---:|
| From Preceding Department (2,000 × $6.08920) | $12,178.00 |
| Added during the Period | |
| Labor (2,000 × 40% × $1.91919) | 1,535.00 |
| Overhead (2,000 × 40% × $0.47980) | 384.00 |
| Total Spoilage | $14,097.00 |

| Allocated to Abnormal: (500 ÷ 2,000) × $14,097 | = | $3,524.00 |
|---|---|---|
| Allocated to Normal: (1,500 ÷ 2,000) × $14,097 | = | $10,573.00 |

Further Allocated Normal Spoilage To:

| Finished Goods: (18,000 ÷ 20,000) × $10,573 | = | $9,516.00 |
|---|---|---|
| Work in Process, Ending: (2,000 ÷ 20,000) × $10,573 | = | $1,057.00 |

**8.12** **FIFO: Materials First Put into Process.** Department I had a beginning work in process inventory of 2,000 units, consisting of: materials, $3,000; labor, $2,500; and factory overhead, $4,000. Costs added by the department during the month were: materials, $19,000; labor, $13,500; and factory overhead, $8,000. During the month, 20,000 units were started and 19,000 units were transferred out. The ending work in process inventory was 3,000 units, consisting of materials 100% complete and conversion costs $33\frac{1}{3}\%$ complete.

Prepare a Cost of Production Report for the Hennessy Company, Department 1 for the month of July, 19X1, using the FIFO method.

**SOLUTION**

*The Hennessy Company*
*Department I*
*Cost of Production Report*
*for the month of July, 19X1*

| Quantities | Physical Units | |
|---|---|---|
| Units to Account For | | |
| Work in Process, Begining Inventory | 2,000 | |
| Started in Process | 20,000 | 22,000 |
| | | |
| Units Accounted For | | |
| Transferred Out | 19,000 | |
| Work in Process, Ending Inventory | 3,000 | 22,000 |

| Equivalent Production | Materials | Conversion Costs |
|---|---|---|
| Units completed and transferred | 19,000 | 19,000 |
| Less: Beginning work in process | ⟨2,000⟩ | ⟨2,000⟩ |
| Units started and completed | 17,000 | 17,000 |
| Add: Work needed to complete beginning work in process | | |
| Materials | 0 | |
| Conversion costs (2,000 × 50%) | | 1,000 |
| Add: Work in process, ending | | |
| Materials | 3,000 | |
| Conversion costs (3,000 × $33\frac{1}{3}\%$) | | 1,000 |
| Equivalent production | 20,000 | 19,000 |

| Costs to Account For | Total Cost | Unit Cost |
|---|---|---|
| Work in Process, Beginning Inventory | $ 9,500 | |
| Cost Added by Department | | |
| Materials | $19,000 | $0.950000 (a) |
| Labor | 13,500 | 0.710526 (b) |
| Factory Overhead | 8,000 | 0.421053 (c) |
| Total Costs to Account For | $50,000 | $2.081579 |

**Costs Accounted For**

Transferred Out

  From Beginning Inventory

| | |
|---|---:|
| Inventory Value, Beginning | $ 9,500 |
| Labor Added (2,000 × 50% × $0.710526) | 711 |
| Factory Overhead Added<br>    (2,000 × 50% × $0.421053) | 421 |
| Total Cost, Beginning Units | $10,632 |
| From Current Production | |
|   Units Started and Finished (17,000 × $2.081579) | 35,386 |
| Total Cost | $46,018 |
| | |
| Work in Process, Ending Inventory | |
|   Materials (3,000 × $0.950) | $ 2,850 |
|   Labor (3,000 × 33⅓% × $0.710526) | 711 |
|   Factory Overhead (3,000 × 33⅓% × $0.421053) | 421 |
| Total Costs Accounted For | $50,000 |

**Computations**

*Unit costs:*

(a)  Materials: $19,000 ÷ 20,000 = $0.950000

(b)  Labor: $13,500 ÷ 19,000 = $0.710526

(c)  Factory overhead: $8,000 ÷ 19,000 = $0.421053

**8.13**    **FIFO: Beginning Work in Process from Preceding Department.** The Hennessy Company's records for July showed that Department II had a beginning work in process inventory of 6,000 units at $18,000; 100% complete as to materials, 33⅓% complete as to conversion costs. Costs added by the department during the month were: labor, $46,000; and factory overhead, $23,000. During the month there were 19,000 units transferred in and 20,000 units transferred out. The ending work in process inventory was 5,000 units, consisting of materials 100% complete and conversion costs 40% complete.

    Prepare a Cost of Production Report for the month, using the FIFO method.

**SOLUTION**

*The Hennessy Company*
*Department II*
*Cost of Production Report*
*for the month of July, 19X1*

| Quantities | Physical Units | |
|---|---:|---:|
| Units to Account For | | |
|   Work in Process, Beginning | 6,000 | |
|   Transferred In | 19,000 | 25,000 |
| | | |
| Units Accounted For | | |
|   Transferred Out to Department III | 20,000 | |
|   Work in Process, Ending | 5,000 | 25,000 |
| **Equivalent Production** (Conversion Costs Only) | | |
| Units completed and transferred | 20,000 | |
| Less: Beginning work in process | 6,000 | |
| Units started and completed | 14,000 | |
| Add: Work needed to complete beginning<br>    work in process (6,000 × 66⅔%) | 4,000 | |
| Add: Work in process, ending (5,000 × 40%) | 2,000 | |
| Equivalent production | 20,000 | |

| Costs to Account For | Total Cost | Unit Cost | |
|---|---|---|---|
| Work in Process, Beginning Inventory | $ 18,000 | | |
| Transferred In (19,000) | $ 46,018 | $2.422 | (a) |
| Cost Added by Department | | | |
|   Labor | 46,000 | $2.300 | (b) |
|   Factory Overhead | 23,000 | 1.150 | (c) |
| Total Costs to Account For | $133,018 | $5.872 | |

| Costs Accounted For | | |
|---|---|---|
| Transferred to Department III | | |
|   From Beginning Inventory | | |
|     Inventory Value, Beginning | $ 18,000 | |
|     Labor Added (6,000 × 66⅔% × $2.30) | 9,200 | |
|     Factory Overhead (6,000 × 66⅔% × $1.15) | 4,600 | |
|   Total Cost, Beginning Units | $ 31,800 | |
|   From Current Production | | |
|     Units Started and Finished (14,000 × $5.872) | 82,208 | |
|   Total Transferred (20,000) | $114,008 | |
| Work in Process, Ending Inventory | | |
|   From Preceding Department (5,000 × $2.422) | $ 12,110 | |
|   Labor (5,000 × 40% × $2.30) | 4,600 | |
|   Factory Overhead (5,000 × 40% × $1.15) | 2,300 | |
| | $ 19,010 | |
| Total Costs Accounted For | $133,018 | |

**Computations**

*Unit costs:*

(a)   From preceding department: $46,018 ÷ 19,000 = $2.422

(b)   Labor: $46,000 ÷ 20,000 = $2.30

(c)   Factory overhead: $23,000 ÷ 20,000 = $1.150

**8.14    FIFO: Materials Added in Subsequent Department.**   Department III had a beginning work in process inventory of 2,000 units at a cost of $8,000, 100% complete as to materials (to that point) and 50% complete as to conversion costs.   Costs added by the department during the month of July were: materials, $25,000 (increasing final units by 3,000); labor, $12,000; and factory overhead, $6,000.   During the month, 20,000 units were transferred in and 22,000 units were transferred out.   The ending work in process inventory was 3,000 units, consisting of materials 100% complete and conversion costs 33⅓% complete.

Prepare a Cost of Production Report for the month, using the FIFO method.

**SOLUTION**

*The Hennessy Company*
*Department III*
*Cost of Production Report*
*for the month of July, 19X1*

| Quantities | Physical Units | |
|---|---|---|
| Units to Account For | | |
|   Work in Process, Beginning Inventory | 2,000 | |
|   Transferred In from Department II | 20,000 | |
|   Additional Units Put into Process | 3,000 | 25,000 |

Units Accounted For

| Transferred Out to Department IV | 22,000 | |
| Work in Process, Ending Inventory | 3,000 | 25,000 |

| Equivalent Production | Materials | Conversion Costs |
| --- | --- | --- |
| Units completed and transferred | 22,000 | 22,000 |
| Less: Beginning work in process | ⟨2,000⟩ | ⟨2,000⟩ |
| Units started and completed | 20,000 | 20,000 |
| Add: Work needed to complete beginning work in process | | |
| Materials | 0 | |
| Conversion costs (2,000 × 50%) | | 1,000 |
| Add: Work in process, ending | | |
| Materials | 3,000 | |
| Conversion costs (3,000 × 33⅓%) | | 1,000 |
| Equivalent production | 23,000 | 22,000 |

| Costs to Account For | Total Cost | Unit Cost | |
| --- | --- | --- | --- |
| Work in Process, Beginning Inventory | $ 8,000 | | |
| Transferred In (20,000) | $114,008 | $5.70040 | (a) |
| Cost Added by Department | | | |
| Materials | $ 25,000 | $1.08695 | |
| Labor | 12,000 | 0.54545 | |
| Factory Overhead | 6,000 | 0.27272 | |
| Total Cost Added | $ 43,000 | $1.90512 | |
| Transferred In Unit Cost (adjusted) | | 4.95687 | (b) |
| Total Costs to Account For | $165,008 | $6.86199 | |

**Costs Accounted For**

Transferred to Department IV

From Beginning Inventory

| Inventory Value | $ 8,000 |
| Labor Added (2,000 × 50% × $0.54545) | 545 |
| Factory Overhead (2,000 × 50 % × $0.27272) | 273 |
| Total Cost, Beginning Units | $ 8,818 |

From Current Production

| Units Started and Finished (20,000 × $6.86199) | 137,240 |
| Total Cost, Transferred Units (22,000) | $146,058 |

Work in Process, Ending Inventory

| Adjusted Cost, Preceding Department (3,000 × $4.95687) | $ 14,871 |
| Materials (3,000 × $1.08695) | 3,261 |
| Labor (3,000 × 33⅓% × $0.54545) | 545 |
| Factory Overhead (3,000 × 33⅓% × $0.27272) | 273 |
| | $ 18,950 |
| Total Costs Accounted For | $165,008 |

**Computations**

*Unit costs:*

    (a)   Transferred in unit cost: $114,008 \div 20,000 = \$5.70040$

    (b)   Transferred in adjusted cost: $114,008 \div 23,000 = \$4.95687$

**8.15**    **FIFO: Spoiled Units during Production.**  In Department IV of the Hennessy Company, the beginning work in process inventory was 3,000 units costing $9,000, 100% complete as to material, $33\frac{1}{3}\%$ complete as to conversion costs. Costs added by the department during the month of July were: labor, $38,000; factory overhead, $9,500. During the month there were 22,000 units transferred in and 20,000 units transferred out. The ending work in process inventory consisted of 2,000 units, 100% complete as to materials and 50% complete as to conversion costs. There were 3,000 units spoiled during production in this department; of these, 1,500 units were considered to be controllable. Inspection point is at 40% of the process. Conversion costs are added evenly. Under FIFO costing, prepare a cost of production report using (a) Method 1 and (b) Method 2 of accounting for spoiled units in equivalent production.

## SOLUTION

(a)   *Method 1:* Spoiled units ignored.

**The Hennessy Company**
**Department IV**
**Cost of Production Report**
**for the month of July, 19X1**

| Quantities | **Physical Units** | |
|---|---:|---:|
| Units to Account For | | |
|   Work in Process, Beginning Inventory | 3,000 | |
|   Transferred In from Department III | 22,000 | 25,000 |
| | | |
| Units Accounted For | | |
|   Transferred Out to Department IV | 20,000 | |
|   Work in Process, Ending Inventory | 2,000 | |
|   Spoiled Units | 3,000 | 25,000 |

| Equivalent Production (Conversion Costs Only) | |
|---|---:|
| Units completed and transferred | 20,000 |
| Less: Beginning work in process | ⟨3,000⟩ |
| Units started and completed | 17,000 |
| Add: Work needed to complete | |
|   beginning work in process $(3,000 \times 66\frac{2}{3}\%)$ | 2,000 |
| Add: Work in process, ending $(2,000 \times 50\%)$ | 1,000 |
| Equivalent production | 20,000 |

| Costs to Account For | **Total Cost** | **Unit Cost** |
|---|---:|---:|
| Work in Process, Beginning Inventory | $ 9,000 | |
| Transferred In (22,000) | $146,058 | $ 6.63900 |
| Cost Added by Department | | |
|   Labor | $ 38,000 | $ 1.90000 |
|   Factory Overhead | 9,500 | 0.47500 |
| Total Cost Added | $ 47,500 | $ 2.37500 |
| Adjustment for Spoiled Units | — | 1.04826 |
| Total Costs to Account For | $202,558 | $10.06226 |

**Costs Accounted For**

Transferred to Finished Goods

  From Beginning Inventory

| | |
|---|---:|
|     Inventory Value | $  9,000 |
|     Labor Added (3,000 × 66⅔% × $1.90) | 3,800 |
|     Factory Overhead Added (3,000 × 66⅔% × $0.475) | 950 |
| Total Cost, Beginning Units | $ 13,750 |
|   From Current Production | |
|     Units Started and Finished (17,000 × $10.06226) | 171,058 |
| Total Transferred (20,000) | $184,808 |
| Work in Process, Ending Inventory | |
|   Adjusted Cost, Preceding Department (2,000 × $7.68726) | $ 15,375 |
|   Labor (2,000 × 50% × $1.90) | 1,900 |
|   Factory Overhead (2,000 × 50% × $0.475) | 475 |
| | $ 17,750 |
| Total Costs Accounted For | $202,558 |

**Computations**

*Spoiled units:*

$$\$146{,}058 \div 19{,}000 = \$7.68726; \; \$7.68726 - \$6.63900 = \$1.04826$$

or       $3{,}000 \times 6.63900 = \$19{,}917; \; \$19{,}917 \div 19{,}000 = \$1.04826$

(b)  *Method 2:* Spoiled units included.

*The Hennessy Company*
*Department IV*
*Cost of Production Report*
*for the month of July, 19X1*

| Quantities | Physical Units | |
|---|---:|---:|
| Units to Account For | | |
|   Work in Process, Beginning Inventory | 3,000 | |
|   Transferred In from Department III | 22,000 | 25,000 |
| Units Accounted For | | |
|   Transferred Out | 20,000 | |
|   Work in Process, Ending Inventory | 2,000 | |
|   Spoiled Units | 3,000 | 25,000 |
| **Equivalent Production** (Conversion Costs Only) | | |
| Units Completed and Transferred | 20,000 | |
| Less: Beginning Work in Process | ⟨3,000⟩ | |
| Units Started and Completed | 17,000 | |
| Add: Work Needed to Complete Beginning | | |
|     Work in Process (3,000 × 66⅔%) | 2,000 | |
| Add: Work in Process, Ending (2,000 × 50%) | 1,000 | |
| Add: Spoiled Units [3,000 × 40% (point of inspection)] | 1,200 | |
| Equivalent Production | 21,200 | |

| Costs to Account For | Total Cost | Unit Cost |
|---|---|---|
| Work in Process, Beginning Inventory | $ 9,000.00 | |
| Transferred In (22,000 units) | $146,058.00 | $6.63900 |
| Cost Added by Department | | |
| Labor | $ 38,000.00 | $1.79245 |
| Factory Overhead | 9,500.00 | 0.44811 |
| Total Costs Added | $ 47,500.00 | $2.24056 |
| Total Costs to Account For | $202,558.00 | $8.87956 |

**Costs Accounted For**

Transferred to Finished Goods

From Beginning Inventory

| Inventory Value | $ 9,000.00 | |
|---|---|---|
| Labor Added (3,000 × 66⅔% × $1.79245) | 3,585.00 | |
| Factory Overhead (3,000 × 66⅔% × $0.44811) | 896.00 | $ 13,481.00 |

From Current Production

| Units Started and Finished (17,000 × $8.87956) | $150,953.00 | |
|---|---|---|
| Normal Spoilage | 10,275.00 | 161,228.00 |
| Total Transferred | | $174,709.00 |

Work in Process, Ending Inventory

| From Preceding Department (2,000 × $6.63900) | $ 13,278.00 | |
|---|---|---|
| Labor (2,000 × 50% × $1.79245) | 1,792.00 | |
| Factory Overhead (2,000 × 50% × $0.44811) | 448.00 | |
| Normal Spoilage | 1,028.00 | 16,546.00 |
| Abnormal Spoilage | | 11,303.00 |
| Total Costs Accounted For | | $202,558.00 |

**Computations**

*Unit costs:*   Labor: $38,000 ÷ 21,200 = $1.79245
Overhead: $9,500 ÷ 21,200 = $0.44811

*Spoilage* (3,000 units):

| From Preceding Department (3,000 × $6.63900) | $19,917.00 |
|---|---|
| Added during the Period | |
| Labor (3,000 × 40% × $1.79245) | 2,151.00 |
| Overhead (3,000 × 40% × $0.44811) | 538.00 |
| Total Spoilage | $22,606.00 |

Allocated to Abnormal: (1,500 ÷ 3,000) × $22,606 = $11,303.00

Allocated to Normal: (1,500 ÷ 3,000) × $22,606 = $11,303.00

Further Allocated Normal Spoilage to:

Finished Goods: (20,000 ÷ 22,000) × $11,303 = $10,275.00

Work in Process, Ending: (2,000 ÷ 22,000) × $11,303 = $1,028.00

# Chapter 9

# Standard Costs I

## 9.1 STANDARD COSTS DEFINED

A carefully prepared predetermined or normal standard cost is expressed in terms of a single unit. It represents a product's planned cost and is generally established well before production begins, thus providing a goal to aim for. Standard cost is concerned with unit cost and serves basically the same purpose as a budget, but on a smaller scale, since the latter is concerned with total rather than unit costs.

## 9.2 TYPES OF STANDARDS

Standards are generally classified as either of two types: basic or current.

(1) *Basic Standard.* This is a base against which both estimated and actual results are compared. It usually remains constant from year to year and is used in the same manner as an index number.

(2) *Current Standard.* This takes any of the following forms:

*Expected actual standard.* Anticipated results for the year, based on foreseeable operating conditions and costs.

*Normal standard.* An average figure based on normal operations aimed at smoothing out absorption of fixed factory overhead.

*Theoretical standard.* A figure based on maximum possible level of output under ideal conditions and with no interruptions. It is generally considered a goal that is not easily attained.

## 9.3 MATERIALS VARIANCES

Materials variances contain two components, as discussed below.

(1) *Price Variance.* This is the difference between the standard cost and the actual cost incurred. It is subject to external forces. Management has little control over such variances because they are caused by changes in the price of items purchased. The price variance is computed from the following equation:

$$\text{Price variance} = (\text{Actual unit cost} - \text{Standard unit cost}) \times \text{Actual quantity}$$

(2) *Quantity Variance.* This is the difference between standard input allowed and actual input. The variance is subject to control by management. The equation is

$$\text{Quantity variance} = (\text{Actual quantity used} - \text{Standard quantity allowed}) \times \text{Standard unit cost}$$

## EXAMPLE 1

Assume the following data: Standard unit cost for materials, $8; purchased, 6,000 units @ $8.20; put in process, 4,000 units; standard allowed, 4,100 units.   The price and quantity variances are computed below.

$$\text{Price variance} = (\$8.20 - \$8.00) \times 6,000 = \underline{\underline{\$1,200}} \text{ unfavorable}$$

$$\text{Quantity variance} = (4,000 - 4,100) \times \$8 = \underline{\underline{\$(800)}} \text{ favorable}$$

## 9.4   LABOR VARIANCES

Labor variances consist of two elements, as described below.

(1)  *Rate Variance.*  This is the difference between the standard rate and the actual rate paid. This variance is subject to external forces (e.g. labor unions) over which management has little control.   The equation is

$$\text{Rate variance} = (\text{Actual rate} - \text{standard rate}) \times \text{Actual hours worked}$$

(2)  *Efficiency Variance.*  This is the difference between the number of standard hours allowed and actual input.   It is a variance subject to management control.   The equation is

$$\text{Efficiency variance} = (\text{Actual hours} - \text{Standard hours allowed}) \times \text{Standard rate}$$

## EXAMPLE 2

Assume the following data: Actual hours, 5,000; actual rate, $4.10; standard rate, $4.20; standard hours allowed, 5,200.

$$\text{Rate variance} = (\$4.10 - \$4.20) \times 5,000 = \underline{\underline{\$(500)}} \text{ favorable}$$

$$\text{Efficiency variance} = (5,000 - 5,200) \times \$4.20 = \underline{\underline{\$(840)}} \text{ favorable}$$

## 9.5   FACTORY OVERHEAD VARIANCES

Variances in factory overhead can be attributed to three possible situations:

(1)  Output exceeding or being less than estimated normal capacity

(2)  Actual factory overhead costs exceeding or being less than budgeted factory costs

(3)  Actual hours worked differing from standard hours allowed for production achieved

The predetermined rate used to allocate factory overhead is generally based on *standard* or *allowed* hours (i.e. budgeted hours based on units produced).   Variances result when *actual hours* (those actually worked during the period) differ from the standard (or allowed) hours, or when costs incurred are greater or less than budgeted.

## 9.6   OVERALL FACTORY OVERHEAD VARIANCE (ONE-VARIANCE METHOD)

The overall or net factory overhead variance is computed as follows:

Actual factory overhead
Less: Overhead applied to production at standard hours and rate
Net overhead variance

The net overhead variance may be further analyzed to identify underlying causes using the two-variance method (see Section 9.7), the three-variance method (see Section 9.8), and the idle capacity variance (see Section 9.10).   The definitions of the variances described are given in Section 9.11.

## 9.7  TWO-VARIANCE METHOD

In the two-variance method, the net overhead variance is analyzed in terms of (1) budget (controllable) and (2) volume (denominator) variances, as follows:

(1)
          Actual factory overhead

          Less: Budget allowance at *standard* hours (fixed + variable* expenses)

          Controllable variance

          * Computation: Standard hours allowed × variable overhead rate.

(2)  (Normal or budgeted capacity − Standard hours allowed) × Standard fixed rate = Volume variance

### EXAMPLE 3

The computations associated with the two-variance method are shown below. The basic data for this illustration will be used also for Examples 4 and 5.

| | |
|---|---|
| Actual direct labor hours | 5,000 |
| Standard allowed | 5,200 |
| Normal capacity | 6,000 |
| Actual factory overhead | $29,500 |

Budgeted Overhead (normal capacity)

| | Total | Rate |
|---|---|---|
| Variable overhead | $12,000 | $2.00 |
| Fixed overhead | 18,000 | 3.00 |
| Totals | $30,000 | $5.00 |

The variances are as follows:

| | | | |
|---|---|---|---|
| *Controllable*: | Actual factory overhead | | $29,500 |
| | Budgeted at standard: | | |
| | Fixed | $18,000 | |
| | Variable (5,200 × $2) | 10,400 | 28,400 |
| | Unfavorable controllable variance | | $ 1,100 |

*Volume*:  (Normal or budgeted capacity − Standard hours allowed) × Standard fixed rate

(6,000 − 5,200) × $3.00 = $2,400 Unfavorable volume variance

The volume variance results from a difference in the denominator (of the estimated fixed overhead rate computation); that is, rather than a fixed rate of $3.00 ($18,000/6,000), a rate of $3.46 ($18,000/5,200) results. Hence, it is often called the *denominator variance*. Using these different rates, the volume variance can also be computed as follows:

($3.00 − $3.46) × 5,200 = $2,392 ($8 difference due to rounding)

## 9.8  THREE-VARIANCE METHOD

The three-variance method involves further analysis of the two-variance method. The budget (controllable) variance is divided into two parts: (1) spending (price) variance and (2) efficiency variance. The volume (denominator) variance is the same as in the two-variance method.

(1)          Actual factory overhead
             Less: Budget allowance at *actual* hours (fixed + variable* expenses)
             Spending variance

             _____

             * Computation: *Actual* hours × variable rate.

(2)     (Actual hours − Standard hours allowed) × Standard variable rate = Efficiency variance

(3)   See Section 9.7 for volume (denominator) variance.

## EXAMPLE 4

Analysis using the three-variance method is shown below.   The data is from Example 3.

| | | | |
|---|---|---|---|
| *Spending*: | Actual factory overhead | | $29,500 |
| | Budgeted at actual: | | |
| | Fixed | $18,000 | |
| | Variable (5,000 × $2) | 10,000 | 28,000 |
| | Unfavorable spending variance | | $ 1,500 |

*Efficiency*:          (Actual hours − Standard hours allowed) × Standard variable rate
                       (5,000 − 5,200) × $2.00 = $(400) Favorable efficiency variance

*Volume*:   See solution to Example 3 in Section 9.7.

## 9.9   FROM THREE- TO ONE-VARIANCE METHOD

As mentioned before, the two- and three-variance methods are further analysis of the net overhead variance (Section 9.6).   Thus, the previous variance calculations are related and can be tied in.

## EXAMPLE 5

The variance relationship can be illustrated as follows, using the results of the previous examples:

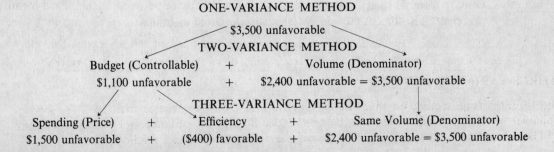

ONE-VARIANCE METHOD
$3,500 unfavorable

TWO-VARIANCE METHOD
Budget (Controllable)      +          Volume (Denominator)
$1,100 unfavorable      +        $2,400 unfavorable = $3,500 unfavorable

THREE-VARIANCE METHOD
Spending (Price)      +      Efficiency      +      Same Volume (Denominator)
$1,500 unfavorable    +    ($400) favorable    +    $2,400 unfavorable = $3,500 unfavorable

## 9.10  IDLE CAPACITY VARIANCE (FOURTH VARIANCE)

This fourth variance is unrelated to the other variances previously mentioned.  It results when a plant is underutilized (idle); production then falls below the expected, budgeted, or normal capacity.

(Normal or budgeted capacity − Actual hours) × Standard fixed rate = Idle capacity variance

### EXAMPLE 6

Assuming the same information as in Example 3, the idle capacity variance is as follows:

$$\text{(Normal or Budgeted capacity − Actual hours)} \times \text{Standard fixed rate}$$
$$(6,000 - 5,000) \times \$3.00 = \underline{\underline{\$3,000}} \text{ Unfavorable idle capacity variance}$$

## 9.11  MEANING OF VARIANCES

The following list of terms is intended to summarize the cost accounting significance of the presentation in Sections 9.7–9.10.

*Controllable.*   Measures variable variances.   Responsibility of supervisor of each department.

*Volume.*   Indicates capacity available and not utilized.   Responsibility rests with top management.

*Spending.*   Variable expenses analyzed.   Responsibility of supervisor, who is expected to keep actual expenses within the budget.

*Idle capacity.*   Indicates overhead underabsorbed because actual hours are less than normal hours upon which overhead rate was based.   Only fixed expenses are included.   Responsibility falls to top management.

*Efficiency.*   Reflects labor efficiency variance of variable expenses when labor cost or hours are used as the basis for applying factory overhead.

## 9.12  MIX AND YIELD VARIANCES

In industries where various grades of materials are used, an analysis of mix and yield variances often results in the production of more profitable products and less waste.  In addition to the mix and yield variances computed for materials, yield variances are also calculated for labor and variable factory overhead, since related expenses for these items are included in finished product costs.

The procedures for calculating mix and yield variances are described below.  The computations are illustrated in Example 7.

*Materials.*   The combination of materials used in production is generally based on predetermined specifications.   Variances often occur when it becomes possible to use a materials mix differing from this standard formula to achieve the same end.   The difference between the standard formula and the actual materials mix, or the *mix variance*, is computed as follows:

Actual materials mix (*individual* quantities used × individual standard unit input costs)

Less: Standard formula (*total* quantity used × standard weighted average unit input cost)

Materials mix variance

See Example 7, Item 1.

The materials mix specified in the standard formula is expected to provide a given amount of output, or *yield*. When the expected, or standard, yield differs from the actual yield, a *yield variance* exists, and is computed as follows:

> Expected yield (total quantity used × standard weighted average unit *input* cost)
>
> Less: Actual yield (total quantity produced × standard weighted average *output* cost)
>
> Materials yield variance

*Note*: In the computation for the materials yield variance given above, the equation for expected yield used the standard weighted average unit *input* cost and is identical to the standard formula equation for the materials mix variance. As such, it is a time-saver when both mix and yield variances are being computed. Expected yield may also be computed using the standard weighted average unit *output* cost and the ratio of standard output quantity to standard input quantity, as follows:

$$\text{Expected yield} = \text{Actual input quantity} \times \frac{\text{Standard output quantity}}{\text{Standard input quantity}}$$

$$\times \text{ Standard weighted average unit } output \text{ cost}$$

See Example 7, Item 2.

**Labor and Factory Overhead.** The standard output/standard input ratio introduced in the discussion of materials yield variances is also used to calculate labor yield and overhead yield variances. The computations are as follows:

> Expected yield (Actual input quantity × output/input ratio × standard labor rate per unit)
>
> Less: Actual yield (Actual output quantity × standard labor rate per unit)
>
> Labor yield variance

> Expected yield (Actual input quantity × output/input ratio × standard overhead rate per unit)
>
> Less: Actual yield (Actual output quantity × standard overhead rate per unit)
>
> Overhead yield variance

See Example 7, Items 3 and 4.

## EXAMPLE 7

The following data represent standard product and cost specifications for 10,000 gallons of white paint.

|                | Gallons Allowed | Unit Price | Cost      |
|----------------|-----------------|------------|-----------|
| Raw material A | 4,000           | $1.20      | $ 4,800   |
| Raw material B | 8,000           | .90        | 7,200     |
| Input          | 12,000          | $1.00*     | $12,000   |
| Output         | 10,000          | $1.20*     |           |

\* weighted average

Standard output/input ratio for materials: 10,000/12,000 = 5/6, or 0.833.

*Additional data*:

Conversion of 12,000 gallons of raw material into 10,000 gallons of white paint requires 50 hours at $3 per hour ($150), or $0.015 per gallon. Actual direct labor hours for the month were 40 at $3.20 per hour, or $128.

Factory overhead is applied on a direct labor hours basis at $4 per hour, or $0.02 per gallon ($200 ÷ 10,000). Normal overhead is $200 at 40 hours.

Actual finished production was 9,500 gallons, from 14,000 gallons total input (5,700 gallons of raw material A and 8,300 gallons of raw material B).

The mix and yield variances are computed as shown below.

**Item 1:** *Materials mix variance*

Actual materials mix

| | | |
|---|---|---:|
| Material A : 5,700 gallons @ $1.20 | | $ 6,840.00 |
| Material B : 8,300 gallons @ $0.90 | | 7,470.00 |
| | | $14,310.00 |
| Less: Standard formula (14,000 × $1) | | 14,000.00 |
| Materials mix variance (unfavorable) | | $   310.00 |

**Item 2:** *Materials yield variance*

Expected yield*

| | |
|---|---:|
| Standard formula (14,000 × $1) | $14,000.00 |
| Less: Actual yield | |
| (9,500 gallons produced × $1.20) | 11,400.00 |
| Materials yield variance (unfavorable) | $ 2,600.00 |

* Expected yield may also be calculated as follows:
14,000 × (10,000/12,000) × $1.20

**Item 3:** *Labor yield variance*

Expected yield

| | |
|---|---:|
| [14,000 × (10,000/12,000) × $0.015] | $   175.00 |
| Less: Actual yield | |
| (9,500 × $0.015) | 142.50 |
| Labor yield variance (unfavorable) | $    32.50 |

**Item 4:** *Overhead yield variance*

Expected yield

| | |
|---|---:|
| 14,000 × (10,000/12,000) × $0.02 | $   233.33 |
| Less: Actual yield | |
| (9,500 × $0.02) | 190.00 |
| Overhead yield variance (unfavorable) | $    43.33 |

# *Summary*

(1) The system which determines what the cost should be in advance of production is called a _____ system.

(2) For materials, the difference between actual quantities at standard prices and actual quantities at standard weighted average input prices is called the _____ variance.

(3) For labor, the difference between actual hours at actual rates and actual hours at the standard rate is called the _____ variance.

(4) Generally the variances are the direct responsibility of the _____.

(5)	Standard costs are not suitable for a job order cost system.  (a) True, (b) false.

(6)	The materials quantity variance is the difference between the actual quantity used at standard cost, and the standard quantity at standard cost.  (a) True, (b) false.

(7)	The labor efficiency variance is the difference between actual hours used at standard rates and standard hours at actual rates.  (a) True, (b) false.

(8)	Standard costs are (a) historical, (b) predetermined, (c) expensive, (d) not very useful.

(9)	Which of the following is not a principal type of standard?  (a) Theoretical or basic standard, (b) normal standard or currently attainable, (c) expected actual, (d) imputed standard cost.

(10)	The cost of a product as determined under standard costs is (a) joint cost, (b) historical cost, (c) expected cost, (d) direct cost.

*Answers:*  (1) standard cost; (2) mix; (3) rate; (4) supervisor; (5) b; (6) a; (7) b; (8) b; (9) d; (10) c.

# Solved Problems

**9.1	Variance Analysis: Materials, Labor, Factory Overhead.** The Reefer Company employs a standard cost system in its operations.  The standard product costs are:

| | | |
|---|---|---|
| Raw materials | 1.5 lbs at $20.00 per lb = | $30.00 |
| Direct labor | 10 hrs at $3.00 per hr = | 30.00 |
| Factory overhead | 10 hrs at $1.25 per hr = | 12.50 |
| Total standard cost per package of 200 units | | $72.50 |

Production for June amounted to 500 packages

| | |
|---|---|
| Budgeted output per month | 92,000 units |
| Raw materials used | 700 lbs |
| Cost of raw materials used | $15,400 |
| Direct labor cost (5,100 actual hrs) | 16,575 |
| Actual factory overhead | 7,375 |
| Fixed overhead for budgeted output | 1,840 |

Prepare variance analyses for (a) materials, (b) labor, and (c) factory overhead.  Use the three-variance method in part (c).

## SOLUTION

### (a)  Materials Variances

$$\text{Price variance} = (\text{Actual unit cost* } - \text{ standard unit cost}) \times \text{actual quantity}$$
$$= (\$22 - \$20) \times 700 = \underline{\$1,400} \text{ (unfavorable)}$$

$$\text{Quantity variance} = (\text{Actual quantity used } - \text{ standard quantity allowed*}) \times \text{standard unit cost}$$
$$= (700 \text{ lbs} - 750 \text{ lbs}) \times \$20 = \underline{\$(1,000)} \text{ (favorable)}$$

---

\* *Computations*
Actual unit cost = $\$15,400 \div 700 = \$22$ per lb
Standard quantity allowed = 500 pkgs $\times$ 1.5 lbs = 750 lbs

### (b)  Labor Variances

$$\text{Rate variance} = (\text{Actual rate } - \text{ standard rate}) \times \text{actual hours worked}$$
$$= (\$3.25 - \$3.00) \times 5,100 = \underline{\$1,275} \text{ (unfavorable)}$$

$$\text{Efficiency variance} = (\text{Actual hours } - \text{ standard hours}) \times \text{standard rate}$$
$$= (5,100 \text{ hrs} - 5,000 \text{ hrs}) \times \$3.00 = \underline{\$300} \text{ (unfavorable)}$$

### (c)  Three-variance Method   (See *Computations below for standard hours and overhead rates.)

(1)  *Spending variance*

| | |
|---|---|
| Actual Factory Overhead | $7,375 |
| Budget Allowance based on Actual Hours | |
| [$1,840 fixed + $4,335 variable (5,100 hrs × $0.85)] | 6,175 |
| Spending variance (unfavorable) | $1,200 |

(2)  *Efficiency variance*

$$(\text{Actual hours } - \text{ Standard hours allowed}) \times \text{Standard variable rate}$$
$$(5,100 - 5,000) \times \$0.85 = \underline{\$85} \text{ Unfavorable efficiency variance}$$

(3)  *Volume (Denominator) Variance*

$$(\text{Normal or budgeted hours } - \text{ Standard hours allowed}) \times \text{Standard fixed rate}$$
$$(4,600 - 5,000) \times \$0.40 = \underline{\$(160)} \text{ Favorable volume variance}$$

---

\* *Computations:*

Standard hours:          92,000 units ÷ 200 units = 460 budgeted packages
10 standard hrs per pkg × 460 standard pkgs = 4,600 budgeted hours

| Overhead rates: | | |
|---|---|---|
| | Total rate | $1.25 |
| | Fixed rate ($1,840/4,600 hrs) | 0.40 |
| | Variable rate | $0.85 |

Standard hours allowed:
10 standard hours per package × 500 actual packages produced = 5,000 standard hours allowed

**9.2    Two-variance from Four-variance Analysis.** Consolidate the four-variance analysis prepared in Problem 9.1(c) into a two-variance analysis.

**SOLUTION**

| | | | |
|---|---|---|---|
| *Controllable variance*: | Spending variance | $1,200 | Unfavorable |
| | Variable efficiency variance | 425 | Unfavorable |
| | Controllable variance | $1,625 | Unfavorable |
| | | | |
| *Volume variance*: | Idle capacity variance | $ (200) | Favorable |
| | Fixed efficiency variance | 200 | Unfavorable |
| | Volume variance | $  0 | |

**9.3    Variance Analysis: Materials, Labor.** Hill Pumps, Incorporated produces pumps for fire departments. They have one main plant and an office complex in Troy, New York. Hill employs a cost accounting department to control and analyze production costs. At the end of the current period the cost accounting department showed the following:

**Actual Data**

| | |
|---|---|
| *Production*: | 18,800 units |
| *Materials*: Purchased | 80,000 lbs @ $0.36 per lb |
| | 100,000 lbs @ $0.40 per lb |
| Requisitioned | 155,600 lbs |
| | |
| *Direct labor*: Actual hours worked | 38,400 |
| Standard hours allowed | 37,600 |
| Average actual labor cost | $4.50 per hour |
| | |
| *Factory overhead*: Variable overhead | $32,900 |
| Fixed overhead | 11,900 |
| Total factory overhead | $44,800 |

The factory overhead rate is based on a normal capacity of 36,000 hours. Budgeted overhead is as follows:

Variable overhead, $30,600
Fixed overhead, $12,600
Total factory overhead, $43,200

The Standard Cost Card showed, for each unit:

| | | |
|---|---|---|
| Direct materials | 16 lbs @ $0.40 per lb | $ 6.40 |
| Direct labor | 4 hours @ $4.40 per hour | 17.60 |
| Factory overhead | 4 hours @ $1.20 per hour | 4.80 |
| Total standard manufacturing costs | | $28.80 |

Prepare variance analyses for (a) direct materials and (b) direct labor.

## SOLUTION

### (a)  Materials Variances

*Materials Purchase Price Variance*

| | |
|---|---:|
| Actual quantity purchased × actual price (180,000 × $0.382*) | $ 68,760 |
| Actual quantity purchased × standard price (180,000 × $0.40) | (72,000) |
| Materials purchase price variance (favorable) | $ (3,240) |

* *Computation of actual purchase price:*

      80,000 lbs @ $0.36 = $28,800
    100,000 lbs @ $0.40 =  40,000
    180,000 lbs           $68,800 ÷ 180,000 lbs = $0.382 per lb

*Materials Quantity Usage Variance*

| | |
|---|---:|
| Actual quantity used × standard price (155,600 × $0.40) | $ 62,240 |
| Standard quantity allowed × standard price (300,800** × $0.40) | (120,320) |
| Materials quantity usage variance (favorable) | $ (58,080) |

** *Computation of standard quantity allowed:*

    Units of production × lbs per unit at standard = 18,800 units × 16 lbs
                              = 300,800 lbs

### (b)  Labor Variances

*Labor Rate Variance*

| | |
|---|---:|
| Actual hours worked × actual rate (38,400 × $4.50) | $172,800 |
| Actual hours worked × standard rate (38,400 × $4.40) | (168,960) |
| Labor rate variance (unfavorable) | $ 3,840 |

*Labor Efficiency Variance*

| | |
|---|---:|
| Actual hours worked × standard rate (38,400 × $4.40) | $168,960 |
| Standard hours allowed × standard rate (37,600 × $4.40) | (165,440) |
| Labor efficiency variance (unfavorable) | $ 3,520 |

**9.4**  **Variance Analysis: Factory Overhead.** Prepare a variance analysis for factory overhead based on the data in Problem 9.3, using (a) the two-variance method and (b) the three-variance method.

## SOLUTION

### (a)  Two-variance Method

*Controllable variance*: Actual factory overhead                  $44,800

                Budget allowance based on standard hours:

| | | |
|---|---:|---:|
|    Fixed expenses | $12,600 | |
|    Variable expenses ($0.85* × 37,600) | 31,960 | 44,560 |
| Controllable variance (unfavorable) | | $ 240   debit |

* *Computation of overhead rates:*

      Fixed rate: $12,600 ÷ 36,000 = $ .35
   Variable rate: $30,600 ÷ 36,000 =   .85
           Total (normal capacity rate): $1.20 per direct labor hour

*Volume variance*:

(Normal or budgeted capacity − Standard hours allowed) × Standard fixed rate

(36,000 − 37,600) × $0.35 = (\$560) Favorable volume variance (credit)

### (b)  Three-variance Method

*Spending variance*: Actual factory overhead        $44,800

Budget allowance based on actual hours:

| | | |
|---|---|---|
| Fixed expenses | $12,600 | |
| Variable expenses (38,400 × $0.85) | 32,640 | 45,240 |
| Spending variance (favorable) | | $  (440)  credit |

*Efficiency variance*:

(Actual hours − Standard hours allowed) × Standard variable rate

(38,400 − 37,600) × $0.85 = $680 Unfavorable efficiency variance (debit)

*Volume variance*:   See answer to two-variance method.

**9.5**  **Factory Overhead Rates.**  The Curtus Association has elected to install a standard cost system and a flexible overhead budget.  The normal capacity hours are 11,500.  Fixed overhead is $19,550 per month.

The company produces only one product, the standard costs for which are:

| | | |
|---|---|---|
| Direct materials | 3 lbs at | $20.00 |
| Direct labor | 8 hrs at | 2.50 |
| Variable overhead | 8 hrs at | 1.80 |

Standard direct hours are 9,000 per month.

Actual data for the month are as follows: variable overhead, $13,800; fixed overhead, $19,200; direct labor hours, 9,200.

Determine (a) the fixed, variable, and total overhead rate per direct labor hour, and (b) the fixed overhead rate per unit.

### SOLUTION

(a)  **Overhead Rates**

$$\text{FOR} = \frac{\text{Fixed overhead}}{\text{Standard direct labor hours at normal capacity}} = \frac{\$19,550}{11,500} = \$1.70$$

$$\text{VOR} = \frac{\text{Variable overhead}}{\text{Standard direct labor hours at normal capacity}} = \frac{\$20,700}{11,500} = \underline{1.80}$$

$$\text{TOR} = \text{Fixed overhead rate} + \text{variable overhead rate} = \$3.50$$

(b)  **Fixed Overhead Rate per Unit**

8 hours × $1.70 = $13.60

**9.6    Three-variance analysis.** Using the data in Problem 9.5, calculate the (a) spending, (b) efficiency, and (c) volume variances.

**SOLUTION**

(a) *Spending variance*:

| | | |
|---|---|---|
| Actual Factory Overhead | | $33,000 |
| Budget allowance based on actual hours | | |
| Fixed expenses | $19,550 | |
| Variable expenses (9,200 × $1.80) | 16,560 | 36,110 |
| Spending variance (favorable) | | $(3,100) |

(b) *Efficiency variance*:

(Actual hours − Standard hours allowed) × Standard variable rate

(9,200 − 9,000) × $1.80 = $360 Unfavorable efficiency variance

(c) *Volume variance*:

(Normal or budgeted capacity − Standard hours allowed) × Standard fixed rate

(11,500 − 9,000) × $1.70 = $4,250 Unfavorable volume variance

**9.7    Factory Overhead Variance Analysis.** The Hopeless Company uses a standard cost system in its operations. The following flexible monthly overhead budget is applied to production based on the normal capacity rate:

| | Capacity | |
|---|---|---|
| **Cost Elements** | **90%** | **100% (normal)** |
| Direct labor hours | 450,000 | 500,000 |
| Fixed overhead expenses | $250,000 | $250,000 |
| Variable overhead expenses | 202,500 | 225,000 |
| **Operating Data for the Current Year** | | |
| Actual direct labor hours | 475,000 | |
| Actual factory overhead | $460,000 | |
| Actual payroll | 688,750 | |
| Standard labor cost | 600,000 | |
| Standard labor cost per hour | 1.50 | |

Compute, at normal capacity, the (a) actual direct labor rate, (b) standard hours allowed, and (c) total overhead rate, showing fixed and variable portions. Analyze the factory overhead variances using the (d) two-variance and (e) three-variance methods.

**SOLUTION**

(a)  **Actual Direct Labor Rate**

$$\frac{\text{Actual payroll}}{\text{Actual direct labor hours}} = \frac{\$688,750}{475,000} = \$1.45$$

(b)  **Standard Hours Allowed**

$$\frac{\text{Standard labor cost}}{\text{Standard labor cost per hour}} = \frac{\$600,000}{\$1.50} = 400,000$$

(c)  **Overhead Rate**

$$\text{Fixed:}\ \frac{\text{Fixed overhead}}{\text{Direct labor hours}} = \frac{\$250,000}{500,000} = \$0.50$$

$$\text{Variable:}\ \frac{\text{Variable overhead}}{\text{Direct labor hours}} = \frac{\$225,000}{500,000} = \underline{\$0.45}$$

Total overhead rate                                   $0.95

(d)  **Two-variance Method**

*Controllable variance:*

| | | |
|---|---:|---:|
| Actual overhead | | $460,000 |
| Budget allowance | | |
| Fixed overhead | $250,000 | |
| Variable overhead (400,000 × $0.45) | 180,000 | 430,000 |
| Controllable variance (unfavorable) | | $ 30,000 |

*Volume variance:*

(Normal or budgeted capacity − Standard hours allowed) × Standard fixed rate

(500,000 − 400,000) × $0.50 = $50,000 Unfavorable volume variance

(e)  **Three-variance Method**

*Spending variance:*

| | | |
|---|---:|---:|
| Actual overhead | | $460,000 |
| Budget allowance | | |
| Fixed expenses | $250,000 | |
| Variable expenses (475,000 × $0.45) | 213,750 | 463,750 |
| Spending variance (favorable) | | $ (3,750) |

*Efficiency variance:*

(Actual hours − Standard hours allowed) × Standard variable rate

(475,000 − 400,000) × $0.45 = $33,750 Unfavorable efficiency variance

*Volume variance:*  See the above solution to the two-variance method.


**9.8    Input and Output Costs.**  The Eat-all Corporation manufactures chocolate candy bars.  It requires 2,000 pounds of raw materials to produce 1,500 pounds of chocolate candy.  Standard product quantities are: 1,000 pounds of cocoa @ $0.75 per pound, 600 pounds of sugar @ $0.60 per pound and 400 pounds of corn syrup @ $0.50 per pound.

   Compute the input price per pound and the output price per pound.

**SOLUTION**

**Cost of Materials**

| Materials | Pounds | × Cost | = Total |
|---|---:|---:|---:|
| Cocoa | 1,000 | $.75 | $ 750 |
| Sugar | 600 | .60 | 360 |
| Corn syrup | 400 | .50 | 200 |
| | 2,000 | | $1,310 |

Input cost per pound:    $1,310 ÷ 2,000 = $0.655 per pound

Output cost per pound:   $1,310 ÷ 1,500 = $0.873 per pound

**9.9** **Mix and Yield Variances.** The Morris Minerals Company uses the following standard costs and quantities of materials to produce one hundred tons of mix:

| Materials | Tons | × Unit Cost | = Amount |
|---|---|---|---|
| Scrap iron | 50 | $12 | $ 600 |
| Limestone | 30 | 15 | 450 |
| Coal | 20 | 9 | 180 |
| Total input | 100 | | $1,230 |

The standard mix, with a cost per pound of $12.30 ($1,230 ÷ 100 tons) should produce 75 pounds of finished product at a standard cost of $16.40 ($1,230 ÷ 75 tons) per ton.

The following raw materials we used during the month of March:

| Materials | Tons | Unit Cost |
|---|---|---|
| Scrap iron | 2,500 | $14 |
| Limestone | 900 | 12 |
| Coal | 600 | 11 |

The finished output was 3,500 tons.

Prepare, for materials, the (a) mix variance, (b) yield variance, and (c) related journal entries.

**SOLUTION**

(a)　**Materials Mix Variance**

| Materials | Tons | × Unit Cost | = Total |
|---|---|---|---|
| Scrap iron | 2,500 | $12 | $30,000 |
| Limestone | 900 | 15 | 13,500 |
| Coal | 600 | 9 | 5,400 |
| | 4,000 | | $48,900 |

| | |
|---|---|
| Actual materials mix | $48,900 |
| Less: Standard formula (4,000 tons × $12.30) | 49,200 |
| Mix variance (favorable) | $ (300) |

(b)　**Materials Yield Variance**

| | |
|---|---|
| Expected yield (4,000 tons × 75/100 × $16.40) | $49,200 |
| Less: Actual yield (3,500 tons × $16.40) | 57,400 |
| Yield variance (favorable) | $(8,200) |

(c)　**Journal Entries**

| | | |
|---|---|---|
| Work in Process | 49,200 | |
| 　Material Mix Variance | | 300 |
| 　Materials | | 48,900 |
| Finished Goods | 57,400 | |
| 　Material Yield Variance | | 8,200 |
| 　Work in Process | | 49,200 |

**9.10    Mix and Yield Variances.**  The Millisam Candy Company uses the following materials and costs for its standard production unit of candy.

| Materials | Pounds | Unit Cost | Amount |
|---|---|---|---|
| Sugar | 125 | $.90 | $112.50 |
| Corn syrup | 50 | .75 | 37.50 |
| Flavoring | 25 | .80 | 20.00 |
| Total input | 200 | | $170.00 |

The following raw materials were used in April to produce 1,200 pounds of candy:

| Materials | Pounds | Unit Cost |
|---|---|---|
| Sugar | 800 | $.95 |
| Corn syrup | 400 | .80 |
| Flavoring | 300 | .75 |

The standard input cost per pound is $0.85 ($170.00 ÷ 200).  The standard output cost per pound, based on 150 pounds of output is $1.13 ($170.00 ÷ 150).

(*a*)  Compute the mix and yield variances.

(*b*)  Prepare the related journal entries.

**SOLUTION**

(*a*)  **Materials Mix Variance**

| Materials | Pounds | Unit Cost | Amount |
|---|---|---|---|
| Sugar | 800 | $.90 | $ 720 |
| Corn syrup | 400 | .75 | 300 |
| Flavoring | 300 | .80 | 240 |
| | 1,500 | | $1,260 |

| | |
|---|---|
| Actual materials mix | $1,260 |
| Less: Standard formula (1,500 pounds × $0.85) | 1,275 |
| Materials mix variance (favorable) | $ (15) |

**Materials Yield Variance**

| | |
|---|---|
| Expected yield | $1,275 |
| Less: Actual yield (1,200 × $1.13) | 1,356 |
| Materials yield variance (favorable) | $ (81) |

(*b*)  **Journal Entries**

| | | |
|---|---|---|
| *Work in Process* | *1,275* | |
| *Material Mix Variance* | | *15* |
| *Materials* | | *1,260* |
| *Finished Goods* | *1,356* | |
| *Material Yield Variance* | | *81* |
| *Work in Process* | | *1,275* |

# Chapter 10

# Standard Costs II

In a full standard cost system all direct materials, direct labor and factory overhead are placed into work in process at standard cost.

## 10.1 JOURNAL ENTRIES FOR MATERIALS

Accounting for direct materials in a standard cost system can be handled by any of the following methods.

*Method 1.* The account Materials is maintained at *standard cost*. Price variances are recorded as materials are received.

*Method 2.* The account Materials is maintained at *actual cost*. Price variances are recorded when materials are put into production.

*Method 3.* The account Materials is maintained at *standard cost*. When purchases are recorded, any price variance is simultaneously recorded in a valuation account, to be allocated when materials are transferred to production.

### EXAMPLE 1

The following data will be used to illustrate the three methods of accounting for direct materials: Standard unit cost, $5.00; purchases: 8,000 units @ $5.10; put into process, 6,000 units; standard allowed, 6,200 units. The journal entries are as follows:

*Method 1*

| | | | Computations |
|---|---|---|---|
| Materials | 40,000 | | (8,000 × $5.00) |
| Materials Price Variance | 800 | | (8,000 × $0.10) |
|     Vouchers Payable | | 40,800 | (8,000 × $5.10) |
| *To record purchase of direct materials.* | | | |
| Work in Process | 31,000 | | (6,200 × $5.00) |
|     Materials | | 30,000 | (6,000 × $5.00) |
|     Materials Quantity Variance | | 1,000 | (200 × $5.00) |
| *To record direct materials put into production.* | | | |

*Method 2*

| | | | |
|---|---|---|---|
| Materials | 40,800 | | (8,000 × $5.10) |
|     Vouchers Payable | | 40,800 | (8,000 × $5.10) |
| *To record purchase of direct materials.* | | | |
| Work in Process | 31,000 | | (6,200 × $5.00) |
| Materials Price Usage Variance | 600 | | (6,000 × $0.10) |
|     Materials | | 30,600 | (6,000 × $5.10) |
|     Materials Quantity Variance | | 1,000 | (200 × $5.00) |
| *To record direct materials put into production.* | | | |

*Method 3*

| | | |
|---|---|---|
| Materials | 40,000 | (8,000 × $5.00) |
| Materials Price Variance | 800 | (8,000 × $0.10) |
|    Vouchers Payable | 40,800 | (8,000 × $5.10) |
| *To record purchase of direct materials.* | | |
| | | |
| Work in Process | 31,000 | (6,200 × $5.00) |
|    Materials | 30,000 | (6,000 × $5.00) |
|    Materials Quantity Variance | 1,000 | (200 × $5.00) |
| *To record direct materials put into production.* | | |
| | | |
| Materials Price Usage Variance | 600 | (6,000 × $0.10) |
|    Materials Price Variance | 600 | (6,000 × $0.10) |
| *To record allocation of purchase price variance.* | | |

## 10.2  JOURNAL ENTRIES FOR LABOR

In a standard cost system, direct labor costs are charged to production using standard hours and rates. Variances result from the difference between payroll (actual hours × actual rates) and standard charges; these must be recognized at the time they are incurred.

### EXAMPLE 2

To illustrate the procedure for recording direct labor costs, the following data will be used: Actual hours, 3,000; actual rate, $2.80; standard hours, 3,200; standard rate, $2.60. The appropriate journal entries are:

| | | |
|---|---|---|
| Payroll | 8,400 | (3,000 × $2.80) |
|    Vouchers Payable | 8,400 | (3,000 × $2.80) |
| *To record direct labor payroll.* | | |
| | | |
| Work in Process | 8,320 | (3,200 × $2.60) |
| Labor Rate Variance | 600 | (3,000 × $0.20) |
|    Labor Efficiency Variance | 520 | (200 × $2.60) |
|    Payroll | 8,400 | (3,000 × $2.80) |
| *To record the distribution and variances* | | |
| *   for direct labor payroll.* | | |

## 10.3  JOURNAL ENTRIES FOR FACTORY OVERHEAD

Entries for factory overhead reflect total charges as well as variances resulting from the various methods of analysis.

### EXAMPLE 3

Journal entries for factory overhead are illustrated below, based on the following data: actual direct labor hours, 3,000; standard allowed, 3,200; normal capacity, 4,000.

| | Total | Rate |
|---|---|---|
| Budgeted overhead (normal capacity) | | |
|    Variable overhead | $ 5,000 | $1.25 |
|    Fixed overhead | 8,000 | 2.00 |
|    Total | $13,000 | $3.25 |
| Actual overhead | $10,500 | |

For a *two-variance method* of analysis, the entries are as follows:

|  |  |  | **Computations** |
|---|---|---|---|
| Factory Overhead Control | 10,500 |  |  |
| Various Credits |  | 10,500 |  |
| Work in Process | 10,400 |  | (3,200 × $3.25) |
| Factory Overhead Control |  | 10,400 | (3,200 × $3.25) |
| Volume Variance | 1,600 |  | [(4,000 − 3,200) × $2.00] |
| Controllable Variance |  | 1,500 | [$10,500 − ($8,000 + $4,000)] |
| Factory Overhead Control |  | 100 | ($1,600 − $1,500) |

For a *three-variance* analysis, the entries are as shown below:

|  |  |  | **Computations** |
|---|---|---|---|
| Factory Overhead Control | 10,500 |  |  |
| Various Credits |  | 10,500 |  |
| Work in Process | 10,400 |  | (3,200 × $3.25) |
| Factory Overhead Efficiency Variance |  | 250 | [(3,200 − 3,000) × $1.25] |
| Factory Overhead Control |  | 10,150 |  |
| Factory Overhead Volume Variance | 1,600 |  | ($11,750 − $9,750) |
| Factory Overhead Spending Variance |  | 1,250 | [$10,500 − ($8,000 + $3,750)] |
| Factory Overhead Control |  | 350 | ($2,000 − $1,250) |

## 10.4  JOURNAL ENTRIES FOR MIX AND YIELD

In the journal entries for mix and yield variances, the debit to work in process is based on the standard yield of actual input.   The yield variances for materials, labor and factory overhead constitute the difference between this standard yield figure and the standard yield of actual output.

**EXAMPLE 4**

The variances calculated in Example 7 of Chapter 9 are used as data in the mix and yield entries below.

| | | | |
|---|---|---|---|
| **Material mix:** | Work in Process | 14,000 | |
| | Materials Mix Variance | 310 | |
| | Materials | | 14,310 |
| **Material yield:** | Finished Goods | 11,400 | |
| | Materials Yield Variance | 2,600 | |
| | Work in Process | | 14,000 |
| **Labor yield:** | Finished Goods | 142.50 | |
| | Labor Yield Variance | 32.50 | |
| | Work in Process | | 175 |
| **Overhead yield:** | Finished Goods | 190.00 | |
| | Overhead Yield Variance | 43.33 | |
| | Work in Process | | 233.33 |

## 10.5  JOURNAL ENTRIES TO CLOSE VARIANCES

Variances may be closed to either (1) the Income Summary or (2) Cost of Goods Sold and Inventory.

*Income Summary.* In this case, variances are treated as period costs. This treatment is based on the assumption that *standard costs* are true costs for inventory valuation and cost of sales.

*Cost of Goods Sold and Inventory.* This method treats variances as product costs. It is based on the assumption that *actual costs* are true costs for inventory valuation and cost of sales.

## EXAMPLE 5

Assume the following end of period data:

|                         |        |
|-------------------------|-------:|
| Goods sold              | 7,000  |
| Ending finished goods   | 2,000  |
| Ending work in process  | 1,000  |
|                         | 10,000 |

Variances for period:

| Materials: | Quantity   | $80 | Unfavorable |
|-----------|------------|-----|-------------|
|           | Rate       | 30  | Favorable   |
| Labor:    | Efficiency | 40  | Favorable   |
|           | Rate       | 10  | Unfavorable |
| Overhead: | Spending   | 120 | Favorable   |
|           | Volume     | 50  | Favorable   |
|           | Efficiency | 70  | Unfavorable |

(1) *To close variances to Income Summary:*

| | | |
|---|---:|---:|
| Materials Rate Variance | 30 | |
| Labor Efficiency Variance | 40 | |
| Spending Variance | 120 | |
| Volume Variance | 50 | |
| Materials Quantity Variance | | 80 |
| Labor Rate Variance | | 10 |
| Efficiency Variance | | 70 |
| Income Summary | | 80 |

(2) *To close variances to Cost of Goods Sold and Inventories:* The net favorable variance of $80 must be allocated to goods sold, ending finished goods and ending work in process. The computations are:

$$\text{Goods sold} = 7/10 \times \$80 = \$56$$
$$\text{Ending finished goods} = 2/10 \times \ 80 = \ 16$$
$$\text{Ending work in process} = 1/10 \times \ 80 = \underline{\ \ 8}$$
$$\$80$$

The entry is:

| | | |
|---|---:|---:|
| Materials Rate Variance | 30 | |
| Labor Efficiency Variance | 40 | |
| Spending Variance | 120 | |
| Volume Variance | 50 | |
| Materials Quantity Variance | | 80 |
| Labor Rate Variance | | 10 |
| Efficiency Variance | | 70 |
| Cost of Goods Sold | | 56 |
| Finished Goods | | 16 |
| Work in Process | | 8 |

# *Summary*

(1) All direct materials, direct labor, and factory overhead are placed into work in process at _____ cost in a full standard cost system.

(2) Variances resulting from differences between actual and standard labor charges are recognized at the time they are _____.

(3) In the journal entries for mix and yield variances, the debit to work in process is based on the standard yield of _____ input.

(4) Variances may be closed to either the _____ or to _____.

(5) Variances when closed to the Income Summary are treated as product costs.   (*a*) True, (*b*) false.

(6) The assumption that actual costs are true costs for inventory and cost of goods sold underlies the treatment of variances as product costs.   (*a*) True, (*b*) false.

(7) An unfavorable materials quantity variance has a debit balance that is credited at the end of the period.   (*a*) True, (*b*) false.

(8) The payroll account is credited for standard labor hours multiplied by the actual rate.   (*a*) True, (*b*) false.

*Answers:*   (1) standard; (2) incurred; (3) actual; (4) Income Summary, Cost of Goods Sold and Inventory; (5) *b*; (6) *a*; (7) *a*; (8) *b*.

# Solved Problems

**10.1**   **Variance Analysis, Journal Entries.**   Operations of the Ralph Corporation are based on the following data: Normal capacity for direct labor hours, 12,500; normal estimated overhead: fixed, $5,000; variable, $9,000.

Actual results were as follows: Direct labor hours, 9,300; overhead: fixed, $5,075; variable, $8,900.

There are 10,300 standard hours allowed for actual production.

Compute (*a*) the variable, fixed and total overhead rates, (*b*) overhead variances using the three-variance method, and (*c*) overhead variances using the two-variance method.   Prepare (*d*) all necessary journal entries for the three-variance method.

## SOLUTION

(*a*)

| | | |
|---|---|---|
| Variable rate: | $9,000 ÷ 12,500 = | $ .72 |
| Fixed rate: | $5,000 ÷ 12,500 = | .40 |
| Total rate: | $14,000 ÷ 12,500 = | $1.12 |

(b)   *Spending variance:*

|  |  |  |
|---|---|---|
| Actual factory overhead |  | $13,975 |
| Budget allowance based on actual hours: |  |  |
| Fixed expenses | $5,000 |  |
| Variable expenses (9,300 × $0.72) | 6,696 | 11,696 |
| Spending variance (unfavorable) |  | $ 2,279   debit |

*Efficiency variance:*

(Actual hours − Standard hours allowed) × Standard variable rate

(9,300 − 10,300) × $0.72 = $(720) Favorable efficiency variance (credit)

*Volume variance:*

(Normal or budgeted capacity − Standard hours allowed) × Standard fixed rate

(12,500 − 10,300) × $0.40 = $880 Unfavorable volume variance (debit)

(c)   *Controllable variance:*

|  |  |  |
|---|---|---|
| Actual factory overhead |  | $13,975 |
| Budget allowance based on standard hours: |  |  |
| Fixed expenses | $5,000 |  |
| Variable expenses (10,300 × $0.72) | 7,416 | 12,416 |
| Controllable variance (unfavorable) |  | $ 1,559   debit |

*Volume variance:* Same as above.

(d)

|  |  |  |
|---|---|---|
| *Factory Overhead Control* | *13,975* |  |
| *Various Credits* |  | *13,975* |
| *Work in Process (10,300 × $1.12)* | *11,536* |  |
| *Efficiency Variance* |  | *720* |
| *Factory Overhead Control* |  | *10,816* |
| *Spending Variance* | *2,279* |  |
| *Volume Variance* | *880* |  |
| *Factory Overhead Control* |  | *3,159* |

**10.2   Variance Analysis: Direct Labor, Factory Overhead.**   The Ludwig Company produces high quality drums for all levels of musical ability at one factory in Germany.   Ludwig employs a cost accounting department in order to control and analyze production costs.   At the end of the current year, the cost accounting department showed the following data:

| Capacity | 85% | 90% | 95% | 100% | 105% |
|---|---|---|---|---|---|
| Direct labor hours | 680,000 | 720,000 | 760,000 | 800,000 | 840,000 |
| Fixed expenses | $468,000 | $468,000 | $468,000 | $468,000 | $468,000 |
| Variable expenses | $214,200 | $226,800 | $239,400 | $252,000 | $264,600 |
| Total factory overhead | $682,200 | $694,800 | $707,400 | $720,000 | $732,600 |

*Additional data:* Actual direct labor cost .......................... $1,089,280
Actual direct labor hours .......................... 736,000
Standard direct labor cost .......................... $1,080,000
Standard direct labor rate per hour .......................... $1.60
Actual factory overhead .......................... $650,000

Analyze the above data for (*a*) direct labor variances and (*b*) three-variance factory over-head.   (*c*) Consolidate the three-variance analysis in part (*b*) into a two-variance analysis.

## SOLUTION

(*a*)                **Labor Rate Variance**
Actual hours × actual rate (736,000 × $1.48*) .......................... $1,089,280
Actual hours × standard rate (736,000 × $1.60) .......................... (1,177,600)
Labor rate variance (favorable) .......................... $ (88,320)

**Labor Efficiency (Time) Variance**
Actual hours × standard rate (736,000 × $1.60) .......................... $1,177,600
Standard hours × standard rate (675,000** × $1.60) .......................... (1,080,000)
Labor efficiency variance (unfavorable) .......................... $  97,600

* Actual direct labor rate per hour =

$$\frac{\text{Actual direct labor cost}}{\text{Actual direct labor hours}} = \frac{\$1,089,280}{736,000} = \$1.48$$

** Standard hours allowed =

$$\frac{\text{Standard direct labor cost}}{\text{Standard direct labor rate per hour}} = \frac{\$1,080,000}{\$1.60} = 675,000$$

(*b*)  **Three-variance Method**

*Spending variance:*
Actual factory overhead .......................... $650,000
Budget allowance based on actual hours:
   Fixed expenses .......................... $468,000
   Variable expenses (736,000 × $0.315*) .......................... 231,840     699,840
Spending variance (favorable) .......................... $ (49,840)

*Efficiency variance:*
(Actual hours − Standard hours allowed) × Standard variable rate
(736,000 − 675,000) × $0.315 = $19,215 Unfavorable efficiency variance

*Volume variance:*
(Normal or budgeted capacity − Standard hours allowed) × Standard fixed rate
(800,000 − 675,000) × $0.585 = $73,125 Unfavorable volume variance

* Normal capacity overhead rates:

Fixed: $468,000/800,000 = $.585
Variable: $252,000/800,000 =  .315
Total normal capacity rate:  $.900

(c)  **From Three- to Two-variance Method.**

    (1)  Budget (controllable) variance

| | |
|---|---:|
| Spending variance (favorable) | $(49,840) |
| Efficiency variance (unfavorable) | 19,215 |
| Budget variance (favorable) | $(30,625) |

    (2)  Volume variance (unfavorable)      $ 73,125

**10.3**    **Variance Analysis: Materials, Labor, Factory Overhead.**  Hardwood Furniture, Incorporated manufactures all types of office furniture.  The company has one giant plant and office complex in California, and employs a full-time cost accounting department to control and analyze production costs.  At the end of the year, the cost accounting department showed the following data:

    The factory overhead rate is based on a normal capacity of 8,000 hours.  Total factory overhead expenses budgeted were $11,560, consisting of variable expenses, $4,960 and fixed expenses, $6,600.

    The standard cost card showed:

| | |
|---|---|
| Direct materials | $5.00 per unit |
| Direct labor | 4.00 per hour |
| Factory overhead | 3,500 units |

### Actual Data

| | |
|---|---|
| *Materials:* Purchased | 10,000 units @ $4.94 |
| Requisitioned | 7,100 units |
| Standard quantity allowed | 7,000 units |
| *Direct labor:* Actual hours worked | 3,760 hours |
| Standard hours allowed | 3,180 hours |
| Actual rate paid | $4.20 per hour |
| *Factory overhead (actual):* | $10,994 |

    Compute the variances for (a) direct materials, (b) direct labor, and (c) factory overhead, showing (1) computation of overhead rates and (2) the three-variance method.

### SOLUTION

(a)  **Materials Variances**

$$\text{Materials price variance} = (\text{Actual price} - \text{standard price}) \times \text{actual quantity}$$
$$= (\$4.94 - \$5.00) \times 10,000 = \$(600) (\text{favorable})$$

$$\text{Materials quantity variance} = (\text{Actual quantity} - \text{standard quantity}) \times \text{standard price}$$
$$= (7,100 - 7,000) \times \$5.00 = \$500 \ (\text{unfavorable})$$

(b)  **Labor Variances**

$$\text{Labor rate variance} = (\text{Actual rate} - \text{standard rate}) \times \text{actual hours}$$
$$= (\$4.20 - \$4.00) \times 3,760 = \$752 \ (\text{unfavorable})$$

$$\text{Labor efficiency variance} = (\text{Actual hours} - \text{standard hours}) \times \text{standard rate}$$
$$= (3,760 - 3,180) \times \$4.00 = \$2,320 \ (\text{unfavorable})$$

(c)  (1)  **Overhead Rates**

$$\text{Fixed rate: } \$6,600 \div 8,000 = \$ \ .825$$
$$\text{Variable rate: } \$4,960 \div 8,000 = \ \ \ .620$$
$$\text{Total overhead rate: } \qquad\qquad \$1.445$$

(2)  **Three-variance Method**

*Spending variance:*

| | | |
|---|---:|---:|
| Actual factory overhead | | $10,994.00 |
| Budget allowance based on actual hours: | | |
| Fixed expenses | $6,600.00 | |
| Variable expenses (3,760 × $0.62) | 2,331.20 | (8,931.20) |
| Spending variance (unfavorable) | | $ 2,062.80   debit |

*Efficiency variance:*

$$(\text{Actual hours} - \text{Standard hours allowed}) \times \text{Standard variable rate}$$
$$(3,760 - 3,180) \times \$0.620 = \underline{\$359.60} \text{ Unfavorable efficiency variance (debit)}$$

*Volume variance:*

$$(\text{Normal or budgeted capacity} - \text{Standard hours allowed}) \times \text{Standard fixed rate}$$
$$(8,000 - 3,180) \times \$0.825 = \underline{\$3,976.50} \text{ Unfavorable efficiency variance (debit)}$$

**10.4    Materials Variance Analysis, Journal Entries.**  On a standard cost card for one of its products, the Tudor Tool and Die Company showed the following information:

| | | |
|---|---|---:|
| Direct materials | 4 lbs @ $ .40 | $ 1.60 |
| Direct labor | 4 hrs @ 2.00 | 8.00 |
| Factory overhead | 4 hrs @ 1.40 | 5.60 |
| Total standard cost per unit | | $15.20 |

Actual data for the period was as follows:

| | |
|---|---|
| Total production | 6,000 units |
| Materials purchases | 75,000 lbs @ $.50 |
| Materials requisitions | 25,000 lbs |

(*a*) Compute the price, usage, and quantity variances for materials (1) at time of purchase and (2) at time of requisition.  (*b*) Prepare the necessary journal entries for items (1) and (2).

**SOLUTION**

(*a*)  **Price, Usage, and Quantity Variances**

(1)   At time of purchase

$$\text{Actual quantity purchased} \times (\text{actual price} - \text{standard price}) = \text{price variance}$$
$$75,000 \times (\$0.50 - \$0.40) = \underline{\$7,500} \text{ unfavorable}$$

(2)   At time of requisition

$$\text{Actual quantity requisitioned} \times (\text{actual price} - \text{standard price}) = \text{usage variance}$$
$$25,000 \times (\$0.50 - \$0.40) = \underline{\$2,500} \text{ unfavorable}$$

$$(\text{Actual quantity requisitioned} - \text{standard quantity}) \times \text{standard price} = \text{quantity variance}$$
$$(25,000 - 24,000^*) \times \$0.40 = \underline{\$400} \text{ unfavorable}$$

---

* Standard quantity = 6,000 units × 4 lbs per unit = 24,000 lbs

(b)   (1)   When the material price variance is recorded at the time of purchase, the entry is

| | | |
|---|---|---|
| *Materials* | *30,000* | |
| *Materials Purchase Price Variance* | *7,500* | |
| *Accounts Payable* | | *37,500* |

The materials quantity variance in this case is recorded as materials are requisitioned. The entry is

| | | |
|---|---|---|
| *Work in Process* | *9,600* | |
| *Materials Quantity Variance* | *400* | |
| *Materials* | | *10,000* |

(2)   When the material price variance is recorded at time of requisition, the entry is

| | | |
|---|---|---|
| *Materials* | *37,500* | |
| *Accounts Payable* | | *37,500* |

When price and quantity variances are recorded at the time of requisition, the entry is

| | | |
|---|---|---|
| *Work in Process* | *9,600* | |
| *Materials Price Usage Variance* | *2,500* | |
| *Materials Quantity Variance* | *400* | |
| *Materials* | | *12,500* |

**10.5**   **Factory Overhead Variances; Journal Entries.**   From the data below prepare (a) an analysis of factory overhead variances using (1) the two-variance method and (2) the three-variance method, and (b) journal entries for the three-variance analysis.

| | **Budgeted (normal capacity)** | **Actual** |
|---|---|---|
| Direct labor hours | 20,000 | 25,600 |
| Factory overhead: | | |
| Fixed | $14,000 | $17,000 |
| Variable | 16,000 | 19,000 |

Standard allowed for actual production: 24,000 hours

### SOLUTION

(a)   (1)   **Two-variance Method**

Controllable variance:

| Actual factory overhead: | | |
|---|---|---|
| Fixed expenses | $17,000 | |
| Variable expenses | 19,000 | $36,000 |
| Budget based on standard hours: | | |
| Fixed expenses | $14,000 | |
| Variable expenses | 19,200 | 33,200 |
| Controllable variance (unfavorable) | | $ 2,800 |

Volume variance:

(Normal or budgeted capacity − Standard hours allowed) × Standard fixed rate

(20,000 − 24,000) × $0.70 = $(2,800) Favorable volume variance

* Computation of overhead rates:

| | | |
|---|---|---|
| Fixed rate: | 14,000 ÷ 20,000 = | $ .70 |
| Variable rate: | 16,000 ÷ 20,000 = | .80 |
| Total overhead rate: | | $1.50 |

**(2) Three-variance Method**

*Spending variance:*

| | | |
|---|---:|---:|
| Actual factory overhead | | $36,000 |
| Budget allowance based on actual hours: | | |
| Fixed expenses | $14,000 | |
| Variable expenses (25,600 × $0.80) | 20,480 | 34,480 |
| Spending variance (unfavorable) | | $ 1,520 |

*Efficiency variance:*

(Actual hours − Standard hours allowed) × Standard variable rate

(25,600 − 24,000) × $0.80 = $1,280 Unfavorable efficiency variance

*Volume variance:* Same as the solution for two-variance method.

(b) The journal entries relating to the three-variance method are given below.

| | | |
|---|---:|---:|
| Factory Overhead Control | | |
| ($17,000 + $19,000) | 36,000 | |
| Various Credits | | 36,000 |
| Work in Process | | |
| (24,000 × $1.50) | 36,000 | |
| Spending Variance | 1,520 | |
| Factory Overhead Control | | 37,520 |
| Efficiency Variance | 1,280 | |
| Factory Overhead Control | 1,520 | |
| Volume Variance | | 2,800 |

**10.6 Variance Analysis for Materials, Labor, Factory Overhead; Journal Entries.** The Perplexed Manufacturing Company's books and records furnished the following data relating to standard costs:

| | Quantity | Price |
|---|---|---:|
| Direct materials | 7.5 lbs at $0.30 per lb | $2.25 |
| Direct labor | 2 hrs at $2.40 per hr | 4.80 |
| Factory overhead | 2 hrs at $1.40 per hr | 2.80 |
| Total standard manufacturing cost per unit | | $9.85 |

**Actual Data**

| | | |
|---|---|---|
| *Materials:* Purchased | 90,000 lbs @ $0.25 per lb | |
| Requisitioned | 63,600 lbs | |
| *Direct labor:* Actual hours | 22,500 | |
| Standard hours | 20,000 | |
| Average actual labor cost | $2.50 | |
| *Factory overhead:* Fixed overhead | $ 6,200 | |
| Variable overhead | 17,500 | |

*Production:* 10,000 units; no work in process inventories.

*Normal capacity:* 8,000 units; fixed expenses, $6,400; variable expenses, $16,000.

Prepare (*a*) an analysis of variance for (1) direct materials, (2) direct labor, and (3) factory overhead, using the two-variance method, and (*b*) all related journal entries.

## SOLUTION

(*a*)  (1)  **Direct Materials**

| | | | |
|---|---|---|---|
| *Price variance:* | Actual quantity × actual cost | | |
| | (90,000 × $0.25) | $22,500 | |
| | Actual quantity × standard cost | | |
| | (90,000 × $0.30) | (27,000) | |
| | Price variance | $ (4,500) | (favorable) |

| | | | |
|---|---|---|---|
| *Quantity variance:* | Actual quantity × standard cost | | |
| | (63,600 × $0.30) | $19,080 | |
| | Standard quantity × standard cost | | |
| | (75,000* × $0.30) | 22,500 | |
| | Quantity variance | $ (3,420) | (favorable) |

* Standard quantity allowed = 10,000 units × 7.5 lbs per unit = 75,000

(2)  **Direct Labor**

| | | | |
|---|---|---|---|
| *Rate variance:* | Actual hours × actual rate | | |
| | (22,500 × $2.50) | $56,250 | |
| | Actual hours × standard rate | | |
| | (22,500 × $2.40) | 54,000 | |
| | Labor rate variance | $ 2,250 | (unfavorable) |

| | | | |
|---|---|---|---|
| *Efficiency variance:* | Actual hours × standard rate | | |
| | (22,500 × $2.40) | $54,000 | |
| | Standard hours × standard rate | | |
| | (20,000 × $2.40) | 48,000 | |
| | Labor efficiency variance | $ 6,000 | (unfavorable) |

(3)  **Factory Overhead.**  The following overhead rates are used in the computation of variances.

FOR:  $6,400 ÷ 16,000* = $ .40
VOR:  $16,000 ÷ 16,000 = 1.00
TOR:  $22,400 ÷ 16,000 = $1.40

* Normal  capacity  hours = 8,000  units  at  normal × 2 hours per unit = 16,000 hours.

**Two-variance Method**

| | | | |
|---|---|---|---|
| *Controllable variance:* | Actual factory overhead | | |
| | Fixed expenses | $ 6,200 | |
| | Variable expenses | 17,500 | $23,700 |
| | Budgeted at standard | | |
| | Fixed expenses | $ 6,400 | |
| | Variable expenses | | |
| | (20,000 × $1.00) | 20,000 | (26,400) |
| | Controllable variance | | $ (2,700)  (favorable) |

*Volume variance:*
(Normal or budgeted capacity − Standard hours allowed) × Standard fixed rate
(16,000 − 20,000) × $0.40 = $(1,600) Favorable volume variance

(*b*)  **Journal Entries**

| Materials | 27,000 | |
| Vouchers Payable | | 22,500 |
| Materials Purchase Price Variance | | 4,500 |

To record purchase of direct materials.

| Work in Process | 18,000 | |
| Materials Quantity Variance | 1,080 | |
| Materials | | 19,080 |

To record direct materials put into production.

| Payroll | 56,250 | |
| Vouchers Payable | | 56,250 |

To record distribution of direct labor payroll.

| Work in Process | 48,000 | |
| Labor Rate Variance | 2,250 | |
| Labor Efficiency Variance | 6,000 | |
| Payroll | | 56,250 |

To record distribution of payroll and associated variances.

| Factory Overhead Control | 23,700 | |
| Various credits | | 23,700 |

To record actual factory overhead.

| Work in Process | 28,000 | |
| Factory Overhead Control | | 28,000 |

To record factory overhead budgeted at standard.

| Factory Overhead Control | 4,300 | |
| Controllable Variance | | 2,700 |
| Volume Variance | | 1,600 |

To record variances under the two-variance method.

**10.7  Factory Overhead Analysis, Journal Entries.** (*a*) Analyze the overhead data in Problem 10.6 using the three-variance method, (*b*) show all related journal entries, (*c*) calculate the idle-capacity variance.

**SOLUTION**

(*a*)  **Three-variance Method**

*Spending variance:*

| Actual factory overhead | | $23,700 |
| Budgeted at actual | | |
| Fixed expenses | $ 6,400 | |
| Variable expenses | | |
| (22,500 × $1) | 22,500 | (28,900) |
| Spending variance | | $ (5,200)  (favorable) |

*Efficiency variance:*
(Actual hours − Standard hours allowed) × Standard variable rate
(22,500 − 20,000) × $1.00 = $2,500 Unfavorable efficiency variance

*Volume variance:*  Same as solution in Problem 10.6.

(b)  **Three-variance Entries**

| | | |
|---|---|---|
| Work In Process, Factory Overhead | 28,000 | |
| Efficiency Variance | 2,500 | |
| Factory Overhead Control | | 30,500 |
| Factory Overhead Control | 6,800 | |
| Volume Variance | | 1,600 |
| Spending Variance | | 5,200 |

(c)  **Idle-capacity Variance**

$$(\text{Budget capacity} - \text{Actual hours}) \times \text{Standard fixed rate}$$
$$(16,000 - 22,500) \times \$0.40 = \underline{\$(2,600)} \text{ Favorable idle-capacity variance}$$

**10.8**    **Variance Analysis: Materials, Labor, Journal Entries.**   The Edwardo Company presents you with the following accounting information from its books:

| | |
|---|---|
| Standard materials price (per lb): | $3.25 |
| Purchased: | 5,500 lbs @ $2.75 |
| Requisitioned: | 2,400 lbs |
| Materials allowed (per standard production order): | 2,100 lbs |
| Actual hours worked | 1,675 |
| Actual rate paid (per hour): | $2.05 |
| Standard hours allowed: | 1,500 |
| Standard rate (per hour): | $2.00 |

(a)   Compute (1) the materials purchase price and quantity variances, and (2) the labor rate and efficiency variances and (b) Prepare the necessary journal entries.

**SOLUTION**

(a)   (1)   **Materials**

$$\text{Price variance} = (\text{Actual price} - \text{standard price}) \times \text{actual quantity}$$
$$= (\$2.75 - \$3.25) \times 5,500 = \underline{\$(2,750)} \text{ favorable}$$

$$\text{Quantity variance} = (\text{Actual quantity} - \text{standard quantity}) \times \text{standard price}$$
$$= (2,400 - 2,100) \times \$3.25 = \underline{\$975} \text{ unfavorable}$$

(2)   **Labor**

$$\text{Rate variance} = (\text{Actual rate} - \text{standard rate}) \times \text{actual hours}$$
$$= (\$2.05 - \$2.00) \times 1,675 = \underline{\$83.75} \text{ unfavorable}$$

$$\text{Efficiency variance} = (\text{Actual hours} - \text{standard hours}) \times \text{standard rate}$$
$$= (1,675 - 1,500) \times \$2.00 = \underline{\$350} \text{ unfavorable}$$

(b)   **Journal Entries**

| | | |
|---|---|---|
| Materials | 17,875 | |
| Purchase Price Variance | | 2,750 |
| Vouchers Payable | | 15,125 |
| Work in Process, Material | 6,825 | |
| Materials Quantity Variance | 975 | |
| Materials | | 7,800 |
| Payroll | 3,433.75 | |
| Vouchers Payable | | 3,433.75 |
| Work in Process, Labor | 3,000.00 | |
| Labor Rate Variance | 83.75 | |
| Labor Efficiency Variance | 350.00 | |
| Payroll | | 3,433.75 |

**10.9 Journal Entries.** The Hofstram Corporation used a standard cost system. Use (a) T-accounts and (b) journal entries to record the transactions for May listed below.

| | |
|---|---|
| Inventories, May 1: | |
| Raw materials | $53,700 |
| Materials in process | 4,300 |
| Labor in process | 1,750 |
| Finished goods | 30,100 |
| Cash purchases in May: | |
| Actual cost | 37,120 |
| Standard cost | 38,950 |
| To Finished Goods: | |
| Standard material cost | 36,000 |
| Standard labor cost | 12,800 |
| Direct labor at standard rates | 13,500 |
| Materials put into process | 42,150 |
| Inventories, June 1: | |
| Raw materials | 50,500 |
| Materials in process | 9,300 |
| Labor in process | 2,100 |
| Finished goods | 17,700 |
| Cost of goods sold (standard labor + materials costs) | 61,200 |
| Payroll | 18,500 |

**SOLUTION**

(a) **T-accounts.** In the T-accounts below, the numbers in parentheses refer to the journal entries in part (b).

**Raw Materials**

| | |
|---|---|
| Bal. 5/1 53,700 | 42,150 (3) |
| (1) 38,950 | |
| Bal. 6/1 50,500 | |

**Materials in Process**

| | |
|---|---|
| Bal. 5/1 4,300 | 36,000 (4) |
| (3) 41,000 | |
| Bal. 6/1 9,300 | |

**Labor in Process**

| | |
|---|---|
| Bal. 5/1 1,750 | 12,800 (4) |
| (2) 13,150 | |
| Bal. 6/1 2,100 | |

**Cash**

| | |
|---|---|
| | 37,120 (1) |
| | 18,500 (2) |

**Finished Goods**

| | |
|---|---|
| Bal. 5/1 30,100 | 61,200 (5) |
| (4) 48,800 | |
| Bal. 6/1 17,700 | |

**Cost of Goods Sold**

| | |
|---|---|
| (5) 61,200 | |

**Materials Quantity Variance**

| | |
|---|---|
| (3) 1,150 | |

**Materials Price Variance**

| | |
|---|---|
| | 1,830 (1) |

**Labor Rate Variance**

| | |
|---|---|
| (2) 5,000 | |

**Labor Efficiency Variance**

| | |
|---|---|
| (2) 350 | |

**Payroll**

| | |
|---|---|
| (2) 18,500 | 18,500 (2) |

(b)  **Journal Entries**

| (1) | Raw Materials | 38,950 | |
| |    Cash | | 37,120 |
| |    Materials Price Variance | | 1,830 |

| (2) | Payroll | 18,500 | |
| |    Cash | | 18,500 |

| | Labor in Process | 13,150 | |
| | Labor Rate Variance | 5,000 | |
| | Labor Efficiency Variance | 350 | |
| |    Payroll | | 18,500 |

| (3) | Materials in Process | 41,000 | |
| | Materials Quantity Variance | 1,150 | |
| |    Raw Materials | | 42,150 |

| (4) | Finished Goods | 48,800 | |
| |    Materials in Process | | 36,000 |
| |    Labor in Process | | 12,800 |

| (5) | Cost of Goods Sold | 61,200 | |
| |    Finished Goods | | 61,200 |

**10.10  Mix and Yield Variances; Journal Entries.** From the data given below, (a) compute (1) the materials mix variance, (2) the materials yield variance, (3) the labor yield variance, and (4) the overhead yield variance. (b) Prepare the necessary journal entries.

Standard product and cost specifications for 500 lbs of Product A:

| | Standard Quantity Allowed | Price | Cost |
|---|---|---|---|
| Raw material X | 200 lbs | $.10 per lb | $ 20 |
| Raw material Y | 400 lbs | $.25 per lb | 100 |
| Input | 600 lbs | | $120 = $0.20 per lb |
| Output | 500 lbs | | $120 = $0.24 per lb |

*Additional data:*

Conversion of 600 lbs of raw materials into 500 lbs of Product A requires 40 hours at $6 per hour ($240.00), or $0.48 per lb. Actual direct labor hours for the month were 45 hours at a cost of $274.50 ($6.10 per hour).

Factory overhead is applied on the direct labor hour basis at $3 per hour or $0.24 per lb ($120 ÷ 500). Normal overhead is $120 at 40 hours.

Actual production was 510 lbs. Total input was 610 lbs, consisting of 190 lbs of raw material X and 420 lbs of raw material Y.

**SOLUTION**

(a)  (1)     *Materials mix variance*

Actual quantities at standard cost
   Material X: 190 lbs at $0.10   $ 19
   Material Y: 420 lbs at $0.25   105       $124.00

Actual quantity at standard material cost
   (610 lbs × $0.20)                      122.00

Materials mix variance (unfavorable)        $ 2.00  debit

(2)    *Materials yield variance*

| | |
|---|---|
| Actual quantity at standard material cost | $122.00 |
| Actual output quantity at standard materials cost (510 lbs × $0.24) | (122.40) |
| Materials yield variance (favorable) | $ (0.40) credit |

(3)    *Labor yield variance*

| | |
|---|---|
| Actual input at standard output of actual input (610 lbs × 500/600 × $0.48) | $244.00 |
| Actual output quantity at standard labor rate (510 lbs × $0.48 per lb.) | (244.80) |
| Labor yield variance (favorable) | $ (0.80) credit |

(4)    *Overhead yield variance*

| | |
|---|---|
| Standard (expected) output (610 lbs × 500/600 × $0.24) | $122.00 |
| Actual output quantity at standard overhead rate (510 lbs × $0.24) | (122.40) |
| Overhead yield variance (favorable) | $ (0.40) credit |

(b)

| | | |
|---|---|---|
| **Materials mix:** *Work in Process* | *122.00* | |
| *Materials Mix Variance* | *2.00* | |
| *Materials* | | *124.00* |
| **Materials yield:** *Finished Goods* | *122.40* | |
| *Materials Yield Variance* | | *.40* |
| *Work in Process* | | *122.00* |
| **Labor yield:** *Finished Goods* | *244.80* | |
| *Labor Yield Variance* | | *.80* |
| *Work in Process* | | *244.00* |
| **Overhead yield:** *Finished Goods* | *122.40* | |
| *Overhead Yield Variance* | | *.40* |
| *Work in Process* | | *122.00* |

**10.11    Disposition of Variances.**  For the year ended December 31, 19X8 the O'Rourke Company income statement was as follows:

| | |
|---|---|
| Sales | $95,000 |
| Cost of Goods Sold | 36,000 |
| Gross Profit | $59,000 |

The company had the following variances (all were unfavorable):

| | | |
|---|---|---|
| Materials Price Variance | $2,800 | |
| Labor Efficiency Variance | 1,600 | |
| Volume Variance | 2,800 | |
| Controllable Variance | 2,000 | |
| Total Variances (Unfavorable) | | 9,200 |
| Gross Profit (Adjusted) | | $49,800 |
| Less: Marketing and Administrative Expenses | | 23,000 |
| Net Profit | | $26,800 |

Prepare the journal entry to close the variance accounts to the Income Summary.

**SOLUTION**

| | | |
|---|---|---|
| Income Summary | 9,200 | |
| Materials Price Variance | | 2,800 |
| Efficiency Variance | | 1,600 |
| Volume Variance | | 2,800 |
| Controllable Variance | | 2,000 |

**10.12** **Disposition of Variances; Adjustment of Cost of Goods Sold and Inventories.** In connection with the data in Problem 10.11, the following summary shows the percentage of cost elements in the cost of goods sold, finished goods and work in process inventories of the O'Rourke Company.

| | Materials | % | Labor | % | Factory Overhead | % |
|---|---|---|---|---|---|---|
| Cost of goods sold | $12,000 | 50.0 | $10,000 | 62.5 | $14,000 | 50.0 |
| Finished goods inventory | 4,000 | 16.7 | 4,000 | 25.0 | 5,600 | 20.0 |
| Work in process inventory | 8,000 | 33.3 | 2,000 | 12.5 | 8,400 | 30.0 |
| Total | $24,000 | | $16,000 | | $28,000 | |

(a) Allocate the variances (price, efficiency, volume and controllable) to cost of goods sold, finished goods, and work in process.

(b) Show the effect the above allocation has on the Income Statement.

**SOLUTION**

(a) **Allocation of Variances.** The following allocation was computed by applying the percentages above to the variances given in Problem 10.11.

| Variances | Cost of Goods Sold | Finished Goods | Work in Process | Total |
|---|---|---|---|---|
| Materials price variance | $1,400 | $ 467 | $ 933 | $2,800 |
| Labor efficiency variance | 1,000 | 400 | 200 | 1,600 |
| Volume variance | 1,400 | 560 | 840 | 2,800 |
| Controllable variance | 1,000 | 400 | 600 | 2,000 |
| Total | $4,800 | $1,827 | $2,573 | $9,200 |

(b) **Adjusted Income Statement**

| | |
|---|---|
| Sales | $95,000 |
| Cost of Goods Sold (Adjusted to actual: $36,000 + $4,800) | 40,800 |
| Gross Profit | $54,200 |
| Less: Marketing and Administrative Expenses | 23,000 |
| Net Profit | $31,200 |

# Chapter 11

# Direct Costing

## 11.1 THE RATIONALE FOR DIRECT COSTING

In absorption costing, when standard volume or capacity (a short-run concept) is compared to normal capacity (a long-run concept), (1) a volume variance or (2) idle capacity and fixed efficiency variances generally result. Closing these variances to cost of goods sold causes a variation in unit cost each period which is due primarily to the effect of applying a long-run measurement tool to a short-run situation.

In contrast, direct costing procedures are designed to present cost-volume relationships and income data in terms of the short run. The need for such information by management is detailed in the following sections.

## 11.2 DIRECT COSTING: PRODUCT AND PERIOD COSTS

Direct costing makes a distinction between *product costs* and *period costs*. Product costs consist only of prime costs for direct materials and direct labor plus variable factory overhead. These are the costs assigned to inventories (work in process and finished goods) and cost of goods sold. Fixed factory overhead is included with other period expenses, such as selling and administrative expenses.

Thus, the primary difference between direct costing and absorption costing is the treatment of fixed factory overhead. Direct costing excludes it as a product cost; absorption costing includes it as a product unit cost in inventories and cost of goods sold.

## 11.3 DIRECT COSTING VS. ABSORPTION COSTING: INCOME STATEMENTS

The conceptual differences between income statements prepared under direct costing and absorption costing procedures are as follows:

(1) *Gross marginal income vs. gross profit.* Under direct costing, the gross marginal income figure represents the difference between sales and variable manufacturing costs. It is the equivalent of the gross profit figure under absorption costing, and reflects the exclusion of fixed costs from inventory valuation and cost of goods sold. Thus, gross marginal income will always be greater than gross profit. It is also important to note that this method allows the cost of goods sold to vary directly with sales.

(2) *Contribution margin.* Also known as marginal income, the contribution margin is the excess of sales over total variable costs (i.e. manufacturing, selling, administrative). Its usefulness as a profit planning device makes this a significant feature of the direct costing income statement (see Section 11.4).

(3) *Inventory costs.* Under direct costing, fixed overhead is eliminated from inventories. This is contrary to the AICPA's view; *ARB No. 43* specifically states that "... exclusion of all overheads from inventory costs does not constitute an accepted accounting procedure." Neither the IRS nor the SEC will accept direct costing until the AICPA approves its use. As a result,

many firms use direct costing for internal reports but adjust inventories to conform with
absorption costing procedures for external reports.

(4) *Net operating profit.*   The difference in net operating profit under the two methods is due to
the amount of fixed costs charged to inventories.   If there are no beginning or ending inventories, the NOP under both methods would be the same.

## EXAMPLE 1

Assume the following information:

| | |
|---|---|
| Units manufactured | 120,000 |
| Sales | 100,000 units @ $15/unit |
| Direct materials | $4/unit |
| Direct labor | $3/unit |
| Variable costs | |
|    Manufacturing overhead | $2/unit |
|    Selling and general expenses | $1/unit |
| Fixed costs | |
|    Manufacturing overhead | $180,000 |
|    Selling and general expenses | $140,000 |

$\frac{180}{120} = 1.50$

Prepare an income statement under (*a*) absorption costing and (*b*) direct costing.

(*a*)   Absorption Costing Method

### Income Statement

| | | | |
|---|---|---:|---:|
| Sales | | | $1,500,000 |
| Cost of goods sold: | | | |
|   Direct materials | | $ 480,000 | |
|   Direct labor | | 360,000 | |
|   Manufacturing overhead: | | | |
|     Variable | $240,000 | | |
|     Fixed | 180,000 | 420,000 | |
|     Cost of goods manufactured | | $1,260,000 | |
|   Less: Finished goods inventory (end) | | | |
|     (20,000 at $10.50 per unit) | | 210,000 | |
|      Cost of goods sold | | | 1,050,000 |
| Gross margin | | | $ 450,000 |
| Selling and general expenses | | | |
|   Variable | | $ 100,000 | |
|   Fixed | | 140,000 | 240,000 |
| Net income for year | | | $ 210,000 |

*Note:*   Variable and fixed overhead portions of items shown above are not generally disclosed in an income
statement.

(b)   Direct Costing Method

***Income Statement***

| | | |
|---|---:|---:|
| Sales | | $1,500,000 |
| Cost of goods sold: | | |
| Direct materials (4 x 120) | $ 480,000 | |
| Direct labor   (3 x 120) | 360,000 | |
| Variable manufacturing overhead | 240,000 | |
| Cost of goods manufactured | $1,080,000 | |
| Less: Finished goods inventory (end) | | |
| (20,000 at $9.00 per unit) | 180,000 | |
| Cost of goods sold | $ 900,000 | |
| Variable selling and general expenses | 100,000 | 1,000,000 |
| Contribution margin | | $ 500,000 |
| Fixed costs and expenses: | | |
| Manufacturing overhead | $ 180,000 | |
| Selling and general expenses | 140,000 | 320,000 |
| Net income for year | | $ 180,000 |

*Note:*  The $30,000 difference from the net income found in part (*a*) is equal to the inclusion under absorption costing [part (*a*)] of fixed manufacturing overhead in ending inventory to the extent of 20,000 units at $1.50 per unit (fixed manufacturing overhead of $180,000 ÷ 120,000 units produced).

## 11.4   USES OF DIRECT COSTING

By distinguishing between product and period costs, direct costing offers a variety of uses for both internal and external purposes.  Some of the benefits accruing from this costing method are described below.

Direct costing is a useful analytic device in budget preparation, since such *profit planning* involves both short- and long-run operations.  The isolation of product costs emphasizes the cost-volume-profit relationship, providing data for such planning problems as breakeven analysis, return on investment, etc.

The simplified techniques associated with the contribution margin also make direct costing a useful tool for product pricing; managerial decisions related to production levels, new products and markets, special activities, etc.   Finally, as a control tool, direct costing facilitates the preparation of responsibility-based income statements for managers, enabling them to recognize and act upon discrepancies and variances occurring in their areas.

The separation of accounts into fixed and variable components under direct costing simplifies the processes of assigning costs to inventory and determining income.  It allows net income to vary more directly with sales since no fixed costs are deferred in inventories.  It also results in clear, easily understood financial reports.   Finally, direct costing guards against profit manipulation.  It reduces the possibility of having increased sales with decreased earnings because fixed expenses are considered period, not product, costs.  With fixed overhead costs remaining constant, an increase in sales will increase profits.

### EXAMPLE 2

If a company wants to show a greater profit, under absorption costing it can increase production at the end of a period, thus reducing the unit cost (since fixed costs are spread over more units).  Such a practice is impossible under direct costing, since a change in production has no effect on unit cost, as the cost of goods sold varies directly with sales.

## 11.5   ADVANTAGES AND DISADVANTAGES OF DIRECT COSTING

**Advantages of Direct Costing**

(1)   Establishes cost-volume-profit relationships.

(2)   Exclusion of fixed overhead from inventories both simplifies the report and leaves it less open to misinterpretation by management.

(3)   Impact of fixed overhead on management is more effective when fixed overhead is shown as a separate charge.

(4)   Provides a basis for comparison of the profitability of different products.

(5)   Conforms to the concept of assigning current out-of-pocket expenditures to the cost of manufacturing a product.

**Disadvantages of Direct Costing**

(1)   No clear-cut distinction between fixed and variable overhead costs—many are hybrid.

(2)   Violates the principle that manufacturing cost should include all manufacturing charges, including fixed overhead.

(3)   An item may be fixed or variable, depending on the (depreciation) method used.

(4)   Is not in accordance with the tax laws.

(5)   Cannot be used for long-range pricing policies, which must include fixed overhead as part of cost.

## *Summary*

(1)   _____ costing assigns only prime costs and variable factory overhead to a product.

(2)   Under _____ costing, a company can affect profits by controlling production.

(3)   Marginal income will always be _____ than gross profit because fixed overhead is excluded.

(4)   Direct costing makes a distinction between _____ costs and _____ costs.

(5)   Product costs under direct costing include (*a*) prime costs only, (*b*) prime costs and variable overhead, (*c*) prime costs and fixed overhead.

(6)   One of the primary differences between direct costing and absorption costing is the treatment of (*a*) variable overhead, (*b*) direct materials, (*c*) fixed overhead.

(7)   The contribution margin is also known as (a) marginal income, (b) net operating profit, (c) net income.

(8)   Under direct costing, cost of goods sold varies directly with sales.   (a) True, (b) false.

(9)   Under direct costing, fixed overhead is eliminated from inventories.   (a) True, (b) false.

(10)   Net operating profit under both costing methods is the same.   (a) True, (b) false.

(11)   The AICPA accepts direct costing for external reports only.   (a) True, (b) false.

*Answers:*   (1) direct; (2) absorption; (3) greater; (4) product, period; (5) b; (6) c; (7) a; (8) a; (9) a; (10) b; (11) b.

# Solved Problems

**11.1**   **Direct Costing: Net Operating Profit.**   The H.R.M. Corporation sells review books to accounting students.   The company noticed a decline in sales for the months of May, June, and July, presumably due to the reduced number of students attending the summer session.

The variable costs to produce each book are as follows:

| Direct materials | $2.00 |
|---|---|
| Direct labor | 1.00 |
| Variable overhead | 1.00 |
| Total | $4.00 |

Fixed overhead is $12,000 per year; selling and administrative expenses are $6,000 per year. The selling price per book is $5.00.   Actual data relating to inventories and sales are as follows:

| Quantity | May | June | July |
|---|---|---|---|
| Inventory (beginning) | 0 | 1,000 | 3,000 |
| Books produced | 5,000 | 4,000 | 2,000 |
| Books sold | 4,000 | 2,000 | 1,000 |
| Inventory (ending) | 1,000 | 3,000 | 4,000 |

Find the net operating profit for May, June and July, using direct costing.

**SOLUTION**

|                                         | May       | June      | July      |
|-----------------------------------------|-----------|-----------|-----------|
| Sales                                   | $20,000   | $10,000   | $ 5,000   |
| Direct Materials                        | $10,000   | $ 8,000   | $ 4,000   |
| Direct Labor                            | 5,000     | 4,000     | 2,000     |
| Variable Overhead                       | 5,000     | 4,000     | 2,000     |
| Cost of Goods Manufactured              | $20,000   | $16,000   | $ 8,000   |
| Beginning Inventory                     | —         | 4,000     | 12,000    |
| Cost of Goods Available for Sale        | $20,000   | $20,000   | $20,000   |
| Ending Inventory                        | 4,000     | 12,000    | 16,000    |
| Cost of Goods Sold                      | $16,000·  | $ 8,000   | $ 4,000   |
| Marginal Income                         | $ 4,000   | $ 2,000   | $ 1,000   |
| Less Fixed Expenses:                    |           |           |           |
|   Factory Overhead            | $ 1,000   | $ 1,000   | $ 1,000   |
|   Selling and Administrative Expenses | 500 | 500       | 500       |
| Total Fixed Expenses                    | $ 1,500   | $ 1,500   | $ 1,500   |
| Net Operating Profit (Loss)             | $ 2,500   | $ 500     | $ (500)   |

**11.2   Direct Costing: Inventory Valuation.**   The Metnick, Meyer C.P.A. firm was asked by Gin Gin, Incorporated to determine the value of its inventory.   The company produces a line of two-piece bathing suits.   In the month of July the company made 90,000 suits.   It was a warm month so sales increased 20% from June (June sales, 50,000).   Costs for the 90,000 suits were: Direct materials, $4; direct labor, $2; and variable overhead, $1.   Fixed overhead was $1.50 per suit.   The ending inventory was 30,000 suits.   The C.P.A. firm used direct costing to value the inventory.

Compute the value of the ending inventory.

**SOLUTION**

| Direct materials          | $4  |
|---------------------------|-----|
| Direct labor              | 2   |
| Variable factory overhead | 1   |
| Total variable costs      | $7  |

Ending inventory = 30,000 suits × $7 = $210,000

**11.3   Income Statements: Direct Costing, Absorption Costing.**   The financial data for the Locke Corporation are as shown below.

|                                           | 19X1    | 19X0    |
|-------------------------------------------|---------|---------|
| Sales (in units)                          | 60,000  | 50,000  |
| Selling price (per unit)                  | $2.00   | $2.00   |
| Beginning inventory (units)               | 15,000  | 10,000  |
| Ending inventory (units)                  | 10,000  | 15,000  |
| Production (units)                        | 120,000 | 100,000 |
| Direct materials (per unit)               | $ .10   | $ .05   |
| Direct labor (per unit)                   | .10     | .05     |
| Variable overhead (per unit)              | .10     | .05     |
| Fixed overhead (per unit)                 | .20     | .10     |
| Selling and administrative expenses (total) | $5,000 | $3,000  |

(a) Using the direct costing method, prepare an income statement for 19X0.   (b) Using the absorption costing method, prepare an income statement for 19X1.   (c) What is the effect on retained earnings in 19X1 if direct costing is used instead of absorption costing?

## SOLUTION

(a)   **Direct Costing Method**

### Locke Corporation
### Income Statement
### Year 19X0

| | | |
|---|---:|---:|
| Sales (50,000 units @ $2.00) | | $100,000 |
| Direct Materials (100,000 units @ $0.05) | $ 5,000 | |
| Direct Labor (100,000 units @ $0.05) | 5,000 | |
| Variable Overhead (100,000 @ $0.05) | 5,000 | |
| Cost of Goods Manufactured | | $ 15,000 |
| Beginning Inventory (10,000 units @ $0.15*) | | 1,500 |
| Cost of Goods Available for Sale | | $ 16,500 |
| Ending Inventory (15,000 units @ $0.15*) | | 2,250 |
| Cost of Goods Sold | | $ 14,250 |
| Marginal Income | | $ 85,750 |
| Less Fixed Expenses: | | |
|    Fixed Overhead (100,000 units @ $0.10) | $10,000 | |
|    Selling and Administrative Expenses | 3,000 | |
| Total Fixed Expenses | | 13,000 |
| Net Operating Profit | | $ 72,750 |

\* Total variable unit cost = Direct materials + Direct labor + Variable overhead.

(b)   **Absorption Costing Method**

### Locke Corporation
### Income Statement
### Year 19X1

| | | |
|---|---:|---:|
| Sales (60,000 units @ $2.00) | | $120,000 |
| Direct Materials (120,000 units @ $0.10) | $12,000 | |
| Direct Labor (120,000 @ $0.10) | 12,000 | |
| Variable Overhead (120,000 @ $0.10) | 12,000 | |
| Fixed Overhead (120,000 @ $0.20) | 24,000 | |
| Cost of Goods Manufactured | | $ 60,000 |
| Beginning Inventory (15,000 units @ $0.25*) | | 3,750 |
| Cost of Goods Available for Sale | | $ 63,750 |
| Ending Inventory (10,000 units @ $0.50*) | | 5,000 |
| Cost of Goods Sold | | $ 58,750 |
| Gross Profit on Sales | | $ 61,250 |
| Selling and Administrative Expenses | | 5,000 |
| Net Operating Profit | | $ 56,250 |

\* Total unit cost = Total variable unit cost + Fixed overhead unit cost.

(c)   If direct costing had been used instead of absorption costing in 19X1, retained earnings would have been reduced by $500 [(15,000 units in beginning inventory × $0.10 19X0 fixed overhead rate) less (10,000 units in ending inventory × $0.20 19X1 fixed overhead rate)].

**11.4    Income Statements: Full Costing, Direct Costing.** The Cap Company produced 10,000 units of its product during April and May of 19X2. During this period, 8,000 of these units were sold at $15 per unit.   The following represent the operations of these two months:

| | |
|---|---|
| Direct materials | $.20 per unit |
| Direct labor | .10 per unit |
| Fixed overhead | 60% of total factory overhead |

For the two-month period, fixed expenses were as follows:

| | |
|---|---|
| Heat | $2,000 |
| Light | 2,000 |
| Equipment | 2,000 |
| Depreciation | 3,000 |
| Maintenance | 1,500 |
| Rent | 5,000 |
| Insurance | 1,500 |
| Indirect labor | 2,000 |
| Repairs | 2,500 |
| Taxes | 2,500 |
| Selling and administrative expenses | 5,000 |

Prepare income statements using (a) full costing and (b) direct costing.

**SOLUTION**

(a)   **Full Costing**

*Cap Company*
*Income Statement*
*for months of April and May, 19X2*

| | | |
|---|---:|---:|
| Sales (8,000 units @ $15) | | $120,000 |
| Direct Materials (10,000 units @ $0.20) | $ 2,000 | |
| Direct Labor (10,000 units @ $0.10) | 1,000 | |
| Variable Factory Overhead ($40,000* − $24,000) | 16,000 | |
| Fixed Factory Overhead | 24,000 | |
| Cost of Goods Manufactured | | $ 43,000 |
| Beginning Inventory | | 0 |
| Cost of Goods Available for Sale | | $ 43,000 |
| Ending Inventory (2,000 units @ $4.30**) | | 8,600 |
| Cost of Goods Sold | | $ 34,400 |
| Gross Profit on Sales | | $ 85,600 |
| Selling and Administrative Expenses | | 5,000 |
| Net Operating Profit | | $ 80,600 |

\* Total factory overhead = $24,000 (fixed factory overhead) ÷ 60% = $40,000.

\*\* Total cost per unit = $43,000 ÷ 10,000 units produced = $4.30 per unit.

38

42238

8487a822

(b) **Direct Costing**

### Cap Company
### Income Statement
### for months of April and May, 19X2

| | | |
|---|---:|---:|
| Sales (8,000 units @ $15) | | $120,000 |
| Direct Materials (10,000 units @ $0.20) | $ 2,000 | |
| Direct Labor (10,000 units @ $0.10) | 1,000 | |
| Variable Factory Overhead ($40,000 − $24,000) | 16,000 | |
| Cost of Goods Manufactured | | $ 19,000 |
| Beginning Inventory | | 0 |
| Cost of Goods Available for Sale | | $ 19,000 |
| Ending Inventory (2,000 @ $1.90) | | 3,800 |
| Cost of Goods Sold | | $ 15,200 |
| Marginal Income | | $104,800 |
| Less Fixed Expenses: | | |
|    Factory Overhead | $24,000 | |
|    Selling and Administrative Expenses | 5,000 | |
| Total Fixed Expenses | | 29,000 |
| Net Operating Profit | | $ 75,800 |

*Note:* The difference in net operating profit under the two methods results from the different unit cost applied to the ending inventory in each case.

**11.5 Comparative Income Statements.** The cost department of the NO-GO Company has established the following standards for manufacturing.

| | |
|---|---:|
| Normal capacity (units) | 200,000 |
| Maximum capacity (units) | 250,000 |
| Standard variable manufacturing cost per unit | $ 15 |
| Variable marketing expenses per unit | 5 |
| Fixed factory overhead | 400,000 |
| Fixed marketing expenses | 250,000 |
| Sales price per unit | 30 |

Operating units for the year ended 19X8 were as follows:

| | |
|---|---:|
| Beginning inventory | 20,000 |
| Sales | 175,000 |
| Production | 180,000 |

Prepare income statements using (a) absorption costing and (b) direct costing.

**SOLUTION**

(a)  **Absorption Costing**

*NO-GO Company*
*Income Statement*
*for year ended December 31, 19X8*

| | | | |
|---|---:|---:|---:|
| Sales (175,000 units @ $30) | | | $5,250,000 |
| Cost of Goods Sold | | | |
|   Beginning Inventory | | | |
|     Variable Cost (20,000 units @ $15) | $ 300,000 | | |
|     Fixed Cost (20,000 units @ $2) | 40,000 | $ 340,000 | |
|   Manufacturing Cost | | | |
|     Fixed | $ 400,000 | | |
|     Variable (180,000 units @ $15) | 2,700,000 | 3,100,000 | |
|   Goods Available for Sale | | $3,440,000 | |
|   Less Ending Inventory: | | | |
|     Variable Cost (25,000 units @ $15) | $ 375,000 | | |
|     Fixed Cost (25,000 units @ $2) | 50,000 | 425,000 | |
|   Total Cost of Goods Sold | | | 3,015,000 |
| Gross Profit from Operations | | | $2,235,000 |
| Less Marketing Expenses: | | | |
|   Fixed | $ 250,000 | | |
|   Variable (175,000 @ $5) | 875,000 | | 1,125,000 |
| Net Operating Income | | | $1,110,000 |

(b)  **Direct Costing**

*NO-GO Company*
*Income Statement*
*for year ended December 31, 19X8*

| | | | |
|---|---:|---:|---:|
| Sales (175,000 units @ $30) | | | $5,250,000 |
| Less Variable Manufacturing Cost: | | | |
|   Beginning Inventory (20,000 units @ $15) | $ 300,000 | | |
|   Variable Manufacturing Cost | 2,700,000 | | |
|   Total Goods Available for Sale | | $3,000,000 | |
|   Ending Inventory (25,000 units @ $15) | | 375,000 | |
| | | $2,625,000 | |
|   Variable Marketing Expenses | | 875,000 | |
| Total Direct Costs and Expenses | | | 3,500,000 |
| Marginal Income | | | $1,750,000 |
| Fixed Costs: | | | |
|   Manufacturing | $ 400,000 | | |
|   Marketing | 250,000 | | 650,000 |
| Net Operating Income | | | $1,100,000 |

**11.6    Comparative Income Statements.**    Fasco, Incorporated makes and sells fire equipment for general use in all fire services.    The company prepares an income statement at the end of each month, which is given to all stockholders.   Actual data for the first four months of 19X2 are given below.

| Actual Data (in units) | January | February | March | April |
|---|---|---|---|---|
| Beginning inventory | 0 | 100,000 | 80,000 | 80,000 |
| Production | 200,000 | 100,000 | 280,000 | 220,000 |
| Sales | 100,000 | 120,000 | 280,000 | 300,000 |
| Ending inventory | 100,000 | 80,000 | 80,000 | 0 |

In addition to the actual data, the following basic data have been provided.

| | |
|---|---|
| Direct materials | $.20 per unit |
| Direct labor | .20 per unit |
| Variable overhead | .20 per unit |
| Total variable costs | $.60 per unit |
| Normal capacity | 200,000 units |
| Fixed overhead | $40,000 per month; $0.20 per unit |
| Selling and administrative expenses | $10,000 per month |
| Selling price | $2.00 per unit |

The company prepares the monthly income statement in two forms.   It uses absorption costing for reporting to stockholders, and direct costing for reporting to management, since it is useful for internal control.

Prepare monthly income statements for (a) the stockholders and (b) management.

**SOLUTION**

(a)   **Stockholders' Statements: Absorption Costing**

*Fasco, Incorporated*
*Income Statement*
*January 19X2–April 19X2*

| | January | February | March | April |
|---|---|---|---|---|
| Sales | $200,000 | $ 240,000 | $ 560,000 | $ 600,000 |
| Direct Materials | $ 40,000 | $ 20,000 | $ 56,000 | $ 44,000 |
| Direct Labor | 40,000 | 20,000 | 56,000 | 44,000 |
| Variable Overhead | 40,000 | 20,000 | 56,000 | 44,000 |
| Fixed Overhead (applied) | 40,000 | 20,000 | 56,000 | 44,000 |
| Cost of Goods Manufactured | $160,000 | $ 80,000 | $ 224,000 | $ 176,000 |
| Beginning Inventory* | 0 | 80,000 | 64,000 | 64,000 |
| Cost of Goods Available for Sale | $160,000 | $ 160,000 | $ 288,000 | $ 240,000 |
| Ending Inventory* | (80,000) | (64,000) | (64,000) | 0 |
| Cost of Goods Sold | $ 80,000 | $ 96,000 | $ 224,000 | $ 240,000 |
| Over- or Underapplied Fixed Overhead** | 0 | 20,000 | (16,000) | (4,000) |
| Cost of Goods Sold, Actual | $ (80,000) | $(116,000) | $(208,000) | $(236,000) |
| Gross Profit on Sales | $120,000 | $ 124,000 | $ 352,000 | $ 364,000 |
| Selling and Administrative Expenses | (10,000) | (10,000) | (10,000) | (10,000) |
| Net Operating Profit | $110,000 | $ 114,000 | $ 342,000 | $ 354,000 |

\* Inventory unit cost = Total variable costs + Fixed overhead per unit.
\*\* Over- or underapplied fixed overhead = Actual fixed overhead ($40,000) − Fixed overhead applied.

(b)   **Managements' Statements: Direct Costing**

*Fasco, Incorporated*
*Income Statement*
*January 19X2–April 19X2*

|  | January | February | March | April |
|---|---|---|---|---|
| Sales | $200,000 | $240,000 | $ 560,000 | $ 600,000 |
| Direct Materials | $ 40,000 | $ 20,000 | $ 56,000 | $ 44,000 |
| Direct Labor | 40,000 | 20,000 | 56,000 | 44,000 |
| Variable Overhead | 40,000 | 20,000 | 56,000 | 44,000 |
| Cost of Goods Manufactured | $120,000 | $ 60,000 | $ 168,000 | $ 132,000 |
| Beginning Inventory* | 0 | 60,000 | 48,000 | 48,000 |
| Cost of Goods Available for Sale | $120,000 | $120,000 | $ 216,000 | $ 180,000 |
| Ending Inventory* | (60,000) | (48,000) | (48,000) | 0 |
| Cost of Goods Sold | $ (60,000) | $ (72,000) | $(168,000) | $(180,000) |
| Marginal Income* | 140,000 | 168,000 | 392,000 | 420,000 |
| Less Fixed Expenses: |  |  |  |  |
| Factory Overhead | $ 40,000 | $ 40,000 | $ 40,000 | $ 40,000 |
| Selling and Administrative Expenses | 10,000 | 10,000 | 10,000 | 10,000 |
| Total Fixed Expenses | $ (50,000) | $ (50,000) | $ (50,000) | $ (50,000) |
| Net Operating Profit | $ 90,000 | $118,000 | $ 342,000 | $ 370,000 |

* Inventory unit cost = Total variable costs.

**11.7**    **Comparative Cost of Goods Sold Statement.**   The Wilson Manufacturing Company produces widgets for large assemblies.   The standard cost for the production of one widget is:

| | |
|---|---|
| Direct materials, 6 units @ $5 | $30 |
| Direct labor, 4 hours | 10 |
| Factory overhead, $6 per direct labor hour ($4 variable, $2 fixed) | 24 |
| Total cost per widget | $64 |

The following information pertains to the production of widgets for the year ending December 31, 19X8:

> Beginning inventory:
> > Work in process: 2,500 units, all materials, 50% completed
> > Finished goods: 1,500 units
> Actual overhead: $402,000
> Ending inventory:
> > Work in process: 1,500 units, all materials, 50% completed
> > Finished goods: 0 units
> Finished goods (transferred to the warehouse): 70,000 units

The company uses the FIFO method of inventory valuation.
   Prepare (a) a quantity schedule, (b) an equivalent production schedule and (c) a comparative

cost of goods sold statement for the data given above. (d) Explain the difference in cost of goods sold under absorption costing and direct costing.

## SOLUTION

(a) **Quantity Schedule**

| | | |
|---|---|---|
| Beginning Inventory | 2,500 | |
| Purchases | 69,000* | |
| Materials Available | | 71,500 |
| Transferred Out | 70,000 | |
| Ending Inventory | 1,500 | 71,500 |

\* Purchases = 70,000 transferred out + 1,500 ending inventory − 2,500 beginning inventory = 69,000.

(b) **Equivalent Production Schedule**

| | |
|---|---|
| Transferred Out | 70,000 |
| Less: Beginning Work in Process | 2,500 |
| Started and Completed (current) | 67,500 |
| Add: Beginning Inventory (2,500 × 50%) | 1,250 |
| Closing Inventory (1,500 × 50%) | 750 |
| Equivalent Production | 69,500 |

(c)

**Wilson Manufacturing Company**
**Comparative Cost of Goods Sold Statement**
*year ending December 31, 19X8*

| | Absorption Costing | Direct Costing |
|---|---|---|
| Cost of Goods Manufactured: | | |
| 70,000 units @ $64 | $4,480,000 | |
| 70,000 units @ $56 | | $3,920,000 |
| Add: Beginning Inventory, Finished Goods | | |
| 1,500 units @ $64 | 96,000 | |
| 1,500 units @ $56 | | 84,000 |
| Total Goods Available for Sale | $4,576,000 | $4,004,000 |
| Less: Ending Inventory, Finished Goods | 0 | 0 |
| Cost of Goods Sold | $4,576,000 | $4,004,000 |

\* Total variable unit cost = $30 direct materials + $10 direct labor + $16 factory overhead (4 hours × $4) = $56.

(d) The difference in cost of goods sold of $572,000 under the two methods reflects the exclusion of fixed factory overhead in product costs under direct costing. Fixed factory overhead of $8 per unit (4 hours × $2) applied to 71,500 units sold (70,000 + 1,500) equals $572,000.

# Chapter 12

# By-product and Joint Product Costing

## 12.1  JOINT COSTS

The nature of by-products and joint products is such that they contain an element called joint costs.  *Joint costs* are those incurred up to the point in a given process where individual products can be identified.   In the case of by-products, this is the point at which the main product and its associated by-products emerge.   For joint products, it is the point at which separate products having relative sales values can be identified.   In both cases, the stage of production at which separate products are identifiable is known as the *split-off point*.

## 12.2  DIFFICULTIES ASSOCIATED WITH JOINT COSTS

The two major difficulties inherent in joint costs are as follows:

(1)  *True joint costs are indivisible.*  Thus, the total of these costs must be allocated to individual products on some logical basis.   For example, a sample of ore usually contains a variety of minerals (i.e. iron, lead, zinc, etc.).   These minerals are joint products in their raw state; until they are extracted by ore reduction, the costs of locating, mining and processing are properly considered joint costs.

(2)  *Joint costs are frequently confused with common costs.*  The difference here is that joint costs are indivisible while common costs are divisible.   That is, the various products resulting from common costs could have each been obtained separately, so common costs can be allocated on the basis of relative usage.

## 12.3  BY-PRODUCTS DEFINED

*By-products* are products of limited sales value produced simultaneously with a product of greater sales value.   The *main product*, as it is called, is generally produced in much greater quantities than the by-products.

By-products generally fall into one of two categories: (1) They may be sold in the same form as originally produced, or (2) they may undergo further processing before sale.   In many cases, salable uses have been found for by-products formerly considered waste or scrap.

## 12.4  BY-PRODUCTS: VALUATION METHODS

The methods for costing by-products fall into the two categories described below.

### Category 1

Methods in this category *do not allocate* specific costs to by-products for costing or inventory valuation purposes.   They include:

*Method 1.*  Under this method, income from by-products is shown on the income statement under one of the following classifications:

(1)  Addition to revenue

    (a)  Sales revenue

    (b)  Other income

(2)    Deduction from main product

       (c)    Deduction from cost of goods sold of the main product

       (d)    Deduction from total production costs of the main product

## EXAMPLE 1

Assume the following facts:

| | |
|---|---|
| Total production costs | $ 94,500 (54,000 units @ $1.75/unit) |
| Sales from main product | 112,500 (45,000 units @ $2.50/unit) |
| By-product revenue | 6,825 |
| Marketing and administrative expenses (main product) | 9,750 |
| Ending inventory (9,000 units × $1.75) | 15,750 |

Income statements for the various classifications are as follows:

(a)    Sales revenue

| | | |
|---|--:|--:|
| Sales | | |
|    Main Product (45,000 × $2.50) | | $112,500 |
|    By-product | | 6,825 |
|      Total | | $119,325 |
| Costs of Goods Sold | | |
|    Total Production Costs (54,000 × $1.75) | $94,500 | |
|    Less: Ending Inventory | 15,750 | 78,750 |
|      Gross Profit | | $ 40,575 |
| Marketing and Administrative Expenses | | 9,750 |
| Net Income | | $ 30,825 |

(b)    Other income

| | | |
|---|--:|--:|
| Sales (main product—45,000 × $2.50) | | $112,500 |
| Cost of Goods Sold | | |
|    Total Production Costs (54,000 × $1.75) | $94,500 | |
|    Less: Ending Inventory | 15,750 | 78,750 |
|      Gross Profit | | $ 33,750 |
| Marketing and Administrative Expenses | | 9,750 |
|    Income from Operations | | $ 24,000 |
| Other Income | | |
|    Revenue from Sale of By-products | | 6,825 |
| Net Income | | $ 30,825 |

(c)    Deduction from cost of goods sold of the main product

| | | |
|---|--:|--:|
| Sales (main product—45,000 × $2.50) | | $112,500 |
| Cost of Goods Sold | | |
|    Total Production Costs | $94,500 | |
|    Less: Ending Inventory | 15,750 | |
|      Total Cost of Goods Sold | $78,750 | |
|    Less: Revenue from Sale of By-products | 6,825 | 71,925 |
|      Gross Profit | | $ 40,575 |
| Marketing and Administrative Expenses | | 9,750 |
| Net Income | | $ 30,825 |

(d)  Deduction from total production costs of the main product

| | | | |
|---|---|---|---|
| Sales (main product—45,000 × $2.50) | | | $112,500 |
| Cost of Goods Sold | | | |
| Total Production Costs (54,000 × $1.75) | $94,500 | | |
| Less: Revenue from Sale of By-products | 6,825 | $87,675 | |
| Less: Ending Inventory (9,000 × $1.6236*) | | 14,612 | 73,063 |
| Gross Profit | | | $ 39,437 |
| Marketing and Administrative Expenses | | | 9,750 |
| Net Income | | | $ 29,687 |

* The revenue from the sale of by-products decreases total production costs
and therefore requires the recalculation of the unit cost, as follows:

$$\frac{\$87,675}{54,000 \text{ units}} = \$1.6236 \text{ per unit}$$

In classification A, B, and C, no attempt was made to distribute the costs associated with the by-
products. The main product's ending inventory is therefore overstated. These classifications are generally used
when by-products are of relatively minor value. In classification D, the total production cost was reduced on the
basis of sales value rather than on an allocation of costs as in joint cost allocation.

**Method 2.** The income statement shows by-product income in the same manner as Method 1,
but the amount of by-product income is adjusted for any marketing and administrative expenses
and any additional processing costs associated with the by-products.

## EXAMPLE 2

Refer to the data in Example 1 and assume the following additional information:

| | |
|---|---|
| Marketing and administrative expenses for by-products | $2,000 |
| Additional processing costs for by-products | 400 |
| Total | $2,400 |

If by-products are accounted for as other income, the income statement would appear as follows:

| | | |
|---|---|---|
| Sales (main product) | | $112,500 |
| Cost of Goods Sold | | |
| Total Production Costs | $94,500 | |
| Less: Ending Inventory | 15,750 | 78,750 |
| Gross Profit | | $ 33,750 |
| Marketing and Administrative Expenses (main product) | | 9,750 |
| Income from Operations | | $ 24,000 |
| Other Income | | |
| Net Revenue from Sale of By-products ($6,825 − $2,400) | | 4,425 |
| Net Income | | $ 28,425 |

**Method 3.** The replacement cost method is implemented in cases where by-products are used in
manufacturing processes rather than sold. Hence, the need to purchase such supplies or materials is eliminated. The appropriate procedure is to credit production costs of the main product at
the going market purchase or replacement rate of the by-products. By-product revenue in this
case does not appear on the income statement.

**EXAMPLE 3**

Assume the following:

| | |
|---|---|
| Total production costs | $ 94,500 (54,000 units @ $1.75/unit) |
| Sales from main product | 112,500 (45,000 units @ $2.50/unit) |
| Replacement cost of by-product used in manufacture of main product | 6,825 |
| Marketing and administrative expenses | 9,750 |
| Ending inventory (9,000 units × $1.75) | 15,750 |

The income statement is as follows:

| | | | |
|---|---|---|---|
| Sales (main product) | | | $112,500 |
| Cost of Goods Sold | | | |
| Total Production (54,000 × $1.75) | $94,500 | | |
| Less: Replacement Cost of By-product | 6,825 | $87,675 | |
| Less: Ending Inventory (9,000 × $1.6236*) | | 14,612 | 73,063 |
| Gross Profit | | | $ 39,437 |
| Marketing and Administrative Expenses | | | 9,750 |
| Net Income | | | $ 29,687 |

\* Adjust unit cost: $87,675 ÷ 54,000 units = $1.6236/unit

Note that the facts in this example are identical to classification D in Example 1, except that we no longer have any revenue from the sale of by-products since they were used in the manufacture of the main product. However, the production cost of the main product is credited for the worth of the by-products.

## Category 2

Some methods attempt to allocate a portion of joint costs to the by-products. The *market value* (*reversal cost*) *method* is the method generally used for assigning joint costs to by-products. The estimated market value (rather than actual sales revenue) of the by-product is shown on the income statement as a reduction in the production costs of the main product, and the by-product carries its associated costs. The term *reversal cost* is commonly used to describe this method because it requires working backward from revenue to cost. The estimated cost of the by-product is computed by deducting from its estimated sales value any estimated gross profit. Total production costs are then reduced by the by-product's estimated cost.

**EXAMPLE 4**

Assume the following data:

| | By-product X | Main Product |
|---|---|---|
| Sales (main product) | | $300,000 |
| Estimated sales value of by-product | $24,000 | |
| Process costs before separation | | 150,000 |
| Process costs after separation | 4,400 | 46,000 |
| Marketing and administrative expenses | 3,000 | 24,000 |
| Units produced | 18,000 | 40,000 |

There are no beginning or ending inventory accounts. The company estimates a 20% gross profit for by-product X.

The market value (reversal cost) method of allocation is applied as follows.

|  | By-product X | Main Product |
|---|---|---|
| Process costs before separation |  | $150,000 |
| Estimated sales value of by-product | $24,000 |  |
| Gross profit for by-product (20% × $24,000) | 4,800 |  |
| Total | $19,200 |  |
| Less: Process costs after separation | 4,400 |  |
| Amount credited to main product | $14,800 | 14,800 |
| Net cost to produce main product at separation |  | $135,200 |
| Add: Process costs after separation | 4,400 | 46,000 |
| Allocation of total costs | $19,200 | $181,200 |

A basic assumption of the market reversal method is that the costs of a by-product are proportional to its market value. The revenue and expense matching lag experienced under Method 2 is eliminated here since costs after separation are now matched to the total units produced, not just those sold. Of all the methods discussed, this method is the one most similar to those employed in joint product costing.

## 12.5  JOINT PRODUCTS DEFINED

The term *joint products* refers to individual products, each of significant sales value, produced simultaneously as a result of a common process or series of processes. *Joint products costs* are those which arise in the course of such common processes involving common raw materials. Note that joint product costs are inherently indivisible, having been incurred simultaneously for all products, and not for each product individually.

Basically, the characteristics of joint products are as follows: (1) An unavoidable physical relationship which requires simultaneous, common processing, (2) a split-off point at which separate products emerge to be sold or further processed, and (3) individual nominal sales values. Joint products manufacturing is found in the meat-packing industry, in natural resource refining industries, and in those where raw materials must be graded before processing.

## 12.6  JOINT COSTS: ALLOCATION METHODS

The methods used to allocate joint materials and manufacturing costs are described below.

### Market or Sales Value Method

The allocation of joint costs on the basis of market or sales values of the individual products is the most popular allocation method. Advocates of this method argue that a direct relationship exists between cost and selling price, namely, that the selling price of a product is determined primarily by the production cost. The procedure used under this method depends on whether or not the market value is known at the split-off point.

*Market Value Known at Split-off Point.* When the market value is known at the split-off point, the total joint cost is allocated among the joint products on the basis of the respective ratios of individual market values to total market value, multiplied by the total joint costs:

$$\text{Joint cost allocation of each product} = \frac{\text{Total market value of } each \text{ product*}}{\text{Total market value of } all \text{ products**}} \times \text{Joint costs}$$

* Total market value of *each* product = Units produced of *each* product × Unit market value of *each* product

** Total market value of *all* products = Sum of all the total market values of *each* product

## EXAMPLE 5

*Joint Cost Allocation*
*Market Value Method—Value Known*
*Total Joint Costs: $310,000*

| | Joint Products | | |
|---|---|---|---|
| | A | B | C |
| Units produced | 40,000 | 80,000 | 20,000 |
| Market value at split-off point: | | | |
| Unit | $4.00 | $5.00 | $3.00 |
| Total | $160,000 | $400,000 | $60,000 |

$$\text{Product A:} \quad \frac{\$160,000}{\$620,000*} \times \$310,000 = \$\ 80,000$$

$$\text{Product B:} \quad \frac{\$400,000}{\$620,000} \times \$310,000 = \phantom{\$}200,000$$

$$\text{Product C:} \quad \frac{\$60,000}{\$620,000} \times \$310,000 = \phantom{\$00,}30,000$$

$$\text{Total Joint Costs} \quad \$310,000$$

* Total market value of all products:

$$\$160,000 + \$400,000 + \$60,000 = \$620,000$$

***Market Value Not Known at Split-off Point.*** When the market value of a joint product cannot be readily determined at the split-off point, as, for example, when a product requires additional processing before it can be sold, a *hypothetical* market value at the split-off point is calculated. The hypothetical market value is determined by subtracting the cost of additional processing from the market value of the completed product. The total cost of each product (allocation of joint costs + after split-off processing costs) is computed as follows.

Total cost allocation of *each* product =

$$\left( \frac{\text{Total hypothetical market value of } each \text{ product at split-off point*}}{\text{Total hypothetical market value of } all \text{ products at split-off point**}} \times \text{Joint costs} \right)$$

$$+ \text{ After split-off processing costs of } each \text{ product}$$

* Total hypothetical market value of *each* product at split-off point = (Units produced of *each* product × Hypothetical market value of *each* product) − After split-off processing costs of *each* product

** Total hypothetical market value of *all* products at split-off point = Sum of all the total hypothetical market values of *each* product

**EXAMPLE 6**

*Joint Cost Allocation*
*Market Value Method—Value Not Known*
*Total Joint Costs: $310,000*

| | Joint Products | | |
|---|---|---|---|
| | **A** | **B** | **C** |
| Number of units produced | 40,000 | 80,000 | 20,000 |
| Market value *after* further processing (no market value at split-off is available) | | | |
| Unit | $4.00 | $5.00 | $3.00 |
| Total | $160,000 | $400,000 | $60,000 |
| Additional processing costs after split-off | $8,000 | $12,000 | $6,000 |

$$\text{Product A:} \quad \frac{\$160,000 - \$8,000}{\$594,000^*} \times \$310,000 = \$\ 79,327$$

$$\text{Product B:} \quad \frac{\$400,000 - \$12,000}{\$594,000} \times \$310,000 = 202,492$$

$$\text{Product C:} \quad \frac{\$60,000 - \$6,000}{\$594,000} \times \$310,000 = \underline{28,182}$$

$$\text{Total Joint Costs} \quad \underline{\underline{\$310,001}}$$

* Total hypothetical market value of all products:

($160,000 − $8,000) + ($400,000 − $12,000) + ($60,000 − $6,000) = $594,000

## Quantitative Unit Method

Under this method, the quantity of output (expressed in units) is used as the basis for allocating joint costs. Since the quantity of output of all the joint products must be stated in the same terms, a common denominator (for example, quantity/ton) must be determined when the measurement basis of output varies from product to product. The joint cost allocated to each product under this method is computed by using the following formula:

$$\text{Joint cost allocation of } each \text{ product} = \frac{\text{Total units of } each \text{ product}}{\text{Total units of } all \text{ products}^*} \times \text{Joint costs}$$

* Total units of *all* products = Sum of all units produced

**EXAMPLE 7**

The information presented in Example 5 is used here to illustrate the allocation of joint costs under the quantitative unit method.

$$\text{Product A:} \quad \frac{40,000}{140,000^*} \times \$310,000 = \$\ 88,571$$

$$\text{Product B:} \quad \frac{80,000}{140,000} \times \$310,000 = 177,143$$

$$\text{Product C:} \quad \frac{20,000}{140,000} \times \$310,000 = \underline{44,286}$$

$$\text{Total} \quad \underline{\underline{\$310,000}}$$

* Total units of all products:

40,000 + 80,000 + 20,000 = 140,000

### Simple Average Unit Cost Method

The basic assumption of this method is that all products produced by a common process should be charged a proportionate share of the total joint costs based on the number of units produced. It is assumed that the products are homogeneous, i.e. each requires no more or less cost than any other product in the group. The formula is as follows:

$$\text{Cost per unit} = \frac{\text{Total joint costs}}{\text{Total number of units produced}}$$

$$\text{Joint cost allocation} = \text{Cost per unit} \times \text{Number of units of } each \text{ product produced}$$

This method produces the same results as the quantitative unit method; the difference lies in the procedures applied. The quantitative unit method allocates joint costs in total, while the average unit cost method reduces joint costs to a unit cost for the computation of the allocation.

### EXAMPLE 8

The information presented in Example 5 is used here to illustrate the simple average unit cost method.

$$\text{Cost per unit} = \frac{\$310,000}{140,000} = \$2.2143$$

$$
\begin{array}{lll}
\text{Product A:} & \$2.2143 \times 40,000 = & \$\ 88,572 \\
\text{Product B:} & \$2.2143 \times 80,000 = & 177,144 \\
\text{Product C:} & \$2.2143 \times 20,000 = & \underline{\ 44,286} \\
& \text{Total} & \underline{\$310,002}
\end{array}
$$

### Weighted Average Unit Cost Method

Joint products and their production may vary in complexity, a consideration not usually reflected by the simple average method. Since any special conditions for production involve time, labor, materials, etc., joint products will vary in production costs to the degree that such factors play a role. In these instances, weight factors may be advantageously used to determine a more appropriate allocation than is possible by the simple average method.

The main difference between these two methods is that in the weighted average unit cost method, the number of units of each product is multiplied by its assigned weight factor to determine the total weighted average units of that product. The formula for the method is as follows.

$$\text{Joint cost allocation} = \frac{\text{Total weighted average units of } each \text{ product*}}{\text{Total weighted average units of } all \text{ products**}} \times \text{Joint costs}$$

---

\* Total weighted average units of *each* product = Number of units produced × Weight factor

\*\* Total weighted average units of *all* products = Sum of all the total weighted average units of *each* product

### EXAMPLE 9

The information presented in Example 5 is used to allocate joint costs under the weighted average unit cost method. Assume the joint products in the example are weighted as follows:

$$
\begin{array}{ll}
\text{Product A} & \text{5 points} \\
\text{Product B} & \text{4 points} \\
\text{Product C} & \text{8 points}
\end{array}
$$

$$\text{Product A:} \quad \frac{40,000 \times 5}{680,000^*} \times \$310,000 = \$\ 91,177$$

$$\text{Product B:} \quad \frac{80,000 \times 4}{680,000} \times \$310,000 = \ 145,882$$

$$\text{Product C:} \quad \frac{20{,}000 \times 8}{680{,}000} \times \$310{,}000 = \underline{\quad 72{,}941 \quad}$$

$$\text{Total} \quad \underline{\underline{\$310{,}000}}$$

\* Total weighted average units of all products:

$$(40{,}000 \times 5) + (80{,}000 \times 4) + (20{,}000 \times 8) = 680{,}000$$

# Summary

(1)  Those costs incurred up to the point where individual products can be identified are called _____ costs.

(2)  The stage of production at which separate products are identified is known as the _____.

(3)  _____ are those of limited sales value produced simultaneously with a product of greater value.

(4)  The _____ product is generally produced in much greater quantities than by-products.

(5)  True joint costs are indivisible.   (*a*) True, (*b*) false.

(6)  Common costs are identical costs, or another name for, joint costs.   (*a*) True, (*b*) false.

(7)  The market value method of apportioning joint costs reduces the cost of the main product on the income statement.   (*a*) True, (*b*) false.

(8)  The quantitative unit method uses units of measurement for allocating joint costs.   (*a*) True, (*b*) false.

(9)  Total manufacturing costs are divided by the total number of units produced to obtain a cost per unit under the (*a*) market method, (*b*) quantitative unit method, (*c*) average unit cost method.

(10)  Weight factors are used in the (*a*) weighted average unit cost method (*b*) quantitative unit method, (*c*) sales method.

(11)  Individual products, each of significant sales value, produced simultaneously are known as (*a*) by-products, (*b*) main products, (*c*) joint products.

(12)  Joint product manufacturing is fundamental in the (*a*) automobile industry, (*b*) meat-packing industry, (*c*) frozen food industry.

*Answers:*   (1) joint; (2) split-off point; (3) by-products; (4) main; (5) *a*; (6) *b*; (7) *a*; (8) *a*; (9) *c*; (10) *a*; (11) *c*; (12) *b*.

# Solved Problems

**12.1    By-product Profit Determination.**   The following income statement of the Lepolstat Manufacturing Company treats revenues from sales of by-products as other income.   Determine the gross profit, the profit from operations, and the net profit by recognizing revenue from sales of by-products as (*a*) additional sales revenue, (*b*) a deduction from cost of goods sold, and (*c*) a deduction from process costs.   (Round to three places.)

| Sales (main product, 10,000 units @ $6) | | $60,000 |
|---|---|---|
| Cost of Goods Sold | | |
| Production Costs (14,000 units @ $3) | $42,000 | |
| Ending Inventory (4,000 units @ $3) | 12,000 | 30,000 |
| Gross Profit | | $30,000 |
| Other Expenses | | 2,000 |
| Profit from Operations | | $28,000 |
| Other Income | | |
| Revenue from Sales of By-product | | 3,000 |
| Net Profit | | $31,000 |

**SOLUTION**

(a)

| Sales (main product, 10,000 units @ $6) | | $60,000 |
|---|---|---|
| Revenue from Sales of By-product | | 3,000 |
| Total Sales Revenue | | $63,000 |
| Cost of Goods Sold | | |
| Production Costs (14,000 units @ $3) | $42,000 | |
| Less: Ending Inventory (4,000 units @ $3) | 12,000 | 30,000 |
| Gross Profit | | $33,000 |
| Other Expenses | | 2,000 |
| Net Profit | | $31,000 |

(b)

| Sales (main product, 10,000 units @ $6) | | $60,000 |
|---|---|---|
| Cost of Goods Sold | | |
| Production Costs (14,000 units @ $3) | $42,000 | |
| Less: Ending Inventory (4,000 units @ $3) | 12,000 | |
| | $30,000 | |
| Less: Revenue from Sales of By-product | 3,000 | 27,000 |
| Gross Profit | | $33,000 |
| Other Expenses | | 2,000 |
| Net Profit | | $31,000 |

(c)

| Sales (main product, 10,000 units @ $6) | | $60,000 |
|---|---|---|
| Cost of Goods Sold | | |
| Production Costs (14,000 units @ $3) | $42,000 | |
| Revenue from Sales of By-product | 3,000 | |
| Net Production Costs | $39,000 | |
| Ending Inventory (4,000 units @ $2.786*) | 11,144 | 27,856 |
| Gross Profit | | $32,144 |
| Other Expenses | | 2,000 |
| Net Profit | | $30,144 |

* $39,000 ÷ 14,000 units = $2.786 (rounded)

**12.2    By-products: Reversal Cost Method.** The Whitcomb Industrial Corporation manufactures one main product and two by-products. During one period of production, the following data were compiled:

|  | Main Product | By-product X | By-product Y |
|---|---|---|---|
| Sales | $300,000 | $21,000 | $11,800 |
| Processing costs before separation | 150,000 | | |
| Processing costs after separation | 46,000 | 4,400 | 3,600 |
| Miscellaneous selling and administrative expenses | 24,000 | 3,000 | 2,200 |

There are no beginning or ending inventories. The corporation allows a 20% gross profit for Product X and a 15% gross profit for Product Y, based on sales and miscellaneous selling and administrative expenses.

Prepare an income statement covering the period described, using the reversal cost method for by-products.

**SOLUTION**

|  | Main Product | By-product X | By-product Y | Total |
|---|---|---|---|---|
| Sales | $300,000 | $21,000 | $11,800 | $332,800 |
| Costs of Goods Manufactured | | | | |
| Costs before Separation | $150,000 | | | |
| Less: Estimated Gross Profit* | | $ 4,800 | $ 2,100 | |
| Total Estimated Manufacturing Costs | | $16,200 | $ 9,700 | |
| Less: Costs after Separation | | 4,400 | 3,600 | |
| Amount to Be Credited to Main Product | $ 17,900 | $11,800 | $ 6,100 | |
| Total Cost for All Products before Separation | $132,100 | $11,800 | $ 6,100 | $150,000 |
| Add: All Costs after Separation | 46,000 | 4,400 | 3,600 | 54,000 |
| Total Cost of Goods Manufactured | $178,100 | $16,200 | $ 9,700 | $204,000 |
| Gross Profit | $121,900 | $ 4,800 | $ 2,100 | $128,800 |
| Less: Miscellaneous Selling and Administrative Expenses | 24,000 | 3,000 | 2,200 | 29,200 |
| Net Income (Loss) | $ 97,900 | $ 1,800 | $ (100) | $ 99,600 |

* $24,000 × 20% = $4,800; $14,000 × 15% = $2,100.

**12.3    By-product Cost Allocation.** The Alpha Oil Company is the leading manufacturer of home fuel and automobile oils. During the process of deriving the finished product from the crude oil, several by-products are produced. One of the by-products thrown off has a market value of $3 a unit for 5,000 units. There are several costs involved in preparing the by-product for sale: Selling and administrative expenses, 15% of the selling price; cost after split-off, $2,500. The gross profit on the by-product is 25% of the selling price.

Using the reversal cost method, calculate the by-product unit cost.

**SOLUTION**

| | |
|---|---|
| Market value (5,000 units @ $3) | $15,000 |
| Gross profit ($15,000 × 25%) | 3,750 |
| Inventory value (total cost) | $11,250 |
| Total number of units | 5,000 |
| Unit cost | $2.25* |

* $11,250 ÷ 5,000

**12.4    Joint Products Costing: Average Unit Cost Method, Market Value Method.** The Adams Company manufactures baseball bats in four sizes.   All bats are shaped in the Cutting Department and are then sent to one of two Painting Departments (A and B).   Two sizes of bats are painted in each department and, in addition, Painting Department B produces a salable by-product of paint chips.

Costs are charged out of the Cutting Department on the basis of average unit costs. In the painting departments, the market value method is used; the costs before separation in Department B are credited with the value of the chips less 10% normal profit based on sales and additional costs of completion.

The company's records show the following data for the month of May:

| Departments | Materials | Labor | Factory Overhead | Market Value | Units Produced |
|---|---|---|---|---|---|
| Cutting | $20,000 | $10,000 | $10,000 | 0 | 50,000 bats |
| Painting A | 0 | 1,000 | 1,000 | 0 | 20,000 ,, |
| Size 30 | 4,000 | 1,000 | 1,000 | $50 | 10,000 ,, |
| Size 32 | 2,000 | 500 | 500 | 25 | 10,000 ,, |
| Painting B | 0 | 10,000 | 10,000 | 0 | 30,000 ,, |
| Size 34 | 4,000 | 8,000 | 8,000 | 30 | 20,000 ,, |
| Size 35 | 0 | 2,000 | 2,000 | 20 | 10,000 ,, |
| By-product | 0 | 100 | 50 | 1 | 1,500 lbs |

(Selling and administrative expenses, $100)

Determine the unit costs for the four joint products and the by-product.

**SOLUTION**

Costs are charged out of the Cutting Department using the average unit cost method.   The calculations are as follows:

$$\text{Average unit cost} = \frac{\text{Total manufacturing costs}}{\text{Total units produced}} = \frac{\$40,000}{50,000} = \$0.80$$

The distribution of Cutting Room costs is:

To Painting Department A:   20,000 units × $0.80 = $16,000
To Painting Department B:   30,000 units × $0.80 = $24,000

The distribution of general costs in Painting Department A and apportionment to products under the market value method is shown below.

## General Costs, Department A

| | |
|---|---|
| From Cutting Department | $16,000 |
| Costs after Separation | |
| Materials | 0 |
| Labor | 1,000 |
| Factory Overhead | 1,000 |
| Total General Costs, Dept. A | $18,000 |

Size 30 bats:

$$\frac{\$50}{\$75} \times \$18,000 = \$12,000$$

Size 32 bats:

$$\frac{\$25}{\$75} \times \$18,000 = \$\ 6,000$$

The same procedure applies to Painting Department B, except that general department costs here are reduced by a credit for the value of the by-product calculated on the basis of reversal costing. Thus,

## General Costs, Department B

| | |
|---|---|
| From Cutting Department | $24,000 |
| Materials | 0 |
| Labor | 10,000 |
| Factory Overhead | 10,000 |
| | $44,000 |
| Less: By-product credit | 1,200 |
| Total General Costs, Dept. B | $42,800 |

## By-product

| | |
|---|---|
| Market Value | $1,500 |
| Less: Normal Profit (10%) | (150) |
| Cost of By-product | $1,350 |
| Less: Labor | (100) |
| Factory Overhead | (50) |
| Credit to Joint Products, Dept. B | $1,200 |

Apportionment of general costs to Department B products is

Size 34 bats:

$$\frac{\$30}{\$50} \times 42,800 = \$25,680$$

Size 35 bats:

$$\frac{\$20}{\$50} \times \$42,800 = \$17,120$$

Total costs are consolidated as follows for computation of unit costs.

| | Size | | | | |
|---|---|---|---|---|---|
| | **30** | **32** | **34** | **35** | **By-product** |
| General costs | $12,000 | $ 6,000 | $25,680 | $17,120 | $1,200 |
| Material | 4,000 | 2,000 | 4,000 | 0 | 0 |
| Labor | 1,000 | 500 | 8,000 | 2,000 | 100 |
| Overhead | 1,000 | 500 | 8,000 | 2,000 | 50 |
| Total costs | $18,000 | $ 9,000 | $45,680 | $21,120 | $1,350 |
| Units | 10,000 | 10,000 | 20,000 | 10,000 | 1,500 |
| Unit costs | $1.80 | $.90 | $2.284 | $2.112 | $.90 |

**12.5   Joint Cost Allocation from Hypothetical Market Value.** The Bounceback Manufacturing Company manufactures two products, Realrubber and Fakerubber, from the same material. The material costs $0.95 per pound and must pass through two departments. In Department 1, the material is split into Realrubber and Fakerubber. Realrubber requires no further processing; Fakerubber must be processed further in Department 2. The costs below pertain to the year ended December 31, 19X8.

| Department | Direct Materials | Direct Labor | Factory Overhead | Total |
|---|---|---|---|---|
| 1 | $144,000 | $21,000 | $15,000 | $180,000 |
| 2 | ... | 10,000 | 18,000 | 28,000 |
| Totals | $144,000 | $31,000 | $33,000 | $208,000 |

| Product | Pounds Sold | Pounds of Finished Goods, Ending Inventory | Sales in $ |
|---|---|---|---|
| Realrubber | 30,000 | 15,000 | $ 52,500 |
| Fakerubber | 45,000 | ... | 150,750 |

There were no materials on hand at year end.

(a)  Compute the unit price and the market value at split-off for Realrubber.

(b)  What is the total joint cost to be allocated to the two products?

(c)  Compute the total cost of Realrubber and Fakerubber, using the hypothetical market value procedure.

**SOLUTION**

(a)
$$\text{Unit price of Realrubber} = \frac{\text{Sales}}{\text{Pounds sold}} = \frac{\$52,500}{30,000} = \$1.75$$

The market value of Realrubber at the split-off point is computed as follows:

| | |
|---|---|
| Sales | $52,500 |
| Ending inventory (15,000 lbs @ $1.75) | 26,250 |
| Market value at split-off | $78,750 |

(b)  The total joint cost to be allocated between the two products is the total of Department 1 costs: $180,000.

(c)  The hypothetical market value for a specified product is the ultimate market value of total production less any costs beyond the split-off point.  Joint costs are allocated on the basis of the hypothetical market value by applying to the hypothetical market value of each product a percentage derived as follows:

$$\text{Allocation \%} = \frac{\text{Joint costs}}{\text{Total hypothetical market value}}$$

Any processing costs beyond the split-off point are then added back to determine total cost.

In this case, the hypothetical market value for Realrubber is $78,750; for Fakerubber, $122,750 ($150,750 − $28,000).  The total hypothetical market value ($201,500) divided into joint costs ($180,000) gives an allocation percentage of 89.33%.  The computations for total costs are shown below.

| | Realrubber | Fakerubber |
|---|---|---|
| Hypothetical market value | $78,750 | $122,750 |
| Cost allocation percentage | ×.8933 | ×.8933 |
| Distribution of joint costs | $70,347 | $109,653 |
| Add: Costs after split-off | 0 | 28,000 |
| Total costs | $70,347 | $137,653 |

**12.6**  **Joint Product and By-product Unit Costs.**  C. M. Company makes two products and a by-product.  The two products are processed first in Department A where the joint costs are allocated at the split-off point using the quantitative unit method and the cost of the by-product is determined by reversal cost.   The cost information is as follows.

| Department A: | Materials | $50,000 |
|---|---|---|
| | Labor | 10,000 |
| | Overhead | 5,000 |
| | Total costs | $65,000 |

| Production: | Product I | 3,000 |
|---|---|---|
| | Product II | 2,000 |
| | By-product | 1,000 |

| Costs added after split: | Product I: Labor | $10,000 |
|---|---|---|
| | Overhead | 10,000 |
| | Product II: Labor | 20,000 |
| | Overhead | 15,000 |
| By-product: | | 2,500 |
| Selling expenses (by-product) | | 1,500 |
| Profit (by-product) | | 10% |
| Selling prices:   Product I: | | $   200/unit |
| Product II: | | 400/unit |
| By-product: | | 10,000 |

Find the unit costs of the two joint products and the by-product.

**SOLUTION**

| | Products I and II | By-product |
|---|---|---|
| Total production costs (5,000 units) | $65,000 | |
| By-product sales | | $10,000 |
| Less: Profit (10%) | | (1,000) |
| | | $ 9,000 |
| Less: Costs after split-off | | (2,500) |
| Value of by-product credited to joint products | 6,500 | $ 6,500 |
| Net cost of joint products | $58,500 | |

Using the quantitative unit method, the joint costs are apportioned to Products I and II as follows:

Product I: $58,500 × (3,000/5,000) = $35,100
Product II: $58,500 × (2,000/5,000) = $23,400

The unit costs of the completed products are calculated below.

| | Product I | Product II | By-product |
|---|---|---|---|
| Costs before split-off | $35,100 | $23,400 | $6,500 |
| Costs after split-off | | | 2,500 |
| Labor | 10,000 | 20,000 | |
| Overhead | 10,000 | 15,000 | |
| Total costs | $55,100 | $58,400 | $9,000 |
| Units | 3,000 | 2,000 | 1,000 |
| Unit cost | $ 18.37 | $ 29.20 | $ 9.00 |

**12.7    Joint Products: Average Unit Cost Method.** The D'Alessandro Corporation produces four products. The corporation produced 10,000 units of A, 20,000 units of B, 15,000 units of C, and 25,000 units of D. The total manufacturing costs for the four products were $140,000.

Using the average unit cost method, (a) calculate the unit cost, and (b) show how the costs would be allocated among the products.

**SOLUTION**

(a)    $\dfrac{\text{Total manufacturing costs}}{\text{Total number of units produced}} = \dfrac{\$140,000}{70,000} = \$2 \text{ per unit}$

(b)    Product A: 10,000 × $2 = $20,000          Product C: 15,000 × $2 = $30,000
       Product B: 20,000 × $2 = $40,000          Product D: 25,000 × $2 = $50,000

**12.8    Joint Products: Weighted Average Unit Cost Method.** The manager of the Milligan Manufacturing Company assigned the following relative weights to its three products.

| Product | Output per Unit of Material Input | Output per Direct Labor Hour | Factory Overhead |
|---|---|---|---|
| X | 5 | 4 | 50% of weight given |
| Y | 3 | 2 | to direct labor hours |
| Z | 2 | 2 | |

The following costs were incurred during the month of January:

| | | |
|---|---|---|
| Materials | $400,000 | 47% |
| Labor | 250,000 | 29% |
| Factory overhead | 200,000 | 24% |
| Total | $850,000 | 100% |

Allocate the joint costs to the three products using the weighted average method.

**SOLUTION**

Materials:

| Product | Weight | Percentage of Total Weight | Percentage of Materials Cost | Material Point Factor |
|---|---|---|---|---|
| X | 5 | 50 | 47 | 23.5 |
| Y | 3 | 30 | 47 | 14.1 |
| Z | 2 | 20 | 47 | 9.4 |
| | 10 | 100 | | 47.0 |

Labor:

| Product | Weight | Percentage of Total Weight | Percentage of Labor Cost | Labor Point Factor |
|---|---|---|---|---|
| X | 4 | 50 | 29 | 14.50 |
| Y | 2 | 25 | 29 | 7.25 |
| Z | 2 | 25 | 29 | 7.25 |
| | 8 | 100 | | 29.00 |

Factory Overhead:

| Product | Weight | Percentage of Total Weight | Percentage of Overhead Cost | Overhead Point Factor |
|---------|--------|----------------------------|-----------------------------|-----------------------|
| X | 2 | 50 | 24 | 12 |
| Y | 1 | 25 | 24 | 6 |
| Z | $\frac{1}{4}$ | $\frac{25}{100}$ | 24 | $\frac{6}{24}$ |

Combined Point Factors:

| Product | Materials | Labor | Factory Overhead | Total |
|---------|-----------|-------|------------------|-------|
| X | 23.5 | 14.50 | 12 | 50 |
| Y | 14.1 | 7.25 | 6 | 27 |
| Z | $\frac{9.4}{47.0}$ | $\frac{7.25}{29.00}$ | $\frac{6}{24}$ | $\frac{23}{100}$ |

Allocation of Joint Costs:

| Product | Combined Point Factor | Total Cost | Allocated Cost |
|---------|-----------------------|------------|----------------|
| X | 50% | $850,000 | $425,000 |
| Y | 27% | 850,000 | 229,500 |
| Z | 23% | 850,000 | 195,500 |
|   | $\overline{100\%}$ |  | $\overline{\$850,000}$ |

**12.9    Joint Products Profit Determination.**   The Pivot Manufacturing Company produces two joint products, X and Y, in five departments (1, 2, 3, 4 and 5).   Materials enter Department 1 and split off at Department 3, where 60% become Product X and 40% become Product Y.   Product X is completed in Department 4; Product Y goes from Department 3 to Department 5, where it is completed.

Materials entering Department 1 cost $0.50 per unit.   Labor and factory overhead per unit of materials are:

| Department | Labor | Factory Overhead |
|------------|-------|------------------|
| 1 | $.25 | $.10 |
| 2 | .30 | .40 |
| 3 | .50 | .25 |
| 4 | .20 | .30 |
| 5 | .50 | .20 |

*Additional data:*   Product X sells for $4 per unit; Product Y sells for $5 per unit.   Other expenses are 10% of the unit sales price.   Sales were 3,000 units for Product X and 4,000 units for Product Y.

Determine the total net profit on each product.

## SOLUTION

**Cost of Product X**

| Department | Labor | | Factory Overhead | | Total |
|---|---|---|---|---|---|
| 1 | $.25 | + | $.10 | = | $ .35 |
| 2 | .30 | + | .40 | = | .70 |
| 3 | .50 | + | .25 | = | .75 |
| 4 | .20 | + | .30 | = | .50 |
| | | | | | $2.30 |

| | |
|---|---|
| Add: Materials cost | .50 |
| Other expenses ($4 × 0.10) | .40 |
| Total cost per unit | $3.20 |
| | |
| Selling price | $4.00 |
| Less: Total cost | 3.20 |
| Net profit per unit | $ .80 |
| Units sold | × 3,000 |
| Total net profit | $2,400 |

**Cost of Product Y**

| Department | Labor | | Factory Overhead | | Total |
|---|---|---|---|---|---|
| 1 | $.25 | + | $.10 | = | $ .35 |
| 2 | .30 | + | .40 | = | .70 |
| 3 | .50 | + | .25 | = | .75 |
| 5 | .50 | + | .20 | = | .70 |
| | | | | | $2.50 |

| | |
|---|---|
| Add: Materials cost | .50 |
| Other expenses ($5 × 0.10) | .50 |
| Total cost per unit | $3.50 |
| | |
| Selling price | $5.00 |
| Less: Total cost | 3.50 |
| Net profit per unit | $1.50 |
| Units sold | × 4,000 |
| Total net profit | $6,000 |

**12.10 Joint Products Profit.** The Kahoud foundry produces two joint products, coke and tar. Raw materials, which cost $100 per ton, pass through four different departments. Materials enter the Mixing Department, then pass to the Furnace Department after which they are separated into the products, coke and tar. Fifty percent of the material becomes coke and goes through the Grinding Department, where it is prepared for sale. The remaining fifty percent is sent to the Finishing and Packing Department, where it is completed as tar.

The following costs are incurred in the manufacture of one ton of the product:

### Departments

| Costs per Ton | Mixing | Furnace | Grinding | Finishing and Packing |
|---|---|---|---|---|
| Labor | $50 | $30 | $40 | $50 |
| Factory overhead | 30 | 50 | 35 | 60 |

The sales prices per ton are: coke, $800; tar, $1,000.
Selling and administrative expenses are 25% of sales price for each product.
Compute the net profit per ton for coke and tar.

## SOLUTION

### Costs per Ton

| | Mixing | Furnace | Total |
|---|---|---|---|
| Materials | $100 | 0 | $100 |
| Labor | 50 | 30 | 80 |
| Overhead | 30 | 50 | 80 |
| Totals | $180 | $80 | $260 |

| Grinding Dept. | | | Finishing and Packing Dept. | | |
|---|---|---|---|---|---|
| Cost from preceding department | | $130 | Cost from preceding department | | $130 |
| Labor | | 40 | Labor | | 50 |
| Overhead | | 35 | Overhead | | 60 |
| Total cost of coke | | $205 | Total cost of tar | | $240 |
| | | | | | |
| Sales Price of Coke | | $800 | Sales Price of Tar | | $1,000 |
| Less: Cost of goods sold | $205 | | Less: Cost of goods sold | $240 | |
| Selling and administrative expenses | 200 | 405 | Selling and administrative expenses | 250 | 490 |
| Net profit for coke | | $395 | Net profit for tar | | $ 510 |

# Index